Biotechnology Development in Fisheries Management

Biotechnology Development in Fisheries Management

Mukesh Sharma

RANDOM

RANDOM PUBLICATIONS

NEW DELHI (INDIA)

Biotechnology Development in Fisheries Management

ISBN 978-93-5111-554-0

Published in 2015 in India by
RANDOM PUBLICATIONS

4376-A/4B, Gali Murari Lal, Ansari Road
New Delhi-110 002
Phone : +9111-43580356, 011-23289044, 011-43142548
e-mail: sales@randompublications.com,
info@randompublications.com, randomexports@gmail.com

Reprinted 2026

Type Setting by : Friends Media, Delhi-110089

Preface

The genetic improvement of fish for aquaculture and related fisheries is a field of research that has seen immense advances in recent years. Yet there is no book which provides an accessible overview of the subject. The growth of worldwide aquaculture has been sustained and rapid, and the explosion of research in genetic biotechnology has made significant impact on aquaculture and fisheries, although potential for much greater progress exists.

The fisheries and aquaculture industries in Asia contribute about 45 percent of world fish production . These industries are significant contributors to the food supply, livelihood, foreign exchange earnings and socio-economic stability in rural areas of several Asian countries.

At the global level fish production is stagnant, at around 100 million tonnes, or has even slightly declined in recent years. Overharvesting of the world's oceans is recognized as a global threat. To obviate this threat, the production of cultured fish must be accelerated.

The ability to produce transgenic fish and shellfish in culture, which grow faster and larger with more efficient utilization of nutrients, is of particular value to developing countries, not only as a source of food, but also as export products.

The use of modern biotechnology to enhance production of aquatic species holds great potential not only to meet demand but also to improve aquaculture. Genetic modification and biotechnology also holds tremendous potential to improve the quality and quantity of fish reared in aquaculture.

There is a growing demand for aquaculture; biotechnology can help to meet this demand. As with all biotech-enhanced foods, aquaculture will be strictly regulated before approved for market. Biotech aquaculture also offers environmental benefits.

The book is an ambitious title with broad coverage of techniques of fishes and their culture. It has been designed for university students scholars and teachers dealing with Genetics, molecular biology, genetic engineering, recombinant DNA technology.

I would like to thank my team for standing beside me throughout my career and writing this book. My special thanks go to "Random Publications" who have published the book.

– Mukesh Sharma

Contents

1

Introduction

The fisheries and aquaculture industries in Asia contribute about 45 per cent of world fish production. These industries are significant contributors to the food supply, livelihood, foreign exchange earnings and socio-economic stability in rural areas of several Asian countries. At the global level fish production is stagnant, at around 100 million tonnes, or has even slightly declined in recent years. Overharvesting of the world's oceans is recognized as a global threat. To obviate this threat, the production of cultured fish must be accelerated. The ability to produce transgenic fish and shellfish in culture, which grow faster and larger with more efficient utilization of nutrients, is of particular value to developing countries, not only as a source of food, but also as export products.

Biotechnology offers great promises for fish disease control and feed production as well. Gynogenetic and polyploid progeny production and the use of growth hormones have significantly contributed to fish production. The application of hypophysation (injecting of pituitary gland extracts into mature fishes for the induction of spawning) has been widely practiced in Asia during the past two decades. The use of purified gonadotrophin hormone synthetic luteinizing hormone-releasing hormone (LH-RH) has further improved induced spawning techniques.

In China, following detailed discussions and workshops in the 1980s, a policy and plan for aquaculture biotechnology were included in the Seventh Five-Year Plan (1985-90). In 1987, they were also listed in the "863 Programmes", the state development programmes on high technologies, and received great attention from the Ministry of Aquaculture. Fish cell culture, sex control, chromosome manipulation, and to some extent transgenic production, have been the main areas of work.

China's success in fish cell culture, of grass carp, was reported in 1979 by the Freshwater Fishery Research Institute of Zhejiang Province. Up to now, more than ten fish cell strains have been cultured for producing vaccines. Bioreactors for industrial fish cell culture are being developed. Seaweed cell culture in China was first reported in 1985 and is being developed for further breeding work. Diploid gynogenesis, coupled with sex control is being used for mass production of all female common and crucian carps. Although triploid hybrids between 4n common carp (male) and 2n grass carp (female) have been obtained, the work is confined to laboratories.

China was one of the pioneers in transplanting of fish cell nucleus. In the mid-1970s, the reciprocal transplant of nucleus was accomplished between common carp and crucian carp. Of the cell hybrid fishes, 30 grew to sexual maturity and produced F2 and F3 progenies. In 1984, the F3 progenies were mass produced and these showed stable heredity and had 30 per cent faster growth than their grandparents. A similar practice was carried out on grass carp and Megalobrama amblycephala; 26 of the hybrids grew well, matured sexually and were mass produced by aquaculturists. In 1988, live fries were produced from the fusion of blastulla cells and eggs in different fishes: Paramisgrunus dacryanus, Megalobrama amblycephala, grass carp, common carp and red crucian carp. This technique holds great promise for fish breeding.

In fishes, the two sexes differ in their productivity and body weight. For instance, in Tilapia males grow faster than the females, the converse of which is true for carps. Of the several methods of sex manipulation, through distant hybrids, hormone treatment, induced diploid gynogenesis, induced triploids, antoimmure castration, surgical castration, and gene technique, in China the first two are commonly used. Hybrid populations between Tilapia nilotica (female) and T. aurea (male) were 95 to 98 per cent male, and on an average yielded about 25 per cent higher than the higher yielding parent (T. nilotica). Moreover, the hybrid fish could tolerate lower water temperatures, and could be harvested more easily. Such all-male populations are already being mass cultured in China, the Philippines, Thailand and other countries. Israel has made comprehensive use of this technique.

As regards the use of hormones, using steroid hormones, induced females of T. mossambicais when crossed with male T. nilotica, produced super males with a "yy" sex chromosome combination. The "super males" crossed with female T. nilotica produced 100 per cent male progenies which possessed the twin superiorities of being hybrid as well as male. The hybrids grew 38.5 per cent faster than T. nilotica and the mass production increased by 43.4 per cent. Although a sizeable gain, the difficulty in identifying the "super male" fish at fry stage is a major constraint to widespread exploitation.

As regards genetic engineering, Chinese scientists have succeeded in identifying and isolating the gene controlling growth hormone (GH) from salmon, common carp, grass carp and silver carp. Transgenic carps carrying human growth hormone gene have been produced. Antifreeze gene has also been identified and used for improving the antifreeze ability of Tilapia. Successful cryopreservation of fish sperm, involving eight species has been established in China.

India, with a coastline of 7 512 km has 2.02 million km^2 of Exclusive Economic Zones, 4.7 million hectares of identified freshwater areas, and 1.7 million hectares of brackish-water areas. Its annual production of fish is around 4 million tonnes, half of it from aquaculture, and there is ample scope for enhancing fish production in the country. To supplement the fish feed resources, the use of bacterial cells as larval fish feed and processed aquatic plants as grow-out feed has been tested with success in India.

In Japan, chromosomal manipulation and modern biotechnology are being widely applied to improved fish production. Gynogenesis, artificial sex reversal and induced polyploidy are being routinely used for increasing productivity as well as the quality of fish.

The growth hormone of salmon and yellowtail is being mass produced through transgenic bacteria and used as a growth promoter on other fish such as rainbow trout. In the field of transgenic fish, the introduction and manifestation of the crystalline genes of chickens into killifish embryos were successfully achieved in 1986 at Kyoto University. Other useful genes are being identified and introduced into commonly used fish species.

New vaccines are also being developed to treat fish diseases. As regards fish feed, the development of microparticulate diets for larval fish to replace live foods in hatcheries is a major achievement. Mass production of ayu and carp fry in Japan with such diet formulates has been successful.

Malaysia has a relatively long coastline, stretching for about 4 334 km and its marine resources contribute about 9.5 per cent of the total value added in the agricultural sector; production has been increasing at a high annual growth rate of about 8 per cent over the past decade.

Moreover, the industry employs about 120 000 fishermen. The country clearly sees the scope for the application of biotechnology in fish production through genetic improvement of cultured fish, disease resistance and improved growth rate. Yet there is a gap in absorption or diffusion of the proven technologies.

Besides fish, marine algae are now recognized as important resources for the production of valuable chemicals in Malaysia and local species of marine macroalgae (seaweed) are being screened for valuable chemicals. Some of the species studied and their products include: Gracilaria changii for agar and Turbinaria conoides, Sargassum baccularia and Sargassum siliquosum for algiric acid and antimicrobial compounds.

Singapore considers its marine bioresources as one of the most important and the government is highly supportive of the marine biotechnology venture. The National University of Singapore (NUS) is playing a leading role in this direction. Its Bioprocessing Technology Unit, established in 1990, concentrates on two main areas: fermentation and cell culture; and thc isolation, separation and production purification technology.

In addition, the Unit also supplies to specific users, especially synthesized antibodies for immunobiological assays and analyses, and custom-made digonucleotide primers for nucleic acid research. In 1992, the NUS and the Economic Development Board (EDB) established a Bioscience Centre in the University, with the following objectives: (i) to provide a multiuser central facility for biotechnology, (ii) to serve as a vehicle for collaborating with industries and other institutions in Singapore or abroad, in areas of common interest, and (iii) to provide training in biotechnology.

The areas of research of the Centre are: bioactive compounds from marine organisms; toxins and venoms research; plant bioactive products; and products from microorganisms. Other related new establishments are the Centre for Natural Product Research and the Centre for Medical Informatics. The Reef Ecology Study Team of the Department of Zoology in NUS is actively surveying the distribution of the various reef organisms and the Bioscience Centre is screening organisms for antifouling, antibacterial, antitumour, antiviral, antifungal, anti-inflammatory and insecticidal compounds. Antibacterial compounds are being isolated and characterized from horseshoe crabs. Biological properties and potential therapeutic application of toxins and other bioactive compounds in two marine species, namely the "Thunder Crab" (Lyphozozymus pictor) and the stonefish (Sysanceja horrida), have been studied.

In addition, a few bioactive compounds have been purified from five local sea anemone species. These include a cytolysin, a trypsin inhibitor and two putative neurotoxins. Transgenics are also being attempted in a few fish species such as Marble Goby, grouper and salmon. The Marble Goby growth hormone gene has been cloned. NUS scientists are now in the process of combining this gene with a heterologous promoter to make a gene construct for transgenesis. Aquaculturists have been advised of the applications of (i) thyroid hormones in enhancing embryo and fry development; and (ii) gonado-tropin releasing hormones to help induce yolk formation and spawning. The hormones are being encapsulated into synthetic capsules for commercial use. Immunologists are studying the immune responses in fish and are developing various disease control methods, including vaccination with attenuated disease agents to develop antibodies.

Singapore is one of the major exporters of tropical aquarium fishes in the world. The DAN fingerprinting technology is being used to identify proper breeder stocks to be used in breeding programmes to maintain the quality and health of the fishes.

Aquaculture is most developed in Thailand. A Marine Biotechnology Unit (MBU) was established jointly by the National Centre for Genetic Engineering and Biotechnology and Aquatic Resources Research Institute of Chulalong Korn University in 1987. The Unit has been screening algae strains for feed purposes. Using cloned mitochondrial DNA, RFLP patterns of giant freshwater prawns

(Macrobrachium rosenberghi) were studied for analysing variation patterns to design appropriate breeding plans. Studies are in progress to manipulate the Gonad Inhibiting Hormones (GIH) for regulating the growth, maturity and reproductive success of prawns.

To control the most common and yield-reducing disease, vibriosis, caused by the bacteria Vibrio anguillarum, of the widely cultured fish seabass, vaccines have been developed. Chromosome manipulation of oyster has also been standardized. Studies on the gametogenic cycle of Thai abalone (Haliotis ovina) are proving helpful for resource regulation and management, and for broadstock conditioning, induction of spawning, control of mating and seed production for land-based production. An outdoor mass culture of benthic diatom, Navicula sp., as a food source of abalone spot was also standardized recently.

Research on marine natural products in Thailand began a few years ago and provides valuable information on the structures and potential applications of the compounds and their derivatives from Thai sponges. Such information could be, apart from the bioactivities of the compounds that can possibly be applied further to pharmaceutical use, helpful in the chemotaxonomy of Thai sponges.

The use of seaweeds as a source of phycocolloids is being promoted. The Biopolymer Research Unit (BU) of the Srinakarinwirot University, established in 1987, has developed a simple and low-cost technique for agar extraction from Gracelaria sp. seaweeds which could be applied at the village level. By developing and using chitin filter medium, the technique has improved the quality of the agar produced. The chitin could also be changed to chitosan, another valued product that is biodegradable and non-polluting and can be used as a binder in recycling paper. This technology changes the shrimp wastes into more value-added products. The Unit is currently operating a project entitled "Technology Development of Shrimp Shell Processing". Other work relates to the development of biomembranes, copolymer membrane and biobeads. Another value-added product is a fluorescence pigment of R-phycoerythrin for protein markers. The Marine Biotechnology Centre at Burapha University is concentrating on population dynamic studies of phytoplankton and zooplankton and identification of new pharmaceuticals from marine organisms. From the various species screened, the Centre found that 21 marine species had shown some degree of antimicrobial action.

Twenty-three extracts from seven species had shown positive results when subjected to haemolytic testing against erythrocytes of 21 species. From the above, it can be seen that the following biotechnology-related research work on marine organisms is in progress: studies on bioactive metabolites from Thai sponges, isolation of pure culture of some marine microalgae, isolation of pure culture of some marine bacteria, and the use of microalgae in biological control of marine animal diseases.

While considerable progress has been made in fish biotechnology in Asia, the following aspects need to be further strengthened:

- Genetic improvement of cultured fish for improved growth, disease resistance and adaptability to new farming systems.
- Development of low-cost but efficient grow-out diets for cultured fishes using locally available feedstuffs and microbiological processes.
- Utilization of detailed and microbial feed sources for pond cultured fish.
- Production of vaccines and monoclonal antibodies for the prevention and control of bacterial and virus diseases.
- Development of drugs and other biotechnological products from marine organisms.
- Improved availability of mother stocks and seeds, especially of brackish water marine fish and shellfish.

STATUS AND CHALLENGES OF FISHERIES

The fisheries administrators have viewed MCS as little more than the policing of the various maritime zones controlled by the State. This chapter attempts to provide a broader view of MCS - a view of MCS as the vital executive arm of fisheries management. The rapid depletion of key fish stocks in the 1980s and 1990s has made it imperative that governments achieve greater control over fishing activities. At the international level, a number of new agreements have created a stronger legal basis on which to develop greater control. At the same time, new technological developments have facilitated the remote monitoring of fishing vessels and the collection of fisheries data.

The 1982 United Nations Convention on the Law of the Sea (UNCLOS), which entered into force in 1994, forms the backbone of the international legal framework for fisheries management. It sets out the rights and duties of coastal, port and flag States in respect of each of the principal maritime zones recognized by international law, namely the territorial sea, the exclusive economic zone and the high seas. It also deals with a range of other important issues that are related, including the legal regimes applicable to internal waters, archipelagic waters, the contiguous zone, the continental shelf, and the right of innocent passage and passage through international straits. The provisions of UNCLOS relating to fisheries, though widely accepted even before the Convention entered into force, did not prevent the depletion of several valuable fish stocks. For this reason, the 1992 United Nations Conference on Environment and Development (UNCED) called urgently for the development of further instruments that would be necessary to re-establish and maintain sustainable fisheries worldwide.

One of these new instruments is the Agreement for the Implementation of the Provisions of the United Nations Convention on the Law of the Sea of 10 December 1982 Relating to the Conservation and Management of Straddling

Fish Stocks and Highly Migratory Fish Stocks. The UN Fish Stocks Agreement sets forth a broad range of obligations designed to create greater control over fisheries for certain valuable stocks, including the strengthening of MCS capabilities.

The pertinent aspects of several other new instruments developed under the auspices of FAO, including:

- The 1993 Agreement to Promote Compliance with International Conservation and Management Measures by Fishing Vessels on the High Seas;
- The 1995 Code of Conduct for Responsible Fisheries (CCRF);
- Four International Plans of Action dealing with various aspects of fisheries management, and particularly the International Plan of Action to Prevent, Deter and Eliminate Illegal, Unreported and Unregulated Fishing;
- Guidelines for the marking and identification of fishing vessels.

Ideally, each State would implement the 1982 Convention and the more recent agreements through the development of a national "oceans policy." Such a policy would establish government priorities and the strategy for the conservation and sustainable use of all marine resources within the maritime zones over which the State exercises sovereignty or sovereign rights, as well as efforts towards cooperative management of fisheries that occur outside these zones. From this oceans policy would flow the integrated oceans planning and management framework under which fisheries management plans would be developed. Most States see this as a long-term development initiative. To shorten the process, they have chosen to develop oceans policy and fisheries management strategies (including MCS strategies) simultaneously. Consequently, although States recognize that fisheries management must be integrated into an overall oceans policy when it is ultimately established, the MCS systems required to implement fisheries management plans are being developed in the interim to address the more immediate need to protect fish stocks and their habitats. This strategy is commendable. A "precautionary approach" recognizes that a first requirement for fisheries resource conservation is to prevent further degradation of the resource base.

The degree to which a government becomes involved in the fishing industry will have an impact on fisheries management and the resultant MCS activities. *For example, a government can*:

- Assume a controlling role, where it actually runs the industry, impacts the potential income of fishers, and micro-regulates the harvesting sector; or
- Maintain a less intrusive or co-management role, whereby the fishers and the fishing industry are encouraged to accept their resource responsibilities and roles within the framework of general government conservation principles and legislation.

Negative results of centralised, micro-management control mechanisms have become evident in both industrialised and developing States. Consequently, there is an emerging trend towards the second, *participatory co-management approach.* Fishers and the fishing industry want, and in fact are demanding, a more active role in management planning and implementation. Central governments are responding by devolving authority to smaller units of government (provinces, districts and municipalities) and by fostering community-based management, stakeholder involvement, and the acceptance of responsibility for the care, conservation and protection of their local marine resources by the fishers and industry. In a growing number of cases, such as the Canadian experience described in Profile 1, the private sector is also becoming involved in MCS activities.

MISPERCEPTIONS OF MCS

Misperceptions surrounding MCS activities continue to impact how fishers and even fishery managers view the process of MCS and enforcement. A common misperception is that all fisheries problems stem either from a failure to control illegal foreign fishing, or from the fishers themselves. While foreign fishing fleets have had documented impacts on fisheries conservation efforts, the greater impact on fisheries often stems from the domestic fishing industry in the coastal and nearshore fishing zones. On the issue of fishers, fisheries administrators must remember that most are hard working individuals often working in a hazardous environment:

While sometimes libellously assumed by the ill-informed to be crooks, [fishers] are perhaps best described as being as honest as the next man, but hard, individualistic businessmen running very competitive and often highly capitalized operations.

It is worth remembering that they do so in the face of a largely unforgiving sea that creates a working environment which... [has one of the worst industrial accident rates in the world], and [that]... they operate increasingly in an economic climate of ever increasing overheads countered only by the proceeds of catches which [are] subjected to [ever greater] quota restriction. All of this is done in the knowledge that the success of their venture and the livelihood of their crews depends entirely on their individual skill, effort and initiative. Given these pressures, it is perhaps not surprising that such independent minds do not always take kindly to bureaucratic controls, especially if these appear to them to have little practical purpose. Another erroneous perception is that MCS is exclusively concerned with enforcement - thus ignoring the other two components of monitoring (data collection) and control (legislation, licensing, and controls on gear, season, areas, etc.). In focussing only on the "surveillance/enforcement" or deterrent aspects of MCS, fisheries administrators and supporting agencies cannot harness the full utility of MCS as the vital executive arm of fisheries management.

Civilian versus Military Involvement in MCS

The expense of MCS activities is often a primary concern of any government designing and implementing an MCS system. Cost-effectiveness and efficiency is important if MCS operations are to be successful. A civilian approach to deterrent fisheries enforcement has proven in many cases to be the most cost-effective and responsive to fisheries priorities. Use of civilian assets also minimizes the political sensitivity of international fisheries incidents by avoiding the use of military equipment and personnel. Those fisheries administrators who must rely on the use of military resources to carry out MCS activities may find that military agencies often accord low priority to that task. Moreover, military involvement, except in a support role, is usually not cost-effective. Military aircraft and vessels are more expensive to build and operate than equivalent civilian equipment. Savings accrue from the use of a civilian vessel with fewer crew, and lower operating costs. For many governments, however, the military can play a significant supporting role in a strong MCS system. The key for such governments is to establish an inter-agency mechanism that enables fisheries administrators to call upon their military counterparts as and when needed.

Fisheries as a Lead Ministry

Effectiveness of operations can be enhanced considerably if a single ministry is designated to take the lead role in MCS activities. This significantly reduces the lines of communications for the command and control of the monitoring and surveillance components of MCS activities, making them more efficient and responsive to management needs. As noted above, however, a number of different agencies may be called upon in a supporting role. In such situations, effective MCS requires a strong inter-agency control mechanism.

In Canada, the federal Department of Fisheries and Oceans (DFO) has been entrusted by the Parliament of Canada through the *Fisheries Act* and the *Coastal Fisheries Protection Act* to administer all laws relating to fisheries. The administration of federal fisheries laws has, by agreement, been delegated to some, but not all, provincial governments. DFO remains responsible for fisheries management in the tidal waters of the Pacific, Atlantic, Arctic, the inland waters of four Atlantic provinces and the salmon rivers in British Columbia. This includes management of Aboriginal, Recreational and Commercial fisheries within Canada's Exclusive Economic Zone (EEZ), in transboundary rivers, and for sedentary species on the continental shelf outside the Canadian EEZ.

Statistics:

- 58 400 commercial fishers (42 700 Atlantic, 8 700 Pacific and 7 000 inland)
- Commercial harvest > 1 000 000 mt
- Landed value approximately $1.9 billion (shellfish account for

approximately 75 per cent of the total landed value, with groundfish and pelagic fisheries making up the remainder)

- 5 million Canadians and 900 000 visitors/year for the recreational fishery
- Catch over 250 million fish in recreational fisheries, with more than half of the fish released under the catch and release regime
- Over 125 fisheries agreements are negotiated with Aboriginal groups in Canada on an annual basis to provide for aboriginal access to fisheries and an orderly management of their fishing activities.

Management Systems/Control Mechanisms

Various management schemes have been applied in different fisheries, but all are based on limited entry licensing, with vessel and gear restrictions. Other measures to limit catches include total allowable catches (*e.g.* groundfish), escapement targets (salmon), or recruitment strategies (*e.g.* lobster). Other management measures include limitations on fishing area, fishing season, gear (*e.g.* mesh size), incidental catch (bycatch) and minimum fish sizes. Rights-based systems - in the form of Enterprise Allocations (EA) and Individual Quotas (IQ) - have been introduced in some fisheries to allow fishers more efficiently to manage the capacity and effort for harvesting.

MCS Programme

The Department of Fisheries and Oceans (DFO) Conservation and Protection programme ensures compliance with the legislation, regulations and fishing plans. This requires an integrated MCS approach and deployment of some 600 Fishery Officers for air, sea and land patrols; independent/private sector observer coverage on fishing vessels; dockside monitoring of fish landings; and remote electronic monitoring of fishing vessel activity.

DFO operates a fleet of patrol vessels on each coast to enforce closed areas and boundary lines, and to conduct inspections at sea for compliance purposes. Contracted aircraft are used to monitor fishing fleets. Sea and aerial surveillance is also supplemented by the Department of National Defence (DND).

VMS and air surveillance provide for more effective deployment of patrol vessels; with the latter also serving as a visible deterrence. Canada deploys private sector, contracted observers, without enforcement powers, on all foreign vessels fishing in Canadian waters and on some Canadian vessels to gather scientific information and provide on-site monitoring of compliance. They are trained to detect and report infractions such as dumping/discarding, fishing in closed areas, catch misreporting, retention of prohibited catch and the use of illegal gear.

The level of observer coverage in domestic fisheries varies depending on conservation risks and management priorities. Contracted dockside monitors/ observers verify the quantity and species/product form of fish landed for scientific, quota monitoring and compliance reasons. This data is cross-checked by random inspections by Fishery Officers at landing sites. At-sea observer costs are shared by the Department and the fishing industry. Dockside monitoring costs are entirely paid by the fishing industry. In 1999, DFOs expenditures on fisheries enforcement amounted to CDN $70 million (including DFOs share of at-sea observer costs).

The Conservation and Protection programme has been significantly re-oriented in recent years. The mix of enforcement resources has been altered to better respond to changing programme requirements. For example, a number of larger patrol vessels have been replaced with smaller programme boats that can be operated more efficiently by the Fishery Officers themselves. Savings from vessel reductions have been partially re-invested in new equipment and surveillance technologies. Significant investments have also been made in the creation of new enforcement data systems and the integration of existing systems, with the goal of providing Fishery Officers and managers with more accurate and timely information that will strengthen the Department's enforcement capabilities. These efforts at improving data integration and analysis will continue to be a priority for the immediate future. The Conservation and Protection programme is closely integrated with DFOs overall Fisheries Management Programme. Input and advice from fisheries enforcement officials is an important consideration in the development of Integrated Fisheries Management Plans (IFMPs). In future these plans will include specific conservation objectives as identified by DFO scientists in consultation with fishers and other technical experts. The new Objectives Based Fisheries Management strategy will require greater involvement by the fishing industry to design management measures that will minimize identified risks to conservation.

Conserve and Utilise Marine resources

Fisheries are critical to the development of a State's plan to conserve and utilise marine resources, as fish and their habitat are significant renewable resources in the territorial sea and exclusive economic zone. The goal of fisheries management, including MCS, is to maximise the economic opportunities and benefits from the State's waters within sustainable harvesting limits. Fisheries MCS needs to be defined in light of this goal. An MCS Conference of Experts organized by FAO in 1981 developed a definition of MCS that is commonly accepted by fisheries personnel:

- Monitoring - the continuous requirement for the measurement of fishing effort characteristics and resource yields;
- Control - the regulatory conditions under which the exploitation of the resource may be conducted; and
- Surveillance - the degree and types of observations required to maintain compliance with the regulatory controls imposed on fishing activities.

Simply stated, MCS is the mechanism for implementation of agreed policies, plans or strategies for oceans and fisheries management. MCS is an aspect of oceans and fisheries management that is often undervalued. In reality, it is key to the successful implementation of any planning strategy. The absence of MCS operations render a fisheries management scheme incomplete and ineffective. Since the 1981 MCS Conference, the definition of MCS has been enhanced to promote the concept that MCS covers more than just fisheries enforcement - it is an integral and key component for the implementation of fisheries management plans. It encompasses not only traditional enforcement activities but also the development and establishment of both data collection systems, the enactment of legislative instruments and the implementation of the management plan through participatory techniques and strategies.

A 1993 workshop in Ghana offered the following clarifications:

- *Monitoring* includes the collection, measurement and analysis of fishing activity including, but not limited to: catch, species composition, fishing effort, bycatch, discards, area of operations, etc. This information is primary data that fisheries managers use to arrive at management decisions. If this information is unavailable, inaccurate or incomplete, managers will be handicapped in developing and implementing management measures.
- *Control* involves the specification of the terms and conditions under which resources can be harvested. These specifications are normally contained in national fisheries legislation and other arrangements that might be nationally, subregionally, or regionally agreed. The legislation provides the basis for which fisheries management arrangements, via MCS, are implemented. For maximum effect, framework legislation should clearly state the management measures being implemented and define the requirements and prohibitions that will be enforced.
- *Surveillance* involves the regulation and supervision of fishing activity to ensure that national legislation and terms, conditions of access, and management measures are observed. *This activity is critical to ensure that resources are not over exploited, poaching is minimized and management arrangements are implemented.*

These wider definitions amplify the importance of all aspects of MCS.

EMERGING TRENDS IN MCS

Trends over in the past decade have significantly altered fisheries management in general and MCS strategies in particular. These have occurred in three areas - viz: *devolution of authority to lower levels of government*; *the encouragement of participatory management*; and *new technology*.

Devolution of Authority

Fisheries management can no longer be the sole responsibility of central governments. Rapid population growth, urbanisation and migration to coastal areas have created a greater need for local governmental units to address local fisheries management concerns. Growing literacy and educational levels, coupled with easy access to mass media, have helped ordinary citizens to acquire more knowledge of government processes and a desire for more transparency and a greater voice in decision-making. Central governments have responded by devolving more authority over fisheries management to provinces, states, districts, municipalities and communities.

This devolution of authority has vitally affected MCS. In the past, central governments controlled, or at least sought to control, all MCS activities on a national basis. Today, a more typical role for a central government is to set national policies and standards and to co-ordinate the implementation of these policies and standards. Responsibility for actually carrying out MCS activities is now typically shared by central governments with smaller governmental units. Central governments also monitor and evaluate local government performance to enhance future coordination and planning. MCS planning and operations still need this national coordination for consistency in implementation of management plans, and for conflict resolution. However, the overall trend is for central governments to devolve responsibility for MCS activities to lower levels of governmental authority.

Namibia, a State six times the size of the United Kingdom and with a population of 1.7 million, is on the West Coast of Africa just north of South Africa. It has a coastline of 700 nautical miles (1 500 km) and an EEZ of 275 000 km^2. Since independence in 1989, Namibia has developed a progressive fisheries administration and a thriving commercial capture fisheries that is increasingly Namibian.

The fishing industry is based on the high productivity of the up-welling Benguela Current system. Fisheries contributed more than US$50 million (10 per cent Namibia's GDP) in 1999 and employed some 15 000 people. By law, all fish are landed in Namibia through its two ports, Walvis Bay and Lüderitz. Namibia is one of the few major fishing nations that earns more income and creates more jobs from the processing sector than from the catching of fish. This is partly due to policies such as the requirement for onshore processing of hake and other species. *Namibia is recovering all expenses related to its fisheries administration and MCS operations through the collection of revenue from the fishing industry.*

The fisheries are exclusively industrial and annual catches are stable or steadily increasing following the overexploitation before independence. Trends for the three major species (hake, horse mackerel and pilchard) are showing the same broadly consistent pattern of increases in biomass up to 1992, a subsequent decline and, recently, a general recovery. The total landed catch in 1999 was approximately 600 000 t.

The key fisheries are as follows (TAC for 2000 in brackets):

- *The Demersal Fisheries*: Hake (200 000 t), monk (16 000 t), kingklip and sole;
- *The Midwater Fishery*: Horse mackerel (410 000 t) pursued by both midwater trawlers and the purse seiners;
- The Purse Seine Fishery: Pilchard (15 000 t) and juvenile horse mackerel with purse seine nets;
- *The Deep-Water Fishery*: Orange roughy (2 400 t) and alfonsino;
- *The Large Pelagic Fishery*: Albacore, big-eye, yellow-fin, skipjack and swordfish;
- *The Rock Lobster Fishery (400 t)*: Small vessels using carrier vessels to bring the live lobster ashore daily;
- *The Crab Fishery (2 000 t)*: A small fishery that uses traps to catch deep-sea crab during the whole year.

Namibia uses a three-part access system to turn its policies of Namibianisation of the fisheries into practise:

i. Rights to exploit the fisheries are allocated;
ii. Quotas are allocated to rights holders; and
iii. Vessels are granted licences.

This allows Namibia to maintain control over the fishing companies, the vessels and the crews in order to assure that policy aims are being met through a differentiated quota fees system that favours Namibian participation, Namibian flag vessels, Namibian employment, and an empowerment aspect in relation to the social inequalities.

Fisheries management controls fall into two categories:

- Input controls that relate to fishing effort and gear, seasons and areas, with the key ones being the limitation of total fishing effort and seasons; and
- Output controls that set quotas and regulations, size limits, and other characteristics of the fish that may be landed. The main output control is by the establishment of annual TAC and quota allocations set on the best scientific advice available, modified by socio-economic factors. TACs are today established for 7 species (hake, horse mackerel, pilchard, orange roughy, monk, red crab and rock lobster).

The MCS system is an integrated system that has stations in the two Inspectorates in Walvis Bay and Lüderitz with each station tasked as appropriate for deploying fishery officers to air, sea or land operations, deploying fisheries observers on board fishing vessels, analysing past operations and outputs or planning future operations.

There is a cross-verification of data where observer and inspector information is checked through port inspections and landings control. MCS activities related to air and sea operations are co-ordinated from the Inspectorate at Walvis Bay through a maritime and fisheries Operations Centre and an air base at Arandis.

The Ministry of Fisheries and Marine Resources operates two larger patrol vessels and one fixed wing aircraft in addition to maintaining 100 per cent observer coverage of the fishing fleet (230 observers are employed in the largest observer programme south of equator). Observers and fisheries inspectors control gear and catches at sea. All catches are finally landed or transhipped in Namibia under the supervision and control of fisheries inspectors. VMS is still in a pilot stage and different systems are under evaluation.

Participatory Management

Similarly, governments at all levels are giving private groups and individuals more opportunity to participate in the management of fisheries that affect them. This trend towards more transparency and openness is changing all aspects of MCS, including the development of fisheries laws and regulations, the collection of fisheries data, etc. As already indicated, enhanced public participation in the fisheries management process brings a number of advantages.

Specifically, it fosters:

- Greater public understanding of the rationale behind MCS activities;
- A greater sense of partnership between the government and fishers and others whose activities are being regulated;
- A greater sense of ownership and acceptance by private groups and individuals in the decisions that are ultimately adopted;
- Voluntary compliance and the use of peer pressure to deter violations of fisheries rules;
- Greater availability of MCS funding and other assets for dealing with cases of non-compliance.

New Technology

Advances in technology, along with reductions in the cost of technology, have revolutionised MCS.

Examples include:

- New vessel monitoring systems (VMS) in use in Argentina, Australia, Canada, Europe, Malaysia, New Zealand, United States, and member States of the South Pacific Forum Fisheries Agency, with systems also being considered in Madagascar, Namibia, Indonesia, and Sri Lanka;
- Inter-linked coastal radar systems in use in Senegal; and
- A combined VMS and satellite imaging system in use in the Maldives.

Cheap cellular telephone and computer technology has also brought MCS into the computer age and has greatly improved the capacity of States to respond rapidly to situations. Over-the-horizon radar technology is evolving as well, but its cost has not yet fallen to a level that is appropriate for general fisheries management. Currently the most popular VMS systems use INMARSAT C (and more recently D) and ARGOS. Others such as POLESTAR and EULTRACS are also making an appearance. FAO has prepared detailed guidelines as part of the *Code of Conduct for Responsible Fisheries* series for Fisheries Administrators contemplating the introduction and use of such technology.

The use of this new technology for coastal fisheries, particularly VMS, may not yet be cost-effective. However, many States can still monitor large numbers of coastal vessels effectively through other means, *e.g.* observers, dockside monitoring, monitoring of industry landings and production records, etc.

BIOTECHNOLOGY IN FISH BREEDING

Gonadotropin releasing hormone (GnRH) is now the best available biotechnological tool for the induced breeding of fish. GnRH is the key regulator and central initiator of reproductive cascade in all vertebrates.It is a decapeptide and was first isolated from pig and ship hypothalami with the ability to induce pituitary release of luteinising hormone (LH) and follicle stimulating hormone (FSH).Since then only one form of GnRH has been identified in most placental mammals including human beings as the sole neuropeptide causing the release of LH and FSH. However,in non- mammalian species (except guinea pig) twelve GnRH variants have now been structurally elucidated,among them seven or eight different forms have been isolated from fish species. The most recent GnRH purified and characterized was by Carolsfeld *et al.*(2000) and Robinson et al.(2000).Depending on the structural variant and their biological activities, number of chemical analogues have seen prepared and one of them is salmon GnRH analogue profusely used now in fish breeding and marked commercially under the name of ÒOvaprimÓ throughout the world. The induced breeding of fish is now successfully achieved by development of GnRH technology.

TRANSGENESIS

Transgenesis or transgenics may be defined as the introduction of exogenous gene/ DNA into host genome resulting in its stable maintenance, transmission and expression. The technology offers an excellent opportunity for modifying or improving the genetic traits of commercially important fishers, mollusks and crustaceans for aquaculture. The idea of producting transgenic animals became popular when Palmitter et al. (1982) first produced transgenic mouse by introducing metallothionein human growth hormone fusion gene (mT-hGH) into mouse egg, resulting in dramatic increase in growth. This triggered a series of attemptson gene transfer in economically important animals including fish. The first transgenic fish was produced Zhu et al. (1985) in China, who claimed the transient expression n putative transgenics, although they gave no molecular evidence for the integration of the transgene. The technique has now seen successfully applied to a number of fish species. Dramatic growth enhancement has been shown using this technique especially in salmonids. Some studies have revealed enhancement of growth in adult salmon to an average of 3 Ð 5 times the size of non Ð transgenic controls, with some individuals, especially during the first few months of growth, reaching as much as 10 Ð 30 times the size of the controls.

The introduction of transgenic technique has simultaneously put more emphasis on the need for production of sterile progeny in order to minimize the risk of transgenic stocks mixing in the wild populations. The technical development has expanded the possibilities for producing either sterile fish or those whose reproductive activity can be specifically turned on or off using inducible promoters. This would clearly be of considerable value allowing both optimal growth and controlled reproduction of the transgenic stocks while ensuring that any escaped fish would be unable to breed. An increased resistance of fish to cold temperatures has been another subject of research in fish transgenics for the past several years. Coldwater temperatures pose a considerable stressor to many fish and few are able to survive water temperatures much below 0-1oC. this is often a major problem in aquaculture in cold climates.

Interestingly, some marine teleosts have high levels (10 Ð 25 mg/ml) of serum antifreeze proteins (AFP) or glycoproteins (AFGP) which effectively reduce the freezing temperature by preventing ice-crystal growth. The isolation, characterization and regulation of these antifreeze proteins particularly of the inter flounder Pleuronectas americanus has been the subject of research for a considerable period in Canada. Consequently, the gene encoding the liver AFP from winter flounder was successfully introduced into the genome of Atlantic salmon where it became integrated into the germ line and then passed onto the off Ð spring F3 where it was expressed specifically in the liver. The introduction of AFPs to gold fish also increased their cold tolerance, to temperatures at which all the control fish died. Similarly, injection or oral administration of AFP to juvenile milkfish or tilapia led to an increase in resistance to a 26 to 13o C. drop in temperature. The development of stocks harbouring this gene would be a major benefit in commercial aquaculture in counties where winter temperatures often border the physiological limits of these species.

The most promising tool for the future of transgenic fish production is undoubtedly in the development of the embryonic stem cell (ESC) technology. There cells are undifferentiated and remain totipotent so they can be manipulated in vitro and subsequently reintroduce into early embryos where they can contribute to the germ line of the host. This would facilitate the genes to be stably introduced or deleted. Although significant progress has been made in several laboratories around the world, there are numerous problems to be resolved before the successful commercialization of the transgenic brood stock for aquaculture.

To realize the full potential of the transgenic fish technology in aquaculture, several important scientific break Đ through are required. There include (i) more efficient technologies for mass gene transfer (ii) targeted gene transfer technologies such as embryonic stem cell gene transfer (iii) suitable promoters to direct the expression of transgenes at optimal levels during the desired developmental stages (iv) identified genes of desireable traits for aquaculture and other applications (v) informations on the physiological, nutritional, immunological and environmental factors that maximize the performance of the transgenics of the transgenics and (vi) safety and environmental impacts of transgenic fish.

Chromosome Engineering

Chromosome sex manipulation techniques to induce polyploidy (triploidy and tetraploidy) and uniparental chromosome inheritance (gynogenesis and androgenesis) have been applied extensively in cultured fish species. These techniques are important in the improvement of fish breeding as they provide a rapid approach for gonadal sterilization, sex control improvement of hybrid viability and clonation. Most vertebrates are diploid meaning that they possess two complete chromosome sets in their somatic cells. Polyploidy individuals possess on or more additional chromosome sets, bringing the total to three in triploids, four in tetraploids and so on. Induced triploidy is widely accepted as the most effective method for producing sterile fish for aquaculture and fisheries management.

The methods used to induce triploids and other types of chromosome set manipulations in fishes and the applications of these biotechnologies to aquaculture and fisheries management are well described. Tetraploid breeding lines are of potential benefit to aquaculture, by providing a convenient way to produce large numbers of sterile triploid fish through simple interploidy crosses between tetraploids and diploids. Although tetraploidy has been induced in many finfish species, the viability of tetraploids was low in most instances.

In teleosts, technique for inducing sterility include exogenous hormone treatment and triploidy induction. The use of hormone treatements, however could be limited by governmental regulation and a lack of consumer acceptance of hormone treated fish products. Triploidy can be induced by exposing eggs to physical or chemical treatment shortly after fertilization to inhibit extrusion of the second polar body triploid fish are expected to be sterile because of the failure of homologous chromosomes to synapse correctly during the first meiotic division.

Methods of triploidy induction in clued exposing fertilized eggs to temperature shock (hot or cold), hydrostatic pressure shock or chemicals such an colchicines, cytochalasin-B or nitrous oxide. Triploid can also be produced by crossing teraploids and diploids. Tetraploid induction involves fertilizing eggs with normal sperm and exposing the diploid sygote for physical or chemical treatment to suppress the first mitotic division.

Gynogenesis is the process of animal development with exclusive maternal inheritance. The production of gynogenetic individuals is of particular interest to fish breeders because a high level of inbreeding can be induced in single generation. Gynogenesis may also be used to produce all Đ female populations in species with female homogamety and to reveal the sex determination mechanisms in fish.

It is convenient to use all female gynogenetic progenies (instead of normal bisexual progenies) for sex inversion experiments. Methodologies combining use of induced gynogenesis with hormonal sex inversion have been developed for several aquaculture species. Androgenesis is the process by which would have commercial application in aquaculture. It can also be used in generating homozygous lines of fish and in the recovery of lost genotypes from the crypreserved sperms. Androgenetic individuals have been produced in a few species of cyprinids, cichlids and salmonids.

BIOTECHNOLOGY AND FISH HEALTH MANAGEMENT

Disease problem area major constraint for development of aquaculture. biotechnological tools such as molecular diagnostic methods, use of vaccines and immunostimulants are gaining popularity for improving the disease resistance in fish and shellish species world over for viral diseases, avoidance of the pathogen in very important.in this context there is a need to rapid method for detection of the pathogen.

Biotechnological tools such as gene probes and polymerase chain reaction (PCR) are showing great potential in this area. Gene probes and PCR based diagnostic methods have developed for a number of pathogens affecting fish and shrimp. In case of finfish aquaculture, number of vaccine against bacteria and viruses have been developed. Some of these have been conventional vaccines consisting of killed microorgansism but new generation of vaccine consisting of protein subunit vaccine genetically engineered organism and DNA vaccine are currently under development.

In the vertebrate system, immunization against disease is a common strategy. However the immune system of shrimp is rather poorly developed, biotechnological tools are helpful for development of molecule, which can stimulate this immune system of shrimp. Recent studies have shown that the non- specific defence system can be stimulated using, microbial product such as lipopolysacharides, peptidoglycans or glucans. Among the immunostimulants known to be effective in fish glucan and levamisole enhance phagocytic activities and specific antibody responses.

Cryopreservation of Gametes or Gene Banking

Cryopreservation is a technique, which involve long-term preservation and storage of biological material at a very low temperature usually at -196 C,the temperature of liquid nitrogen. It is based on the principle that very low temperature tranquilize or immobilize the physiological and biochemical activities of cell, thereby making it possible to keep them viable for very long period. The technology of cryopreservation of fish spermatozoa (milt) has been adopted for animal husbandary.

The first success in preserving fish sperm at low temperature was reported by Blaxter (1953) who fertilizes Herring (Clupea herengus) eggs with frozen thawed semen.The spermatozoa of almost all cultivable fish species has now been cryopreserved. Cryopreservation overcomes problems of male maturing before female, allow selective breeding and stock improvement and enables the conservation One of the emerging requirement for that can be used by breeders for evolving new strains. Most of the plant varieties that has been produced are based on the gene bank collections. Aquatic gene bank however suffers from the fact that at present it is possible to cryopreserve only the male gametes of finfishes and there in no viable technique for finfish eggs and embryos. However, the recent report on the freezing of shrimp embryos. However, the recent report on the freezing of shrimps embryos by subramoniam and newton (1993) and Diwan and kandaswami (1997) look promising. Therefore, it is essential that gene banking of cultivated and cultivable aquatic species be undertaken expeditiously.

BIOTECHNOLOGY IN FISHERIES DEVELOPMENT

The gap between human demand and the availability of livestock products is huge in Africa, and imports have been increasing fast. The productivity of African breeds is very low: mature beef cattle of 4-5 years hardly weight 300 kg (as against 400 kg at one year for exotic animals); the best African cows produced 300 litre/lactation (as against 5 000 litres and more in Europe); 100 African ewes produced 50 lambs every two or three years (as against 150 lambs a year in developed countries).

Retrospectively, production policies that aimed at developing livestock through cross-breeding of exotic grade cattle with indigenous ones have generally failed. The new approach is not to make selection of local performant animals. Biotechnology offers good methods both for selection and cross-breeding schemes, essentially through Multiovulation Embryo Transfer (MOET) and the field diagnosis of pregnancy. Yet, there is wide diversity among the countries to use new technologies. For instance, even if simpler techniques such as Artificial Insemination (AI) are considered, it is seen that in East Southern Africa the technique is widely used, whereas in West and Central Africa, because of the predominance of nomadic transhumant livestock production, the technique is least developed.

MOET is well developed in few countries such as Zimbabwe and South Africa. Cattle farmers in these countries import frozen embryos from overseas. MOET is promising especially in the development of dairy cattle farms around large cities. Both AI and MOET are being used in Open Nucleus Breeding Systems (ONBS) to improve animal production. Small-scale ONBS projects are being carried out by FAO in small ruminants in Ghana and the Gambia. Moreover, by using semen from bulls, with genetic resistance to high temperature, diseases and insects common to African countries, embryos could be produced from superior cows of other regions and then implanted into surrogate mothers within the environment where improved livestock are needed. In animal feeding, biodegradation of low-quality forage is also a promising technology. It can be associated with chemical degradation techniques (use of urea and ammonia) to improve animal feeds during dry seasons.

In some of the countries, farm diagnosis of pregnancy is also being used by field workers by using a kit based on the difference of levels of progesterone in cow's milk.

In the field of animal health, Sterile Insect Technology (SIT) is well known in Africa. Sterile males of glossina are being reared in Bobo-Dioulasso and Burkina Faso for field application. Successful field projects in tsetse control have been carried out in Nigeria (BICOT Project) and in Burkina Faso. Newworld screwworm was eradicated in the Libyan Arab Jamahiriya in 199091 by the use of SIT.

In disease diagnosis, ELISA is being used to evaluate rinderpest immunity in vaccinated animals. Monoclonal Antibody Techniques (MAB) is not commonly used. The two techniques are very promising because they are very simple and most effective. Trials are under way to use the ELISA test in trypanosomiasis diagnosis. In vaccine production recombinant rinderpest vaccine trials done in the United States seem ready to be utilized in a mass vaccination campaign against rinderpest in Africa. There is an increasing level of activity in hybridoma work in sub-Saharan countries.

The work of ILRAD in Kenya is addressing the problem of diseases and parasites that affect cattle. Some of the common cattle diseases are East Coast Fever, tickborne diseases and trypanosomiasis. The focused approaches to researching on these diseases is expanding to yield results that will significantly benefit cattle breeders. The development of rinderpest vaccines remaining stable at ordinary temperatures was of high practical value.

Biotechnology in fisheries is recent in Africa and it is being applied essentially in private fisheries sector. Work is mostly confined to hormonal treatments for sex reversal and pawning, detection of fish and shrimps disease and development of fish feed.

RESPONSES TO THE CHALLENGES OF FISHERIES USE

The very reality that the root causes of the over-use of fish stocks are structural makes it nearly impossible to completely alleviate the pressures of rising demand, increasing abilities to pay for high-value species, and more effective ways to capture fish on an open-access resource. But people, organizations, and governments have responded to these realities in many ways, their responses sometimes improving the situation, but often exacerbating it. Two of the most prominent and important responses have been subsidies and management schemes.

The first, subsidies, occur when trade measures directly influence the income or reduce the costs of production for industry. Management schemes, the second, encompass the ways in which fisheries are governed and monitored. In practice, the way this is done often highlights a lack of effective management. Subsidies and management, which can be seen as responses by individuals, groups, or governments to the root causes of fisheries depletion, are also the areas where the most opportunities for change in the way fisheries resources are used exist. Effective management regimes are considered by many to be key in the sustainable use of fisheries resources. Theoretically, effective management encourages a sustainable use of resources through providing conservation regulations and incentives for responsible use of the resource. They are especially beneficial under the pressures of international integration; responses by producers to the economic incentives from trade liberalization, for example, can be better regulated when effective management schemes exist so that over-exploitation and destruction are less likely to occur. Unfortunately, the prevalence of such management has been scant in real-world fisheries.

As the United Nations Environment Programme (UNEP) reports, "very few fisheries management systems have demonstrated the ability to keep catches below levels that put pressure on stocks." As noted in a study by the World Conservation Union (IUCN), "national and international progress on trade expansion and liberalization outpaces progress on fisheries management and articulation of sustainable development strategies." Fisheries management, crucial to sustainable use of the world's fisheries, has been difficult to implement effectively and has often left fisheries open to influences from other sources such as state trade measures.

Subsidies, one of these trade measures, have played a proven role in aggravating the causes of fisheries depletion. Theoretically, subsidies can lead to overuse of a resource by altering the behaviour of producers. Revenue-enhancing or cost-reducing subsidies, such as those that will be examined in this chapter, increase marginal profits at each level of effort and therefore theoretically lead to an increased overall effort. This may have the short-term effect of creating additional economic rent for producers, but either new entrants or increased effort by existing producers, also encouraged by the subsidy, will shift the level of effort so that rent is eventually dissipated. Assuming that the management programme does not effectively impose a sustainable level of resource use, cost-reducing and revenue-enhancing subsidies will push the level of overcapacity and overall effort even further than would an open-access resource in the absence of subsidies. The main theoretical effects of cost-reducing, rent-increasing subsidies are increased capacity, a delay in exit by producers from the sector, and increased effort by producers. These effects can cause the overuse of a resource, which can have many other significant impacts such as threats to food, livelihood, and resource security.

FISHING SUBSIDIES

In the real world of governments, fishers, fisheries resources, and the incentives that link them all together, a subsidy can take many forms. Fishing subsidies currently account for large portions of many industrialized country budgets; a 1998 World Bank study estimated annual budgeted expenditures on global fisheries subsidies to be between $14 and $20 billion, and that subsidies account for 20 to 25 per cent of the sector's revenues.

One type of subsidy, domestic assistance programmes, form a clear example of government endorsement of the fishing sector. These programmes are defined as budgeted assistance to fishing production, and often enhance operations and capacity. Japan, one of the biggest subsidizers of fishing activities in the world, has used domestic assistance programmes to recruit young fisherman, give aid to fish cooperatives and boat owners, support marketing, and encourage price stabilization. A 1998 World Bank report estimated that Japan budgets $270 million a year for these types of programmes, and a total of $750 when aid for fishing vessel insurance is included. The European Union (EU), another major subsidizer, supports such structural programmes as fleet renewal and modernization, processing and marketing, aquaculture, maintenance of port facilities, and genetic product promotion in their fisheries sector.

In addition, it pays for market supports to the sector in the form of a minimum import price programme and measures to support price floors. Costs of these programmes to the EU in 1996 were estimated to be about $530 million. While estimates of exactly what types of domestic subsidy programmes the Chinese government uses are hard to determine due to scant data, they have clearly aggressively promoted the expansion of their fishing sector in the last 15 years (and have become the world's leading producer) and are estimated to budget between $500 and $750 million annually for domestic subsidies. While other countries subsidize their domestic fishing industries, they have comparatively small budgets for such programmes as so do so on a smaller scale. The shear magnitude of the domestic subsidies in industrialized countries suggests the possible impacts on the behaviour of fishers their presence may cause.

A less obvious, but yet potentially just as influential, type of subsidy occurs when a country pays the access fees for their fleets to fish in foreign waters. Unlike domestic subsidies, these payments are not made directly to fishers or even domestic programmes, but to the foreign governments who have jurisdiction over the fish stocks. The EU is one of the major subsidizers of distant-water fishing through its numerous access agreements with developing countries, mostly in West Africa.

For example, the EU signed a five-year access agreement with Mauritania in 1996 that lifted an EU embargo on fishery imports from Mauritania and specified EU payments of almost $350 million over five years to the Mauritanian government. In return, the Mauritanian government granted increased access for EU fishing vessels in their waters, authorization of higher EU total harvests, and the specific allowance of EU-directed fishing of highly valued squid and octopus.

The monetary benefits to the "cash-strapped" nation were described as a "windfall;" in consequence, the number of eligible EU boats rose from 165 to 240 and allowable EU harvests from 76,050 to 183,392 tons. The EU has similar agreements with other West African nations, as well as others in East Africa, the Indian Ocean, and South America. Another distant-water fleet subsidizer, Japan, currently budgets about $200 million a year on distant water arrangements with foreign countries and foreign fisheries assistance programmes (which often help secure fishing rights). These payments went mostly to developing countries in the Pacific Ocean and elsewhere. The subsidization of distant water fleets from industrialized nations can have serious effects on the coastal communities of the developing countries with whom these agreements are typically made.

Possible Impacts of Perverse Subsidization

The impacts of government subsidies of fishing are at least as complex and numerous as the types of subsidies themselves, but in the context of sustainable development those related to market access due to trade measures and resource, livelihood, and food security are the most relevant. The trade implications of the subsidization of the fishing industry arise when the lower costs producers see as a result of the subsidies repress world prices for fish products.

Those producers, who are often from developing countries that cannot afford subsidies, are then excluded from the market because they cannot afford to produce at the world price.

For example, when Japan subsidizes its fleets to fish in the waters of Chile, Japanese fishers bring the fish back to Japan and sell them on their domestic market. Chilean fishers try to enter the Japanese market and sell these same Chilean fish to Japanese consumers, but are kept out of the market because their costs are higher and the prices on the Japanese market are too low. In effect, Japanese fishers push Chilean producers out of the market for the sale of their own fish. This example illustrates the way in which subsidies in the fishing sector can exclude those who are outside the national subsidy regime from participating in the market.

Due to numerous examples where the presence of subsidies seemed to increase the capacity in the sector and, in turn, deplete available resources, fishing subsidies have also been blamed for a tendency to encourage overcapacity and overfishing.

The case of stock depletion in Canada's Northwest Atlantic fisheries in the 1950s and 1960s illustrates how subsidies can increase capacity and lead to depletion. Between 1954 and 1968, Canadian subsidies increased the capacity of the Northwest Atlantic offshore fishing fleet by more than 18 times, creating twice as much capacity as could capture fish if resources were to be used sustainably. In 1970, the Canadian government "acknowledged explicitly that its subsidies for vessel construction and modernization over the previous two decades had led to the rapid expansion of larger vessels, creating serious overcapitalisation." An Organization for Economic Cooperation and Development (OCED) study reported that subsidies also contributed to overcapacity in the fishing sector in many member states: New Zealand in the 1970s and early 1980s, Spain's Galician fisheries in the 1980s, Norway in the 1960s, the EU during the 1980s, and the United States (US) in the late 1970s and 1980s. These examples of the history of fishing fleet subsidization in industrialized countries and the resulting depletion of their stocks illustrates how overcapacity in a sector can encourage overuse of a fragile resource and lead to its exhaustion, posing threats to the surrounding ecosystem and human environment.

In addition to threatening the resources on which humans depend for their incomes, fishing subsidies may pose direct threats to crucial aspects of human and national development such as livelihood and food security. These threats are seen most strikingly in the interaction between developing nations and the industrialized countries with whom they sign access agreements. Frequent realities of EU-West African access agreements, for example, include a disregard of African fishing regulations and international agreements by distant water fleets, an inability by African states to monitor activities or catch levels of EU fleets, a lack of direct linkage between access payments and money spent on fisheries-related activities, a lack of enforcement of management efforts by African governments due to a fear of losing compensations, and the challenge of depletion of valuable fisheries stocks. There are also often many adverse effects on African coastal communities such as threats to the livelihoods of artisanal fishers and food security of those who depend of local fish stocks for protein intake. While EU payments often constitute important sources of revenue for West African governments, the security of fishing resources, vital to so many aspects of these countries, are often threatened.

The case of one West African country that signed an access agreement with the EU, Senegal, illustrates how subsidies and trade agreements can lead to threats on food and livelihood security. The Senegalese government initially implemented subsidies as a way to encourage fish production to supply domestic consumers with a protein source; fish accounts for 75 per cent of the population's protein needs. But the use of subsidies has since become incompatible with this goal since the end result has been a re-orientation towards encouraging the exportation of fisheries resources and agreements with the EU for access to Senegalese fisheries.

The combination of domestic export subsidies, which lower the costs of production for those fishers who chose to export, and trade advantages granted under the Lomé Agreement of 1982, which authorized customs exemptions to products originating in African, Caribbean, and Pacific (ACP) countries and increased the competitiveness of Senegalese piscatorial products in the European market, have encouraged small-scale fishers in the country to both intensify their efforts in response to international demand as well as orient themselves towards the export market.

These developments in subsidy policy, along with several fisheries agreements that have been signed with Japan and the EU, have threatened livelihood and food security in Senegal.

The impact of growth in subsidy-driven exports has lead to a "breakdown in the supply of cheap protein to the population," since local producers began to switch their activities towards the capture of species of high market value in European economies rather than those affordable to local consumers. The increasing scarcity of fisheries resources has also affected the traditional, artisanal fishers, whose techniques, which require low technology and employ many people, are beneficial for local resource and employment security. Since fish have become scarcer, foreign fishing fleets have become a larger presence, and local fishers lack the equipment and fuel to travel farther out to sea where the remaining catches are located, they have been forced to make deals with European or Asian boats to remain employed.

In return, locals allow the foreign boats access to areas originally reserved for their needs and use. This trend threatens local control of the resource as well as livelihood security. In a country where fish provides a vital source of sustenance for the local population, in terms of both food and employment, the way in which subsidies encourage a reorientation of resources to foreign markets is a matter of much concern for the sustainable development of the country.

CAPABILITIES OF DEVELOPING COUNTRIES IN FISHERIES

Clearly, the needs and capabilities of developing countries in fisheries vary widely. In this report we have identified the main strategic issues and trends in fisheries and aquaculture from a global perspective. The strategy that we advocate for USAID is to identify and address the common needs within and among countries to benefit the greatest number of people for the resources available.

Considering the issues and future trends we have identified in this study, we recommend the following strategic approaches to USAID:

USAID needs to substantially increase its programmatic emphasis and enlarge its *financial and human resource commitments to global fisheries and aquaculture.*

Given the importance of fish and fisheries to the global economy and their importance in poverty alleviation and food security, USAID has ample justification to increase its global profile in fisheries and aquaculture. We strongly recommend that USAID substantially increase its programmatic emphasis, funding, and enlarge its staff commitments to global fisheries and aquaculture issues.

If USAID cannot increase its core commitments in these areas, the Agency should consider augmenting its core staff by rotating into USAID mid-and senior level professionals from state and federal governments, academia, NGOs, and industry. USAID needs to make more prominent the importance it gives to the sustainability of fisheries and aquaculture at all levels of its bureaucracy: at its DC headquarters, and in all of its missions, and its regions. In addition, USAID needs to give a higher profile to capture fisheries and aquaculture issues in descriptions of its overall agriculture and natural resources portfolios. We find the word "fisheries" missing from these; and we believe aquaculture is too "buried" in lists describing a wide range of agricultural issues that interest the USAID.

USAID needs to play a central role in mobilizing America's considerable human *and institutional resources in fisheries and aquaculture to assist developing countries.*

Our vision is one in which the USAID is a world leader in channeling high quality, "needs directed" kinds of technical assistance in fisheries and aquaculture to developing countries, mainly in the form of capacity building though education and training opportunities, but also in applied research. In order to achieve this vision, we believe that the USA needs to increase its competence and competitive position in dealing with fisheries and aquaculture issues in developing countries.

USAID needs to play a central role in mobilizing America's considerable human and institutional resources in fisheries and aquaculture to assist developing countries. This can be brought about by a variety of initiatives, but the basic requirement is for US applied science and outreach professionals to work more often and for longer durations in developing country fisheries and aquaculture situations in a way that focuses more closely on collaborative solutions to common issues.

A key element of USAID approaches must be the leveraging its organizational and leadership strengths in fisheries and aquaculture by utilizing the considerable array of expertise and talent that exists in America's government (USDA, NOAA-OAR, NOAA-Sea Grant, NOAA-Fisheries, USGS, etc.), universities, state agencies, industry, and NGOs. We encourage USAID to develop innovative ideas/proposals to link with the interests of the US State Department and the Peace Corps to develop additional policy, research, and extension capabilities. In addition, the USAID needs to better insure that its multi-lateral and bilateral investments make the most use of American expertise in fisheries and aquaculture, especially in regards to instruments and relationships with The World Fish Center, various UN organizations, The World Bank, and The Asian, African, and Interamerican Development Banks.

The Pond Dynamics/Aquaculture CRSP (PD/A CRSP) is one notable example of how the USAID can play an enhanced role in mobilizing America's considerable human and institutional resources in fisheries and aquaculture to assist developing countries. The PD/A CRSP has been involved with over 50 institutions and NGOs in 27 host countries. Since the inception of the PD/A CRSP over 200 researchers have been involved and over 400 graduate and undergraduate students supported.

During the past eight years the PD/A CRSP has worked (or is currently working) with 18 US universities in 16 states. This vital capacity-building has enhanced and strengthened host countries' abilities to further develop aquaculture and provide an additional and much needed protein source to the local and regional populations.

However, USAID funds have been far too limited to develop long-term University centers of excellence in capture fisheries and aquaculture; plus the CRSP lacks a broader mandate in order to engage fully in the urgent issues of nearshore and inland fisheries, marine aquaculture, coastal area management, and the comprehensive, systems-based natural resource management approaches we recommend that would ensure a sustainable future for capture fisheries and aquaculture.

The USAID needs to examine how the CRSP, the USAID Cooperative Agreements, and other current/past administrative initiatives in coastal management and aquaculture could be used as models to expand long-term engagement in critical regional issues that have place-based centers and can involve an expanded collaboration between USAID/Government/Universities that could build on America's strengths and competitive position.

Foreign nationals need specialized short and long-term training in the US. Trained human resources are essential to resource management, which require, inter alia: multi-disciplinary expertise in fishery resource assessment; bio-economic and socio-economic analysis; management techniques; fishing technology, marketing and quality control; resource monitoring; fishery surveillance; and fisheries legislation.

The USAID Cooperative Agreements in aquaculture, fisheries and comprehensive coastal area management with American universities were very effective programmes for capacity building worldwide. These Agreements created an impressive cadre of globally important leaders—and good will—in fisheries and aquaculture throughout the academic and governmental institutions of many nations. We urge USAID to enhance its commitments to the building of additional leadership capacities in developing nations by elevating overall human resource capabilities to better manage fisheries and aquaculture. Additional Cooperative Agreements for training on a variety of concepts and skills are needed in order to have a chance at sustaining and rehabilitating fisheries and aquaculture ecosystems in many nations, to strengthen institutions, and to improve individual performance. We recommend USAID to:

- Increase funding to and the participation of American scientists in The World Fish Center, and more generally, in the current and planned activities in fisheries and aquaculture of the Consultative Group in International Agriculture Research (CIGAR),
- Participate actively in the UN/FAO Associate Professional Officer programme, so that young professionals can gain varied and broad global experiences in international settings,
- Increase the recruitment of fishery and aquaculture graduates into USAID missions and train them more extensively in pre-service at American universities,
- Fund or facilitate additional foreign student degree and certificate programmes in fisheries and aquaculture and associated resource sciences at US institutions (both at universities and at US government organizations),
- Fund or facilitate additional targeted technical assistance missions (social science, economics, fisheries management, processing, labeling, GIS, HACCP, etc.),

We recommend that USAID lead a planning process that could result in establishment of formal collaborations with a suite of US government/University centers of excellence— possibly using an expanded and better funded CRSP mechanism—in order to develop additional applied science and extension/

outreach capabilities in capture fisheries and aquaculture, and to better organize long-term, strategic and medium-term implementation plans and regular impact assessments of an expanded USAID portfolio in capture fisheries and aquaculture.

USAID needs to bridge the "digital divide" to develop solutions to fisheries and aquaculture issues in developing countries.

The Internet, supported via cable and satellite, can be an outreach pipeline, not only for spatial analyses, but also for moving more general information on fisheries and aquaculture to developing countries. There is a vast storehouse of fisheries and aquaculture information in the form of on-line technical reports and publications from US government and state agencies, NGOs, universities, professional organizations, and industry that could be "piped" abroad via the Internet. In many cases, simply raising awareness of the availability and location of the material would suffice as a useful intervention. Distance learning via the Internet, TV and radio is increasingly being used for training in developing countries. Even though, the US possesses the means to be effective in these media, training on fisheries and aquaculture using these media is not yet common. Solutions to the problems of fisheries and aquaculture share a fundamental need of basic comparative information on causes and pathways. Nearly all of the issues are not isolated; rather they are shared by neighbouring communities and countries, or topically right around the globe. Furthermore, many of them already have been experienced and treated in many areas of the world, prominently in the USA.

A fundamental problem is that the applied science that has been employed and experience gained in surmounting the issues is not yet readily available to the developing world at acceptable costs.

Therefore, an important advancement of USAID could be an initiative to help bridge the "digital divide" by increasing its emphasis on identifying, compiling and packaging solutions to fisheries and aquaculture issues of developing countries, and by broadening USAID involvement with many organizations specialized in technical, social and economic solutions in fisheries and aquaculture for which the USA has a comparative advantage—especially by taking advantage of the latitude within USAID for developing a broad variety of initiatives that include the US federal government and state agencies, commercial firms, NGO's, Land/Sea Grant universities, regional aquaculture centers, and international organizations. Several kinds of USAID initiatives are required to:

- Synthesize, package, and deliver applied research information by enhancing extension systems to move information to developing countries and to disseminate it in an effective manner;
- Assess the potential of distance learning to significantly improve technical and managerial competences in fisheries and aquaculture in developing countries;

- Facilitate information flow via choosing methods of information delivery that are appropriate for different audiences in different regions (increasing Internet access, radio, CDs, DVDs, videos, etc.);
- Sponsor collaborative in-country research between US professionals and applied fisheries and aquaculture professionals in developing nations on problems that are indigenous to the country or region.

DEVELOPMENT OF THE AMAZON AQUAFORUM

We applaud the Pond Dynamics/Aquaculture CRSP in its development of the Amazon Aquaforum, an Internet-based information exchange aquaculture network in South America which supported development of a variety of technologically appropriate information delivery methods. The CRSP also maintains an invaluable, comprehensive, standardized database of information collected from throughout the world. The CRSP developed a web-based resource for small and medium-scale farmers in Latin America called the Web-based Information Delivery System for Tilapia (WIDeST), a decision-making tool that enables users to gain access to useful resources when deciding on appropriate, site specific methods and aquaculture practices.

USAID should prioritize the improved management of coastal marine and inland fisheries by providing technical assistance to evolve innovative fisheries management schemes in developing countries including but not limited to: property rights, co-management, and the use of marine protected areas; plus assist in the development of more accurate and reliable fisheries and aquaculture data reporting systems.

USAID needs to invest additional resources to assist in achieving the long-term goal of sustaining the world's invaluable marine and inland capture fisheries, which are disproportionately located in developing countries. Additional investments in capture fisheries could positively impact and better leverage USAID's current and planned investments in coastal area management and aquaculture.

Additional assistance is needed to engage users and government institutions to bolster management and governance structures to address issues of overcapacity, access, marine tenure, critical habitats and nurseries, and a priority range of social issues such as gender relations. Investigations are needed into conservation engineering (innovative gears and management); roles of reserves, protected and conservation areas; plus investigations regarding how best to protect freshwater flows to estuaries (and rivers to lakes)—especially the timing, volume, quality and pulsing of freshwater flows to critical estuaries.

In addition, the USAID could play a major role in analyzing and promoting effective fisheries management, government policies, reforms, market/trade policies, and reductions of subsidies. In comparison to the long-standing emphasis on technical investments in fisheries for stock assessments, etc., comparably little attention has been paid to the users of fishery resources. This is despite the fact that the observed successes, failures, and constraints experienced in marine and inland capture fisheries management are social and economic in nature.

Another problem is that fishery researchers often have a low status and income in a given national context, have limited facilities and resources, few opportunities for in-service training, and have limited access to outside scientific research information. We recommend that the USAID expand its investments in the community-based management of marine protected areas, property rights, and overall investments in social ecology and ecosystems-based management of fisheries.

Illegal, unreported and unregulated fishing is found in all capture fisheries, irrespective of the location, species targeted, fishing gears employed or level and intensity of exploitation. USAID should work with the reporting countries to improve fishery statistics, primarily to meet national needs with regard to food security and fisheries management. Unlike capture fisheries, the separate monitoring of aquaculture is relatively new in most countries, and often there are less well-established systems of data collection as compared to capture fisheries.

USAID needs to substantially increase its support to develop more comprehensive, sustainable, ecologically and socially compatible, environmentally-friendly and economically viable aquaculture systems in developing countries that have the long-term goals of poverty alleviation and food security.

To meet global demands for fisheries products, aquaculture will continue to grow at a rapid pace over the next 10 years; then, its rate of growth will slow until the considerable environmental constraints it faces are solved. Aquaculture faces a number of important problems, including access to appropriate technologies, lack of comprehensive, inter-sectoral planning, and a lack of financial resources for the poor, information on its environmental and social impacts and diseases. The priority areas for further applied research support include:

- Land, water and feed/nutrient use in aquaculture in comparison with other animal protein production systems;
- Sustainable intensification and non-consumptive water use in freshwater aquaculture production;
- Participatory management approaches to the comprehensive development of aquaculture ecosystems as sustainable means of rural development;
- Sustainable coastal aquaculture development, especially technologies that avoid user conflicts;
- Social and economic research to add insights into the adoption of aquaculture by poor rural households;

- Genetically advanced technologies for sustainable stock enhancement and ranching programmes, plus the domestication, selective breeding, and genetic improvement of existing aquaculture species;
- Technologies to solve disease problems and innovative management solutions to improve the health of aquatic animals;
- Development of low cost, non-fish meal based feeds;
- Training in the quality and safety of aquaculture products; and
- Research in making emerging technologies cost-effective, including recirculating systems, and offshore aquaculture systems.

The appropriate role for the USAID in fisheries and aquaculture biotechnology is to support applied research and outreach activities that engage in well-known, conventional genetic improvement techniques, such as selective breeding, etc., as opposed to research support to advanced biotechnologies, such as transgenics. USAID support for The World Fish Center's programme on the genetic improvement of farmed tilapias (GIFT)—and the development of international protocols for product dissemination—is an excellent example of the types of biotechnology investments the merit USAID's future consideration. However, it is also very important that USAID engage nations who have large and active programmes in advanced fisheries/aquaculture biotechnology—such as China—in issues of policies, protocols, environmental, market and other social impacts of transgenics.

USAID should prioritize its assistance to capture fisheries and aquaculture activities that are more integrated, comprehensive, community-based, and use "systems approaches"—such as ecological and integrated farming/fishing systems research and extension approaches—in both rural and urban settings. The current agriculture emphasis of USAID is on plant commodity research, not on a comprehensive, agro/aqua-ecosystems research/extension approach. We urge the USAID to support long-term, applied research and development that makes expanded use of participatory ecological and social science tools to empower community control of fisheries and aquaculture systems; and to better integrate aquaculture and fisheries activities into the comprehensive management of natural and social resources of its missions, target nations and regions.

The kinds of assistance provided by USAID should be based on a combination of: (1) assessed needs and capabilities in developing countries, and (2) the comparative advantages held by the USA in technical expertise, education, communications, business management and commercial products. Assistance focused on US comparative advantages provides a way to get around duplication of effort among competing international organizations, while still fully supporting the Code of Conduct for Responsible Fisheries. The top priority for USAID should be the sustainable development of community-based, integrated farming and fishing systems with the long-term goals of poverty alleviation and food security.

AQUACULTURE AND FISHERIES ACTIVITIES

Aquaculture and fisheries activities are frequently poorly planned and considered; funded separately from activities that greatly impact them; and are generally neglected by all levels of government. Fisheries activities should be planned as a continuum, and comprehensively as part of the planning for integrated natural resources management (water, wastes, agriculture, etc.), and the sustainable development of human communities.

Fisheries and aquaculture information should be linked/coordinated with activities in other sectors (*e.g.*, agriculture, forestry, food processing, distribution, etc.). Fisheries and aquaculture should be planned up-front—not as an afterthought—in all water resource development projects such as reservoir and irrigation projects. Coordination is both justified and essential because of shared issues with other sectors of sustaining biodiversity, maintaining water quality and quantity, the management and development in coastal areas and in river and lake basins, and addressing environmental degradation, mitigation and restoration, and the need to improve governance. USAID is encouraged to prioritize its support to applied research and development activities that articulate well with the natural and social resource and farming systems contexts of a nation/region, and (a) plan for the activities as one part of a comprehensive management strategy for the non-consumptive, multiple uses of water; and (b) use ecosystems-based management approaches that promote the more comprehensive, long-term stewardship of marine and freshwater environments. We urge the USAID to support the expanded use of participatory tools to empower community controls over fisheries and aquaculture systems; to use innovative co-management methods to sustain local water and coastal resources, and the community-based management of water bodies for fisheries and aquaculture. Fisheries and aquaculture provide foods of very high nutritional value for households.

When resource-poor fishers and farmers combine fisheries, agriculture, aquaculture and the conservation/rehabilitation of natural resources in innovative "ecosystems approaches"' they improve their food supplies, increase their incomes, and become better able to withstand environmental and economic fluctuations; thereby decreasing risks, increasing fishing and farm sustainability, and contributing greatly to rural social and economic development.

We encourage the USAID to incorporate additional, applied social science and micro-economics research into innovative ecosystem-based methods that empower communities to better manage and control fisheries systems, and to develop more environmentally and socially compatible aquaculture systems (protected areas, property rights, innovative co-management approaches, etc.). Most of the modern aquatic resource crises have roots in social issues that are poorly known, such as the "shifting nature of modern survival" in developing nations. Millions of people do not only fish or farm, rather, they derive income from multiple activities and sources, and in some cases, conduct long distance seasonal migrations between inland farming systems and fisheries systems, and vice versa. USAID is encouraged to support the development of aquaculture systems that are well integrated into existing water resource systems, are virtually non-consumptive of water, and make multiple uses of water.

SMALL BUSINESS DEVELOPMENT

Aquaculture has the potential for small business development but additional technical assistance is needed by business professionals familiar with economics, labour dynamics, opportunity costs, issues of price and volume competition, and other commercial and competitive contexts of other sectors such as agriculture, etc.

The recent activities of the Pond Dynamics/Aquaculture CRSP (PD/A CRSP) are notable in this regard. In 2002, the CRSP conducted regional meetings in Latin America, the Caribbean, Africa, and Asia, plus commissioned a report to explore the current status of aquaculture in Eastern Europe/Central Asia. Participants represented diverse areas of expertise; gender diversity was also a criterion of panel composition.

During the meetings, participants were asked to identify and prioritize constraints to aquaculture development in the region of their expertise. Three central needs-directed programme areas emerged after analyzing the results of the meetings. This movement of the PD/A CRSP to become more of a "system-oriented" network as opposed to a "commodity" collaborative is noteworthy and laudable; and if additional resources were available, these concepts could be developed further.

We cannot emphasize more strongly that poorly-funded, short-term projects with broad, "global" goals will not make lasting impacts on the conservation and sustainable development of fisheries and aquaculture systems in developing countries; and that these approaches do not serve the strategic interests of the United States. Research, education and extension assistance must target the long-term engagement of institutions, and deliver approaches, findings and insights towards these institutional systems and organizations that will continue the long-term engagement with farmers/fishers that can weather the invariable fluctuations in development assistance that will occur over time.

USAID needs to develop comprehensive strategic and implementation plans and regular impact assessments of an expanded capture fisheries and aquaculture portfolio. USAID missions and regions worldwide should include capture fisheries and aquaculture into their strategic plans for the management of natural resources—or they will be incomplete—especially in regards to USAID plans for involvement in the issues of water allocation and quality, and plans for the comprehensive management of marine and inland coastal areas.

USAID needs to sustain a strategic, long-term commitment to fisheries and aquaculture as parts of comprehensive natural, aquatic resource management. Short-term projects should be part of larger, longer-term strategic frameworks for directed action that have adequate accountability to measure strategic progress and impacts. USAID needs to conduct regular, transparent processes that result in the publication of strategic and implementation plans for fisheries and aquaculture over 5 to 10-year time frames. The movement from short term projects to longer term investments in centers of excellence, for example, will require the USAID to develop strategic planning and assessment processes that are much more comprehensive and "living". With more stable investments strategic plans have a shorter "shelf life" and require more frequent review and evaluation in order to make the necessary "mid-course changes". We recommend a process similar to that used by Standing Committees of the U.S. National Research Council where external expert advisors regularly measure progress on investment portfolios.

Within the fisheries sector, USAID should take advantage of shared needs for land and water resources and issues in common to identify sub-sector groupings for directed technical assistance and development activities. We identify two groups that require distinct interventions: (1) offshore (*i.e.*, within the EEZs) and high seas fisheries share common issues of resource and fisheries management that include shared resources, over harvesting, and excess capacity, and (2) coastal and inland fisheries as well as aquaculture to a great extent, may interact both positively and negatively with one another, sometimes competing for space, resources and markets, but they also share many common issues that are external to the fisheries sector, most importantly the environment and poor governance.

2

Embryonic and Genetic Manipulation in Fish

EMBRYOGENESIS FERTILIZERS

Embryogenesis begins when a sperm fertilizes an egg and creates a single cell that has the potential to form an entire organism. In the first hours after fertilization, this cell divides into identical cells. Approximately 4 days after fertilization and after several cycles of cell division, these cells begin to specialize, forming a hollow sphere of cells, called a blastocyst. The blastocyst has an outer layer of cells, and inside this hollow sphere, there is a cluster of cells called the inner cell mass. The cells of the inner cell mass will go on to form virtually all of the tissues of the human body.

Although the cells of the inner cell mass can form virtually every type of cell found in the human body, they cannot form an organism. Therefore, these cells are referred to as pluripotent, that is, they can give rise to many types of cells but not a whole organism. Pluripotent stem cells undergo further specialization into stem cells that are committed to give rise to cells that have a particular function. Examples include blood stem cells that give rise to red blood cells, white blood cells, and platelets, and skin stem cells that give rise to the various types of skin cells. These more specialized stem cells are called multipotent—capable of giving rise to several kinds of cells, tissues, or structures.

CLEAVAGE FERTILIZATION

After fertilization, the zygote proceeds immediately to the first cleavage (cell division) and subsequent cell divisions follow rapidly. The zygote is a very large cell, but the first waves of rapid cell division occur without increase in cell volume.

The result is a closely bound mass of cells each of more typical cell size. At this stage the cells are called blastomeres, and the organism as a whole is called a morula from the time it has 16 blastomeres to the next stage. As it is undergoing this very rapid cell division, the organism is also migrating down the uterine tube towards the uterus.

Vertebrates, such as humans, have bilateral symmetry and therefore polarity in three dimensions (head-tail, or back-front, and left-right). Establishing polarity is one of the most basic manifestations of emerging specialization. But the egg is roughly spherical, and it is not readily apparent how polarity is established. Although it had been shown long ago that the point of sperm entry determines the plane of first cleavage (and thus subsequent ones) in amphibian eggs, mammals were believed until recently to remain spherically symmetrical until later in development. Recent data on mammalian zygotes, however, suggests that the point of sperm entry may similarly determine the cleavage plane. Even the first two cells resulting from the first cleavage may have different propensities, which persist through the next divisions as the progeny of one cell tend to become the body of the offspring and progeny of the other cell become the embryo's contribution to the placenta and other supporting structures. The word "fate," however, might be too strong, because the cells of such very early embryos are resilient to perturbations—if one cell is removed, the remaining ones can compensate.

GASTRULATION ACCUMULATE

Gastrulation begins when fluid starts to accumulate between the blastomeres of the morula. The fluid-filled spaces run together, forming a relatively large fluid-filled cavity. At the point when the cavity becomes recognizable, the organism is called a blastocyst. The outer cells of the blastocyst, especially those around the blastocyst cavity, assume a flattened shape. The flattened cells of the exterior blastocyst are the trophoblast. They become the embryo's contribution to the placenta and other supporting structures. On one side of the blastocyst is a group of cells that project inside into the blastocyst cavity; this is the inner cell mass, or embryoblast, and its progeny form the body of the new offspring.

The cells of the inner cell mass can give rise to progeny differentiating into all the types of cells in the adult body, so they are called pluripotent. They have not usually been described as totipotent because, the inner cell mass having already differentiated from trophoblast, the cells of the inner cell mass were believed to be no longer able to give rise to the cells of the trophoblast. Recent work, however, describes culture conditions under which human embryonic stem cells can differentiate to trophoblast cells. Although the new offspring itself develops only from the inner call mass, the trophoblast is not just passive padding. Its progeny are the essential and specialized connection between the embryonic and maternal systems. Embryonic stem cells can be isolated from the inner cell mass.

ORGANOGENESIS STRUCTURES

The basic structures and relations of all the major organ systems of the body emerge during the fourth through the eighth weeks of embryonic development. First, the embryo folds in several ways so that the flat linear structure distinguished by neural tube flanked by somites become roughly C-shaped.

The effect of this is to bring the regions of the brain, gut, and other internal organs into their familiar anatomical relations. During the fourth week the neural pores, the ends of the neural tube "zipper," close. First the one at the cranial or head end, which is called the anterior or rostral pore, closes, and later the caudal or tail-ward pore closes.

Closure of the neural pores completes the closure of what will become the central nervous system. Also during the fourth week, limb buds become visible, first buds for arms and later for legs. Further, two accumulations of cells along the neural tube become distinguishable: the alar plate and the basal plate. Cells of the alar plate go on to become mostly sensory neurons, while basal plate cells give rise mostly to motor neurons. Already while the neural tube is closing, its walls along the cranial area are thickening to form early brain structure. Cranial nerves, for example the nerves for the eye and for the muscles of the face and jaw, also are beginning to develop at this time. The embryonic brain develops rapidly in both size and structure especially during the fifth week, and the optic cup that will form the retina of the eye becomes visible as well.

HOMOLOGY ORGANISMS

Similarities that exist between different organisms are cited by evolutionists as one of the most compelling lines of evidence for their theory. *Homologous* features are shared design concepts that are generally assumed by evolutionists to be the result of a shared ancestry and therefore offering support for the Darwinian theory of common descent. In The Origin of Species, Darwin referred to the *similar bones in the same relative positions* in the hand of a man and several other mammals as *specifically what the theory of common descent would expect*. The 2008 edition of Prentice Hall Biology by Miller and Levine illustrates that this concept is commonly held wherein it states: *In their early stages of development, chickens, turtles, and rats look similar, providing evidence that they shared a common ancestry*.

Much like gene comparisons, the similarities that are evident during embryo development (*von Baer's law*) are assumed outright to be due to phylogenetic relationships and therefore homologous. Furthermore, embryo homology is considered to be such powerful evidence of common ancestry that patterns during embryogenesis are used to determine if shared morphological structures are truly homologous (due to shared ancestry) or merely analogous (due to convergent evolution). Miller and Levine define homology in such terms: *structures that have different mature forms in different organisms but develop from the same embryonic tissues*.

The reemerging of the early 19th century *"Von Baer's law"* has stimulated a new biological discipline called Evolutionary Developmental Biology, which is a collaboration of Evolutionary Biology and Developmental Biology, popularly known as Evo-devo. This area of scientific enquiry draw from the beliefs of Darwinism that all organisms have descended from the same ancestor, and generally assumes that embryonic developmental mechanisms should be shared (conserved). Drawing from these assumptions, evolutionary developmental biologists compare the developmental processes of different animals and plants in an attempt to determine the ancestral relationship between organisms.

Developmental biologist William Ballard a well known elder developmental biologist at Dartmouth College comments on the impact of *von Baer's law* on modern embryology.

"Thus, the energy of investigators and particularly students is diverted into the essentially fruitless 19th century activity of bending the facts of nature to support second-rate generalities of no predictive value. Though enthusiasm for Haeckel's recapitulation `law' died out, unfortunately the popularity of Von Baer's `laws' of 1828 was renewed. In order to defend the latter's descriptive statements that general characters appear before special characters as an egg develops and that the less general and finally the specific characters trail along later, we have to decide intuitively that certain characters are of `morphological significance' and others are not. When referring to vertebrates, we have to use words like blastula and gastrula in such a way as to imply that things that are vastly different from each other are really very much the same. "

Differences among organisms have traditionally been assumed to become more significant as development proceeds, and therefore earlier embryonic stages should resemble one another more than latter stages. This view can be found presented in popular biology textbooks. Although these assumptions have persisted into modern times, it has been recognized by embryologists since Darwin that this doctrine of developmental biology *"is not in accordance with the facts of development"*, according to British embryologist Adam Sedgwick who also stated: *there is no stage of development in which the unaided eye would fail to distinguish between them with ease"*. Modern embryologists confirm this as well, and have further challenged the erroneous nature of these assumptions.

Recent work has revealed that embryos are not more similar during the earlier stages of cleavage and gastrulation, but in fact, are most alike at the later stage illustrated by Haeckel and recently photographed by Richardson. In the gastrulation stage, fish show dramatic differences when compared to amphibians, and neither are similar to reptiles, birds, or mammals. Organisms begin life very dissimilar, then become somewhat alike during embryo development, then diverge again as adults. Evo-devos (evolutionary developmental biologists) refer to this pattern as the *developmental hourglass*. William Ballard adds that *only by semantic tricks and subjective selection of evidence can we claim that "gastrulas" of shark, salmon, frog, and bird are more alike than their adults*.

Ballard continues:

"In fact, the most obvious structural characteristics of either the eggs or the cleavage stages of a shark, a salmon, a frog, a bird, or a mammal are unique each to its own class, not generally shared. We would not consider them very much alike unless we had been taught so at a very early age. Very few vertebrates pass through a stage which can strictly be called a blastula. The embryo in its period of most active morphogenetic movements is usually called a gastrula, but as all agree this word has no morphologic meaning anymore. Each class of vertebrates (in mammals we might almost say each particular order) develops and then loses its own set of temporary structures-like the parade ground `formations of maneuver' during this period. "

Another significant challenge for evo-devo is the recognition that organs and structures develop from different groups of embryo cells in organisms that are believed to share a common ancestry. Fundamental structures, like the alimentary canal, kidney, or forelimb are commonly found to form from different embryological tissues. The alimentary canal (digestive tract) is formed from the roof of the embryonic gut cavity in sharks; whereas in frogs it is formed from the gut roof and floor; and in birds and reptiles it is derived from the lower layer of the embryonic disc or blastoderm. Vertebrate forelimbs, which were used as an example of homology by Darwin and can be found in hundreds of textbooks as proof for evolution, also develop from different body segments in different species. Rather than being proof of Darwinism, recent embryological studies have shown that forelimbs are not developmentally homologous. The forelimbs in the newt develop from embryo trunk segments 2 through 5; in the lizard they develop from segments 6 to 9; in humans they develop from segments 13 through 18. The development of the vertebrate kidney also conflicts with the view of homology. Evolutionist Michael Denton notes these conflicts in Evolution: A Theory in Crisis.

"In fish and amphibia the kidney is derived directly from an embryonic organ known as the mesonephros, while in reptiles and mammals the mesonephros degenerates towards the end of embryonic life and plays no role in the formation of the adult kidney, which is formed instead from a discrete spherical mass of mesodermal tissue, the metanephros, which develops quite independently from the mesonephros.

Studies of the genes governing development have added even further difficulties for evo-devo. According to the views of neodarwinists, homologous features are produced by genes that have been passed down by common ancestors. Because similar genes are unlikely to have originated independently through random mutation, sequence similarity between organisms indicates they share an ancestral relationship (they are homologous). Features produced by similar sequences are then also inferred to be phylogenetically homologous. For decades it has been recognized that homologous organs were frequently produced by different genes, but more recently, evo-devo biologists discovered that certain developmental genes were highly conserved (similar) in radically different organisms. These homeotic genes are short sequences that act as regulatory switches affecting the development of structures such as eyes and legs. When mutated, homeotic genes can transform one body part into another, such as an antenna into a leg. In organisms as vastly different as mammals and fruit flies, these genes are so similar that the mouse gene can regulate the development of the compound eye of the fruit fly. In such examples, the conflict with Darwinian assumptions lies in the fact that non-homologous structures are produced (or at least regulated) by supposedly homologous genes. As Jonathan Wells states very poignantly: *homology, whether defined morphologically or phylogenetically, cannot be attributed to similar developmental pathways any more than it can be attributed to similar genes.*

The famous embryologist Sir Gavin de Beer challenged his colleagues with the following question which remains unanswered to this day.

"But if it is true that through the genetic code, genes code for enzymes that synthesize proteins which are responsible (in a manner still unknown in embryology) for the differentiation of the various parts in their normal manner, what mechanism can it be that results in the production of homologous organs, the same "patterns", in spite of their not being controlled by the same genes? I asked this question in 1938, and it has not been answered.

Worldviews

While Darwin was convinced that embryological homology was the *strongest single class of facts* to support his views. Modern embryology has instead challenged the Darwinian theory of common descent by illustrating that seemingly homologous structures, such as the mammalian forelimb, developed along different pathways, and are therefore not homologous at all.

While the Darwinists see these similarities as evidence of common descent, the creationist belief system causes us to generally conclude that shared structures, processes, or genes are merely reflections that they were designed by the same creator. Rather than being evidence of shared ancestry, homologies are examples of brilliant and well functioning designs that have been applied to multiple organisms, much in the same way as human designers apply concepts.

FIRST MONOGRAPH OF FISH CULTURE

Lives on earth first appeared over 3 billion years ago. As a result of evolution, vertebrates are the utmost advanced life form distributing from seabed to high-mountain. Fishes, at the lower stage of evolution but being the biggest community in vertebrates, include about 21,700 to 28,000 species that take over almost half of the total number of vertebrates. Fishes are also models for experimental study as the eggs are large, fertilization and development are externally and the embryos are transparent. In addition, mono-sexual breeding and crossbreeding between many distantly related species could be done in fishes. Fish culture is one of the earliest activities of human civilization.

This is the first monograph of fish culture in the world. Since then, Chinese farmers enjoyed a long tradition of selective domestication resulting in very valuable "four farming species" of fish for pond culture. These are black carp (Mylopharyngodon poceus), grass carp (Ctnopharyngodon idellus), silver carp (Hypophthalmichihys molivrix) and big-head carp (Aristichthys nobilis). Based on the feeding habits of these fishes, Chinese farmers also invented "multi-culture method" of stocking the four farming species together in the same water body. This is in fact a sustainable ecological system by that farmers are able to gain maximum output with minimum cost. These domesticated species and the multi-culture method have been favourably adopted by other nations abroad.

In addition to the traditional experiences of fish farming, scientists in China initiated some fundamental research in fish cell and developmental biology and molecular genetics leading to a break-through in fish biotechnology. The major achievements are pointed as follows. In 1960's, Professor Tung T. C. first introduced the art of nuclear transplantation with fish to study the interaction between nucleus and cytoplasm. Tung and his colleagues succeeded in generation of "nuclear-cytoplasmic hybridized fish" between different species (reviewed in). In early 1980's, the first somatic cell cloned fish was derived from kidney cells by nuclear transplantation. In 1984, the first batch of transgenic fish was also generated. The development and combination of technologies of nuclear transplantation and gene transfer in fish predicate that a new era in fish breeding is coming; fish directional breeding will revolutionize the traditional fish farming industry.

LIMB DEVELOPMENT

In developmental terms, the human upper limb is divided into the zeugopod, the stylopod, and the autopod, corresponding approximately to the arm, forearm, and hand, respectively. This tripartite structure is ancient and was even expressed, in a primitive form, in certain Devonian sarcopterygian fish. In 2006, the Devonian "fishapod," *Tiktaalik roseae* was discovered in the Canadian Arctic; at 375 million years old, it represents the earliest example of this structure. The development of the chick embryo exhibits this tripartite structure with 3 morphologically discrete digits, making it a popular model of limb development.

In the first phase of limb development, *HOXD9* and *HOXD10* are primarily expressed as the zeugopod develops. In phase II, development progresses distally into the stylopod, and *HOXD11, HOXD12,* and *HOXD13* expression dominate. With the development of digits and the autopod, *HOXD13* expression becomes dominant. As development progresses down the limb, the *HOXD* genes are expressed in successive overlapping fields, wherein each dominant wave of expression gives way to the next, consistent with the colinear ordering of the genes (*HOXD9* to *HOXD13*). The *HOXA* genes are expressed sequentially in a similar way but demonstrate less of an anteroposterior gradient than the expressed *HOXD* genes. This system of orderly, integrated genetic regulation is the current basis of our understanding of the regulation of upper limb development. This nested process of expression is sometimes referred to as a developmental cascade, a term that implies the concept that expression of just a few proteins may result in multiple subsequent events.

The first problem in human limb development is not outgrowth, but locating the point of outgrowth on the body wall. Little is known about the actual mechanism of placing the "presumptive limb field" along the body wall, but it may be related to *TBX5* expression in the lateral plate mesoderm. *HOXC6* is also expressed in the mesoderm limb primordium before any morphologic changes occur. A tumor suppressor related transcription factor may allow mesodermal-ectodermal interaction and induction. The somites also may participate in determination of the limb field.

Although the presumptive field of outgrowth cannot otherwise be distinguished morphologically, experiments demonstrate that much has already occurred before limb outgrowth actually takes place. Even at this early stage, the ectoderm and mesenchyme interact, setting the stage for outgrowth. The ectoderm of the imaginal field may already be committed to the formation of the AER through the transient expression of *FGF*.

Dorsoventral polarization is already established before limb bud projection, perhaps through dorsalizing influences of the somites and ventralizing influences of the lateral somatopleure. The limb bud develops in the Wolff crest, a ring of thickened ectoderm. The mesoderm is believed to be the prime mover. Experiments that removed the mesoderm produced no limbs, while experiments that transplanted the mesoderm resulted in ectopic limbs.

The ectoderm and mesoderm form a highly regulated primordium, which displays the characteristics of a cleaving embryo. If a portion is removed, the primordium reorganizes to form an entire limb. If the imaginal fields are juxtaposed, superimposed, or disaggregated, they also reorganize to form one complete limb. However, if it is split and a barrier is placed between the 2 halves, 2 limbs form.

The first outgrowth of the limb bud occurs with ectodermal expression of *FGF8*. *HOXB6* expression is also involved. As the bud grows, the original overlying ectoderm becomes the AER, and both dorsal and ventral polarized mesoderm is recruited for outgrowth.

Once initiated, outgrowth of the limb bud to limb completion is a function of the PZ (the undifferentiated, dividing mesenchyme). The PZ underlies and is influenced by the AER. As always, ectoderm and mesenchyme interact and maintain each other. This functional, self-sustaining loop is an important mechanism that is repeatedly employed in the process of limb development.

In this case, the ectodermal AER is linked to the mesenchymal zone of polarizing activity (ZPA). This feedback loop involves sonic hedgehog expression by the ZPA and *FGF4* expression by the AER. Without the ZPA, the AER degenerates, and vice versa. The AER, in turn, promotes outgrowth by maintaining the proliferative zone in an undifferentiated and proliferative state. If the AER is removed, the limb is truncated at a level corresponding to the age of the AER removed.

TISSUE DIFFERENTIATION

Skeletal System

The tissues of the skeletal system are the first major tissues to show overt differentiation in the developing upper limb. As cells migrate from the PZ, they become differentiated mesodermal cells and undergo the process of chondrogenesis. Differential growth after migration from the PZ determines the ultimate size of the skeletal element fashioned. This growth may occur in accordance with positional information. In the fourth week, these cells condense proximally to distally to form a centrally located blastema.

Ectoderm has an inhibitory effect on cartilage formation, which may help explain the central location of the blastema. In the fifth week, chondrification occurs proximally. Chondrification of the blastema then proceeds distally, reaching the phalanges in the sixth week. The sesamoids chondrify in the seventh week. As chondrification occurs, the central diaphyseal cells hypertrophy, radially compressing the surrounding mesenchymal cells, which condense into the periosteum and perichondrium. Matrix secretion aids in this process. Radial growth becomes restricted, but longitudinal growth remains uninhibited.

The process of compaction does not occur in the epiphysis, perhaps explaining the enlarged diameter in this area. By day 48, all of the skeletal cartilaginous models except the terminal phalanges are in place.

Ossification begins in the periosteal collars within the central areas of the cartilaginous models destined to become tubular bones. It is initiated in the humerus and shoulder girdle at day 38-40. The process proceeds distally, reaching the radius and ulna in the seventh week and the metacarpals and distal phalanges in the eighth week. The proximal and middle phalanxes begin to ossify at the 11th week.

The earliest sign of joint formation is dense cellular areas without hypertrophy within the blastema from the fifth to sixth weeks. These areas are referred to as the interzones. Capsular structures condense from the surrounding mesenchyme before actual joint cavitation. Large joint formation begins at the seventh week, with the condensation of the 2 dense plates within the interzone separated by a layer continuous with the synovium.

These plates chondrify to form the articular surfaces of the joint. Subsequent cavitation occurs between the articular surfaces. Cavitation coincides with and is dependent on the development of muscular activity and movement. If no movement occurs, the space fills with fibrovascular tissue and subsequently forms cancellous bone.

Formation of the wrist is a complex process. The distal radius is ossified at the sixth week. At first, the lunate lies between the radius and ulna. Differential growth removes it from this position while extracting the distal ulna from the early wrist joint. The triangular fibrocartilaginous complex is formed simultaneously. Fusion of the centrale ulnare distale and the centrale radiale distale forms the scaphoid at the seventh week. Only the trapezium, trapezoid, and capitate arise from the blastema in their distinctive mature geometries.

Molecular Aspects of Digital Chondrogenesis

In order to fashion a digit (or any bone/cartilage/ligament of the body), the actual tissue (bone, cartilage, etc) must first be made (chondrogenesis) and then be "sculpted" through final differentiation and *morphogenesis*. Regulation of the formation of the cartilaginous anlage is attributed to three primary factors: (1) chondrogenic triggering signals (TGFbs, Activins, and BMPs); (2) cartilage identity genes (group E Sox genes, etc); and (3) chondrogenic extracellular matrix. The matrix forms a scaffold for chondrogenic aggregation of cells but also seems to regulate local delivery of chondrogenic triggering signals in precise concentrations and temporal relationships.

In order to focus on molecular relationships, Montero and Hurle identify a zone beneath the AER and progress zone (PZ) conceptualized as a "distal aggregating region," in which exists a zone of early differentiation and a more proximal region of later differentiation resulting in a segmented digital ray. The idea is that cells proliferating in the progress zone leave it and follow one of two pathways: incorporation into the growing ray cartilage or apoptosis. The distal aggregating region is where differentiation into the ray cartilage occurs. The earliest step in chondrogenesis is condensation of the undifferentiated mesenchymal cells into aggregates.

TGFbs and Activins may play redundant signalling pathways specific for triggering chondrogenesis of the rays (rather than unspecific chondrogenic signalling). This process involves upregulation of ALK6 (BmpRIb), which seems to be the main chondrogenic receptor for the limb bud as it is expressed in the prechondrogenic aggregates of all limb skeletal elements.

BMPs have opposite growth-promoting and apoptic effects, which probably depend on the finely tuned local expression of different receptors. They exhibit well-defined expression domains in the developing digits but not at the tip, except for GDF5. Combinations of BMPs are differentially implicated in the distinct skeletal elements of the limb.

Chondrogenic effects of BMPs include the promotion of cell adhesion in prechondrogenic aggregates, the upregulation of Sox genes, and the production of matrix. The earliest sign of chondrogenic commitment is the expression of Sox9 which may also be a protector against the apoptic-promoting effects of BMPs. The BMP receptor ALK3 (BmpRIa) may be a key modulator of joint formation and interdigitation via apoptosis. Overactivation of the TGFb pathway via Smad2 is present in autopodial anomalies such as arachnodactyly, camptodactyly and polydactyly.

Extracellular matrix has a central role in chondrogenesis. At first, it acts as a scaffold for aggregation. It probably also effects the local delivery of growth factors, both in terms timing and in terms of concentration differentials. Components of the ECM are themselves differentially concentrated within the developing ray. For instance, the proteoglycan Syndecan-3 is highly expressed in prechondrogenic aggregation restricted to the perichondrium and the developing joints (after differentiation). Components of the ECM include fibronectin, proteoglycans, tenascin, elastin, fibrillins, etc. Of interest, severe disorganization of the interdigital scaffold of elastin and fibrillin precedes the induction of ectopic digits.

Musculature

Myogenic mesodermal cells originate in the somites. They migrate from the somites at approximately the fourth week. These cells do not appear to be guided intrinsically, but probably follow the lead of connective tissue. They express extracellular fibrils that allow them to interact with the extracellular matrix. These cells coalesce into 2 common muscle masses, one ventral and one dorsal. The myoblasts grow by hypertrophy and fuse into myotubules. The common muscle masses then split to fashion the definitive muscles. Every muscle is identifiable by 7 weeks. The muscles differentiate from superficial to deep. First, the flexor digitorum profundus, flexor carpi radialis, and flexor carpi ulnaris split off, followed by the flexor pollicis longus. The flexor digitorum superficialis originates from a superficial palmar blastema and thus ascends the arm. The palmaris longus ascends only after it has reached its origin. Cell death is involved in shaping the definitive musculature. Viable muscle requires innervation.

Tendons develop independently and are derived from limb bud mesoderm rather than from somites. In fact, tendons develop in the absence of muscle, but they disintegrate later. The intrinsic muscles of the hand arise from 5 embryonic layers: the interossei dorsalis accessorii, intermetacarpals, flexoris breves profundi, contrahentes, and lumbricals. Initially, a common blastema divides into superficial and deep layers. Interossei and a contrahentes muscle are formed from the deep layer.

The contrahentes recedes from the ulnar half of the hand in weeks 7-9 to become the adductor pollicis. The second, third, and fourth dorsal interossei develop from the fusion of 3 layers: the interossei dorsalis accessorii, intermetacarpals, and flexoris brevis profundi. This pattern is unique to the human hand. In association with the tendons and synovial sheath, the pulley system has been recognized by week 9 as condensing mesenchyme. The pulleys are well-developed by week 12.

Innervation

Motor nerve outgrowth from the spinal cord occurs in an orderly fashion around the third week. Nerves from the medial cord grow to innervate the ventral muscle mass, while those of the dorsal cord supply the dorsal mass. In general, the craniocaudal origin of the nerves also correlates with an anteroposterior axis of final innervation; the nerves that are most rostral supply the muscles that are most anterior. By the fourth week, these motor nerves reach the brachial plexus, where they mix and enter the limb by the fifth week.

The process by which the nerves make their way to the target cells is not fully known. The nerve trunks advance with a roughed leading edge termed the pioneer growth cone.

The filopodia of the growth cone allow for close contact with the mesenchymal cells, which may act as signalling cells for guidance. Motor nerves are not guided by their target muscles, nor are they guided by matrix fibrils as are muscle cells. Manipulating the position of the target muscle does not alter the nerve's ability to locate it. Ventral axonal attraction may be mediated by the binding of chemoattractants, termed netrins, to an axonal receptor encoded by *DCC.* Ultimately, contact with a target muscle is necessary for survival of the nerve. Nerve cell death then adjusts the number of nerves to the target size. Sensory cells are derived from the neural crest and follow the motor cells for guidance.

Vasculature

A nascent network of capillaries coalesces from hemangioblastic stem cells in the limb mesenchyme to form a submarginal vein beneath the AER in the third week. This vein is connected to the cardinal vein. Branching from the aorta establishes a central brachial artery axis that then extends into a dominant medial artery. This axis also produces the interosseous artery. At 6 weeks (14-mm embryo), the ulnar artery branches from the brachial artery and reaches the palm by the 16-mm stage. The radial artery branches from the axis last, at the 17-to 18-mm stage. Once the radial artery is established, the median and interosseous arteries regress. The digital arteries arise from capillary networks that regress and split during the process of clefting, such that each border of the resultant interspace contains a digital vessel; this is of clinical significance. In syndactyly, regression of the network does not fully occur, which can result in variable complex vascular patterns in the residual interspace web.

ESTABLISHING AXES

Anteroposterior Axis

As the limb grows, 3 axes are established: anteroposterior, dorsoventral, and proximodistal. Transplantation experiments with chicks established the existence of a small area located in the base of the posterior limb that, when transposed to the anterior margin, resulted in an extra mirror image limb structure with posterior digits along the leading edge. This zone, the ZPA, is believed to be responsible for polarization along the anteroposterior axis. This axis was along the plane of the fingers, with the little finger posterior and the thumb anterior. Retinoic acid beads mimicked the results of the ZPA transplantation experiments, causing the development of a mirror image limb. Therefore, the polarizing effect was postulated to fit a morphogen model of tissue induction.

The ZPA may express a diffusable morphogen that polarizes cells along a concentration gradient. In this model, high concentrations of the morphogen (a retinoic acid analogue) signal for posterior polarization and the development of appropriate posterior digits, while low concentrations signal for anterior position and structures. Retinoic acid is found in high concentrations in the posterior portion of the chick wing. Retinoic binding proteins and receptors are also located here, implicating a role for retinoic acid in anteroposterior polarization.

The morphogen theory demonstrates how individual cells may be exposed and even imprinted with position information (in this case, a point along a concentration gradient). The positional information theory is used to explain how cells identify their position and then appropriately differentiate into the definitive shape and function of the extremity.

Dorsoventral Axis

In classic descriptions, dorsoventral polarization has been attributed to the dorsal ectoderm. When an ectodermal jacket is transposed from a left-sided limb bud to a right-sided mesenchyme, a limb grows with left-sided dorsoventral polarity. In addition, when an AER is placed on a purely dorsal side of a bud, the resulting outgrowth has a jacket of 2 dorsal surfaces; when it is placed on a purely ventral side of a bud, the resulting outgrowth has a jacket of 2 ventral surfaces.

The current model states that dorsal ectoderm expresses *WNT7A,* which induces mesodermal *LMX1B,* instituting polarization of the mesenchyme. Ventral ectoderm expresses *EN1,* which suppresses *WNT7A* expression, thereby allowing the default ventral phenotype to develop.

Dorsoventral polarization may begin within the presumptive limb field before outgrowth. Opposition of dorsalizing signals of the somites and ventralizing signals of the lateral somatopleure may polarize limb field ectoderm. As limb outgrowth recruits this ectoderm, the underlying mesenchyme, in turn, is polarized via *WNT7A, LMX1,* and *EN1.* In addition, localization of the AER is tied to dorsoventral polarization, as the AER occurs at the border of dorsal and ventral cells. The AER develops at the border of radical fringe (*RFNG*)–expressing and non– *RFNG*-expressing cells. Also, in addition to its role in suppressing dorsalizing *WNT7A, EN1* may be involved in limiting the ventral border of the AER.

Proximodistal Axis

The last axis, the proximodistal axis, is believed to be defined as a function of outgrowth and the PZ. As development proceeds down the limb, cells leave the PZ and differentiate into appropriate mesenchymal structures (skeleton, connective tissue, vessels). The gene *MSX1* (formerly known as *HOX7*) may be involved in keeping the PZ cells undifferentiated. The cells leaving the PZ may, in a sense, be polarized in the proximodistal axis by dwelling time within the PZ or the number of mitoses undergone.

Apoptosis

Lastly, the process of apoptosis (programmed cell death) is involved in the development of the upper limb. This process occurs in the interdigital spaces, the axillary fold, within joint spaces, and in certain primitive embryonic muscle layers.

Patterning the Limb

Sculpting of the hand is a complex, poorly understood process. The outgrowing limb flattens into a hand plate capped by the AER. The number of digits that develop is proportional to the length of the AER. In the past, the breakup of the AER was believed to initiate interdigital clefting; but now, the process appears to be primarily a function of the interdigital mesoderm within the interdigital necrosis zones.

The genetic mechanism of programmed cell death has yet to be identified. Apoptosis may occur by the cellular mechanism of lysosomal enzyme release. This would explain why steroids, which stabilize lysosomal enzyme membranes, may produce syndactyly. A large study by Man and Chang found that maternal cigarette smoking during pregnancy increases the risk of having a child with congenital digital anomalies (polydactyly, syndactyly, adactyly); this results in an adjusted odds ratio of 1.31.

DEVELOPMENT OF FISH EMBRYOLOGY

Fish embryonic development begins after inception with the zygote period. During this time the embryo develops one cell that looks like a half bubble. This lasts on average for 45 minutes with a cell.7 mm in diameter. The chorion, also known as the egg shell, will swell and lift away from the fertilized egg.

It is particularly appropriate to write about the history of fish embryology at this time. History is often said to move in cycles, and this seems to be true of the study of fish development.

After a period of prominence during the nineteenth and early twentieth centuries, the study of fish development, except in the hands of a stalwart few such as Oppenheimer and Trinkaus working with Fundulus and Ballard and Devillers working with the trout and other fishes, was overshadowed by developmental studies of other organisms, such as amphibians, the domestic fowl, sea urchins, and assorted invertebrates.

For obvious reasons, the study of fish development continued to be pursued by fisheries biologists. With the popularization of the zebrafish Danio rerio as a "model of vertebrate development" and a revival of interest in the relationship between development and evolution, the cycle has come full turn and the study of fish development again has a place in the sun. My objective is to present an outline of the historical development of the science of fish embryology in the nineteenth century, broadly defined as 1789-1914. My plan is to assess the state of knowledge at the outset of the period, to document the advancement of descriptive embryology of teleosts and elasmobranchs, to consider the rise of comparative embryology of fishes associated with evolutionary studies, and to search out the beginning of experimental, physiological, and biochemical analyses of fish development.

DIVERSE GROUP OF VERTEBRATES

When discussing the development of fishes, it is prudent to recall that fishes are the most diverse group of vertebrates. They should not be treated as a distinct, relatively homogeneous taxonomic unit. Rather, the term "fishes" applies to a grade of ectothermic, aquatic craniates and vertebrates and not to a distinct taxonomic group.

Extant fishes are divided into five classes, namely Myxini (hagfish), Cephalaspidomorphi (lampreys), Chondrichthyes (cartilaginous fishes), Sarcopterygii, and Actinopteryg. Chondrichthyes contains two taxa, namely the subclass Elasmobranch (living sharks, rays, and skates) and the Holocephal (ratfishes or chimaeras) that diverged at a relatively early time, *i.e.*, the Devonian-Carboniferous boundary.

The class Sarcopterygii (flesh-finned fishes) contains the Actinistia (the living coelacanth), the Dipnoi (lungfishes) and the tetrapod vertebrates. The class Actinopteryg (ray-finned fishes) comprises five groups, namely Cladistia (bichir and reedfish), Chondrostei (sturgeons and paddlefish), Ginglymodi (gars), Halecomorphi (Amia calva, the bowfin), and the Teleostei (teleost fishes). Thus, the five classes of fishes contain eleven major taxonomic groups with an estimated total of 25,000 species. Each class is as distinct from the others as it is from the four other classes of vertebrates. The theme of eleven major taxonomic groups of fishes that is used in the ensuing presentation to emphasize the broad phylogenetic relationships of fishes and other vertebrates, tends, however, to obscure the extraordinary phylogenetic diversity within the teleosts.

Teleostei, a monophyletic group, contains 24,000 species in 38 orders and 126 families compared to the 1,000 species, 19 orders, and 56 families in the ten other groups of fishes and the 25,000 species of tetrapods. Not only are fishes the most diverse group of craniates, but they also display the greatest diversity of life history styles. Most fishes are oviparous, but viviparity is estimated to have independently evolved 42 times in five of the eleven major groups of fishes, all within the Chondrichthyes and Osteichythes.

The phylogenetic diversity of fishes is reflected in the diversity and variability of their developmental patterns. Craniate development based on cleavage and subsequent patterns of gastrulation and embryogenesis is holoblastic, meroblastic, or transitional between the two. In holoblastic eggs, cleavage of the ooplasm is complete by the blastula stage. The morphogenetic movements of gastrulation occur in the three-dimensional space of the entire egg and involve most of the embryonic mass.

They often lead to the occlusion of the blastocoele. Neurulation is synchronous in time and space. Holoblastic development is considered the less specialized and more primitive craniate developmental pattern because it is characteristic of most echinoderms and non-craniate chordates as well as the more primitive representatives of various craniate lineages, namely lampreys, sturgeons, bichirs, lungfish, and most amphibians. In the meroblastic egg, most of the yolk mass remains uncleaved at the blastula stage.

EVOLUTION OF THE MEROBLASTIC PATTERN APPEARS

Morphogenetic movements are confined to a portion of the egg volume, *i.e.*, the blastoderm, and involve only a portion of the embryonic mass. Gastrulation and neurulation tend to be spatially and temporally asynchronous. Evolution of the meroblastic pattern appears to have involved qualitative and quantitative changes in the ooplasm and yolk components of the egg, namely an increase in total yolk content, an increase in the amount of yolk relative to ooplasm, a change in the type of yolk, and a change in the relative disposition of ooplasm and yolk. Not only did the changes in yolk-cytoplasm relationships of the egg affect cleavage patterns, but they also imposed a set of physical or physiological constraints on the morphogenetic movements of embryo formation, the so-called holoblastic-meroblastic barrier.

Consequently, new or highly modified patterns of gastrulation and embryogenesis co-evolved with the evolution of the meroblastic egg. The meroblastic pattern of development appears to have independently evolved in six craniate lineages, namely hagfish, sharks and chimaeras, teleost fishes, the living coelacanth (?), one group of amphibians (the caecilians) and amniotes. In each instance, different morphological patterns of gastrulation and embryogenesis have evolved. Thus, although meroblastic cleavage is superficially similar in hagfish, elasmobranchs, and teleosts, the morphological events of embryo formation differ considerably. These points and others are summarized in part by Collazo *et al.* who present a phylogenetic perspective and an evolutionary scenario for teleost gastrulation. Paradoxically, whether development proceeds according to a holoblastic or meroblastic pattern, the end product is a stereotypic craniate embryo. Recent advances in the study of the molecular basis of embryogenesis should help resolve this paradox.

NATURAL COLLECTIONS OF FISHES

When considering early studies of fish development, one soon realizes that many of these studies were carried out on viviparous species of elasmobranchs and teleosts rather than oviparous ones, and that both egglaying and livebearing elasmobranchs received a disproportionate amount of attention, considering their relatively low diversity compared to teleosts. First, elasmobranch eggs are considerably larger than those of most teleosts and their development can be easily observed with either the unaided eye or with a hand lens.

Secondly, it has always been relatively easy to obtain gravid specimens of viviparous fishes as part of routine fishing efforts. Moreover, as museum or natural history collections of fishes were made during the course of explorations, specimens of curious, new species of gravid viviparous fishes became available for study, *e.g.*, the four-eyed fish Anableps. In contrast, the eggs of oviparous teleosts are small and not easily collected in the wild. Artificial fertilization of teleost eggs did not begin until the late eighteenth century and the regulated spawning of captive fish species and the rearing of their eggs under "controlled" conditions for scientific purposes was first used only towards the mid-nineteenth century.

In addition, the technology for maintaining fishes in aquaria and the possibility of spawning them under aquarium conditions did not emerge until the mid-late nineteenth century. In passing, one should recall that the Chinese have been rearing captive goldfish, including mutant strains, for over a thousand years. Other factors also influenced decisions to study certain viviparous instead of oviparous fishes. Viviparity in fishes, especially when there is a placental relationship, is an intrinsically interesting process. Finally, as a subject for the general study of development, oviparous teleosts have been secondary to the chicken egg ever since the Renaissance because of the greater size of the chicken's egg and its ready availability as an article of food.

DEVELOPMENT OF FISH EMBRYOLOGY

Because the research of early naturalists provided the foundation for the development of fish embryology in the nineteenth century, a brief outline of their work is presented here, beginning with Aristotle. Aristotle, the founder of the science of embryology, was the first to recognize and record many important features of fish reproduction and development. He distinguished oviparous (egg-laying) animals from viviparous (livebearing animals. Aristotle described viviparity in the dogfish shark (Mustelus), the thresher shark (Alopias), and the electric ray (Torpedo).

He did not know of viviparity in teleost fishes because there are no viviparous teleosts in the coastal waters of the Mediterranean or the fresh waters of Europe and Asia Minor. His attribution of viviparity to the needlefish, a teleost, is actually a case of misinterpretation. The needlefish of Aristotle is a pipefish or sygnathid.

Male pipefishes brood embryos in a pouch of abdominal skin. This form of parental care is analogous to viviparity and in its most highly evolved forms, the parentalembryonic relationships can be as complex as in viviparous fishes. The body of Aristotle's observations concern chondrichthyan fishes and include: (1) the distinction between oviparous and viviparous modes of reproduction in sharks, rays, and skates; (2) description of the female reproductive system; (3) description of shark and skate egg cases; (4) description of egg structure and some observations on embryonic development; (5) first description of the oviducal or nidamental (=shell) gland but without any knowledge of its function in egg case formation or sperm storage; (6) hatching from the egg case in utero in viviparous species; (7) description of the male reproductive system; (8) notes on breeding seasons and inshore migration of gravid females for "pupping"; and (9) description of the yolk sac placenta in sharks.

Writing of the smooth dogfish Mustelus canis in the 5th century B.C., Aristotle states, "the young are produced with the umbilical cord attached to the uterus so that as the substance of the egg gets used up, the embryo's condition appears to be similar to what is found in quadrupeds. The umbilical cord, which is long, is attached to the lower parts of the uterus; each one is, as it were, fastened to a cotyledon and is attached to the embryo by the middle where the liver is situated. Each embryo has a chorion and membranes of its own round it, just as in quadrupeds. If the embryos are cut open, a situation is disclosed exactly similar to quadrupeds; whatever internal organs they have, such as the liver, are large and supplied with blood". Aristotle's observations on teleosts are in large part concerned with reproduction, *e.g.*, his exquisite account of brood protection by male catfish. He realized that in contrast to the chondrichthyans, the overwhelming majority of teleosts are oviparous. His observations on the development of teleosts are more limited, due primarily to the small size of most teleostean eggs. Aristotle observed developing teleost eggs, recording their small size and rapid development. He states, "The embryo appears at the upper end of the egg and is enveloped in a membrane; the eyes, large and spherical, are the first organs visible.

The embryo and the egg (yolk) are enveloped by a common membrane, and just under this is another membrane that envelops the egg (yolk) by itself; between the two membranes is a liquid". He described the organization of the teleost egg, distinguishing the perivitelline fluid from the yolk mass. Lastly, in comparing the development of teleostean and avian eggs, Aristotle recognized that teleosts lack the allantois. Relatively little was added to the pioneering efforts of Aristotle by subsequent Greek and Roman scholars. With the decline of classical civilization, the study of science in general as well as the study of fish development languished for almost 1,000 years.

Slowly the tide turned. According to Needham (1959), the first account of fish development in medieval Europe was given by Albertus Magnus, a thirteenth century scholastic. During the Renaissance, there was a revival of interest in natural history. The early zoological encyclopedists, especially Belon, Rondelet, and Aldrovandus, investigated fishes and described aspects of their reproduction and development. Again, there was a decided bias towards viviparous chondrichthyans. Rondelet illustrated an egg case and dissection of the female reproductive system of an oviparous catshark. He also illustrated part of the ovary and an egg case of a skate. He depicted a female shark, probably Mustelus canis, connected to a welldeveloped pup by an elongated yolk stalk that passes from the pup through the cloaca of the female. Although the placenta is not illustrated, Aristotle's research on the shark yolk sac placenta is cited in the text. Progressing to the seventeenth century, Fabricius, who is best known for his studies of the chick, described and illustrated the female reproductive system and uterine embryos with large yolk sacs in a non-placental species of dogfish shark. By 1673, Niclaus Steno had rediscovered the yolk sac placenta in the smooth dogfish, M. canis, investigated its anatomy, and published an illustrated account of it. He also distinguished between placental viviparity in the smooth dogfish shark, and aplacental viviparity in the spiny dogfish shark, Squalus. In the latter, he discovered that the yolk stalk terminates in an intestine characterized by a spiral valve.

His rediscovery appears to have gone unappreciated. During this period, inability to distinguish among species of dogfish sharks that had either aplacental or placental modes of viviparity caused the very existence of a yolk sac placenta in sharks to be doubted. This controversy was not fully resolved until the time of Johannes Muller. Steno's studies on shark development had important ramifications for the study of mammalian reproduction. On the basis of his observation of large eggs in the uterine oviduct and large eggs in the ovary of the spiny dogfish, he concluded that the embryo does not form de novo in the oviduct, but comes form an egg released by one of the ovaries. From this, he postulated that mammalian development proceeded in a similar fashion, except that the mammalian egg is much smaller.

In his examination of the mammalian ovary, unfortunately, he mistook the entire follicle for the mammalian egg. These studies were undertaken at a time when a controversy had arisen between animalculists and ovists with respect to the primacy of the sperm in reproduction and the absence of any knowledge of the mammalian egg. Steno's observations, although flawed, brought mammalian development in line with that of other vertebrates. In essence, he used sharks as a "model" system for mammals. In 1678, Stephen Lorenzini, a pupil of Steno and Redi, published a set of observations on the viviparous electric ray Torpedo. This appears to be the first monographic treatment of a single fish species. Lorenzini's work is of considerable interest because almost one third of it is devoted to an account of urogenital anatomy, reproductive biology, and development of Torpedo, as well as several other rays.

Amongst his observations, those of primary interest concern oogenesis and ovulation, the blastoderm, and embryonic nutrition. Describing the ovary, he notes differences in size and structure between young and mature fishes. Maturing oocytes and ova vary in size, composition, and colour. Oocytes are connected to the ovarian matrix by a stalk through which several blood vessels pass, an arrangement similar to that described by Fabricius in the hen's egg. He states that these vessels provide nutrients to the eggs.

Pole constitutes

The maturing egg is invested by a "membrane" except for the pole opposite the site of attachment to the stalk. This pole constitutes the pore or stigma through which the mature egg is released from the follicle. During oocyte maturation, changes in membrane adhesion were documented. Lorenzini speculates that mature eggs are released from the follicle by contraction of fibres in the ovarian stroma.

The ovulated egg is "received" by the oviduct and passes into the uterine region where embryonic development is completed. Following Fabricius, De Graaf, and Harvey, Lorenzini refers to the residual portion of the follicle as the "calyx." Calyces, which apparently are the corpora lutea, occur in various sizes and shapes throughout gestation, and are lost or regress some time after parturition. Lorenzini found a correlation between the number of young in a brood and the number of calyces in the ovary. Ovulation in the Torpedo is considered to conform to De Graaf's account in other species. Among the more interesting of Lorenzini's observations are those made on the early stages of embryonic development. He describes and illustrates two neurula stages.

The earlier stage depicts an early neural groove on the surface of the blastoderm. He describes the characteristic chondrichthyan blastoderm, "a leaden gray disc" that is clearly distinct from and surmounts the "yellow yolk mass." In another egg, he describes and depicts a slightly more advanced neurula stage. Here Lorenzini correctly shows the splayed, outspread cephalic margins of the medullary plate, a characteristic feature of chondrichthyan embryos. Lorenzini also observed the blastoderm in three other species of rays. Lorenzini seems to be the first to have depicted the chondrichthyan blastoderm. His observations appeared only six years after Malphighi's initial account of the avian (chick) blastoderm.

Lorenzini made one of the first major contributions to the knowledge of embryonic nutrition in non-placental viviparous fishes. Late stage embryos with yolk sacs lie free in the uterine region of the oviduct where they are bathed by uterine fluid. A yolk stalk passes from the external yolk through the abdominal wall and empties into a large internal yolk sac that in turn empties into the intestine. The intestine is filled with yellow material apparently derived from the yolk and brown globules. The same brown globules occur in the uterine fluid and in the mouth, esophagus, and stomach of the embryos.

Lorenzini concluded that advanced embryos are nourished both by yolk passed to the intestine and by uterine fluid which they imbibe. He believed that the nutrients in uterine fluid are derived from the blood and conveyed to the uterine fluid by vascularized glandular structures which he compared to chorionic villi. These structures are now known as trophonemata. Villi increase in size during gestation; their size is correlated with the amount of uterine fluid. They regress and are absent in non-gravid fish. In addition, Lorenzini also made significant observations on the male reproductive system, reproductive cycles, and the duration of gestation.

In the closing years of the seventeenth century, Willughby and Ray summarized much of what was known of fish reproduction and development in a work primarily devoted to systematics. Considering its promising beginning, it is surprising that the study of chondrichthyan development made relatively little progress in the eighteenth century. There are many possible reasons. Those scholars interested in fish biology may have been attracted to systematic studies because of the revolutionary efforts of Willughby and Ray, Artedi, and Linnaeus as well as the influx of new species of fishes from the tropics. Changing fashions in science also enter the picture, especially the rise of microscopy and microscopic anatomy. Perhaps in terms of the material, questions, and technology, research on chondrichthyans had reached an impasse. There are some exceptions. Bohadsch investigated the structural organization of eggcases.

Monro published detailed descriptions accompanied by elegant illustrations of the urogenital anatomy of the oviparous skates.

He also described and illustrated for the first time the spermocysts, spherical aggregations of Sertoli cells and differentiating sperm cells that are a characteristic feature of chondrichthyan spermatogenesis. Descriptions and illustrations of microdissections of the internal anatomy of mid-and late-stage embryos are given.

The extensive vitelline circulation and the connection of the yolk sac and the small intestine are documented. External gill filaments, another feature of chondrichthyan development, are described for the first time. The eighteenth century concluded with Bloch's magnum opus (1782-95) which added little to the study of chondrichthyan development other than information on the embryos of the viviparous sawfish Pristis. The study of teleostean development, as previously noted, lagged well behind that of both oviparous and viviparous chondrichthyan fishes, and little was done prior to the mid-late eighteenth century.

To be more accurate, the little that was done was done with viviparous teleosts. Schoenveld first described viviparity in the embryos of the eelpout, Zoarces viviparus, a fish common to the marine waters of northern Europe. Late stage embryos are illustrated. Impressed by the substantial growth of the embryos during gestation, Schoenveld postulated that they obtain nutrients by ingesting ovarian fluid. (In viviparous teleosts, an oviduct or uterus is absent and gestation takes place in the ovary. Cf. Wourms, *et al.*, 1988).

Somewhat later, Willughby and Ray apparently observed the development of live Zoarces embryos. Interest in teleost development during the seventeenth and eighteenth centuries seems to have been generated by the viviparity of exotic species discovered during the explorations of the Old and New World Tropics.

Anableps, the four-eyed fish, conspicuous because of its size, unusual anatomy, and behaviour in its Central and South American habitats, was described as viviparous as early as 1738. Gronovius was the first to illustrate advanced embryos of Anableps with their characteristic rugose "yolk sac" (actually the abdominal trophoderm). Gronovius may also have been the first to describe viviparity in the clinid, Clinus superciliosus. Bloch described and illustrated the external and internal reproductive anatomy of Anableps, its embryos in situ, and the embryos themselves. He also depicted the adults and embryos of Zoarces and Clinus. One of the first sets of field observations was made by de Alzate — Ramyrez in 1769 who discovered viviparity in a Mexican poeciliid and made microscopic observations of blood circulation in living, near-term embryos.

During this period, the foundations were laid for the study of early development, *i.e.*, fertilization through embryogenesis. In 1763, Jacobi published an extensive letter in which he reported that he had artificially fertilized the eggs of trout and salmon by removing the ripe eggs and adding sperm to them.

Although this is the first known written account of artificial fertilization, it is probable that the technique had been in use for some time, for fish culture had been practiced in Europe since the late fifteenth century. Jacobi may have observed the entry of sperm into the egg. He also recorded the formation of double embryos in artificially fertilized eggs, a condition that he attributed to the entry of two spermatozoa.

In 1787, Cavolini published a monograph on the "generation" of fishes and crabs. The bulk of this work was devoted to the description of spawning habits, hermaphroditism, fertilization, and contemplations on the nature of development.

However, he did make one observation of considerable significance. In the eggs of the pipefish, he described a structure on the egg which he referred to as the "cicatrix" or in modern terminology, the blastoderm. He identified the blastoderm with the same structure in the chick and assumed that the embryo originated from the blastoderm.

The study of teleost development in the eighteenth century was brought to a close with the appearance of Bloch's massive, twelve-volume monograph on the natural history of fishes. This work is one of the linchpins of systematic ichthyology and summarized what was known about fishes up to that time. It contains much information on fish reproduction and development. As previously noted, aspects of the development of viviparous chondrichthyans and teleosts are described and illustrated.

Of greater interest are his pioneering studies of the early stages of development of an oviparous teleost. For the first time, he describes and illustrates consecutive stages in development, from post fertilization through hatching to a late larval stage, and provides a time base for the description of developmental stages.

He appreciated the eccentric position of the yolk mass relative to the blastoderm. He made observations on the development of the heart, and illustrates the contractile, simple tubular stage of heart development. There were, of course, errors of interpretation, one of which was the identification of the perivitelline fluid of the teleost egg with the albumen layer of the avian egg.

EMBRYONIC DEVELOPMENT

30 minutes after fertilization the blastodisc begins to form over the yolk, following first, second and third cleavage. Sixty four cell stages were observed after 70 minutes postfertilisation followed by morula stage in two hours. Yolk plug stage appeared after five hours. The cephalic and caudal end of the embryo

had differentiated after 10 — 15 hours. After 16 —21 hours the gut had faintly appeared posterior to the yolk sac, leading to the anus, and movement of the embryo could be seen within the egg. After 22 hours movements of the embryo were observed. The eggs began to hatch after 23 hours.

LARVAL REARING

Newly hatched larva can be reared in fibre glass tanks and cement cisterns as well as in nurseries using pond water. Suitable water parameters are temperature 25±3° C, alkalinity 120-150 mg l^{-1} and dissolved oxygen in the range 3 - 5 mg l^{-1}.

Initially the water level of containers was maintained.at 3 - 4 cm, and gradually increased to 15 - 20 cm after one week. Water levels were adjusted at different stages of rearing to minimize the stress to larva. Aquatic weeds such as Hydrilla can be provided to give cover for the larvae.

FEED

Yolk sacs were absorbed in around three days. Early spawn were cannibalistic, attacking and devour others. It was necessary to reduce the density of the stocked population to reduce cannibalism. Mixed zoo plankton, Tubifex worm, and egg custard were provided as larval feed. Larvae accept zooplankton up to day 15.

In fry stages and onwards the fish can be fed with compound feed (rice polish, silk worm pupae and boiled egg) at 100 per cent of body weight of the population. The average size of fry was 1.1 - 2.0 cm in length and 0.6 - 2.0 g in weight.

Fry can also can be reared in fibre glass tanks and cement cisterns fed with both zooplanktons 2.0 - 3.0 Embyonic development at 1 hour and 10 minutes. Embryonic development at 1 hour and 42 minutes. Embryonic development at 11 hours and 40 minutes. Fry attained 5.0 - 6.0 cm and 3.0 -5.0 g after a rearing period of 40 days, which is a good size for stocking in grow out ponds.

BREEDING OF MURRELS

The important cultured species are:

- Channa marulius
- C. panctatus
- C. striatus

Among freshwater fish species, murrels (snakeheads) and catfishes secure the top rank economically. Murrels have long been commercially cultured in Thailand, Taiwan and Philippines. But fish farmers in India are not much familiar with murrel culture due to want of breeding, feeding and culture techniques. The common species are Therefore it is imperative to make murrel culture popular among fish farmers and unemployed youths for income generation. Females with soft and swollen bellies are suitable for breeding. However a gentle pressure on the belly for oosing of eggs could check prime maturation. Males are selected by external examination of genital papilla since they do not ooze milt by pressure. The fecundity of Channa punctata ranges from 2,200 in a specimen of 12·1 cm TL to 33,873 in a specimen of 22·3 cm TL.

Murrels are induced to spawn by injecting natural (pituitary, human chorionic gonadotropin) or synthetic (ovaprim, ovatide) hormones intramuscularly.

Among the hormones tested a synthetic product of SGnRHa marketed by Glaxo Ltd. is recommended at a single dose of 0.5 ml/ Kg.

Each breeding set consists of one female and two males. Immediately after injection each breeding set is introduced into a breeding tank (6m x 5m x1m) having sides pasted with cement and bottom filled with clay. Aquatic weeds (*e.g.*, water hyacinth) are introduced into the breeding tank for hiding purposes. Spawning activities are observed after 6-10 hrs of hormone injection. Courtship behaviour continues till the complete release of eggs and milt (24-30 hrs). Fertilization is external and the fertilized eggs are usually floating. An egg mass of about 6-14 cm diameter consists of 5000-10,000 eggs (diameter 1.2mm - 1.5mm).

The rate of fertilization ranges between 70-90 per cent. Hatching takes place 24-30 hrs after fertilization and the hatchlings (2.8mm - 3.2mm in length) are guarded by the parents especially by the male parent. From a single spawning 4000-8000 hatchlings/female are obtained.

REARING OF SPAWN

The yolk sac is completely absorbed on the 3rd day and the mouth is fully formed. At that time the larvae start exogenous feeding especially on small plankton like rotifers. The young ones are allowed to stay with parents in the breeding tanks for one or two weeks. To avoid cannibalism the fry are removed from breeding tanks after two weeks. The fry are fed with boiled and finely ground chicken intestine or fish waste. After a month the fry (15mm length) attains red colour.

The fry are reared in cement tanks (3m × 1m × 1m) with a stocking density of 500/m^2. Whenever the young ones are reared, they should be of equal size to avoid cannibalism.

Fry survival may be 65-80 per cent in the cement tanks. Water quality (29 ±°C, 0.06 - 6.52mgO2/l pH 7.5 - 8.2) and feeding are the deciding factors for the survival of the young ones.

A flow through system is always preferred for better survival. The fry are reared in medium (3m × 1m × 1m) or large cement (5m × 4m × 2m) tanks upto the fingerling stage. The fry reaches 4 to 5 cms after 2 months and the fingerlings are collected from the cement tanks for commercial culture.

Table. Effect of Different Doses of Two Hormones on Induced Spawning in C. punctatus and H. fossilis. The Low, Medium and High Dosages with Different Superscripts are Significantly Different (P<0.05)

Hormone	Fish mass (g)	Dosage	Latency period (h)	Fertilization rate (%)	Egg output kg/bw	Hatching rate (%)	Survival rate of hatchlings (%)
C. punctatus							
Ovaprim	65 – 80	0.1 ml	–	–	30 ± 8	–	–
	65 – 80	0.3 ml	28 – 34	73.5	3276 ± 75	65.0	30
	75 – 85	0.5 ml	28 – 34	75.0	198 ± 10	50.0	10
	60 – 70	1000 IU	–	–	102 ± 20	–	–
HCG	70 – 80	2000 IU	28 – 34	75.5	699 ± 78	65.5	50
	65 – 85	3000 IU	28 – 34	78.0	1253 ± 126	70.5	65
H. fossilis							
	100 – 105	0.3 ml	18 – 24	70.0	258 ± 85	50.5	10
Ovaprim	90 – 105	0.5 ml	18 – 24	75.0	1052 ± 220	60.0	30
	90 – 100	0.7 ml	18 – 24	70.0	6692 ± 790	50.0	15
	80 – 105	1000 IU	18 – 24	78.0	6336 ± 800	75.0	60
HCG	90 – 100	2000 IU	18 – 24	75.0	18376 ± 1020	60.5	50
	110 – 115	3000 IU	18 – 24	70.0	82922 ± 5432	60.0	55

SMALL INDIGENOUS FISHES (SIFS) AND THEIR BREEDING

Small indigenous fishes traditionally occupy an unenviable position and an inseparable link in the life, livelihood, health and the general well being of the rural mass, especially the poor.

It has been reported that some species such as mola (A. mola), dhela (O. cotio cotio), darkina (E. danricus) and kaski (C. soborna) contain a high amount of vitamin A and other micronutrients and minerals.

Studies in Bangladesh and Cambodia showed that small fish species make up 50- 80 per cent of all fish eaten during the production season. Two species from the genus Esomus (E. danricus, E. longimanus) are rich in high iron content.

Small scale aquaculture of A. mola, Puntius sophore, Osteobrama cotio, Cirrihinus reba, Labeo bata, Gudusia chapra, Notopterus nototerus, etc., along with Indian major carps have been reported in India.

Successful captive breeding of several SIF's have been reported under National Agricultural Technology Project (NATP) -NBFGR projects and also by several workers. Many of the SIF's are self breeders and need proper management practices to facilitate natural breeding mostly in monsoon.

EARLY IDEAS IN EMBRYOLOGY

Prior to the mid-1800s, scientists believed that development was the result of preformation. Preformation means that animals develop from an already existing miniature animal that merely required the right conditions to unfold and grow into a new organism. Scientific debates over whether the miniature animal was contained in the egg (ovum) or the sperm raged for decades. Scientists who believed that the miniature animal was in the egg were called ovists; those who believed that the miniature animal was in the sperm were called spermists.

In 1675, Marcello Malpighi (1628–1694), an ovist, reported seeing a miniature chick in the chicken egg. Anton Leeuwenhoek (1632–1723), a spermist, reported seeing a miniature human (homunculus) in each sperm. In 1775, Lazzaro Spallanzani (1729–1799) demonstrated that both egg and seminal fluid were needed to produce a new individual. He conducted a series of experiments using amphibian eggs and seminal fluid. When the eggs were exposed to seminal fluid, they began to develop. However, if the eggs were exposed to filtered seminal fluid, fewer eggs developed. The more highly the seminal fluid was filtered, the fewer eggs developed. If the eggs were combined with the material left on the filter paper, they began to develop. Although Spallanzani correctly concluded that both egg and seminal fluid were necessary for development, he believed that the sperm seen in the seminal fluid were parasites. He postulated that the fertilizing agent was composed of the proteins and fats in the fluid.

William Harvey (1578–1657) viewed embryological development as a continuing process of remodeling and growth from unspecialized tissues to specialized structures. This theory, which is termed epigenesis, was largely ignored until 1759 when Kaspar Friedrich Wolff (1733–1794) offered empirical evidence of epigenesis from his detailed studies of chick development. In 1828, Karl von Baer (1792–1876) described four fundamental concepts of development. These four concepts, referred to as von Baer's law, are: (1) general features such as appendages appear earlier in the embryo than specialized features such as fingers; (2) development proceeds from general to specific characteristics; (3) as an embryo develops, it becomes increasingly different from other species; and (4) the early embryo of a higher animal is never like an adult of a lower animal, but only similar to the lower animal's embryo. Because they delineated the basic concepts of development, Wolff and von Baer are considered founders of modern embryology.

FERTILIZATION DEVELOPMENT

The process of development begins with the fusion of gametes: egg (ovum) and sperm. The motile sperm swims to the egg, pierces its cell membrane and enters the cell. Fertilization is the fusion of the nuclei of the egg and sperm, and the single cell that results from this fusion is called the fertilized egg or zygote. During fertilization, the genetic material of the sperm and egg are combined. Each gamete is haploid, that is, it contains one-half of the normal number of chromosomes for the species. At fertilization, the gametes combine to produce a zygote with the full number of chromosomes for that particular species. Another way to say this is that fertilization restores the diploid number. For example, haploid human gametes have twenty-three chromosomes; when the egg and sperm fuse, the diploid state of forty-six chromosomes is restored to the zygote. Thus, each parent contributes one-half of the chromosomal complement of the new individual, resulting in a new organism with genetic characteristics of both parents. This single cell, the fertilized egg, gives rise to all the organs of the individual—muscles, brain, liver, eyes—through highly regulated and timed processes.

The stages from fertilization to the birth or hatching of an individual organism are identical to those of all individuals of the same species. Developmental stages include rapid cell division or cleavage; formation of the germ layers through the process of gastrulation; and differentiation and growth of the organs and organ systems. These stages are categorized as the periods of embryogenesis (cleavage and gastrulation) and organogenesis (formation of organs and organ systems).

Cleavage

As soon as the sperm enters the egg, the cell membrane of the egg undergoes changes that prevent the entrance of additional sperm. Meanwhile, the chromosomes from each parent come together and, within a few hours, the first cell division begins. The egg degrades the cytoplasm and organelles of the sperm; only the chromosomes of the sperm contribute to the fertilized egg.

The early cell divisions of the fertilized egg are called cleavage. The fertilized egg divides into two daughter cells called blastomeres. These two blastomeres divide into four blastomeres, the four blastomeres divide into eight, and so on. During cleavage, the total number of cells increases, but the size of each cell decreases. The reason for this strange situation is that cell division occurs so rapidly that there is not enough time for the individual cells to grow bigger. The constant doubling of cells during cleavage results in a multicellular embryo very quickly. In a short period, the embryo has over one hundred cells arranged as a solid ball of blastomeres called a morula. The cells of the morula rearrange themselves into a single layer of cells surrounding a fluid-filled central cavity; the embryo at this stage is called a blastula.

Gastrulation

The next step in development is the formation of the gastrula by invagination, the folding in of the cells of the blastula at a point called the blastopore. The resulting gastrula is a double-layer cup of cells. The outer layer of cells is termed the ectoderm and the inner layer of cells is termed the endoderm. The inner endodermal layer surrounds a new cavity, the primitive gut. A third layer of cells, the mesoderm, develops between the ectoderm and endoderm in most animals. Ectoderm, mesoderm and endoderm are the three germ layers from which all cells, tissues and organs develop. Cells of the ectoderm differentiate into the epidermis, hair, nails, claws, sweat glands, tooth enamel, brain, and spinal cord. Mesoderm differentiates into muscles, blood, blood vessels, heart, spleen, reproductive organs, and kidneys. Endoderm differentiates into the cells lining the digestive and respiratory systems, the liver, gallbladder, and pancreas.

Induction

One of the more fascinating aspects of development is the determination of body form, pattern, and differentiation. Put simply, how does a cell know what it is supposed to grow up to be? How do cells of the endoderm know they are supposed to form the digestive and respiratory systems? Induction is the process during which individual cells are "told" what they are supposed to become.

Hans Spemann (1869–1941) received the Nobel Prize in 1935 for over twenty years of research on development in amphibians.

In a series of elegant and delicate "baby hair loop" experiments, he demonstrated that when cells invaginate during gastrulation, they are induced to form specific cells and organs and that the primary inducer is a specific region of the blastopore.

Spemann tied a strand of baby's hair around a fertilized newt egg so that the nucleus and some cytoplasm were on one side of the ligature while the other side contained only cytoplasm. After several cell divisions, Spemann loosened the ligature and allowed a nucleus to pass over into the other side. When cell divisions began on the side with the transported nucleus, the ligature was again tightened to separate the two masses of cells. The result was the production of two newt larvae, one a bit older than the other.

These experiments demonstrated that all the nuclei of an early embryo are capable of producing embryos. This ability is the basis for much current practice of cloning agriculture or lab animals.

In later experiments, Spemann found that the location of the ligature was important. If the ligature were placed so that each half of the fertilized egg contained the certain cells (called the gray crescent because of their colour) from the region destined to become the blastopore, two newts would develop.

However, if the ligature were placed so that the gray crescent was only on one half of the cell, that part would form a newt, but the half without the gray crescent would remain a formless mass of cells he called the belly piece. Further experimentation demonstrated that during gastrulation cells became committed to their developmental fates.

Spemann and his graduate student Hilde Mangold (1898–1924) demonstrated that specific cells of the blastopore are the only determining region in the gastrula. When these cells were transplanted to other embryos, the embryos were induced to undergo gastrulation and form a second embryo.

These experiments that Mangold performed for her doctoral dissertation formed the foundation for much of Spemann's later work. Mangold died at age twenty-six when the heater in her apartment exploded. She could not share the Nobel Prize awarded to Spemann eleven years later because the prize is not awarded posthumously.

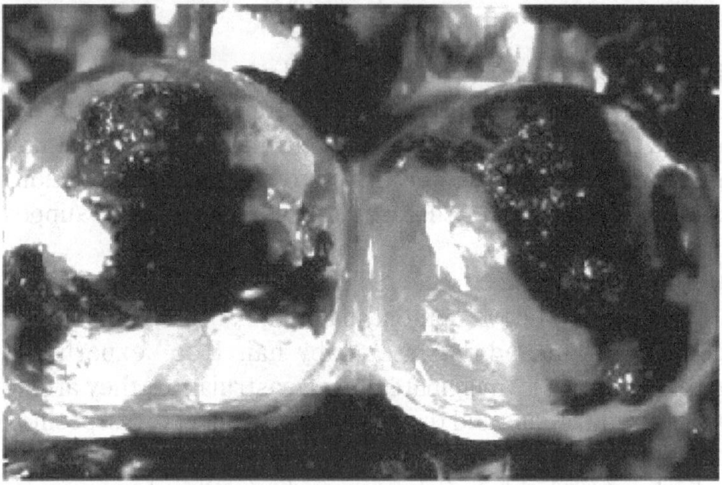

Frog embryos begin their development inside eggs.

PROTOSTOMES AND DEUTEROSTOMES

The fate of the blastopore is used to classify animals that have three germ layers into two large categories, protostomes and deuterostomes. Most adult animals have two external openings, the mouth and the anus, into the digestive tract.

During gastrulation, the blastopore is the opening into the primitive gut. During further development, the blastopore becomes the mouth in animals classified as protostomes; the blastopore becomes the anus in deuterostomes. Organisms belonging to the phyla Mollusca (clams and snails), Arthropoda (insects and crustaceans) and Annelida (earthworms) are protostomes; members of the phyla Echinodermata (starfish) and Chordata (fish and humans) are deuterostomes.

The type of cleavage and the development of the body cavity are other important differences between the protostomes and deuterostomes. Protostomes exhibit spiral cleavage in which the blastomeres divide at acute angles to one another and are not aligned over one another. If one of these blastomeres is removed from the embryo, neither the removed blastomere nor the remaining cells develop into an individual.

This type of determinate cleavage indicates that the fate of the daughter cells is determined early in development. A final characteristic of protostomes is that the body cavity, or coelom, develops as a split within the middle of the mesodermal layer. This type of coelom formation is termed schizocoelous development. Deuterostomes, on the other hand, exhibit radial cleavage in which the blastomeres divide perpendicular or parallel to one another and are aligned over one another. If one of these blastomeres is removed from the embryo, both the removed blastomere and the remaining cells can develop into individual organisms. This type of indeterminate cleavage indicates that the fate of the daughter cells is determined later in development.

Identical twins are possible because of indeterminate cleavage. Genetic testing of human embryos is possible because of indeterminate cleavage: One blastomere can be removed from an eight-celled embryo and tested without interfering with the normal development of the remaining seven cells. In deuterostomes the coelom develops as buds from the primitive gut. This type of coelom formation is termed enterocoelous development.

BIOGENETIC LAW

Ernst Haeckel (1834–1919), a physician, was so influenced by Charles Darwin's *The Origin of Species* that he gave up medicine and devoted himself to comparative anatomy.

He disagreed with Darwin's theory of natural selection, and suggested that the environment acted directly on organisms, producing new species. In 1868, he proposed the biogenetic law, which sought to explain evolution as a series of stages in which the new characteristics of the next animal to evolve are simply added on to the lower animal.

Briefly put, his biogenetic law stated that ontogeny recapitulates phylogeny embryological development of a particular species repeats the evolutionary history of that species). Although Haeckel is best remembered for his "ontogeny recapitulates phylogeny" statement, he also coined the terms phylum, ecology, and phylogeny. Modern scientists do not subscribe to the biogenetic law as postulated by Haeckel. However, there are elements of recapitulation that are important in comparative embryology.

In 1828, Karl von Baer pointed out that vertebrates share common characteristics during development. Examination of vertebrate embryos reveals that during corresponding stages of early development, the embryos appear to be very similar. For example, all vertebrate embryos pass through stages in which they have gill pouches. The pouches eventually develop into the gill apparatus in fish; in later evolving vertebrates that do not have gills, the gill pouches undergo further refinement and develop into structures associated with the head and neck. Similarly, all early vertebrate embryos have tails, which persist in some animals but regress during the later stages of development of humans. Thus, the individual development of an animal occurs through a series of stages that paint a broad picture of the evolutionary stages (phylogeny) of the species to which it belongs.

APPROACHES THE GENETICS OF BEHAVIOUR

We describe in order of increasing complexity how a researcher might approach the genetics of a behaviour of interest. For each method, I describe its aim, the general approach, its strength and weaknesses and the kinds of traits and animals for which it is most suited.

'Low tech' approaches

The first step in approaching the genetics of a behavioural trait is to determine if the behaviour is repeatable, which involves measuring the same behaviour on the same individual several times. Repeatability is the proportion of phenotypic variance attributable to the individual, which could be caused by additive genetic variance or environmental variance with long-lasting effects. Evidence that a behaviour is repeatable indicates that it might have a heritable component and is amenable for further genetic dissection.

The repeatability of a trait sets an 'upper bound' to heritability. However, it is worth considering that non-genetic effects can also produce stable behaviour; repeated reinforcement including learning can also lead to stability. Another indication that there might be a heritable component to the behaviour is if it is consistent across contexts; in this case, the stability occurs via a correlation between individual behaviours in different contexts, or a behavioural syndrome.

Another relatively low-tech approach to the genetics of a behaviour is to ask if it differs across populations that occur in different kinds of environments. If so, then population differences in the behaviour could reflect an evolved response to differing selective pressures. Alternatively, the differences could reflect environmentally-induced changes within individuals.

A way to disentangle these two hypotheses is to rear animals from the different populations in a 'common garden', or in the same environment. If population differences in the behaviour are preserved under common environmental conditions, then the difference between populations might be genetic in origin.

A common garden experiment represents the first step towards approaching the genetics of complex traits such as behaviour, but there are at least two important factors to consider before concluding that population differences are genetic in origin. The first is that F1s reared in a common garden could still experience parental effects from their wild-caught parents. To control for such environmental effects, it is preferable to rear the offspring of lab-born individuals and to compare the phenotype of the F2s. Second, GxE interactions should also be considered when populations do not differ in a common environment. For example, individuals from both populations might converge in their response to the common garden environment, but the extent of response might have a genetic component. A reciprocal transplant experiment might reveal genetic differences that are not apparent in a common environment.

An advantage to using population differences as a clue to which behaviours are likely to be heritable is that traits that differ across populations in different environments are probably linked to fitness. Several common garden studies on fishes have shown that population differences in behaviour are often preserved in a common garden. For example, Lahti *et al.* 2001 found evidence for a genetic basis to aggressive behaviour in brown trout by comparing different types of populations. The authors reared fish from 10 populations in a common environment. The populations can be grouped into the following types: resident (non-migratory), sea-run (migratory) or lake-run (migratory), so there were replicate populations for each type. Contrary to the expectation that resident trout are more aggressive than migratory forms, they found that sea-run populations were consistently more overtly aggressive towards opponents than the other types of populations.

There is a rich literature comparing domesticated and wild populations of salmonids, which has revealed genetic influences on several types of behaviour (reviewed in). When reared in a common garden, hatchery fish show reduced antipredator responses are more bold towards a novel object and are frequently more aggressive. However, wild Atlantic salmon (*Salmo salar*) became dominant over hatchery salmon if they were given an opportunity to establish residence, suggesting that the expression of genetic differences between hatchery and wild salmon depends on the environmental context.

Quantitative Genetic Approaches

There is a long history of examining the genetic basis of continuously distributed traits using quantitative genetic techniques, which are based on the phenotypic resemblance among relatives due to shared genes. Unlike some of the reverse methods, quantitative genetic techniques measure phenotypes, not genes, and rely on the resemblance among relatives to infer genetic effects. Quantitative genetic approaches assume that many genes of small effect influence the phenotype, thereby producing a continuous distribution (however, recent QTL studies have called this assumption into question). By measuring the phenotype on individuals of known relatedness, we can partition the phenotypic variation into environmental, genetic and gene x environment variance components.

The simplest quantitative genetic approach is to ask whether the trait of interest runs in families, which would suggest that there might be a genetic component to it. However, families often share a common environment so cross fostering experiments are useful here. Like repeatability, a demonstration of full-sib resemblance sets an upper limit to the heritability. More complicated breeding designs involve estimating the resemblance of parents and offspring using regression, or generating full and half-sib families to disentangle parental effects from genetic effects using ANOVA-based approaches, which are thoroughly described elsewhere. These approaches estimate heritabilities, genetic correlations, parental effects and non-additive genetic variance.

The most powerful quantitative genetic experiments estimate the G matrix. The G matrix refers to the multivariate matrix of genetic variances and covariances between several different traits. Although laborious to quantify, obtaining a G matrix allows us to predict the consequences of selection on any given trait, and, with a few assumptions about the stability of the G matrix through time, allows us to retrospectively analyze selection in the past. In addition to satisfying the assumption of stability required for retrospective selection analysis, it is also desirable to compare G matrices to determine whether genetic constraints are limiting. If genetic correlations can be uncoupled, then the relationship between traits might respond to selection, and the G matrix will, itself, evolve. Alternatively, genetic correlations might limit the number of different configuration of traits that are possible, which would be reflected in an invariant G matrix through time. Fortunately, there are several different techniques available to compare the structure of G matrices but there is debate about the best method.

A relatively new powerful technique known as the animal model allows us to estimate genetic variances and covariances without performing breeding experiments in the lab. Therefore this method is particularly useful for field studies. The animal model is powerful because it takes advantage of all types of resemblance between relatives to partition variance components; it uses all the available information about relatedness from a pedigree. Moreover, this method is suitable for unbalanced datasets, and can accommodate missing values.

Another approach for estimating genetic variances and covariances is to perform an artificial selection experiment, which involves selective breeding of individuals.

Selection experiments have shown that many behavioural traits can respond to selection. Artificial selection experiments are only suitable for organisms that can be kept in the lab, and which ideally have a short generation time. Selection experiments should only be undertaken when different selected lines can be replicated and when sample sizes are sufficient to control for drift and inbreeding. The pitfalls and perils of selection experiments are reviewed in.

Artificial selection experiments can be particularly insightful when they vary the environmental context in which selection occurs. For example, in a very interesting series of selection experiments on medaka (*Oryzias latipes*, Ruzzante and Doyle (1991, 1993) showed that the correlated response of aggressiveness to selection for fast growth depended on the ecological context in which the selection took place. In these experiments, Ruzzante and Doyle selected for fast growth under two different conditions: when food was clumped and could be defended, and when food was dispersed. The same limited amount of food was added to each treatment. Selection for fast growth produced a correlated response to selection on aggressiveness, but only when food was defensible. Interestingly, levels of aggressiveness *decreased* in the fast-growth lines, which they interpret as reflecting indirect selection for 'social tolerance'.

One of the strengths of a selection experiment is that it can tell us whether there are packages of traits that are linked together and respond to selection in concert. For example, selection for increased and decreased stress responsiveness, as measured by the change in circulating concentrations of cortisol in response to handling stress, produced several correlated effects on physiological and behavioural measures in rainbow trout. Relative to trout that did not release very much cortisol in response to handling stress, 'high responding' trout were more aggressive in a new environment were more active in the presence of an intruder and took longer to acclimate to a new environment. Moreover, these behavioural differences were also accompanied by changes in the brain monoaminergic systems. These results suggest that an entire suite of physiological and behavioural changes accompanied modifications to stress responsiveness. Interestingly, the packages of physiological and behavioural traits that changed together are analogous to different 'coping styles' that have been identified in other vertebrates.

Candidate Gene Approaches

Over the past few decades, there has been increasing evidence that the molecular functions of many genes are highly conserved across species. For example, studies on transgenics have revealed that genes from one species accomplish similar functions in distantly-related species. The incredible conservation of gene function in living things allows us to apply genetic information about other species to the organism of interest. This means that we can apply the genetic information gained from studies on model organisms to non-traditional models for which genomic information is not available.

Genes could become candidates based on genetic studies in other species (*i.e.* when polymorphism has already been identified and associated with behavioural variation, Fitzpatrick *et al.*, 2005), or because a physiological pathway leading to behaviour of interest is well-understood, suggesting hypotheses about which genes to examine. For example, the neuroendocrine mechanisms underlying circadian rhythms are well described for several mammalian species. Therefore, we can ask whether the expression or structure of genes along those pathways differ among individuals or among groups. Candidate gene expression approaches typically involve measuring the abundance of mRNA transcript in a particular tissue (usually brain, in the case of behaviour) using quantitative real-time PCR or Northern blots.

One of the attractions of the candidate gene approach is that detailed genomic information on the species is not necessary, therefore this technique can be applied to non-model organisms by designing degenerate primers based on other species. Another attraction of the candidate gene approach is that unlike quantitative genetic approaches, it does not require complicated breeding designs or data on the relationships among individuals – comparisons can be made across individuals of unknown relatedness because the genes are being measured directly. Therefore this approach is suitable for organisms that do not readily breed in the lab.

Summaries of using the candidate gene approach for studying behaviour are well-described elsewhere. Notable examples include work on the *for* gene and foraging behaviour, and the 'fruitless' gene and mating behaviour in Drosophila and the promoter region of the vasopressin gene and parental behaviour. The candidate gene approach for studying the genetics of fish behaviour is a relatively unexplored but promising future research direction. While the candidate gene approach is very attractive and has great appeal especially for non-model organisms, there are some drawbacks. First, candidate gene studies are biased; what if the ultimate source of genetic differences between groups lies further up or downstream of the particular candidate gene? One approach to this issue is to choose a pathway that is probably associated with the behaviour and look at gene expression at several points in the pathway. Second, candidate gene studies are purely correlative. Concluding that the gene is really associated with the behaviour requires further experimentation. Perhaps most seriously, candidate gene approaches work best when the trait is influenced by just few genes of major effect, which is probably the exception rather than the rule for behavioural traits.

GENOMICS

'Genomics' refers to the study of the structure, content and evolution of genomes, including the analysis of the expression and function of genes and proteins. What distinguishes genomics from other branches of genetics is that it looks at the whole genome simultaneously, rather than focusing on one gene at a time. Luckily, doing genomics does not require a full genome sequence, and there are already several good examples of applying whole-genome approaches to non-model organisms and ecologically-relevant traits, including behaviour. Genomics has been hailed as an opportunity to integrate mechanistic and evolutionary approaches to studying behaviour because information about genes provides neuroscientists and behavioural ecologists with a 'common language'.

BEHAVIOURAL ECOLOGIST STUDY THE GENETICS OF BEHAVIOUR

In a classic paper, Alan Grafen proposed that with a few simplifying assumptions, behavioural ecology might be able to ignore genetics. He argued that the aim of behavioural ecology is to uncover the selective forces that shape characters, and that our method will work almost regardless of which genetic system underlies the character. He proposed 'the phenotypic gambit', which was 'to examine the evolutionary basis of a character as if the very simplest genetic system controlled it'. Here, I take seriously Grafen's challenge to find cases where an understanding of the genetic mechanisms makes a difference. I highlight cases where different genetic mechanisms occur and change the evolutionary dynamics. I make the case that we often need to understand at least a little about the genetic mechanisms underlying behaviours if we are really interested in predicting the response to selection, inferring evolutionary history and understanding how animals cope with a non-equilibrial world.

However, for some questions, the phenotypic gambit might be justified. That is, if our interest is purely in the current utility of a trait rather than the evolutionary history or fate of it, the genetic mechanisms underlying the trait might not be informative. For example, if we want to know whether females prefer males with particular ornaments, then we do not need to know the genetics underlying female preference or the male ornament.

But there are several reasons why a behavioural ecologist might be interested in the genetics of behaviour. We cannot understand the selective forces that have produced adaptive variation without studying genetics in some form. In fact, many of our models either implicitly or explicitly include a genetic component to the behaviour of interest. Optimality models, for example, the simplest models in behavioural ecology, assume the presence of heritable variation for selection to act upon. Therefore, if we want to know if the behaviour has responded to natural or sexual selection in the past, and if it has the potential to evolve, we need to exclude the possibility that variation is not entirely environmentally-induced; we need to know if the trait is heritable.

If we are interested in obtaining more detailed information about the rate and direction of past and future evolution, then knowing more about the genetic architecture underlying a trait becomes important. In what follows, I describe what we can learn about the past and future evolution of a particular behaviour by elucidating its genetic architecture, including the number of loci, the number of alleles at a given locus, the distribution of effect sizes of the genes, whether the trait is genetically correlated with other traits, the relationship between loci (epistasis) and the relationship between alleles at a particular locus (dominance). Understanding genetic architecture is important for behavioural ecologists interested in tracing the evolutionary history of a particular behaviour, as well as for those trying to predict how animals will respond to a changing environment, including anthropogenic-induced change.

First, the number of genes affecting a behaviour and the distribution of their effect sizes determines how the behaviour can respond to future environmental change. For example, if a single gene of major effect is responsible for variation in the behaviour, the behaviour can quickly respond to selection. While traits that are affected by just a few genes might respond faster to selection, it has also been argued that polygenic traits might be more 'evolvable' because many genes of small effect effectively increases the opportunities for a beneficial mutation to arise. This additional pool can act as a reservoir for genetic variation, possibly allowing a population to respond to novel selection pressures.

Second, we frequently want to know whether there is additive genetic variation (V_a, reflected in the number of alleles at a given locus) for a trait because this can tell us about the past selective regime and the potential for future evolution. Theoretical models predict that natural selection will erode additive genetic variation, therefore small values of V_a) can indicate that the trait has been subject to selection in the past. This reasoning should be treated with some caution, however, because the data actually suggest that there is still substantial genetic variation for fitness-related traits, which presumably have been subject to strong directional selection in the past. A possible resolution to this paradox is that fitness-related traits are probably affected by many loci, thereby providing a bigger target for mutation to maintain genetic variation. As far as the fate of traits under selection goes, a trait will not respond to natural selection unless there is additive genetic variation for it, so knowing V_a can tell us whether the trait can respond to selection in the future. For example, global warming is causing disruption to animals that rely on seasonal cues for timing reproduction and migration. If populations do not harbour sufficient genetic variation for re-setting the timing of these critical behavioural decisions, then the viability of these populations might be threatened.

A third important component of the genetic architecture is how traits are genetically related to each other. A significant genetic correlation between two traits might indicate that the traits have been subject to correlational selection in the past. Correlational selection occurs when a trait's fitness effect depends on its interaction with another trait. Alternatively, a genetic correlation might be the result of a fundamental constraint that links two traits together, *i.e.* pleiotropy. Genetic correlations can also tell us about future responses to selection of a behaviour of interest). The response to selection on a particular trait depends on more than just the amount of genetic variation present for it;

it also depends on the sign and magnitude of genetic covariance between traits as well as on the force of selection acting on correlated traits. In some cases, the response to selection on a given trait can actually be in the opposite direction that we would predict if we did not consider genetic correlations.

There is another reason why researchers studying animal behaviour might be interested in genetic correlations. That is because genetic correlations hold a central place in sexual selection theory, arguably the most popular and controversial topic in animal behaviour. Different theories have been proposed to explain the evolution of exaggerated male ornaments used to attract mates. Fisherian models of sexual selection explain 'runaway' evolution of male ornaments by a genetic correlation between ornament and female preference for that ornament. In other words, brothers which have the exaggerated ornament have sisters with a strong preference for that ornament. It has proven difficult to empirically test this model, but some of the best evidence showing support for the Fisherian process comes from studies of fishes. For example, female guppies prefer to mate with males with particular coloration patterns (especially increased orange area), and evidence from both population comparisons and selection experiments support the hypothesis that there is a significant genetic correlation between female preference and different male ornaments in this species. This correlation has also been found in threespined sticklebacks.

Fourth, non-additive effects such dominance and epistasis, which are common for behavioural traits, also affect our ability to infer past selective regimes and to predict evolutionary potential. In a recent review, Merila and Sheldon reported that non-additive genetic effects (and environmental effects) are the most important genetic determinants of fitness in nature. Dominance refers to the relationship between alleles at a given locus; a dominance relationship implies that one allele is dominant to its partner. At the opposite end of the spectrum, if two alleles contribute equally, then the relationship between alleles is said to be additive.

Directional selection can favour the evolution of directional dominance for the allele that corresponds to the favored phenotype. Therefore, a dominance relationship between alleles at a given locus might indicate that the gene has been subject to directional selection in the past. Similarly, because a dominant allele will reach fixation faster than a recessive allele, the dominance relationship among alleles influences how quickly the trait can evolve.

Epistasis refers to interactions between loci affecting a trait. Selection can favour particular interactions between loci, resulting in coadapted epistatic gene complexes within populations. Epistasis is important for evolution because outbreeding depression can occur when populations that differ in their coadapted gene complexes are crossed. The breakdown of coadapted gene complexes can result in reproductive isolation between populations with different genetic backgrounds. Therefore, epistasis could be a mechanism for maintaining postzygotic reproductive isolation between populations according to the 'Dobzhansky-Muller model'.

For some people studying the genetics of complex traits, the real trophy is to find genes. If genes associated with adaptation can be identified, that can allow us to trace the evolutionary history of the gene through time. When did the gene originate? What are the functions of the gene in phylogenetically-distant relatives? Are similar behaviours related to the same gene in distant relatives? Is the same gene used over and over again to accomplish similar functions? Does this occur via *de novo* mutation in particular 'hot spots' of the genome, or is there standing genetic variation for it? We are beginning to get a glimmer of answers to these perennial questions for non-behavioural traits and it is only a question of time until we can answer those kinds of questions about behavioural traits as well.

Finally, we might want to find genes so that we can manipulate them. This is desirable, of course, for clinical applications, including psychopharmacology but it could also be a powerful experimental tool for the behavioural ecologists' toolbox.

3

Reproduction in Fisheries

REPRODUCTION

In biology, reproduction is the process by which new individual organisms are produced. Reproduction is a fundamental feature of all known life; each individual organism exists as the result of reproduction. Although the term reproduction encompasses a great variety of means by which organisms produce new offspring, reproductive processes can be classified into two main types: Sexual reproduction and asexual reproduction.

REPRODUCTION IN FISHES

The methods of reproduction in fishes are varied, but most fishes lay a large number of small eggs, fertilized and scattered outside of the body. The eggs of pelagic fishes usually remain suspended in the open water. Many shore and freshwater fishes lay eggs on the bottom or among plants. Some have adhesive eggs. The mortality of the young and especially of the eggs is very high, and often only a few individuals grow to maturity out of hundreds, thousands, and in some cases millions of eggs laid.

Males produce sperm, usually as a milky white substance called milt, in two (sometimes one) testes within the body cavity. In bony fishes a sperm duct leads from each testis to a urogenital opening behind the vent or anus. In sharks and rays and in cyclostomes the duct leads to a cloaca. Sometimes the pelvic fins are modified to help transmit the milt to the eggs at the female's vent or on the substrate where the female has placed them. Sometimes accessory organs are used to fertilize females internally-for example, the claspers of many sharks and rays.

In the females the eggs are formed in two ovaries (sometimes only one) and pass from the ovaries to the urogenital opening and to the outside. In some fishes the eggs are fertilized internally but shed before development takes place. Members of about a dozen families each of bony fishes (teleosts) and sharks bear live young. Many skates and rays also bear live young. In some bony fishes the eggs simply develop within the female, the young emerging when the eggs hatch (ovoviviparous). Others develop within the ovary and are nourished by ovarian tissues after hatching (viviparous). There are also other methods utilised by fishes to nourish young within the female. In all live-bearers the young are born at a relatively large size and are few in number. In one family of primarily marine fishes, the surfperches from the Pacific coast of North America, Japan, and Korea, the males of at least one species appear to be born sexually mature, although they are not fully grown.

Some fishes are hermaphroditic, an individual producing both sperm and eggs, usually at different stages of its life. Self-fertilization, however, is probably rare. Successful reproduction and in many cases defence of the eggs and young is assured by rather stereotyped but often elaborate courtship and parental behaviour, either by the male or the female or both. Some fishes prepare nests by hollowing out depressions in the sand bottom (cichlids, for example), build nests with plant materials and sticky threads excreted by the kidneys (sticklebacks), or blow a cluster of mucus-covered bubbles at the water surface (gouramis).

The eggs are laid in these structures. Some varieties of cichlids and catfishes incubate eggs in their mouths. Some fishes, such as salmon, undergo long migrations from the ocean and up large rivers to spawn in gravel beds where they themselves hatched (anadromous fishes). Others undertake shorter migrations from lakes into streams or in other ways enter for spawning habitats that they do not ordinarily occupy.

TYPES OF REPRODUCTION

Generally two types of reproduction are seen, these are-

1. Sexual reproduction
2. Asexual reproduction

SEXUAL REPRODUCTION

A from of reproduction that involves the fusion of two reproductive cells (ova and sperm) in the process of fertilization normally especially in animals, it requires two parents, one male and the other female. The female of the species produces an egg which is fertilized by sperm from the male.

Depending on the species, fertilization takes place either within the female's body or externally, after the female lays her eggs and the male releases his sperm close by. When the egg is fertilized the genes of both parents are combined to produce zygote which develops into a new individual. Nearly all animals reproduce sexually.

Bisexual

Which is the prevalent kind; sperm and eggs develop in separate male and female individuals.

Hermaphrodites

Both sexes are in one individual and, as among certain errands and a dozen or more other families. Self-fertilization or true functional hermaphrodites sexists. Hermaphroditic sex glands are known for several species, including some trout relatives (salmonoids), perches (Perca), walleyes (Stizostedion). Darters (Etheostoma). And some of the black basses (Micropterus).

ASEXUAL REPRODUCTION

Reproduction in which new individuals are produced from a single parent without the formation of gametes. Asexual reproduction enables animals to reproduce without a partner. It occurs chiefly in lower animals, microorganisms, and plants. Many invertebrates reproduce asexually, including coral and starfish. Coral grow small buds that break off to become separate organisms, whilst starfish are able to generate an entirely new being from a fragment of their original body.

OTHER TYPES

Without above classification, another three types of reproduction are also possible.

Parthenogenesis

Is the development of young without fertilization, and a condition that has been called parthenogenesis (more properly gynogenesis) occurs in a tropical fish, the live-bearing Amazon molly (poecilia Formosa), and is also known in poeciliopsis. Mating with a male is required, but the sperm serves only one of its two functions, that of inciting the eggs to develop; it does not take any part in heredity. The resultant young are always females, with no trace of parental characters.

Sexual Reproduction

Sexual reproduction is a process of biological reproduction by which organisms give rise to descendants that have a combination of genetic material contributed by two different gametes, usually, *i.e.*, two different individuals, male and female. A gamete is a mature reproductive or sex cell. Sexual reproduction results in increasing genetic diversity, since the union of these gametes produces an organism that is not genetically identical to the parent(s).

Sexual reproduction is characterized by two processes: meiosis, involving the halving of the number of chromosomes to produce gametes; and fertilization, involving the fusion of two gametes and the restoration of the original number of chromosomes. During meiosis, the chromosomes of each pair usually cross over to achieve genetic recombination. Once fertilization takes place, the organism can grow by mitosis.

While typically sexual reproduction is thought of in terms of two different organisms contributing gametes, it also includes self-fertilization, whereby one organism may have "male" and "female" parts, and produce different gametes that fuse. Sexual reproduction is the primary method of reproduction for the vast majority of visible organisms, including almost all animals and plants. The origin of sex and the prominence of sexual reproduction are major puzzles in modern biology.

Overview: Gametes, Meiosis, Fertilization, and Mitosis

In the first stage of sexual reproduction, 'meiosis', a special type of that takes place in gonads prior to the a production of gametes, the number of chromosomes is reduced from a diploid number (2n) to a haploid number (n). During 'fertilization', haploid gametes come together to form a diploid zygote and the original number of chromosomes (2n) is restored in the offspring.

Sexual reproduction involves the fusion or fertilization of gametes from two different sources or organisms. Typically, a gamete or reproductive cell is haploid, while the somatic or body cell of the organism is diploid. A diploid cell has a paired set of chromosomes. Haploid means that the cell has a single set of unpaired chromosomes, or one half the number of chromosomes of a somatic cell. In diploid organisms, sexual reproduction involves alternating haploid (n) and diploid (2n) phases, with fusion of haploid cells to produce a diploid organism. Some organisms, however, exhibit polyploidy, whereby there are more than two homologous sets of chromosomes.

Meiosis and mitosis are two diverse type of cell divisions. Mitosis occurs in somatic (body) cells. The resultant number of cells in mitosis is twice the number of original cells. The number of chromosomes in the daughter cells is the same as that of the parent cell. Meiosis occurs in reproductive or sex cells and results in gametes. It results in daughter cells with half the number of chromosomes present in their parent cell. Essentially, a diploid cell duplicates it's chromosomes, then undergoes two divisions (tetroid to diploid to haploid), in the process forming four haploid cells. This process occurs in two phases, meiosis I and meiosis II.

Fertilization involves the fusion of haploid gametes to give a diploid organism, which can then grow by mitosis. Thus, in sexual reproduction, each of two parent organisms contributes half of the offspring's genetic makeup by creating haploid gametes that fuse to form a diploid organism. For most organisms, a gamete that is produced may have one of two different forms. In these anisogamous species, the two sexes are referred to as male, producing sperm or microspores as gametes, and female, producing ova or megaspores as gametes. In isogamous species, the gametes are similar or identical in form, but may have separable properties and may be given other names. For example, in the green alga, Chlamydomonas reinhardtii, there are so-called "plus" and "minus" gametes. A few types of organisms, such as ciliates, have more than two kinds of gametes.

Sexually reproducing organisms have two sets of genes (called alleles) for every trait. Offspring inherit one allele for each trait from each parent, thereby ensuring that offspring have a combination of the parents' genes. Having two copies of every gene, only one of which is expressed, allows deleterious alleles to be masked.

As with the other vertebrates, sexual reproduction is the overwhelming dominant form of reproduction. However, there are several genera of fish that practice true or incomplete parthenogenesis, where the embryo develops without fertilization by a male.

Although vertebrates in general have distinct male and female types, there are fish species that are both males and females gonads(hermaphrodites), either at the same time or sequentially. For example, the amenone fish spend the first part of their lives as males and later become females, and the parrot fish is first female and then male. Some members of the Serranidae (sea basses) are simultaneous hermaphrodites, such as the Serranus and their immediate relatives, Hypoplectrus (the synchronoous hermaphroditic hamlets). Fertilization may be external or internal. In the yellow perch, eggs are produced by ovaries in the female and sperm is produced by the testes, and they are released through an opening into the environment, and fertilization takes place in the water (Towle 1989). In some live bearers, such as guppies and swordtails, females receive sperm during mating and fertilization is internal. Other behaviours related to sexual reproduction include some species, such as the stickleback, built nests from plants, sticks, and shells, and many species that migrate to spawn.

Asexual Reproduction

Asexual reproduction is a form of reproduction in which an organism gives rise to a genetically-similar or identical copy of itself without a contribution of genetic material from another individual. It does not involve meiosis, ploidy reduction, or fertilization, and only one parent is involved genetically. A more stringent definition is agamogenesis, which refers to reproduction without the fusion of gametes.

Asexual reproduction is the primary form of reproduction for single-celled organisms such the archaea, bacteria, and protists. However, while all prokaryotes reproduce asexually (without the formation and fusion of gametes), there also exist mechanisms for lateral gene transfer, such as conjugation, transformation, and transduction, whereby genetic material is exchanged between organisms. Biological processes involving lateral gene transfer sometimes are likened to sexual reproduction (Narra and Ochman 2006). The reproductive variances in bacteria and protists also may be symbolised by +

and - signs (rather than being called male and female), and referred to as "mating strains" or "reproductive types" or similar appellations.

Many plants and fungi reproduce asexually as well, and asexual reproduction has been cited in some animals, including bdelloid rotifers, which only are known to reproduce asexually, and various animals that exhibit parthenogenesis under certain conditions.

In parthenogenesis, such as found in some invertebrates and vertebrates, an embryo is produced without fertilization by a male. Generally, parthenogenesis is considered a form of asexual reproduction because it does not involve fusion of gametes of opposite sexes, nor any exchange of genetic material from two different sources however, some authorities classify parthenogenesis as sexual reproduction on the basis that it involves gametes or does not produce an offspring genetically identical to the parent (such as a female domestic turkey producing male offspring).

A wide spectrum of mechanisms may be exhibited. For example, many plants alternate between sexual and asexual reproduction, and the freshwater crustacean Daphnia reproduces by parthenogenesis in the spring to rapidly populate ponds, then switches to sexual reproduction as the intensity of competition and predation increases. Many protists and fungi alternate between sexual and asexual reproduction.

A lack of sexual reproduction is relatively rare among multicellular organisms, which exhibit the characteristics of being male or female. Biological explanations for this phenomenon are not completely settled. Current hypotheses suggest that, while asexual reproduction may have short term benefits when rapid population growth is important or in stable environments, sexual reproduction offers a net advantage by allowing more rapid generation of genetic diversity, allowing adaptation to changing environments.

Hermaphroditism

A hermaphrodite is defined as any individual organism that possesses both male and female reproductive organs during their life span. The main advantage of hermaphroditism is the assurance of a reproductive partner. Although hermaphroditism is quite common in invertebrates and plants, it is an exceedingly rare occurrence in vertebrates. Hermaphroditism in mammals and birds are almost always a pathological condition (often leading to infertility). Only in Perciforms (fish) does hermaphroditism occur naturally and in high frequency. Hermaphrodites are divided into two main categories: synchronous hermaphrodites, and sequential hermaphrodites. In the synchronous hermaphrodites, organisms possess both active male and active female reproductive organs at the same time. In sequential hermaphrodites, both male and female reproductive organs may be present, but only one is active and viable at any given time.

Synchronous, or simultaneous hermaphrodites in reef fish are relatively atypical. A few Serranids (sea basses, *e.g.* Serranus sp.) and Hamlets are known synchronous hermaphrodites. During mating, one individual will lay eggs while another fertilizes the eggs, after which both will reverse roles and perform fertilization again. Synchronous hermaphrodites do not fertilize themselves; Self-fertilization does not promote genetic diversity, and can amplify genetic defects from parent to offspring. The interesting fact is most synchronous hermaphrodites form monogamous pairs.

Sequential hermaphrodites are so named because they are capable of transforming from one sex to another. Theses transformations entail a full conversion of gonads from one sex to another. The gonads of sequential hermaphrodites possess the genetic information to produce both male and female reproductive organs, but only the dominant gene is expressed at any giventime. Different cues - varying from species to species - may induce sex changes.

Sequential hermaphrodites are further categorised into two main categories: protogynous and protandrous. Protandrous hermaphrodites are those that develop into males first, then possibly to females. Protogynous hermaphrodites are the exact opposite, with juveniles first developing female reproductive organs that may possibly change into male reproductive organs in select circumstances.

It should be noted that hermaphrodites do not necessarily have to change sexes, but by definition, are capable of this feat. Protandrous hermaphrodites are the rarer of the two types. Pomacentrids (damselfish) are the most famous of these hermaphrodites. For example, clownfish of the genus Amphiprion live in communities that consist of one dominant female specimen and several smaller male (or asexual juvenile) specimens. If the female should be removed, a male will convert to a female, insuring a reproductive partner for the community.

Protogynous hermaphrodites are most often haremic fish. These fish form monoandric harems comprising of 1 male overseeing numerous females for life. The two primary responsibilities of the male are to defend its territory against other conspecific males, and to court and fertilize females of its territory. If the male should die (either of natural causes or conflict-related mortality), the dominant female of the harem will undergo a sex change from female to male. This sex change may take as little as 5 days. The new male will then resume the full responsibilities of the previous male until he should die. Protogynous hermaphrodites that form harems include the wrasses of the genus Cirrhilabrus and Paracheinlinus, Dwarf Angelfish of the genus Centropyge, and Anthias (*e.g.* Pseudoanthias sp.). Some protogynous fish do not form harems, but may form pairs. The dottybacks (Pseudochromis sp.) are presumably protogynous hermaphrodites that fall under this category. There are also sequential hermaphrodites that waver between sexes with no discernable order.

The sexes of these fish are often determined by the ratio of sexes in an immediate community. These types of hermaphrodites include numerous gobies.

MODES OF REPRODUCTION AND DEVELOPMENT

The ability to produce new living individual is a basic characteristics of all plants and animals. All reliable evidence indicates that new life comes only from pre-existing life; this is the process of biogenesis or reproduction. The different modes of reproduction can be classified according to the environment in which the embryos develop, and the sources of the nutrients supporting embryonic growth. These are mentioned into the following term:

OVIPARITY

Oviparity or egg laying refers to the situation where the development or the fertilized of egg occurs outside the body of the female. The young hatch when the egg envelope, shell or capsule is broken. Oviparous fish may be further categorised as being either ovuliparous or zygoparous.

ovuliparity refers to the release of ova from the reproductive tract of the female followed by fertilization or activation in the external environment. Thus, all organisms that have external fertilization and this includes most teleost are said to be ovuliparous. Zygoparity refer to the oviparous condition in which the zygotes (*i.e.*, fertilized ova products of fusion between the eggs and sperm) are retained within the body of the female for a short period of time before being released into the environment. Obviously, zygoparous species display internal fertilization with their being a transfer of male sperm to the reproductive tract of the female. Zygoparous reproduction characterises all skates some sharks and a small number of teleost. Irrespective of weather the fertilization of the eggs occurs internally or the egg yolk provides externally the nutrient for the developing embryos of oviparous species.

Oviparity in Fishes

Amongst fish which reproduce by ovipartity, there are several groups.

Egg Scatterers

Fish which breed in this way either spawn in pairs or in groups. Males and females release milt (the sperm and spermatic fluid of the male) and eggs into the water at the same time. These mix together, fertilising the eggs. The fertilised eggs are broadcast (or spread) into the plankton column and float away in the current or sink to the bottom. No parental care is given, so large amounts of eggs are produced. It is easy to produce many eggs and because they are in the water, they don't dry out - necessary oxygen and nutrients aren't scarce. When theoffspring settle out of the plankton, they might be in totally new environments: this gives the young a chance to survive across a wide area. The main disadvantage of this method is that the fish must go through a larval stage before they transform into adults. In this larval stage, they are very vulnerable while they try to find food and avoid predators. Also, they may not find a suitable environment when they settle out of the plankton column. The survival rate for individual eggs is very low, so the parent has to produce millions of eggs.

Egg Depositors

These fish either lay eggs on a flat surface, like a stone or plant leaf or may even place them individually among fine leaved plants. The parents usually form pairs and guard the eggs and fry (young fish) from all danger. The Cichlids such as Koi are the best known species for this. Some Catfish and Rainbow fish are also egg depositors.

Nest Builders

Many fish species build nests. These might be a simple pit dug into gravel (trout do this) or an elaborate bubble nest. When they are ready to spawn, the fish may construct a nest by blowing bubbles, and they often use vegetation to anchor the nest. The male will keep the nest intact and keep a close eye on the eggs. The Gouramis, Anabantids and some catfish are the most common of this type.

Mouthbreeders

These are particularly odd, since eggs are fertilised externally, but raised internally. The females usually lay their eggs on a flat surface where they are then fertilised by the male. After fertilization the female picks up the eggs and incubates them in her mouth. Broods tend to be small, since by the time the fry are released by their mothers they are well formed and suffer minimal losses. The best known mouthbreeders are the African lake Cichlids.

Egg Buriers

The annual Killifish reproduce in this way. As the pools they live in dry out, the fish spawn, pressing their eggs into the mud. The pools eventually dry out completely, killing the adults, but the eggs remain safe in the dried mud. When it rains and the pool refills the eggs hatch and the cycle is repeated. Killifish eggs can survive for many years in dried out mud.

Ovoviviparity

In the ovoviviparous species the eggs usually develop within the uterus (modified oviduct) of the female. Fertilization of the egg occurs internally and the eggs are retained until hatching or beyond. The developing embryos do not receive any supply of foodstuffs from the female but must rely on the yolk of the egg for nutrition. This form of nutrition is known as lecthotrophy. The developing embryos must, however, rely on the female for supply of oxygen. During pregnancy the wall of the oviduct becomes enlarged and richly supplied with blood vessels.

Viviparity

Viviparous species have eggs, which develop either within the uterus (*i.e.*, several species of shark), or within the ovary (*i.e.*, teleosts). The developing embryos receive some nutrient supply from the female in edition to that provided as yolk in the egg.

This form of nutrition is known as matrotrophy. The additional nutrient can be supplied in various forms. in some species of female secrets a nutrient-rich fluid which is taken up by the developing young has a form of 'soup'. In other species some form of 'placenta' may develop allowing a more direct transfer of nutrient from the blood of the female to the developing embryo. A distinction is sometimes made between viviparous animals in which the embryos derives nourishment from the mother's tissues as in most mammals and animals that are called ovoviviparous in which the embryo is nourished entirely by food stored in the egg, the hatching before being laid.

Viviparity in Fishes

Fishes provide a key to understanding vertebrate viviparity in as much as the first viviparous vertebrates were fishes and they display the most diverse maternal fetal relationships of all the live bearing vertebrates. Viviparity occurs in three major fish groups: the chondrichthyans, the teleosts, and the actinistians.

Although widespread, it represents the dominant mode of reproduction only among the sharks and rays. Approximately 420 of the estimated 600-700 species of chondrichthyan fishes are viviparous in contrast, only 510 of the estimated 20,000 species of teleost fishes are viviparous. The coelacanth, the only extant species of actinistian, is viviparous.

Semelparity and Iteroparity

Semelparity and Iteroparity refer to the reproductive strategy of an organism. A species is considered semelparous if it is characterised by a single reproductive episode before death, and iteroparous if it is characterised by multiple reproductive cycles over the course of its lifetime. Some plant scientists use the parallel terms monocarpy and polycarpy. In truly semelparous species, death after reproduction is part of an overall strategy that includes putting all available resources into maximizing reproduction, at the expense of future life. In any iteroparous population there will be some individuals who die between their first and second reproductive episodes, but unless this is part of a syndrome of programmed death after reproduction, this would not be called semelparity.

Semelparity

The word semelparity comes from the Latin semel, once, and pario, to beget. It is also known as "big bang" reproduction, since the single reproductive event of semelparous organisms is usually large, as well as fatal. A classic example of a semelparous organism is Pacific salmon (Oncorhynchus spp.), which lives for many years in the ocean before swimming to the freshwater stream of its birth, for laying eggs, and dying. Other semelparous animals include many insects, including some species of butterflies, cicadas, and mayflies, some molluscs such as squid and octopus, and many arachnids. Semelparity is much rarer in vertebrates, but in addition to salmon, examples include smelt, capelin, and a few lizards, amphibians, and didelphid and dasyurid marsupial mammals.

Iteroparity

The term iteroparity comes from the Latin itero, to repeat, and pario, to beget. An example of an iteroparous organism is a human-though many people may choose only to have one child, humans arc biologically capable of having offspring many times over the course of their lives.

Iteroparous vertebrates include all birds, most reptiles, virtually all mammals, and most fish. Among invertebrates, most mollusca and many insects (for example, mosquitoes and cockroaches) are iteroparous. Most perennial plants are iteroparous.

Fecundity

Fecundity, the number of eggs ripened by female fish during a spawning season, or event, varies from a few dozen in some continuously reproducing livebearing fishes to millions in some species that spawn pelagic eggs on an annual basis.

In general, fecundity varies among species inversely with the amount of "care" given to the individual progeny: viviparous fishes have lower fecundity than ovoviviparous fishes, which in turn have lower fecundity than oviparous fishes, and nest builders have lower fecundity than pelagic spawners. Within species fecundity is positively related to size; generally it is close to a function of the cube of fish length.

Although fish eggs range from about 0.5 to 20 mm in diameter, the size of the adult limits the fecundity in smaller species. In most species with high fecundity, several batches of eggs are usually produced at intervals of a few days to weeks during the spawning season.

Some general reasons for determining fecundity is that it is useful for making total population estimates, it is useful in studies of population dynamics or productivity, and it is useful for characterising specific populations, subpopulations, and/or stocks of fishes.

- *Absolute fecundity:* is the number of ripe eggs produced by a female in one spawning season or year (this is the usual meaning when the general term "fecundity" is used, although on occasion it might also mean the number of eggs produced in a lifetime).
- *Relative fecundity:* is the number of eggs produced in a season per unit somatic weight of the fish (*i.e.*, eggs/gram), and is useful if it is shown that the fecundity of a fish is proportional to its weight, which is not uncommon.
- *Population fecundity:* is the number of eggs spawned by the population in one season, is the sum of the fecundities of all females, and is usually expressed as the product of the expected fecundity of an average female, the number of breeding females in the population (an example of why classifying maturity stages may be useful).

SPAWNING

Spawning refers to the release of unfertilized planktonic eggs by female fish, which is the reproductive pattern for most marine fishes. The eggs are fertilized shortly after release by males. Some fishes also deposit unfertilized Fish Reproduction eggs in nests where they are fertilized and develop. Fishes with internal fertilization release free-swimming larvae, or juveniles. The ripening of eggs and spawning are controlled by hormones, nutrition of the female, and external (ecological) factors (Hempel 1979). Usually maturation and spawning are controlled by a combination of endogenous and exogenous controls and are not governed by any specific factor.

TERMINOLOGY USED IN DISCUSSING SPAWNING

- *Mating:* pairing (one-on-one) for the purpose of fertilizing eggs; copulatory organ present.
- *Spawning:* release of unfertilized eggs into the environment or release of larvae into the environment; mating and spawning need not occur simultaneously (*e.g.*, surfperches). Spawning can occur without true mating (*e.g.*, herring, which are broadcast spawners).
- *Fertilization:* fusion of eggs and sperm (creating diploids from haploids); mating and fertilization need not occur simultaneously (*e.g.*, surfperches and rockfishes).
- *Incubation time:* time from egg fertilization to hatching. Gestation applies only to live-bearing fishes; it is the time young stay within the female.
- *Hatching:* when the larva frees itself from the egg.
- *Breed:* to produce offspring by hatching (or gestation).
- *Brood:* guard and groom eggs until they hatch.

DESCRIPTION OF MATURITY STAGES

Male

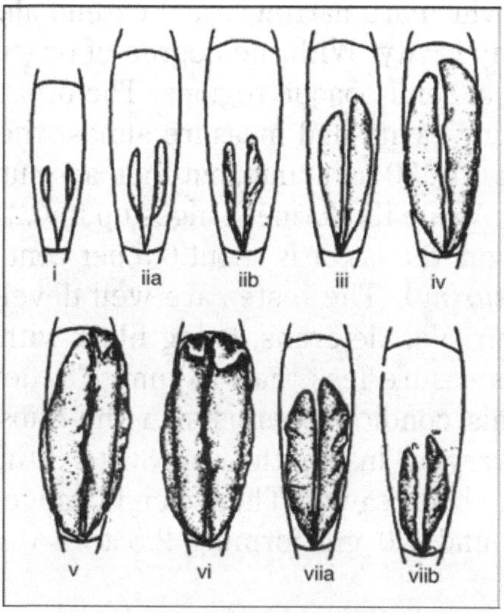

Fig. Diagrammatic representation of different maturity stages of male

- *Stage I (Immature):* The testes are extremely small, often recognised only as translucent filamentous strands in the early stages. Later, when easily visible, they are small, opaque, pinky-white, leaf-like structures with a fairly long vas deferens, which get easily snapped when the testes are removed. There is very little asymmetrical development and, if any, the left testis is slightly longer. The testes with the vas deferens occupy roughly 50 per cent of the length of the body cavity or occasionally slightly more, measuring a maximum overall length of about 35 mm, of which the testicular portion may form 10 to 15 mm only. The gonad weight ranges up to 0.2 gm, but it is usually less than that. Their relative weight to body weight is normally below 0.8 per cent.
- *Stage II-A (Developing Virgin):* The testes are thicker and more elongated. They are opaque, pink or white in colour, with vas deferens reduced but thread-like. Asymmetrical development has set in and the left testis is almost always longer. The testes with the ducts extend to 50-60 per cent of the body cavity and measure 30 to 40 mm and the testicular portion measures about 25 to 30 mm. Their weight ranges from 0.2 to 0.5gm, but it is usually around 0.4gm. The relative weight varies from 1.0 to 1.7 per cent.
- *Stage II-B (Spent-resting):* The testes are pinkish or brownish-white in colour but different from the previous stage in having shrunken and wrinkled appearance when viewed against light, showing that the

organs are not compactly filled with germ cells. The left testis is usually longer. The vas deferens is a much wider duct than the thread-like passage of the previous stage and is covered by the lower halves of the testes which are narrower and extend almost to the posterior end of the body cavity. With the degree of opacity varying, there are a few patches of semi-opaque regions. The organs fill up 50 to 55 per cent of the body cavity and measure almost the same length as the previous stage, *i.e.*, 30 to 40 mm, but theif absolute and relative weight are much less. While the former ranges up to 0.29 gm with an average of about 0.15 gm, the latter is about 0.5 per cent.

- *Stage III (Maturing):* The testes are well developed and thickened, white in colour. Vas deferens, being filled with spermatogonia, are reduced and measure less than 15 mm. The left testis is distinctly longer and this condition persists in the subsequent stages also. The gonads varying in length from 36 to 50 mm occupy 70 to 75 per cent of the body cavity. Their weight ranges up to 2.0 gm but it is usually around 1.0 gm forming 2.5 to 4-0 per cent as relative weight.
- *Stage IV (Maturing):* Quite massive and creamy-white are the testes with vas deferens hidden under them. The organs, while extending to the entire breadth of the body cavity, occupy 85 to 90 per cent of the body cavity length, measuring 40 to 70 mm. Their absolute weight ranges from 2.5 to 5.0 gm, but in majority of cases it is around 3.5 gm. Their relative weight varies from 5.0 to 7.0 per cent.
- *Stage V (Mature):* The testes are opaque white in colour, soft, more extensive than Stage IV and occupy the entire length of the body cavity but very often even more with the result their anterior ends tend to fold down along the ventral body wall. On a little pressure internally at the posterior end, spermatic fluid oozes out. Their usual length is 65 to 70 mm but can attain even 80 mm sometimes. Their absolute weight ranges from 6.0 to 8.0 gm, with an average around 7.0 gm. The relative weight works up to 10.0 to 14.0 per cent.
- *Stage VI (Running):* The testes are very extensive, white in colour and fill the entire space of body cavity displacing the intestines to a fraction of space. Not only the anterior tips are folded down along the ventral body wall but even the outer margins extending along the sides of the body wall curve towards the middle so much so very often an insertion along the mid-ventral line cuts through the outer edges of the testes. Under a slight pressure externally on the flanks of the fish or even while handling, milt extrudes out. The organs always measure more than 70 mm and weigh from 9.0 to 13.0 gm

with an average around 10.0 gm and the relative weight ranges between 15 and 20 per cent.

- *Stage VII A (Partially Spent):* The testes are meat-coloured, a bit leathery in texture, shrunken with wrinkles and semi-opaque spaces visible when viewed against fight. Measuring 40 to 60 mm, they occupy 70 to 80 per cent of the body cavity and weigh usually 2.0 gm but may range from 1.0 to 2.5 gm, which forms 2.5 to 4.5 per cent as relative weight.
- *Stage VII B (Spent):* The testes are deep flesh-coloured, shrunken, flat, strap-like, shrivelled with translucent patchy regions. They occupy 50 to 60 per cent of the body cavity and measure 30 to 45 mm. Their weight is around 0.5 gm, forming about 1.5 per cent as relative weight.

Female

- *Stage I (Immature):* The ovaries are soft cylindrical and almost translucent, pink or flesh-coloured. Sometimes due to post-mortem changes they appear purple in colour. The surface of the ovary is smooth with no distinct blood vessels. There is very little asymmetry in the size of the ovaries. The oviduct is fairly long and completely transparent with the result, the ovarian bodies look like detached stubs, short and plump. The entire length of the ovaries with their ducts occupies about or slightly more than 50 per cent of the body cavity and measures up to about 35 mm of which the length of the ovary alone ranges from 10 to 25 mm. Their absolute weight may be about or below 0.25gm forming a maximum of 0.8 per cent as relative weight. The ovaries are compactly filled with oocytes, not visible to naked eye. The oocytes are yolkless and transparent and measure up to 0.13 mm with the majority of them in the size range of 0.07 to 0.09 mm.
- *Stage II A (Developing Virgin):* Cylindrical, soft, translucent ovaries pink or flesh-coloured. Asymmetry is not quite distinct yet. Oviducts, thin and thread-like, are a little reduced in length and not more than 10 mm. The overall length of the gonads ranges from 30 to 35 mm forming 55 to 60 per cent of body cavity. The ovaries alone measure about 20 to 25 mm in length and usually weigh around 0.4 gm, but may range from 0.3 to 0.6 gm. The relative weight is 1.0 to 1.5 per cent. Majority of the ova are transparent with signs of yolk formation in some, which are mostly semi opaque but sometimes fully opaque with or without translucent periphery. However, even these do not appear as distinct grains to be easily recognised with naked eye. Maximum diameter of ova recorded is 0.30 mm with a large number of ova ranging in size from 0.15 to 0.18 mm.

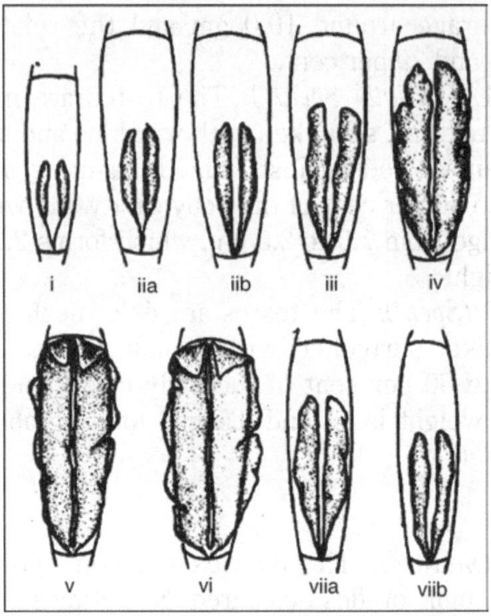

Fig. Diagrammatic representation of different maturity stages of female

- *Stage II B (Spent-resting):* The ovaries are dark-red or brownish red or deep flesh-coloured, having a collapsed and flattened appearance. External surface is wrinkled. The tunica is thicker and the Oviducts much wider and shorter than in the previous stage. The length of the organs is 30 to 45 mm occupying 55 to 60 per cent of the body cavity. Their weight is commonly around 0.2 gm, forming less than 0.5 per cent as relative weight. Occasionally, late spawners resting in January-February period may record a maximum gonad weight of about 0.4 to 0.5 gm with their relative weight of about 0.8 per cent. Majority of ova are transparent, not visible to naked eye and measure 0.07 to 0.11 mm. A few scattered opaque ova may be present without transparent periphery and measure up to 0.15 mm. This stage is characteristically distinguished by the presence of clots of blood cells appearing as brownish masses in between the oocytes.
- *Stage III (Maturing):* The ovaries are turgid, opaque and yellow in colour with granular appearance. Development of blood vessels is perceptible. The oviducts are very much reduced. Usually there is asymmetrical development in the size of the ovaries, either gonad longer than the other. This condition persists in the subsequent stages also. The ovaries occupy about 65 to 70 per cent of the body cavity and measure from 35 to 50 mm. Their weight ranges from 0.8 to 1.5 gm, but usually it is below 1.0gm. The relative weight may accordingly vary from 2 to 4 per cent. The maximum diameter of ova recorded is 0.54 mm. The size frequency distribution of ova normally shows one

distinct mode of maturing ova around 0.35 to 0.40 mm, which are opaque with translucent periphery and visible to naked eye. In these ovaries, some semi-opaque ova with yolk deposition around the centre measure 0.15 to 0.17 mm and form a good percentage. Sometimes, ovaries advanced a little further but not entered into Stage IV show two modes of maturing ova, an advance one 0.42 to 0.47 mm and a minor one around 0.22 to 0.27 mm. Both sets of ova are opaque and are provided with translucent periphery.

- *Stage IV (Maturing):* The ovaries are compact, vascular with conspicuous blood vessels on the tunica and bright yellow in colour. Oviducts are not quite distinct. The organs almost extend to the entire body cavity forming 80 to 90 per cent of the latter's length, with its own length varying from 45 to 65 mm. They weigh about 2.0 to 4.5 gm with an average of 3.0 gm, forming 4.5 to 7.0 per cent as relative weight. The largest ova may measure about 0.67 mm and the size frequency polygons show two distinct modes, one Any where between 0.51 and 0.57 mm and the other around 0.27 to 0.34 mm. The former are completely opaque, while the latter are provided with translucent periphery.
- *Stage V (Mature):* The ovaries are orange-yellow in colour, fully vascular with prominent blood vessels ramifying on the surface. Tunica is very thin and bursts at slight pressure. Ovaries are very often more than the length of the body cavity with the anterior tips taking a loop down. Their normal length is 65 to 70 mm, but according to the size of fish may even extend up to 80 mm. Their average weight is 6.5 gm with a range of 5.5 to 7.5 gm. Relative weight ranges from 9 to 13 per cent. Maximum diameter of ova observed is 0.82 mm. The distribution of ova shows two groups, an advanced mature one anywhere between 0.62 and 0.67 mm. and a maturing group around 0.35 to 0.47 mm. The ova of former group Present varying appearances; some are completely opaque, some provided with narrow or wide transparent periphery, some vacuolated, some partly Transparent and a few fully. Completely transparent ova have one big Oil globule or two-three smaller droplets of oil globule which measure from 0.054 to 0.109 mm and the other partly transparent and vacuolated ova have a number droplets of oil globule. The ova of less advanced mode are fully opaque.
- *Stage VI (Running):* The ovaries appear as a sort of cream-coloured cellophane bags filled with boiled sago. At a slight prick, a gelatinous mass of transparent ova flows out, the tunica being so thin. Ova can be extruded on slight pressure externally on the flanks of the fish or even while handling. The ovaries measure more than 70 mm and fill the entire-space of abdomen cavity displacing the intestine to a narrow

space in between the two ovaries- They may weigh from 8.0 to 12.0 gm, but ordinarily around 9.0 gm, forming 13 to 17 per cent as relative weight. The largest ova are transparent and jelly-like reaching a maximum diameter of 1.2 mm, but the majority of these range from 0.80 to 0.91 mm in diameter with one or two oil globules very rarely cleaved into three which measure 0.091 to 0.127 mm. There is a significant number of medium-sized ova forming another distinct mode between 0.46 and 0.51 mm, which are completely opaque or provided with transparent periphery.

- *Stage VII A (Partially Spent):* The ovaries are dark red in colour either throughout the length or only at the posterior half They are a bit flaccid and collapsed with slight wrinkles on the surface. The ovarian lamellae are clearly seen as book leaves especially at the posterior region indicating that the lamellae are not compactly filled with maturing ova and that some have been shed. The ruptured blood capillaries produce blood clots which appear as brownish or reddish masses. Blood capillaries penetrate deeply into the interior. Although the ovaries are shrunk in volume and reduced in breadth, they extend to 70 to 80 per cent of the body cavity measuring 40 to 60 mm. Their weight ranges from 1.5 to 3.0 gm but is usually around 2.0gm, amounting to 2.5 to 5.0 per cent as relative weight. The maximum diameter of ova is about 0.60 mm and the frequency distribution shows only one distinct mode anywhere within 0.35 to 0.51 mm. These ova are completely opaque but a few of these perhaps in the process of resorption are translucent with greyish yolk in the centre within which may be found a few droplets of oil-globule.
- *Stage VII B (Spent):* The ovaries are elongated, honey-coloured, bloodshot, flabby, limp and gelatinous with wrinkles on surface due to collapsed condition. The tunica is leathery and the wide oviduct is now Recognisable. The ovaries measure about 30 to 45 mm and occupy 55 to 60 per cent of the body cavity. They almost always weigh around 0-5 gm with a maximum limit of 1.0gm, forming 0.6 to 1.5 per cent as relative weight. Recently, spent fish have remnants of mature ova, measuring a maximum diameter of 0.47 mm, as resorbing and disintegrating opaque structures. The blood cells from ruptured capillaries appear as reddish clots. Sometimes, there may be a few scattered droplets of oil globule. The resorbing eggs are sometimes translucent in appearance, with the yolk in the form of small spherules, light grey or brownish in colour with man droplets of oil globule clustering around the centre. These ova form a small mode in the size frequency distribution around 0.27 to 0.31 mm. At a later stage, a few blood-coloured or brownish masses are seen which

represent the unspawned ova broken down and covered up by the blood cells. In this state, the ovaries appear deep flesh-coloured. The rest are all immature transparent oocytes less than 0.25 mm in diameter.

Nutrition of the Female

The feeding condition of the mother can have an important effect on the final maturation of the eggs. Two examples from Hempel show that in some of the Atlantic herring populations spawning may occur only every other year if environmental conditions, particularly those affecting food supply, are poor. Also, it has been found in the laboratory that in Atlantic sole (Solea solea) no spawning occurred when the flatfish were fed a diet (mussels only) deficient in certain amino acids; however, when the flatfish were force-fed the missing amino acids they spawned, indicating the ovary had been unable to obtain the needed amino acids from maternal tissue when the nutrition of the female had been inadequate.

Physiological Factors

Hormones govern migration and timing of reproduction, morphological changes, mobilisation of energy reserves, and elicit intricate courtship behaviour. The pituitary is the major endocrine gland that produces gonadotropin, which controls gametogenesis, the production of gametes, namely sperm (spermatogenesis) and eggs (oogenesis), by the gonads. The pituitary also controls the production of steroids (steroidogenesis) by the gonads; once the gonads are stimulated by the pituitary they begin producing steroids, which in turn control yolk formation (vitellogenesis) and spawning. The control of spawning by the pituitary is often used in fish farming such as in the production of caviar from sturgeon (Acipenser spp.) where spawning is induced by injecting pituitary extract at a late stage of gonadal development, usually in combination with changes in temperature and light periodicity.

Ecological Factors

Often ecological factors are associated with timing so that food availability is optimal for the larvae. Some ecological factors important to spawning are temperature, photoperiod, tides, latitude, water depth, substrate type, salinity, and exposure.

- *Temperature:* An important factor in determining geographical distributions of fishes. Although little is known about the mechanism by which temperature controls maturation and spawning in fishes, for many marine and freshwater fishes the temperature range in which spawning occurs is rather narrow, so that in higher latitudes the minimum and maximum temperature requirement for spawning is often the limiting factor for geographical distribution and for the successful introduction of a species into a new habitat. For example, Pacific halibut (Hippoglossus stenolepis) are found spawning primarily in areas with a 3-8°C temperature on the bottom and therefore do not spawn in Puget Sound, although the adults are caught in the northern areas of Puget Sound. In fact, even in highly migratory tuna, spawning is restricted to water of specific temperature ranges.

- *Photoperiod and periodicity:* The day length (photoperiod), in some cases at least, is thought to influence the thyroid gland and through this the fishes' migratory activity, which is related to gonadal development (maturation). In the northern anchovy, by combining the effects of temperature and day length, continued production of eggs under laboratory conditions was brought about by keeping the fish under constant temperature conditions of 15°C and a light periodicity of less than 5 hours of light per day (Lasker personal communication). In high latitudes, spawning is usually associated with a definite photoperiod (and temperature), which dictates seasonal pulses of primary production in temperate regions to assure survival of larvae. In low latitudes, where there is little variation in day length, temperature, and food production, other factors may be important such as timing with the monsoons, competition for spawning sites, living space, or food selection.
- Reproductive periodicity among fishes varies from having a short annual reproductive period to being almost continuous. There is a tendency for the length of the reproductive period to shorten with increasing latitude. Thus tropical fishes spawn nearly continuously, whereas subarctic fishes spawn predictably during the same few weeks each year. Presumably times of spawning have evolved so larval development will coincide with an abundant food supply. Within spawning seasons, fish may spawn on a daily or monthly tidal cycle or on a diel cycle, or in association with some other environmental cue, such as a change in daylength, temperature, or run-off. A notable instance of spawning periodicity associated with the tidal cycle is the California grunion (Leuresthes tenuis), which spawns intertidally at the peak of the spring high tides. Within species, spawning times may vary with latitude: Generally, in species that spawn as daylength increases, spawning occurs earlier in the year in lower latitudes than at higher latitudes. In species that spawn as daylength decreases, spawning takes place earlier in the year at higher latitudes than at lower latitudes.
- *Tides (moon cycles):* The dependence of spawning on moon cycles in California grunion spawning on California beaches is an extreme

example of external factors controlling reproduction in fishes. Grunion are adapted to spawning on the beach every two weeks in the spring during a new or full moon. Spawning is just after the highest high tide; therefore, eggs deposited in the sand are not disturbed by the surf for 10 days to a month later. Eggs will hatch when placed in agitated water (which simulates surf conditions). In Puget Sound, surf smelt (Hypomesus pretiosus) spawn year-round, except in March. Surf smelt deposit eggs at high tide in sand and gravel (but not necessarily at the highest tide). On the open ocean shores, spawning occurs at midtidal heights (for different subpopulations) (Dan Pentilla personal communication).

- *Latitude and locality:* Pacific herring show a definite relationship between latitude and spawning time. Spawning is early in San Francisco (December, January); later in Washington State (February, March, April, May); and still later in Alaska (April, May, June). These fishes are perhaps of different, distinct subpopulations. In temperate waters a biomodal distribution of eggs is usually seen, which indicates discontinuous spawners. The smaller-sized mode represents resting eggs for a future spawning, and the larger mode represents maturing eggs (oocytes), which will presumably be spawned within the year. Temperate water fishes are also usually deterministic, which means all eggs to be spawned are determined at the start of the year. A polymodal distribution of eggs is typical of tropical areas and some temperate water fishes, which signifies continuous or serial spawners, and indicates several spawnings. A well-known temperate example would be Pacific sardine (Sardinops sagax), which spend 7 months spawning and 2 months developing/maturing. Batch spawning has been described for northern anchovies. Tropical spawners are usually non-deterministic, which means the eggs to be spawned are not determined at the start of the year but are produced throughout the year; however, non-deterministic can also represent the spawning potential for successive years, an example being the Atlantic cod (Gadus morhua), which will have several years' spawn in the ovary.
- In general, older fish usually spawn first and younger fish later, which means that a prolonged spawning period for a population may not be true for individual fish. Once a set of eggs is mature and hydrated, the female may release them all at once or in several batches. An example of releasing several batches is plaice (Pleuronectes platessa), where a single female two weeks after releasing one batch of eggs releases more eggs, and then three weeks later she releases the remaining eggs. Another example is the Pacific herring, which spawn once a year and females lay about 100 eggs per spawning act, which

they repeat several hundred times over a few days. In the lab, walleye pollock spawned an average of nine times in an average period of 27 days.

- It also needs mentioning that a long duration of the spawning season of a population cannot necessarily be taken as an indication of prolonged spawning of the individual fish. The prolonged period may be due to differences in spawning time between age groups since older fish tend to spawn earlier in the season. Furthermore, the coexistence of different spawning subpopulations must be taken into account, since winter and summer spawners may be distinct stocks, although shifts from one seasonal spawning pattern to the other may occur. An example of how unpredictable this can be is that certain Atlantic herring of low fecundity have been found to always spawn in the winter, regardless of whether they originated from winter or summer spawning.
- *Water depth:* Pacific herring spawn along beaches, marine grasses, and algae. Atlantic herring do not spawn along shore but in deeper water up to 200 m (the clearest difference between the Pacific and Atlantic herring, which are usually designated distinct species on the basis of genetic analysis). Of course fishes often spawn at one depth but live at different depths during other times of the year. For example, petrale sole (Eopsetta jordani), in which spawning occurs in a specific offshore area 300-400 m deep, were found by fishermen and eventually had to be protected with regulations to prevent overfishing (A.C. Delacy personal communication).
- *Spawning substrate type:* Pacific herring spawn on vegetation whereas Atlantic herring spawn on solid substrate (*e.g.*, gravel). Lingcod spawn on rocks, pilings, and cracks in solid substrate; this species protects the egg mass. Some species such as buffalo sculpin (Enophrys bison) and plainfin midshipman (Porichthys notatus) spawn intertidally and will stay with the egg mass even when they are exposed at a low tide.
- *Salinity:* Also a factor affecting spawning. There are varying salinities in many areas of estuaries. Some species will shift spawning sites because of salinity changes. Various degrees of mixing, precipitation, and freshwater run-off may alter spawning habits.
- *Exposure and temperature:* A clear example of shifting spawning sites in response to temperature and exposure is the black prickleback (Xiphister atropurpureus), where spawning is shifted from winter in protected areas to spring in exposed areas. The complex effects of lower or higher wave action and lower or higher temperatures on courtship, gonadal development, and spawning behaviour that result in the spawning site shift.

CONTROL OF PEJERREY REPRODUCTION IN CAPTIVITY

A series of studies were performed in order to optimize pejerrey reproduction in captivity, including the increase of sperm volume and the synchronization of spawning by hormonal treatments.

In pejerrey, the sperm volume obtained by stripping of males either in natural conditions or captivity is very scarce, being necessary several males to fertilize the eggs produced by a single female.

In pejerrey males it was possible to increase sperm volume by environmental and hormonal treatments practically during all the year around without affecting the sperm concentration and motility. These treatments included: increase of the light phase of photoperiod, human chorionic gonadotropin (hCG), heterologous pituitary extracts and GnRH superactive analogues (GnRHA) injection. In order to compare all hormonal treatments, an experiment using the doses previously demonstrated to induce a 5 time increase of expressible milt was performed. The treatment with sGnRH-A was the most effective. However, the use of hCG is recommended because of its effectiveness to stimulate pejerrey spermiation in low doses, its low cost and availability.

In the case of females, a commercial sustained release system (Ovaplant, Syndel, Vancouver, Canada) was used in order to synchronize spawning. Pejerrey females (250 g) in late vitellogenesis with no signals of final oocyte maturation, were intraperitoneally implanted either with pellets having 75 g of a sGnRH-A or blank pellets. The first groups of eggs were obtained after 60 hours in the sGnRH-A group and one week later it was shown that 82 per cent of sGnRH-A implanted females had spawned meanwhile none of the control implanted females spawned during that period. Although much work is necessary in order to find easier and non expensive ways to control pejerrey reproduction in captivity, these results demonstrated that is possible to use hormonal manipulation to induce reproduction in this species. In this context, it is important to think that even though the use of endocrine agents can be use to induce reproduction in this species, the study of environmental and maintenance conditions can also be effective to synchronize reproduction in pejerrey.

EVIDENCE FOR FEMALE HOMOGAMETY IN CHANNEL CATFISH

The mechanism of sex determination in channel catfish Ictalurus punctatus was evaluated by hormonal and genetic methods. Aromatizable and non-aromatizable androgens, as well as an estrogen, caused feminization in fish fed steroids for 21 days after yolk-sac absorption. The effectiveness of 60 g of ethynyltestosterone/g food decreased markedly when the experimental feeding period was shortened and was ineffective when the treatment lasted less than 12 days. Females from all-female populations produced by treatment with sex hormones were mated with normal males resulting in nine spawns with a sex ratio different from 1:1. The sex ratios were statistically similar to 3 male:l female in five spawns, both 2:1 and 3:1 in two spawns, and 2:1 in two spawns. These data are consistent with a model for female homogametic sex determination in channel catfish and suggest that the YY equivalent genotype is viable.

The phenotypic sex of many fish species can be experimentally altered during early development to produce monosex populations. Generally, in teleosts, treatment with androgens results in masculinization and treatment with estrogens results in feminization. Paradoxical feminization (production of allfemale populations by treatment with androgens) has been reported in cichlids. Channel catfish, Ictalurus punctatus, were feminized by a wide range of concentrations of 17-ethynyltestosterone as well as 17-estradiol. Hormonal manipulation of phenotypic sex has been accomplished by injection into the egg, by dissolving the hormone in the water during the period of gonadal indifference, or by feeding hormone to young fish. Treatment with hormones often produces fish that are sterile, intersex (ovotesticular), or have abnormalities of the genital ducts that prevent spawning. Morphological anomalies that would prevent spawning have not been observed in feminized catfish.

Genotypic sex cannot currently be determined in channel catfish by chromosomal analysis. However, the sex genotype and the genetic sex determination model can be determined by mating sex-reversed females with normal male fish and evaluating the sex ratio of the progeny. This study evaluates the influence of a variety of androgens and time of treatment on sex determination in channel catfish. Breeding evidence is provided that supports a female homogametic sex determination model.

METHODS OF HORMONE TREATMENTS

Hormone treatments. Channel catfish were spawned by traditional methods (Dupree and Huner, 1984). Hatched larvae were transferred in groups of 200 to 40-litre glass aquaria held at about 21°. Experimental diets were prepared by dissolving hormones in 95 per cent ethanol, spraying the food with the solution to obtain the desired concentration of hormone, and airdrying to evaporate the alcohol. Hormones were tested by feeding fish to satiation three times daily for 21 days starting after yolk-sac absorption. The first day that fish began to feed was designated as Day 1. The hormones tested were 17-ethynyltestosterone (17-ET), 17-methyltestosterone (17-MT), 1,4 17-methyltestosterone (1,4 17-MT), 5-dihydrotestosterone (DHT), 1-methyldihydrotestosterone (1-MDHT), 17-methyldihydrotestosterone (17-MDHT), 11-ketotestosterone (1l-KT), 11-hydroxytestosterone (1l-HT), norethisterone (NE), and NE plus 17-ET.

In a second set of experiments a diet of 60 μ g 17-ET/g food, prepared was administered at selected intervals within the first 21 days of feeding to delineate the minimum effective treatment period. Treatment intervals were from Days 1, 5, 9, 13, or 17 through Day 21, or from Days 1 through 8, 5 through 12, or 9 through 16. Sac-fry were treated in a third experiment with 17-MT, 17-ET, or DHT on Days 1 and 2 after hatching and exposed under static conditions to 10 or 100 g/litre of hormone for 2 hr. Water flow was stopped and sufficient hormone solution was added to the tank to produce the desired concentration. After 2 hr, water was turned on and the hormone washed out of the tank.

Progeny sex ratio evaluation. Four-year-old fish from all-female populations produced by 17-ET or 17-estradiol were individually paired and spawned with normal males in wire cages placed in a pond. A spawning container was placed in each cage. Egg masses were removed and incubated in indoor hatching troughs. Spawning success from mid-May through mid-June under these conditions is normally about 60 per cent.

Progeny from each treatment group were maintained and reared separately. Sex was verified in 10-to 15-cm fish by dissection. Females had paired tubular ovarian structures; in males, gonadal structures were either not discernible or consisted only of opaque convoluted lines on the ventral surface of the kidney.

Statistical analysis. Sex ratios of control and hormone-treated groups were evaluated by x2 analysis based on an expected 1 male:l female sex ratio. The sex ratios of the progeny of hormone-treated females were tested for homogeneity by x2 analysis. When homogeneity was not indicated, groups were tested individually by x2 using Yates correction term with expected ratios of 1:1, 2:1, and 3:1. A probability of 0.05 was considered to be significant.

RESULTS OF HORMONE TREATMENTS

Every hormone fed to fry for 21 days (except 11-HT, which was ineffective) resulted in a significantly higher percentage of females than that in control populations. Those most effective at producing females were NE, NE plus 17-ET, 17-ET, 17-MT, and 1,4 17-MT; 17-MDHT, DHT, 1-MDHT, and KT were markedly less effective. Treatment of yolk-sac fry with DHT, 17-MT, or 17-ET added to the water at 10 or 100 g/litre did not alter the sex ratio. The feminizing effect of 17-ET (at a concentration of 60 g food) decreased when fish were fed for less than 21 days and was absent when fed for less than 12 days. Sex ratios were not significantly affected in fish fed from Days 13 to 21 or from Days 17 to 21, nor by 8-day treatments at the beginning, middle, or end of the 21-day period.

Progeny Sex Ratio Evaluation

Six of 15 spawns produced by crossing hormone-treated females with normal males grouped into a statistically homogeneous set and had a sex ratio of 1:1. The other 9 spawns were not statistically homogenous; however, when tested individually, 7 of the 9 spawns were not significantly different from a 3 male: 1 female sex ratio. Two of those 7 spawns and the remaining 2 spawns were not significantly different from a 2 male:1 female sex ratio.

SEXUAL PHENOTYPE OF DEVELOPING CHANNEL

Although the sexual phenotype of developing channel catfish could be altered by a variety of androgens and dosage rates, deviations from normal sex ratios were limited to feminization. Goudie *et al.* suggested that paradoxical feminization in channel catfish may be caused by endogenous aromatization of dietary androgens to compounds with estrogenic properties. Conversion of testosterone by aromatase is part of the normal biosynthesis of estrogen.

Some natural and synthetic androgens are not susceptible to aromatization due to their molecular structure. Aromatizable androgens used in the present study were 17-ET and 17-MT; while DHT, 11-KT, and 11-HT were non-aromatizable. The two other forms of DHT-1-MDHT and 17-MDHT-are thought to be non-aromatizable due to their similarity to DHT and to the addition of methyl groups at positions that interfere with aromatase activity. Norethisterone, an estrogen component of contraceptive pills, has been found to inhibit the aromatase enzyme in vitro by some investigators, but not by others. Further, 1,4 17-MT has molecular similarities to both non-aromatizable androgens and to aromatase inhibitors. Predominantly female populations were obtained by treatment with non-aromatizable androgens, suggesting that androgen aromatization may not be necessary for paradoxical feminization in channel catfish.

However, Nakamura reported that 11-KT in the diet produced all-male populations of Tilapia mossambica, a species that exhibited paradoxical feminization when sexually undifferentiated animals were treated with aromatizable testosterone propionate in the water. Furthermore, 11-KT treatment caused precocious appearance of male secondary sex characteristics, but no change in gonadal differentiation. Norethisterone was expected to have prevented the aromatization of 17-ET; however, NE when used alone had a feminizing effect. Treatment with non-aromatizable androgens resulted in the lowest percentage females of any of the feminizing treatments. Higher doses or earlier treatment with any of the feminizing non-aromatizable androgens might produce different sex ratios; however, these androgens apparently have a feminizing effect during the first 21 days.

The minimum effective treatment period for production of all-female populations with 60 g 17-ET/g food must be close to the first 21 days of exogenous feeding. Reducing the duration of the treatment within any portion of the 21-day period reduced the percentage of females produced. This contrasts with phenocritical periods that are as short as 3 days in Hemihaplochromis multicolour. The six spawns resulting from pairing normal males with females from an all female population had a sex ratio of 1:1 and must have been produced by genotypic females that were unaffected by the steroid treatment. Progeny from the nine spawns that had a sex ratio different from 1:1 must have resulted from breeding genotypic male-phenotypic female fish with normal males.

These data are important for two reasons. First, they demonstrate that the hormone treatment does not differentially affect survival of genotypic males, leaving only female fish to develop. Second, this sex ratio is possible only if the genotypic sex determination model is equivalent to a homogametic female condition (XX). The resulting populations would have been composed of all-male offspring if males were the homogametic sex. Additional support for female homogamety is available: all channel catfish progeny produced by gynogenesis were females, and the sex ratio of triploid channel catfish produced by second polar body retention was 1:1. This female homogametic condition should be used only as a model because neither sex chromosomes nor sex-determining genes have been identified in channel catfish. The 3 male: 1 female ratio of the progeny obtained from seven of nine sex-reversed females indicated that the male phenotype included both XY and YY genotypes. The normal male genotype (XY) should be present in two-thirds of the males and the YY genotype in one-third. Therefore, the YY equivalent male genotype must be viable in channel catfish, as has been reported in other fish species. The YY genotype may not be as hardy as the normal XY genotype in all catfish families, which may explain why two of the populations were statistically similar to only a 2:1 sex ratio. In mammals, some non-sex-related genes essential for survival are located on the X chromosome; consequently, the YY genotype is lethal. Variability in YY viability has been found among families of medaka Oryzias latipes. The YY genotype is rare in families homozygous for xanthic coloration, but occurs with predictable frequency in families heterozygous for this trait.

Identification of the YY equivalent males in channel catfish can now be accomplished only by progeny testing. All-male progeny should be produced by the spawning of YY males with normal (XX) females or with sex-reversed (XY) females. In the first case, all offspring would have the XY genotype, and in the latter case, half of the progeny would be expected to have the XY genotype and half would be YY males. These techniques could be useful to the aquaculture industry because male channel catfish grow faster than females. All-male populations could be produced without sex steroids being administered to fish reared for food.

4

Biotechnologies in Fishery Management

INTRODUCTION

The role that the application of genetic principles can play in the sustainable use and conservation of living aquatic resources is being increasingly appreciated by resource managers, policy makers and the international community. Fishery management requires information on the fishery resources in order to be effective. Primary information needs include:

- an identification of the resource;
- the breeding or stock structure of the resource;
- an estimate of the size of the resource; and
- the identification of key habitat that the resource requires.

Genetic analysis of the resources can address these information needs. Gene and genotype frequencies of different markers can provide information on, inter alia, species identification, population stock structure, hybridisation and gene flow.

Often, data from other sources, *e.g.* studies of tagged fish or of external characters of fish, cannot provide such information or are extremely difficult to collect in certain areas such as large river systems, floodplains or marine areas. The use of protein and DNA data in fishery management requires collection of baseline (or background) genetic information. Genetic data were used to determine how sub-groups of Pacific salmon differed from each other in the Pacific Northwest.

This required the analysis of hundreds of stocks of salmon but, once completed, endangered stocks were identified, levels of migration were estimated, and the contribution of different stocks to a mixed stock ocean fishery was estimated. Protein and DNA information has been used to identify endangered species that are either inadvertently captured in wild fisheries or that are purposefully taken illegally. DNA analysis of legally sold whale meat revealed that many samples came from protected species of whale and dolphin. Species of shark are often difficult to identify because it is only the fins or flesh that are for sale; DNA analysis can be used to identify the species that provided the tissue and has the added advantage that dried tissue or less than fresh samples from markets can be studied.

MANAGEMENT OF RESERVOIR FISHERIES

The fish production from the reservoirs is low, emphasizing the need for attention to shape and develop the reservoir fisheries from the survey and planning stage to achieve high rate of production and better returns for the fishermen, who represent the weaker section of the society. Majority of these water bodies are not scientifically managed. Only a handful has so far been harnessed on scientific lines, while the others are either half-heartedly managed or even not managed at all.

There are marked variations in the fishery management practices which are followed in various reservoirs within the country. Even though the reservoirs are owned by the Government or Corporate agencies in most of the states, their fishing rights and exploitation systems vary considerably. The fishing systems can be divided into the following broad categories: a). privately owned and managed reservoirs, b). Public water bodies, c). Community water bodies and d). Water bodies managed by the Government. After a scrutiny of the various management practices followed in the country, it is difficult to miss a common underlying spirit of the common property norm. Majority of Indian reservoirs are public properties where a fixed number of licensed fishermen make their living.

The exceptions are the small reservoirs in some states like Karnataka and Uttar Pradesh, which are auctioned to private individuals on annual basis. The following steps are to be taken for the development of reservoir fisheries. Some of them are

1. Pre-impoundment survey of the reservoir
2. Removal of obstacles like tree stumps.
3. Fish farm construction at the dam site for stocking of fish seed adequately.
4. Organization of fishermen co-operative society for harvesting the fish in the reservoir and to take up fish marketing.
5. Implementation of conservation methods to prevent over exploitation and to prevent catching of small fish.

Pre – impoundment survey: Before formation of reservoir studies and investigations were taken up in the rivers connected to know the possible effects of fisheries. In case of the dams constructed, the dam constructing authorities should facilitate necessary fish ways for fish migration. The authorities also assess the fishermen living in the villages and their craft and tackles that are going under the submergence of the reservoir. The above measures are to be taken up before formation of the reservoir to assess and to plan for future development of fishery in the reservoir.

Removal of obstacles under submergence: After formation of the reservoir, it should facilitate easy fishing with modern fishing methods. To facilitate the above, the trees, buildings, boulders are to be removed either by mechanical means or manually.

Construction of fish seed farms at dam site: Some of the reservoirs have got river connection as such, they will have natural stocking of fish seed (auto stoking). The reservoirs, which will have a deep column of water, will greatly affect the breeding grounds of the fish. Further more the height of the dam is another major obstruction for the movement of the fish from the lower stretch of the river to upper stretches.

All these factors leads to low productivity, which drags the attention of many authorities towards the fish seed stocking every year in the reservoirs. Keeping in view of this, planning has to be done for establishment of a fish seed farm near the dam site. The Department of fisheries, Govt. of Andhra Pradesh made an attempt to promoting the fishery wealth in the reservoirs, by constructing the fish seed farms at Thandva, Wyra, Kinnerasani, Palair, Nagarjuna Sagar, Nizam Sagar, Dindi, Jurala, Kadam, Araniyar, Bahuda, Somasila, Sriram Sagar and Lower Manair dam.

Stocking of the fish seed in reservoirs: An adequate sized fish seed should be stocked in the reservoirs. The tender stages of fish seed like fry (22-25 mm), fingerlings (40-50 mm) are susceptible and are to be eaten by the carnivorous fishes. Hence the reservoirs to be stocked with an advanced fingerlings (100-120 mm). Stocking of reservoirs with fingerlings of economically important fast growing species to colonies all the diverse niches of the biotype is one of the necessary prerequisites in reservoir fishery management. This has proved to be a useful tool for developing fisheries potential of such small aquatic systems.

Agarwal recommended the following stocking rates in reservoirs.

1. Large reservoirs (1000-5000 ha) – 500 fry/ha/yr.
2. Medium reservoirs (100-1000 ha) – 1000 fry/ha/yr.
3. Minor reservoirs (10-100 ha)-2000 fry/ha/yr.
4. Small reservoirs (below 10 ha) – 10000 fry/ha/yr.

Srivastava recommended the following stocking rates of fingerlings for reservoirs in India.

1. Large reservoirs (5000-10000 ha) – 200 fry/ha/yr.
2. Medium reservoirs (1000-5000 ha) – 400 fry/ha/yr.
3. Minor reservoirs (up to 1000 ha)-1000 fry/ha/yr.

IMPLEMENTATION OF CONSERVANCY METHODS TO PREVENT OVER EXPLOITATION

It has been observed that fishes of mature major carp fishes migrate to the rivers for breeding, where the fishermen lead to catch them and destroy their breeding grounds. The breeding grounds of these fishes are to be identified and necessary protective measures are to be taken up. It is also observed that during rainy season, the big fishes migrate towards the dam site along the canals and congregate at the gates, which has been catch by the fishermen folk. This is to be reduced.

The conservancy methods like mesh size regulation, observing the closed season for fishing, strict observation of prohibiting the unethical means of fishing are to be implemented strictly by the Government.

Species enhancement: Decline of indigenous fish stocks due to habitat loss, especially that caused by dam construction, is a universal phenomenon. Planting of economically important, fast growing fish from outside with a view to colonising all the diverse niches of the biotope for harvesting maximum sustainable crop from them is species enhancement. It can be just stocking of a new species of introductions. Here introduction means one time or repeated stocking of a species with the objective of establishing its naturalised populations. This widespread management practice has more relevance to larger water bodies where stocking and recapture on a sustainable basis is not feasible.

Introduction of exotics: In India, the fish transferred on trans-basin basis within the geographic boundaries of the country is not considered as exotic and there are no restrictions on them. Thus, catla is not regarded as exotic to peninsular rivers. This is despite the fact that the peninsular rivers have habitats distinctly different from those of Ganga and Bhrahmaputra. Catla, rohu. and mrigal have been stocked in the peninsular reservoirs for many decades now. with varying results. In some of the south Indian reservoirs, they have established breeding populations. The hallmark of the Indian policy on introductions is the heavy dependence on Indian major carps.

There is evidence that the Gagetic major carps have affected the species diversity of peninsular cyprinids. The Indian policy on stocking reservoirs, though not very explicit, disallows the introduction of exotic species into the reservoirs. However, common carp is very popular in reservoirs of the northeast where it enjoys a favourable microclimate and a good market. Silver carp and grass carp are not normally encouraged to be stocked in Indian reservoirs, though they are stocked regularly in a few small reservoirs. The three exotic species brought in clandestinely by the fish farmers, bighead carp..Aorichthys nobilis, Oreochromis niloticus and African catfish Clarius gariepinus have not gained entry into the reservoir ecosystems. They still remain restricted to the culture systems.

Environment enhancement: The improvement of the nutrient status of water by the selective input of fertilizers is a very common management option adopted in intensive aquaculture. If similar environmental enhancement is adopted in small reservoirs, stocks can be maintained at levels higher than the natural carrying capacity of the environment.

However, scientific knowledge to guide the safe application of this type of enhancement and the methods to reverse the environmental degradation, if any. is still inadequate. On account of all these, this is not a very common management tool. China is known to have used this instrument in a big way to augment production from small reservoirs. Cuba, taking a clue from China has tried manuring of small reservoirs using both organic and inorganic fertilizers. This is also practised selectively in the community water bodies of Thailand.

Fertilisation of reservoirs as a means to increase water productivity through abetting plankton growth has not received much attention in India. Multiple use of the water body and the resultant conflict of interests among the various water users are the main factors that prevent the use of this management option. Surprisingly, fertilisation has not been resorted to even in reservoirs which are not used for drinking water and other purposes. Documentation on fertilisation of reservoirs in India is scarce. Sreenivasan and Pillai attempted to improve the plankton productivity of Vidur reservoir by the application of super phosphate with highly encouraging results. As soon as the canal sluice was closed, 500 kg super phosphate with P,O5 content of 16 to 20 per cent was applied in the reservoir when the water spread was 50 ha with a mean depth of 1.67 m.

As an immediate result of fertilisation, phosphate content of water increased from nil to 1.8 ppm and that of soil from 0.242 to 0.328 per cent. Similar improvements in organic carbon nitrogen have been reported from soil and water phases on account of fertilisation. Experiments were also conducted with urea in the same reservoir. Fertilisation can play a key role in many small reservoirs of India which require correction of oligotrophic tendencies. A number of reservoirs in Madhya Pradesh. the Northeast and the Western Ghats receiving drainage from poor catchments show low productivity, necessitating artificial fertilisation. Chinese experience in fertilising the small reservoirs for increasing productivity has been reassuring.

Fertilizers are less effective in soft water with total alkalinity less than 20 ppm. Soft waters have inadequate carbon usually in the form of carbon dioxide and can often be enhanced by applying lime to low alkalinity impounded waters. The application of lime equivalent to 2,000 to 6.000 kg/ha calcium carbonate is generally sufficient to maintain total alkalinity above 20 ppm.

Suggestive Model for Management of Reservoirs

The concept of fishery-business model was developed by Desai in 1984. The main components of this model are macro-fisheries and micro – fishery systems. Macro-fishery system again composed with fish supply system, fish production system and fish marketing system. The micro –fishery system contains fishery input sub system, fishery credit subsystem, fishery extension subsystem, fishery education sub system, fishery habitat sub system, fishery research subsystem, fishery regulation subsystem, fishery administration subsystem, fishery exploitation subsystem, fishery processing subsystem and fishery distribution sub system.

Natural Fishery in Reservoir

The following fishery wealth is available in the major reservoirs of Andhara Pradesh. The Fishes like Wallago attu; Mystus species; Heteropneustes fossilis; Clarias sp; Major carps like – Catla catla; Labeo rohita; Cirhinus mrigala and other carps like C. reba; Thynicthus sandkhol etc. The fresh water Eel, fresh water prawns, Murrels are also available in the reservoirs.

Planning Criteria

In keeping with the need for rapid assessment of the country's small reservoir resources, the following planning criteria are suggested for the resource assessment at the State level for the preparation of an inventory of such small reservoir ecosystems along with the estimates of their potential yields under the categories-a. Reservoirs which are best developed as capture fisheries, b. Reservoirs mostly of local interest having significant potential for fish culture; and c.Reservoirs intermediate in size and potential yield.

These under-utilised fishery resources offer immense scope and potential for generating additional national income of the order of more than ₹ 100 crores per year and providing additional employment to lakhs of fishermen and others through fishing, handling, transport, marketing and ancillary industries. A systematic and integrated approach towards scientific studies and planning criteria for undertaking fish culture in small reservoirs should be so directed as to have an understanding of the following factors.

- The reservoir morphometry and water residence time.
- The physico-chemical characteristics of water and soil.
- The animal and plant inhabitants.
- Growth rate of commercially important fish species, and
- The relation between the inhabitants and the physico-chemical aspects of the environment in terms of population and community dynamics.

It is felt that under the prevailing socio-economic conditions, such short-range studies undertaken for small reservoirs would provide a rapid assessment of their fisheries potential to take up fish culture in them.

RESERVOIR FISHERIES MANAGEMENT IN INDIA

The present low level of fish production in Indian reservoirs can be attributed to inadequate management inasmuch as many of them have high propensities of production from a limno-chemical point of view. In many of the reservoirs, the high rate of the primary and secondary productivity is not channelled to fish production. Insufficient understanding of the reservoir ecosystem often comes in the way for adopting effective management measures. Since fish production from reservoirs is essentially extractive in nature, the essence of management strategy lies in exploitation of natural stocks. Nevertheless, the ecosystem management provides different degrees of freedom for stock maniputation, depending on the size and class of the water body.

One of the possible criteria that can be used to differentiate between capture and culture fisheries is the extent of human intervention in the ecosystem management. While aquaculture systems provide maximum avenues for the man to monitor and change the habitat variables and the biotic communities at will, this freedom attenuates as we proceed from aquaculture to the culture-based and capture fisheries. In a large water body, managed on capture fishery norms, there is little room for altering the habitat variables and the scope for effecting change in biotic communities is limited to stocking and ranching, which have uncertain chances of success.

Relative contribution of culture and capture norms in management vary, depending on the category of the reservoir. Medium and large reservoirs are predominantly capture fisheries systems and the management norms are based on the principle of stock manipulation, adjustment in fishing effort, observance of conservation measures and gear selectivity. Selective stocking is resorted to for correcting imbalances in species spectrum and to fill the vacant ecological niches.

The small reservoirs, on the other hand, are generally managed as culture-based capture fisheries, akin to extensive aquaculture, where the main accent is on stocking, fattening and harvesting. An imaginative stocking and harvesting schedule and right species mix hold the key for effective management of small reservoirs.

STOCKING

Inducting fast-growing extraneous species into the ecosystem to colonise the diverse niches is a necessary prerequisite of reservoir management. Since one of the primary aims of stocking is to ensure utilization of the enhanced food reserves, the ideal time to stock new species is the period of trophic burst. Any lapse in this important management measure causes the proliferation of trash fishes by taking advantage of the increased availability of fish food organisms, which in turn, may provide forage base for catfishes. Nagarjunasagar, Tungabhadra, Hirakud and a number of other large reservoirs in India are examples where the minnows, catfishes, murrels and other uneconomic fishes gained grounds in the early years, leading to establishment of long food chains. These reservoirs harbour good standing crops of plankton and benthos, which are not reflected in the fish output. Even intensive stocking at a later stage has failed to reverse the situation.

Since large and medium reservoirs are to be developed on the principles of capture fisheries, it is desirable to stock the species that may breed and ultimately get naturalised in the system through autostocking. This is imperative to meet the long-term objective of obtaining a sustained yield rate. Management involving persistent stocking in large water bodies not only pushes up the input cost, such systems also create many practical difficulties in raising the stocking material in adequate quantities. However, naturalisation of introduced species is quite often beset with many problems. The alien species should find the habitat conducive to its biological and physiological requirements. It should have an edge in the competition for food and finally, the environmental conditions should favour its requirements of spawning and larval development.

Recruitment failure due to the erratic hydrographic conditions that break the breeding rhythm have been found to be the single major factor responsible for the failure of stocked fishes to hold out in reservoir.

In Konar, strong currents wash down the carp eggs into the deep zones of the reservoir leading to their destruction and resultant recruitment failure. But more often, the fishes do not find suitable spawning grounds as in the case of many south Indian reservoirs. Since the breeding of major carps is governed to a great extent by the magnitude of monsoon floods, annual variations in this parameter affect their breeding and recruitment.

Selection of species for stocking

Jhingran has summarized the principles to be followed in the selection of species for stocking as:

1. The species should find the environment suitable for growth and reproduction.
2. It should be quick growing, ensuring high efficiency in food utilization.
3. A fishery comprising herbivores with a short food chain is preferable, as they have a better conversion of primary production to fish flesh.
4. The stocking density should be such that the food resources of the ecosystem are fully utilized and optimum population maintained, consistent with normal growth.
5. The size of the fingerlings to be stocked should be so chosen to get the desired results.
6. Seed should be readily available with minimal transportation cost.
7. Cost of stocking and managing the species must be such that the operation is economically viable.

One of the important considerations is to know the amount of food available in the new environment. This factor has a considerable bearing in determining stocking rates and hence production.

Fish production from unit area is a product of individual growth rate and population density.

From a study of growth rate of various species in a particular body of water, it is possible to assess their optimal stocking density. Efficient utilization of fish food communities increases the carrying capacity and therefore calls for a higher population density which is achieved by addition of species to the original fish populations. In addition, information on differences, if any, in the growth rates of the endemic and introduced species, and the time taken by the introduced species in attaining harvestable size would provide insight into the production dynamics of the system.

Competition

Both intra-and inter-specific competitions are to be considered in the stocking programme. Situations where two or more species use a similar resource, such as food or space, lead to overcrowding and poor growth rate. Under a higher than optimum stocking rate, though production may be high, the individual growth rate will be so small that to attain a marketable size a long growing period will be needed.

On the other hand, if bigger fishes are needed, the rate of stocking should be lowered and a low production will have to be accepted. Similarly, when a marketable size is to be attained in a shorter period, stocking rate will have to be lowered to allow faster growth. Thus, a desired balance among stocking rate, population density and growth is to be maintained with enough flexibility so as to swing it to suit the changes in environmental factors. Such a plan must determine tentative stocking rates and population thinning, depending on the need.

The sizes of fingerlings that are stocked in Indian reservoirs come under the pre-recurit phase and so, up to the size of entering the exploited phase they are prone only to natural mortality. Therefore, a knowledge of the natural mortality rate is essential as due compensation can be provided for it while computing optimum stocking rates. Jhingran and Natarajan, while evaluating the stocking rates of Damodar Valley Corporation (DVC) reservoirs, arbitrarily recommended a compensation factor for natural mortality @ 25 per cent for reservoirs with no large predaceous fishes and 50 per cent for those harbouring large predators. While estimating optimum stocking rates for such populations, about which no reliable estimates of natural mortality are available, it is felt that assumption of higher natural mortality rate would be desirable as a little overstocking would be less harmful than understocking. Fish Seed Committee of the Government of India recommended the stocking rate for reservoirs at about 500 fingerlings ha^{-1} of the size range 40 to 150 mm.

TRENDS IN FISHERIES MANAGEMENT

Poorly defined property rights, increasing effort and decreasing catches are resulting in conflict in fisheries throughout the world. While these effects are common and well documented in highly regulated fisheries in the European Union (conflicts over allocation of quota for example) and North America (for example conflicts over access to salmon stocks between the USA and Canada); the effects upon fisheries in developing countries, while under-researched are invariably more dramatic and can have long-term implications for the promotion of sustainable livelihoods. While there is as yet little evidence of a sharp increase in natural resource conflicts it is apparent, however, that the consequences of conflict in the management of natural resources are becoming more detrimental to long-term sustainable exploitation and are effecting an increasingly large number of people.

Although there is an extensive literature on natural resource conflicts, little work has been done on a) analysing the causes of conflict beyond the case-study arena or b) applying economic tools to the study of conflict. In an attempt to redress the balance, this chapter sets out some initial findings from an on-going study into the management of conflict in tropical fisheries. Drawing on New Institutional Economics and common property resource management theory, it analyses how and why fisheries institutions adapt to changing circumstances and the role of conflict in the process. Using evidence from Ghana it examines the emergence of fisheries management institutions under differing access regimes and analyses the factors which appear to have influenced institutional change.

The paper argues that conflict can be the result of rising transaction costs and the inability of natural resource institutions to manage these changes. It also argues that conflict can be both a positive and negative force and should not necessarily be eliminated altogether. The chapter is divided into four sections.

First, it locates fishing as an economic activity within developing countries and looks at the interactions between local, national and international policy objectives and how these can impact upon the development and exploitation of the resource. In the second section, conflicts are described and why they emerge in natural resources management is discussed. Focusing on the role of institutions it looks at how changes in institutions might affect the management of common property resources.

Section three draws on initial findings from field research conducted in Ghana between March and May 2000. In the final section, the paper presents a number of conclusions as to the process of conflict formation and the possibilities for managing it. The role of fisheries in developing economies Fisheries play an important role in the local and national economies of many developing countries where they provide food, income and employment for large sections of the population. However, the framework within which they operate is often complex and vulnerable to failure. The absence of clearly defined property rights, the trade-offs between national and local needs and the impact of rising pressures on the economy can, however, all contribute to the failure of fisheries to positively contribute to the development process. The national perspective: Following the second world war the rapid expansion of fishing capacity in many developing countries was promoted through the so-called Blue Revolution.

New fishing technologies and fishing methods coupled with a desire to improve nutrition and generate foreign exchange led many countries to build on fishing activity already present. Some of this development was as part of national development programmes, in other cases, international loans and funding programmes helped promote the development of national fishing industries. As a direct result of this drive to build up national fishing capacity, the participation of developing countries in global fishing activity rose dramatically between 1955 and the 1980s. The rewards to be gained from participating in the global fishing market were potentially large, and many benefited, albeit in the short-term, from their forays into fishing. Increased export-revenues and the multiplier effects associated with expanding industries all helped boost the development of many developing coastal states.

The long-term consequences of such developments, have, however, had a dramatic effect. Rising incomes and increased borrowing of cheap petro-dollars contributed to chronic debt problems as the global economy staggered to a halt in the early 1980s; an attitude of positive speculation on fish-stocks, lack of proper assessment and regulation led to the over-exploitation of a number of important stocks (Schurman, 1996; Thorpe et al 2000).

As a consequence of the international debt burden and the strictures placed on the economy by the Structural Adjustment Programmes, trade-offs between local and national needs put further pressure on resources.

The downsizing of the state and the increased role of the market as the resource allocation mechanism saw many developing countries expand their export fisheries to generate revenue whilst at the same time the power to regulate such activity was hampered bythe limited capacity of Fisheries Departments to undertake interventions. The push for export revenue and the renting of grounds to Distant Water Fleets has resulted in spatial conflicts between industrial and artisanal fleets, state support for local fisheries has been constricted and external economic pressures now drive national policy formation.

From a local perspective: In agricultural-based economies, natural resources form the social safety-net that supports large parts of the population. Access to common property natural resources such as timber, fuelwood, grazing land, fisheries, forest products and irrigation water are fundamental to the livelihoods of many of the world's poor. These natural resources are often held as common property and the survival of rural populations has traditionally relied upon a complex set of institutional arrangements that govern use of and access to these resources.

The formation of institutional access and use arrangements is well-documented. Whilst many communities have succeeded in maintaining their common property resources through collective action, in some cases pressures internal and external to the community have caused arrangements to collapse. The outcome of a resource becoming open-access is likely to be over-exploitation and the dissipation of resource rents. In terms of development, then, as the ability of a community of users to exercise rights over their resource is eroded so the role of the resource as a safety-net is undermined.

The pressures that lead to the erosion and collapse of common property resources are diverse. They can result from a rapid rise in population (either through natural growth or an influx of migrants); changes to the ecological status quo (through droughts or flooding, for example); national policy changes that affect rural employment rates; technological change that results in higher harvesting potential and social change that can alter income differentials, systems of property rights and market systems.

An important outcome of the breakdown of common property arrangements is the emergence of conflict between stakeholders. However the precise mechanism is not fully understood. A review of the conflict literature reveals numerous theoretical approaches to describing and explaining conflict.

Conflict is a function of social structure (sociology), of power or class relations (political science) and of individual utility maximisation (economics). It is both positive and negative, constructive and destructive, violent, coercive and non-violent. Thisdiversity of approaches reflects the wide range of disciplines that have addressed the subject. There are many possible definitions of conflict, the following synthesis of definitions is used in this chapter: Conflict is a situation of non-cooperation that involves groups of people with differing goals and objectives and yet Conflict is dynamic and can be a positive catalyst for change Although the term 'conflict' often has negative values attached to it, this is not necessarily the case.

Conflict can be described as negative when the outcomes are a zero-sum game (no-one benefits) rather than a positive sum-game (everyone benefits) or where there is a deadweight loss of social resources as a result of the 'guns vs butter' argument. However, it is also important to bear in mind that conflict can be positive and attempts should never be made to eradicate it completely or to prevent it emerging. Conflict encourages goods to be produced more cheaply, government to become more efficient, flaws in the set-up of institutions to be ironed out and allows society to function efficiently by resolving small conflicts often.

At this point, the question of the difference between conflict and competition arises. Competition implies the existence of rules, conflict arises when those rules are, for whatever reason, disbanded or ignored. In order to help clarify whether conflict is positive or negative it is often helpful to look at what the conflict is over and how fundamental that disagreement is to the social status quo. Aubert (1963), Boulding (1966) and Powelson (1972) all differentiate between conflicts that are 'within consensus' and those that are 'over consensus'. In the former case the parties to the conflict agree about the value of what they seek but not the means of achieving it. In the latter case the parties to the conflict are unable to agree on the value of what they seek nor on how to achieve it.

The potential impact of conflict is thus dictated by the degree of consensual framework within which they are contested and the degree of conflict over basic consensus.

AN ECONOMIC EXPLANATION FOR CONFLICT

Economic theory provides two reasons why conflicts emerge over natural resources:

(a) the allocation of scarce resources requires trade-offs which become increasingly difficult as the demand for and supply of resources changes and

(b) Short-term personal gain wins out over long-term social needs or benefits.

The resource allocation issue: Natural resource conflicts occur when the resource in question has become so scarce or degraded as to raise issues of allocation amongst the community of users. Under perfect environmental conditions, as the ratio of users to resource grows so expansion takes place: extra land is brought into cultivation, new areas of forest are exploited, different species are fished or fishery activity moves along the coast or further out to sea. Powelson argues that so long as the answer to 'who gets how much' is resolved by producing more, conflicts over allocation are positive because they encourage growth. When the ecological boundaries of the resource have been reached, further expansion is no longer possible (without adverse consequences) and the division of the metaphorical cake has to change because the option of increasing the size of the cake is no longer possible. At this point, resource allocation mechanisms come under increased pressure to satisfy all users. The equity of resource allocation tends to diminish as the ability to expand production decreases.

As government departments attempt to placate all the stakeholders, so resource allocation decisions have to change and conflict ensues as certain stakeholders gain precedence over others. This is of course nothing new. The trade-offs between equity and efficiency occur in all markets and are faced by all governments. In the developing world however, where democracy may be weak and where powerful interest groups are able to co-opt and unduly influence the decision making process, managing the trade-offs is difficult. Short-term gain vs social needs: There is a large body of literature that uses game theory and behaviour modelling to explain why common property management institutions (in particular) can fail. The Nash Equilibrium and the Prisoner's Dilemma illustrate this point neatly: in the classic decision making model-the Prisoner's Dilemma-the best possible move for player A given the best possible move for player B is to not co-operate.

Thus the socially optimal outcome of the 'game' is not a Nash Equilibrium. McKean (1992:248) notes, in a similar vein that the short term benefits of cooperating are often outweighed by the costs.

Consequently a community opts for the least-cost option which is to withhold their contribution to the collective goal. A third explanation for the emergence of conflict has also arisen from the more recent New Institutional Economics school, this sees institutions and transaction costs as a key element.

From a new institutional economics perspective, institutions exist to minimise transaction costs and are a means of transcending the social welfare dilemmas that arise out of individual action and help maximise collective welfare. They are also the mechanism for dealing with 'gaps' left by market failure in insurance and risk assessment. Transaction costs are literally the costs involved in negotiating a transaction and have been described as the economic equivalent of friction in the world of physics. Transaction costs are the costs associated with gaining information, making decisions and carrying out decisions.

In terms of fisheries, they can be divided into the ex-ante costs of collecting information and making collective decisions in the fishery and the ex-post costs associated with implementing collective decisions. Kuperan et al (1999) argue that transaction costs in fisheries arise, mainly, from the fact that the fishery involve multiple stakeholders and differing objectives and long-term goals. Institutions are important as resource allocation mechanisms-markets and fisheries departments, for example, both have a role to play in allocating scarce resources. What is more, it is now recognised that institutions matter for economic development and recent development research has recognised the need to 'get the institutions right' if effective economic development is to be achieved.

Katterman (1998:294) points out that the OECD has finally recognised that technical co-operation, the long-time philosophical foundation of development practice, can amount to nothing if the institutions that it relies upon for success are weak. Thus for both successful natural resource management and economic development institutions able to adapt to changing circumstances are needed. There are two explanations about why institutions might fail in the face of change.

The first relates to the supply and demand for institutional change, the second to transaction costs. Thomson, Feeny and Oakerson (1992: 132) and Feeny (1988) discuss the supply and demand model for institutional change: when the demand for institutional change (to capture gains not possible under existing arrangements) outstrips the ability to supply change, failure emerges. They list relative factor or product prices, the size of the market, technological change and fundamental decisions of government as causes of change that lead to what they term 'institutional disequilibrium'. However, they also recognise that change depends on the State's willingness and ability to help new institutions emerge.

This is a particularly pertinent issue in the developing world where, as discussed before, state capacity may be underdeveloped. Because in the NIE perspective institutions evolve to minimise transaction costs (through minimising uncertainty)-when it is no longer able to do this effectively its position is weakened and it is increasingly unable to deliver services effectively or be allocatively efficient. Using the NIE paradigm and the supply and demand argument above it could, therefore, be argued that a rise in transaction costs, over and above the institution's ability to accommodate this change leads to inefficient operation. This rise in transaction costs could be due to development pressures (political and economic), environmental scarcity (perceived or otherwise) and structural problems (political and economic) which increase the costs mentioned earlier: the costs of collective decision making, information gathering and collective operation.

In the case of fisheries management, strong and flexible institutions are required at both the national and local level. Arguably, the more nested the structure, the lower the transaction costs between the top and the bottom of the system and the more efficient the institution in its allocation role.

In many developing countries this may not be the case. Communication between the different layers of fisheries management are frustrated, the legitimacy of the ruling body to assign resources is often missing or contested and political factions and the action of rent-seeking elites influence the vertical relationship. Institutions, conflicts and fishing in Ghana The political and economic context

Ghana, the former British colony of the Gold Coast, became the first African colonial state to gained independence in 1957. It has had a number of military coups, but is set, in December 2000 to become the first African state in which a military ruler has handed power to a civilian government through the ballot box. Unlike many other countries in the region, Ghana has experienced comparatively little unrest with its neighbours or amongst its diverse tribal and linguistic groups, and it is perhaps this aura of stability and peace at a national level which influences conditions at a local level. In the 43 years since independence Ghana has made some remarkable advances in development and has also suffered some serious set-backs.

Despite significant advances made in improving some of the standard development indicators (life expectancy has risen by 4 years since 1995; adult literacy has risen by 44 per cent since 1970), Ghana is currently struggling with the dual effects of economic adjustment measures and external shocks. Economic reforms have seen public sector budgets slashed and the impact in the natural resources sector, to name but one, has been devastating. All departments are under funded, and in the fisheries department, this has lead, in particular to a reduced ability to monitor fisheries effectively and enforce regulations. The need to raise revenue has seen the introduction of VAT at 10 per cent which is set to rise to 12.5 per cent later this year. Despite well intentioned publicity campaigns to educate the public as to the need for VAT, this is unlikely to ease the blow of a significant price rise on all VATable goods-particularly on basic grains that have shown sharp price rises since last year. Coupled to this is the rapidly devaluing national currency which, while making Ghanaian exports cheaper, makes servicing the national debt (currently $580 million) more expensive daily and dramatically increases the costs of vital industrial inputs.

Ghana is an oil importer, and recent OPEC price rises have also hit the economy hard. While exports have grown aided by improving terms of trade and export initiatives put in place as a result of economic reforms, these have tended to concentrate on cash crops such as cocoa.

In the context of fisheries, the prevailing economic conditions are having a number of effects. Firstly the day to day costs of fishing are rising. Fuel prices not only impinge on the length of fishing trips, but exchange-rate depreciation has increased the costs of imported inputs such as nets, ropes and outboard motors.

The knock-on effects of such price rises are widespread. Education and health at the local level both suffer as more and more income is diverted away from the 'add-on luxuries' into the basic needs for survival. Although things have not reached crisis level as yet, there is evidence of malnutrition in fishing villages and primary schools lack basic teaching materials (supplied by the community). Despite this catalogue of economic problems, some very interesting results emerged from a recent study of the causes and management of conflict in coastal Ghanaian fishing villages.

EVOLUTION OF VIEWS OF FISHERY MANAGEMENT

Fishing is an old activity, and concern about its effects also is old. As early as the fourteenth century, people in England were worried about fishing with a *wondyrchaum* (a fine-meshed trawl), which they feared was killing enormous numbers of small fish. By 1716, minimum mesh sizes and minimum size limits for various fish species were in effect. Many forms of fishery management have evolved based on traditional knowledge gained by fishing peoples. They included cultural practices, community agreements, and government controls. But in general, and despite early regulations, management of marine fisheries was minimal before the middle of the twentieth century, with a few notable exceptions such as the International Pacific Halibut Commission. Although there has long been concern over the effects of fishing, that concern—like fishing itself—was largely confined to coastal waters until recently. The famous scientist Thomas Huxley expressed his opinion in 1883 that probably "all the great sea-fisheries are inexhaustible", although some great sea-fisheries were already depleted by then. The Atlantic halibut fishery had collapsed by the early 1880s and has not yet recovered. And the U.S. Fish Commission had been established a dozen years earlier (1871) to find the causes of declining New England fisheries. By 1919, W.F. Thompson (1919) recognized that sea fisheries were not inexhaustible, but he identified a difficulty that remains critical to this day: "Proof that seeks to modify the ways of commerce or of sport must be overwhelming."

He developed research to concentrate on what "is necessary to the perpetuation and prosperity of the fishery." To protect the Pacific halibut (*Hippoglossus stenolepis*) from the fate of the Atlantic halibut, the International (United States and Canada) Pacific Halibut Commission was established in 1924 with "a competent man as director of investigations": W.F. Thompson. While and before Thompson was investigating the North Pacific halibut fishery, Heincke was developing catch-curve analyses as a basis for proposed minimum size limits for North Sea plaice (*Pleuronectes platessa*) and demonstrating racial differences in North Sea herring. The International Council for the Exploration of the Seas was formed in 1902, motivated by the desire to understand and predict fluctuations in fish stocks.

North Sea fish increased in size and numbers during both World Wars I and II, because naval action forced a reduction in fishing. That phenomenon led to wider recognition that fishing did affect fish stocks and that the effects were at least partly reversible. Those observations led Graham to explain how increases in fishing power allowed catches to be maintained or increased even when fish stocks declined, leading to a waste of time and money by comparison with fishing at a maximum sustained yield. Gordon (1954) provided the economic theory to support Graham's observations.

In the 1950s and 1960s, scientific methods of stock assessment and estimation of fishery yields were developed based on growth rates and age composition of the catch. At the same time, fishing vessels based many hundreds or thousands of miles from fishing grounds ("distant-water fleets") changed the face of fishery management, leading to exclusive economic zones, international treaties, international fishery-management bodies, and continued international disputes about fishing. One of those international bodies, the U.S.-Canadian International Commission for Northwest Atlantic Fisheries, implemented an early attempt at incorporating ecosystem management into fisheries. When it set catch limits for a particular species, it took into account the expected bycatch of that species in fisheries for other species. It also concluded that the total sustainable catch rate for all species was less than the sum of sustainable catch rates for the individual species.

Many factors have reduced the effectiveness of management and prevented the adoption of scientific advice. In a few cases the advice itself was not correct. Progress in developing better scientific perspectives for management and more equitable and effective ways of implementing management goals continues, but it has been slow. In some cases the obstacles seem to be overwhelming. Significant societal, commercial, and governmental economic incentives and pressures often lead to unsustainable fishing practices. It is difficult, for example, for a poor, hungry family to stop or even reduce fishing if its basic food needs depend on fishing and it has no resources with which to supplement reduced food from fishing. In addition, most such families live in countries whose governments have limited resources to apply to the problem. In wealthier societies, economic pressures can be as great as the basic need for food. But it is clear that the long-term costs of overexploitation of fishery resources are even greater than the short-term costs of reducing catches. Options for achieving sustainable fishing are the topic of this report.

VIEWS OF FISHERY MANAGEMENT EVOLVE

As views of fishery management evolve, the importance of terms becomes apparent. For example, it is common to refer to fishing as "harvesting the resource." But the term *harvest* usually includes the idea that an investment has been made in a crop, which is not true of most marine-capture fisheries. Another term often used is *underutilized*, which implies that greater exploitation of a particular fish stock is desirable. This term probably reflects one purpose of many fishery-management institutions—that is to promote fisheries. In this report those terms and some others are avoided; in general, the committee has sought to use the terms *catch* or *landings* instead of *harvest* and *lightly fished* or *subject to low fishing mortality* rather than *underutilized*. The term *stock* might be linked by analogy to stock of a commodity. It also is difficult to define biologically, and so the committee has used the term *population* where possible. It is extremely difficult to find terms that do not express any societal values. Thoughtful evaluation of the values implicit in many terms and replacement of some of them could be an important part of achieving sustainable fishery management.

Report Organization

The stage by reviewing information on the state of marine fisheries. The committee attempted to be comprehensive although not exhaustive. Thus, enough information is presented for a general overview, but not all relevant. The effects on ecosystems of fishing and of environmental changes. What is known about the factors that contribute to the conditions. These include incomplete scientific information, scientific errors, failure to heed scientific advice, conflicting and unresolved goals and values, failure to consider all ecosystem components, institutional failures, social and economic incentives that do not favour sustainable resource use, changes in perspectives, new information, and perhaps a failure to recognize the limits of science.

The potential usefulness and practical application of an ecosystem-based approach, alternative institutional structures, social and economic arrangements that hold promise for improving sustainable fishing, marine protected areas, scientific questions, and research needs. The emerging recognition that marine ecosystems have values in addition to their production of food and the importance of that recognition in developing ecosystem-based approaches to sustainable fishery management.

DEGREE OF FISH-STOCK UTILIZATION

FAO periodically reports the degree of utilization of global fish stocks, classifying fisheries as underexploited, moderately exploited, heavily to fully exploited, overexploited, depleted, and recovering. The largest number of fisheries (44 per cent) are classified as heavily to fully exploited. Twenty-five per cent of stocks have been fished beyond sustainable limits (overexploited, depleted, and recovering).

For the United States during the period 1992–1994, the picture was similar despite slight differences in terminology: 12 per cent of 275 stock groups were classified as underutilized, 34 per cent as fully utilized, 23 per cent as overutilized, and 31 per cent were of unknown status. Of the 191 stock groups whose status was known, 82 per cent were fully utilized or overutilized. A U.S. example of a formerly overexploited and now recovered stock is striped bass (*Morone saxatilis*): Georges Bank haddock (*Melanogrammus aeglefinus*) represents a depleted stock.

Globally, some increase in exploitation might be possible for 32 per cent of the landed species, but Garcia and Newton (1997) noted that, given past experience, heavily to fully exploited fisheries are likely candidates for future overfishing. This assertion is demonstrated by Alverson *et al.* (1994), who reported (based on FAO data) that from 1980 to 1990 the number of overexploited fisheries increased by 250 per cent, whereas the number of underexploited fisheries decreased by about 75 per cent. Depleted species are being replaced in today's catches by species that were less heavily fished in the past.

For example, the Chilean Inca scad (*Trachurus murphyi*), Japanese pilchard (*Sardinops sagax melanosticus*), South American pilchard or Chilean sardine (*Sardinops sagax sagax*), and skipjack tuna (*Katsuwonus pelamis*) replaced chub mackerel (*Scomber japonicus*), Atlantic mackerel (*Scomber scombrus*), Atlantic cutlassfish (*Trichiurus lepturus*), and saithe (Atlantic pollock, *Pollachius virens*) in the top-10 species list between 1973 and 1993. In the United States, skates and dogfish have replaced more commercially valuable fish on Georges Bank. This process of depletion of one resource and replacement by another is limited by the number of potentially catchable and usable species; depleted species may not return to previous abundance levels. For example, Atlantic halibut (*Hipploglossus hippoglossus*) and spring-spawning Icelandic herring (*Clupea harengus*) have not recovered from overfishing, although they probably would if mortality were reduced. Many shark populations appear to be declining as well. For instance, Van der Elst (1979) described the impact of South African antishark nets on local populations of oceanic sharks, and the resultant and unanticipated decline in nearshore bony fishes. On a global scale, Manire and Gruber (1990) concluded that sharks were overfished by approximately 30 per cent per year in U.S. waters; and cited domestic demand for shark meat; wasteful fisheries practices, especially discarded bycatch of sharks; irrational dread; and an increasing global demand for shark fins as major factors contributing to excess fishing mortality of sharks.

In addition, unexploited fish populations that are long lived and slow growing cannot support high exploitation rates, unlike populations of faster-growing, short-lived species. For example, the five species of the genus *Sebastes*, including the Pacific Ocean perch itself (*S. alutus*) and the northern (*S. polyspinus*), rougheye (*S. aleutianus*), sharpchin (*S. zacentrus*), and shortraker (*S. borealis*) rockfishes off the northwestern and Alaskan coasts of the United States and the coast of British Columbia, are all slow-growing and were severely overfished, although they have now largely recovered. The marbled rockcod (*Notothenia rossi*) in the Southern Ocean also has been severely overfished.

Catch Per Ton of Fishing Vessel

Approximately 3.5 million vessels are engaged in fisheries worldwide; about two-thirds are small undocked vessels, but the total also includes about 24,000 high-seas fishing vessels of more than 500 gross tons. The gross tonnage of the world's fishing fleets (decked vessels only) increased by an average of 2.9 per cent annually from 1970 to 1992. This rate of increase in gross tonnage exceeded the rate of increase in catch (1.8 per cent annually) during the same period: the ratio of metric tons of fish caught per ton of fishing vessel decreased from 4.3 in 1970 to 3.0 in 1992.

Assuming that additional fishing capacity has at least the same average fishing power per ton as the pre-existing fleet—almost certainly true—and that the new vessels are used at least as much as the older ones—probably the case—the decreased ratio of catch to fishing tonnage provides further evidence that fish populations declined on average during this period. The discrepancy between fishing capacity and catch is even greater when one considers the increase in fishing power of vessels as a result of technological improvements.

Based on an analysis conducted by Fitzpatrick (1995), the rate of increase in fishing power resulting from technological improvements has averaged 4.4 per cent annually since 1965. Garcia and Newton (1997) fit a production model to global catch and gross tonnage data, adjusted for fishing power increases. Their analysis indicates that catch is higher than the maximum sustainable yield of world fisheries and that fishing capacity is too large to be economically efficient.

The decline in the per-ton catch rate of fishing vessels also indicates an economic problem, although lower catches have probably been partially offset by price increases. The economic problems also include the substantial debt service or depreciation of fishing vessels. Government subsidies have been used worldwide to increase employment and food supply. Subsidies have probably stimulated excess growth in the world's fishing fleet and must be a major factor in poor economic performance. They may amount to as much as $27 billion per year, although information about subsidies and how people and organizations react to them is not readily available.

UNITED STATES OVERVIEW

Fishing Sectors

Marine fishing activities in the United States are divided among commercial, recreational, subsistence, and indigenous sectors. The balance of activity among these sectors depends on the areas and species fished and whether the comparison is made in terms of weight or number of fish landed or dollars injected into the U.S. economy. All sectors are subject to fishery management in the United States through the regional fishery management councils and, in some cases, through state and international agreements as well. Fisheries are important to the culture and social structure of their practitioners and can have a major economic impact, at least regionally.

Commercial Fisheries

The United States has the largest exclusive economic zone (EEZ) of any nation, covering about 11 million km^2.The United States was the fifth-largest fish producer in 1993, following China, Japan, Peru, and Chile. The first-sale value of U.S. commercial landings (4.47 million t^6) in 1997 was estimated at $3.5 billion, with a direct contribution to the gross domestic product (GDP) of $20.2 billion. The United States is also one of the world's largest fish-trading nations, with a deficit of $4.6 billion in 1994 resulting from $12 billion in imports and $7.4 billion in exports.

U.S. commercial landings were relatively stable at about 2 million per year from 1935 until 1977, when the United States extended its jurisdiction over fisheries to 200 miles from the coast and increasingly excluded foreign vessels. At present foreign fishing is not permitted in the U.S. EEZ, although in some cases—for example, menhaden (*Brevoortia tyrannus*) in the Gulf of Maine—

foreign processor vessels receive catches from the U.S. EEZ. Since 1977, landings have more than doubled, to 4.47 million t in 1997. The rapid rise in U.S. catch in the late 1980s was due primarily to the walleye pollock fishery that resulted from displacements of foreign vessels during the 1970s and into the 1980s. About half of the U.S. landings are from the fishing grounds off Alaska, primarily walleye pollock (*Theragra chalcogramma*). Pacific cod (*Gadus macrocephalus*), and various salmon (*Oncorhynchus*) species. As is true for most fishing nations, U.S. fishers are dependent on a small number of species, with almost 50 per cent of the catch composed of walleye pollock from the Pacific Ocean and menhaden (*Brevoortia tyrannus* and *B. patronus*) from the Gulf of Mexico and Atlantic Ocean.

Recreational Fisheries

Recreational fishing also is important in the United States. Although the recreational catch is only about 2 per cent as large as commercial landings for all species combined (90,000 t in 1994), there are more than 17 million marine recreational fishers, who in recent years made more than 66 million fishing trips per year, caught about 360 million fish, and spent $25.3 billion per year on fishing-related activities, comparable to the contribution to the GDP of commercial fisheries. For some fisheries in which both commercial and recreational fishers participate (*e.g.*, summer flounder [*Paralichthys dentatus*] and bluefish [*Pomatomus saltatrix*]), the recreational catch is a significant portion or even a majority of the total.

Recreational and commercial fishers often conflict over management goals and methods for various fisheries. In some cases, recreational fishers are effective at influencing policy, as for example recent restrictions they supported on the use of nets in coastal waters of various states (including a legislative ban on gillnets in Texas in 1988: California's Proposition 132, which banned net fishing starting in 1990: a Florida legislative ban on coastal nets that passed in 1993: and a Louisiana legislative restriction on nets passed in 1994). In other cases, they are not successful. The allocation of available marine fisheries resources between commercial and recreational sectors is a major issue for regional fishery management councils and in the political arena. Some of the disputes and the differences—and occasional agreements—between commercial and recreational fishers are described in almost every issue of *National Fisherman* and *Saltwater Sportsman*. The resolution of such disputes and allocation controversies is made more difficult because recreational landings often are underreported or not surveyed. Serious allocation disputes have been limited thus far primarily

INDIGENOUS PEOPLE'S FISHERIES

Indigenous people's fisheries are a minor part of total catches but are particularly important in cultural and social terms. Indigenous marine fisheries in the United States—primarily in Washington, Oregon, California, and Alaska—are subject to treaties between the United States and tribal groups. Tribal fisheries for salmon include commercial, ceremonial, and subsistence uses. The Northwest Indian Fisheries Commission handles treaty rights related to salmon in the Puget Sound area.

The Columbia River Inter-Tribal Fisheries Commission represents four tribes in the Columbia River basin of Oregon. Fishing by three tribes in the Klamath River Basin in California is not protected by treaty, but 50 per cent of Klamath River chinook salmon are allocated to these tribes by government regulation. The Pacific Fisheries Management Council, as well as its Scientific and Technical Committee and its Salmon Technical Team, have Native American tribal representatives. There is also a Native American allocation for sablefish (*Anoplopoma fimbria*) off the coast of Washington. For communities in western Alaska, which are largely populated by Alaska natives, Section 305 of the Magnuson Fishery and Conservation Act and Section 111 of the 1996 amendments provide for a Community Development Quota Programme. The programme allots varying percentages of the total allowable catch (TAC) of several fisheries to these communities; by 1999 those communities will be allotted 7.5 per cent of the TAC of Bering Sea groundfish and crabs. The amendments also allow the establishment of a similar programme in the Western Pacific Regional Fishery Management Area (Hawaii and other U.S. Pacific islands).

Subsistence Fisheries

Subsistence fisheries—fisheries conducted for food, material, and fuel but not primarily for commerce or recreation—occur in many parts of the world, most commonly in non-industrialized and tribal societies. Although the sale of fish for cash is not included in subsistence fishing, trading fish for other food or services is an important part of subsistence economies in many places, and cash from activities in market economies is used to finance subsistence fishing. Subsistence fishers, like others but perhaps to a greater degree, develop a large store of traditional knowledge. Subsistence fishing is recognized in many laws and regulations. It does not usually constitute a major portion of the landings except locally.

Status of U.S. Fisheries

In its most recent assessment of the condition of U.S. fisheries, NMFS (1996a) evaluated 275 stocks caught by fishers in nearshore coastal waters, the EEZ, and the high seas beyond the EEZ for the period 1992–1994. Of the 191 stocks for which information was available, 33 per cent were overutilized and 49 per cent were fully utilized, leaving only 18 per cent underutilized. Forty-six per cent were below the level of abundance required to produce the greatest long-term potential yield. The long-term potential yield of the U.S. fisheries within the U.S. EEZ is estimated on a single-species basis to be 8.1 million t per year, which is much greater than the recent yields. Based on the calculations in that estimate, for the United States to achieve its potential increase in long-term potential yield, some ("underutilized") fisheries would need to be fished more heavily, but, more importantly, fishing on overutilized stocks, bycatch, and unaccounted mortality will need to be reduced so that stocks can rebuild. The estimated long-term potential yield and maximum sustainable-yield levels can be used as reference points to help guide the sustainable development and prosecution of fisheries or the rebuilding of marine fish stocks that have been overfished.

Although there is limited information available regarding the overall economic performance of U.S. fisheries, they are undoubtedly suffering from over-capitalization at a national level (with some regional exceptions), as has been reported by FAO for fisheries worldwide. NMFS (1996b) reported that there were about 23,000 commercial fishing vessels in the United States in 1987 (the latest year for which there is good information), which is more capacity than is required to achieve the long-term potential yield from U.S. fisheries. For example, the capacity off Alaska has been estimated to be two and a half times that necessary to catch the available resources (North Pacific Fishery Management Council [NPFMC] 1992). Major losses in revenue from New England fisheries have resulted from overfishing, driven in large part by excess capacity.

A Canadian Example: Northern Cod

The case of the northern cod is an example of the effects of overfishing as well as institutional difficulties in applying scientific findings to management. This overfishing occurred despite reasonably conservative target fishing mortalities; the problem was largely due to systematic errors in stock assessments exacerbated by unreported (illegal) discarding of small fish and perhaps unreported catches, and later to a failure of management to respond quickly to corrected assessments.

The fisheries of the Atlantic Canada region have been dominated by groundfish; the cod fishery was unquestionably of greatest importance. Cod (*Gadus morhua*) served as the base of the fishing industry in Newfoundland, Nova Scotia, and other provinces in the region (*e.g.*, New Brunswick). The northern cod fishery is an instructive example of overexploitation of a fishery. It has been much discussed, recently by Walters and Maguire (1996) and Hutchings and Myers (1994), who focused on fishery biology, and by Neis (1992), Steele *et al.* (1992), and Finlayson (1994), who focused on the sociology of science. A combination of lack of data, improper handling of available data, and overconfidence in methods led to overfishing and the collapse of the fishery. The offshore catch of northern cod expanded from approximately 240,000 t annually in the mid-1950s to a peak of 700,000 t in 1968. Total catches of northern cod declined steadily thereafter. By the early 1970s, distress in the northern cod inshore fishery also was evident.

The Canadian government planned to rebuild the resource through reduced fishing by the distant water fleets. As the resource rebuilt, the total allowable catch (TAC) for northern cod would gradually be increased. The management strategy adopted was expected to result in sustainable catches averaging 20 per cent of the exploitable biomass by the late 1980s—roughly 400,000 t annually. In the years immediately following implementation of this plan, the northern cod resource appeared to be rebuilding as planned, but the actual landings never achieved even 260,000 t per year. The offshore sector of the cod fishery always succeeded in taking its allocation, but the inshore sector landings declined by 35 per cent from 1982 to 1986.

In response to these trends, the Canadian Atlantic Fisheries Scientific Advisory ommittee (CAFSAC) undertook in 1988 a review of its stock-assessment methods. CAFSAC concluded that the northern cod stock was in fact substantially smaller than previously believed, a view confirmed by an independent Northern Cod Review Panel, which estimated that the actual fishing mortality rates had been at least double those projected in the Canadian management strategy. CAFSAC concluded that the northern cod TAC for 1989 should be reduced from the continuing 266,000 t to 125,000 t. The Canadian government, fearful of the economic disruption and dislocation that such a draconian reduction in the TAC would entail, reduced it only to 235,000 t. In mid-1992, after poor catches, a moratorium was established on all directed commercial fishing for northern cod for a period of two years, during which deterioration of the stock continued. The moratorium was extended, remains in place, and is expected to remain in effect for the indefinite future. Recent reports indicate that the northern cod stock is at a historically low level and that there are, as yet, no significant signs of recovery of the stock.

The causes of the resource management catastrophe are the focus of intense debate in Canada, although the proximate cause is clearly overfishing supported by erroneous assessments of stock size and fishing mortality. The reasons for the errors in stock assessments are complex. Overcapitalization in the fishery may have exerted pressure to interpret stock-assessment data in an excessively optimistic manner, as did an overreliance on the science and culture of quantitative stock assessment. The northern cod stock-assessment procedures appear to have been flawed from 1977 until at least 1985, owing to statistical inadequacies of the biomass model used, overreliance on catch-per-unit-effort data, variability of the data set, and relatively short and unreliable data series. Ironically, the northern cod is one of the few examples that seems to show a clear and positive relationship between parent stock and recruitment. Although the intuitive expectation is that the more spawning adults there are in the population, the more recruits there will be, most fish populations do not show such a relationship. For the northern cod, estimates of recruitment were not corrected for changes in spawner biomass, which themselves were overestimated. Fishing mortalities were underestimated, probably because of unreported discards of young fish—a significant source of mortality—and perhaps unreported or underreported catches of adult fish.

Recent analyses indicate that the cod populations in the western Atlantic are not the only ones in danger of being overfished. For example, Cook *et al.* (1997) concluded that there is an urgent need to reduce the exploitation rate on North Sea cod to avoid risk of collapse (they also found a significant relationship between parent stock and recruitment). Several NMFS assessments of cod in the Gulf of Maine also reached this conclusion, recently confirmed by the National Research Council.

BIOLOGICAL CRISIS OF FISHERY MANAGEMENT

From this point, fishery sciences itself are progressively switching their attention from single species to ecosystem approach, from micro to macro perspectives, increasing the need for measuring the impact of fishing on natural and man-made systems. Consequently, Cochrane argued that the problems currently experienced in fishery management throughout the world occur in four realms, namely biological, ecological, economic and social crises. Biological crisis of fishery management started during the last decade after awareness grew about the alarming status of fishery resources. Ludwig for example, drew attention to collapses of fish stocks such as those of the Pacific salmon, the Californian sardine, and the Peruvian anchovy. In 1994, FAO showed, in an analysis, of global fish landings, that there had been reduction in the annual growth in landings in 1980s, and that in 1990 there had been 3 per cent reduction in the global annual catch from the previous year. Garcia and Newton analyzed that this trend continued over the next few years and in between 1990 and 1992, global landings fell by an average of 1.5 per cent per year.

In an economic perspective, fisheries actually exist to meet social and economic demands and one would expect to find that the impact on the resources has resulted in a measurable social and/or economic benefit. Unfortunately, some evidences suggest that the expected benefits have not been in the form of economic gain.

Christy estimated that the gross revenues from the total global marine landing in 1989 was US$ 70 billion, giving a deficit balance since the global operating costs were estimated at a level of US$ 92 billion. With an annual capital costs of US$ 32 billion per year, the total deficit in global fisheries was estimated to be US$ 54 billion per year.

At a country level, Japan for example, a deficit gross cash flow was also founded for cause of purse seine fisheries. In this type of fisheries, the volume of production was estimated to be lower than its MYS, OSY as well as MEY level. However, due to its high operating cost and low price of fish caught by the purse seine, it resulted in a deficit cash flow. Matsuda called this phenomenon the poverty in large catch. Nevertheless, the recent study undertaken by Tietze shows that in some fisheries, they perform a positive gross cash flow in their global operation. Out of 108 types of vessels from 15 countries throughout the world, 97 per cent had a positive gross cash flow and fully recovered their operating costs. When also considering the annual cost of capital, 85 per cent showed a net profit after deducting the cost of depreciation and interests. However, in terms of sustainability issues, some symptoms of economic crisis in some fisheries should be considered in order to come up with the solution for economic sustainability in the system.

From a social point of view, fisheries are rarely seen as simple tools for generating economic returns. The role of fisheries as a source of employment, particularly in rural or more remote areas, has also widely been given high priority. Moreover, McGoodwin elaborated that fisheries actually are a human phenomenon which essentially are places where human activities are linked with marine ecosystems and renewable resources. Human fishing activities defined the attribute of fishery, since without it there would only be an aquatic realm where various marine species live. Therefore, it has been strongly argued that clearly the fisheries are much more than geographic regions, fishing methods, types of fishing gear, fish species, or economic-domains— it is something more human.

SOCIAL ASPECTS IN FISHERIES

In this regard, social aspects in fisheries would be very important to be understood. One of the major features of fisheries in recent decades, related to the social crisis, has been the introduction of modern fishing technologies and also the increasing globalization of trade affecting the fishing communities. Modernization in fisheries has two faces of which actually one contributed to the welfare of fishing communities, while the other has led to the social problem related to the depletion of fishery resources. According to Crean and Symes, in the North Atlantic and Mediterranean, there has been a decline in the quality of life and standard of living among many fishing communities, as also experienced in some parts of South East Asia. This symptom of social crisis in fisheries should seriously be taken up when we consider the sustainability in this sector. We argue that the need for measuring and evaluating the sustainability of fishery activities in a system perspective has acquired its highest importance and should be undertaken at various levels involving all aspects in the fishery system.

As also strongly argued by Charles that critical concern about sustainability arises not only in terms of catch level or even biomass level, but in all aspects of the fishery: from the ecosystem, to the social and economic structure, to the fishing communities and management institutions, as well as fish stocks themselves. Moreover, the pursuit of sustainable fisheries is best seen as requiring, more than keeping the catch of fish, to keep a level that is not too large.

Instead, sustainability can be viewed comprehensively as the maintaining or enhancing of four key components, namely ecological, socioeconomic, community and institutional sustainability indicators. In Chuenpagdee and Alder, there have been some methods for analyzing and evaluating fishery sustainability, such as RapFish method, FAO Code of Conduct Compliance, and International Instrument Compliance. RapFish is a rapid appraisal technique designed to allow an objective, transparent, multi-disciplinary evaluation. It uses multidimensional scaling, and ordination method to appraise the relative sustainability of fisheries. RapFish relies on a defined-scoring of a number of attributes in five dimensions, namely of ecological, economic, social, technological and ethical. As its characteristics of a rapid appraisal, this method has a slightly top-down approach by employing the defined-score and criteria for the fishery system evaluation. The application of RapFish can be seen, for example, in the Gulf of Maine fisheries, in the North Atlantic Fisheries and recently in the case of Jakarta coastal fisheries, Indonesia.

Similar to RapFish, compliance with the FAO Code of Conduct required multidimensional scaling approach. In this case, four different sets of attributes articulate the clauses in the Code. This evaluation method reflects national management intentions and management practices for each fishery system that is assessed. The application of this method has been carried out in Australian fisheries, Australian multi-species trawl fishery, and Gulf of Maine fisheries. International Instrument Compliance method focuses on measuring either qualitatively or quantitatively the level of compliance with the fisheries management provisions contained within an instrument. In this method, criterion scores ranged from 0 (low compliance) to 3 (high compliance) and the total criteria were limited to approximately six per instrument. An example of this method is presented by Chuenpagdee and Alder in the case of Gulf of Maine fisheries.

It could be said that the above methods rather focus on relatively static approach from the top (top down approach). The fishery in question is just used like the static object which will be evaluated using such methods. They do not involve stakeholders to evaluate their fishery. By these methods, a straight forward analysis could be done but should be treated as preliminary results only. We then argue that it is necessary to confirm dynamic complex systems of the fishery by using a bottom-up approach.

This study attempts to evaluate sustainability indicators of a fishery system by involving the local stakeholders rather than by straightforward analysis (top down) as shown in other measurement methods previously described. We assess what we call ¯local accepted fishery sustainability by examining local sustainability indicators, their importance, interactions, connections, linkages, and assess sustainable state indicators using a cognitive approach involving fishery stakeholders in the area studied. Indicators of sustainability in this case could be defined as a variable that can be used to measure the status or condition of a system.

Information on cumulative impacts of indicators is important because those indicators are often linked together and consequently may impact sustainability directly and indirectly. It is also argued that although individual indicators appear to be good, fishery sustainability may be compromised due to cross-criterion or cross-indicators interactions. Further, the overall risk of a fishery system is not only affected by the risk associated with each indicator, but also by the ecosystem-wide risk that emerges from cross-indicator linkages. Therefore, while being an indicator in and by itself may not be a risk but it may eventually be compromised because of its linkages either directly or indirectly to other indicators that are at risk.

In this study, we used the fishery system of Yoron Island, Kagoshima Prefecture, Japan as the case study. This island is located in the southernmost of Kagoshima Prefecture which is bordered by Okinawa Prefecture in the south, Okinoerabu Island in the north, South China Sea in the west, and Pacific Ocean in the east. Geographically, this island is included in the group of Amami Islands together with Okinerabu Island, Amami Oshima, Tanegashima, and Kikai Island. Among these islands, Yoron Island is the smallest and in terms of area as is estimated to be 20.5 and 23.7 km of coastal line. In terms of population, this island is also small with only 6210 people inhabiting in year 2000. This island is also considered to be relatively vulnerable in terms of its economy according to Adrianto and Matsuda.

Fishery sector in Yoron Island was considered as one of the main areas of economic activities compared to other islands in the group of Amami Islands. Using location analysis approach, fishery sector in Yoron Island has been considered to have very high representation of its economy with location quotient (LQ) value of 1.82, compared with the LQ values of other islands that have lower than 1.0 except Amami Oshima. In terms of production, during the 10 years of analysis, fishery sector in Yoron Island was considerably stable and tended to be growing. In 1988, the fishery production was 321 ton and increased to 384 ton in 1998. In 2002, the total production was recorded to be 540 ton.

Beyond the statistic performance of fishery production, it was important to have an in-depth analysis on the importance of sustainability issues in fishery development in the island. First, as previously elaborated, fishery sector has been an important sector in Yoron Island, so that such efforts to maintain the performance of fisheries in this island are considerably important in terms of its economic function to increase the gross island products. Secondly, it is a matter of fact that fishery sector in Yoron has an important role in the food supply of the islanders. In 2003, almost a half of the fishery production was consumed locally. Out of the 540.139 ton total production, 139.638 ton went to local market as food supply for the local islanders. From these two reasons, we may argue that analysis of sustainable fishery system in Yoron Island is considerably needed from ecological, socioeconomical, and institutional point of views.

THE WORKING PRINCIPLES OF FISHERIES MANAGEMENT

A complex and possibly confusing picture of all the tasks which need to be considered by the fisheries manager. Some of this complexity can be reduced by attempting to highlight the underlying key issues. There are both benefits and risks in attempting to simplify a subject and over-simplification can lead to neglect of important details. However, simplification can facilitate understanding important principles and highlighting the broad areas which need attention. Arising from the considerations, a number of key principles can be identified which may serve to focus attention on the starting points for effective fisheries management.

WHO IS THE FISHERY MANAGER

The Technical Guidelines (FAO, 1997) suggest that fisheries management institutions have two major components: the fisheries management authority and the interested parties. The fishers and fishing companies would usually be the major participants amongst the interested parties. The fisheries management authority is that entity which has been given the mandate by the State (or States in the case of an international authority) to perform specific management functions.

In many countries that authority would be a Department of Fisheries or, within a broader Department, a Division of Fisheries. However, a fisheries management authority does not have to fall directly within central government, and could be, for example, provincial, local, parastatal or private. Any one of these arrangements can function effectively, given an adequate legal framework in which to operate and the resources necessary to fulfil their function.

Who, then, within this authority is the fisheries manager and to whom is this Guidebook addressed? In fact, despite the fact that we have deliberately used the term in the title, we suggest that in modern fisheries management, there is rarely a single individual who fulfils the functions of "fisheries manager". The head of the authority, for example, a Director of Fisheries, may have overall responsibility for implementing fisheries management and, as well as being accountable and responsible for the advice passed on from his or her Department to the political decision-maker, may act in an overall coordinating role. However, this individual is unlikely to, and generally should not, have sole responsibility for receiving information, formulating advice and making and implementing decisions. Fisheries management is a complex and multi-faceted discipline and requires input from a range of perspectives. It is therefore inappropriate to expect any individual to fulfil this function on their own. Fisheries management should involve the legitimate interested parties in the management process.

Perhaps the closest we can come to a "fisheries manager" is the management authority as a whole, including technical experts, monitoring, control and surveillance (MCS) units, administrative units, the executive body of the formal authority, the consultative mechanisms, the advisory body where one exists, and the responsible political head who is often a Minister. Each member of these functional bodies is, to some extent, a fishery manager and this Guidebook is aimed at all of them. It is not designed to go into great technical and operational detail on each function or task as this would require a set of Guidebooks. Instead, it is intended to give a holistic picture of how the different functions should interact in a fisheries management authority in order to develop appropriate objectives, management strategies and plans, and how to encourage all those participating in a fishery to collaborate in and adhere to the agreed strategy.

CONSTITUTES A MANAGEMENT AUTHORITY

The responsibility for fisheries management rests with the designated fisheries arrangement or organisation which, in this Guidebook, we have referred to without distinction as the fisheries management authority. Following the practice used in the Technical Guidelines on Fisheries Management (FAO, 1997) the term is used broadly here to describe that legal entity which has been designated by the State as having the mandate to perform specified fisheries management functions. In practice, it may be a national or provincial ministry, a department within a ministry, or an agency and could be governmental, parastatal or private. In the case of shared resources it should be international.

The area of competence, geographical area, fish resources and fisheries for which a given management authority is responsible must be precisely specified in each case in the appropriate legislation. The task of an authority is diverse and complex and as a result, fisheries management authorities are normally divided into institutional support structures: the fisheries management institutions. The institutions need to encompass the basic tasks and functions of fisheries management. The actual institutional structure and mechanisms may differ from authority to authority and it would be inappropriate for us in this Guidebook to attempt to prescribe any specific set of characteristics as representing the 'best' institutional structure and processes. What is best in each case will depend in large part on the specific circumstances and context. What is universal, however, is that it is essential for the different institutions concerned with management of any fishery or fisheries to be able to interact effectively, requiring good channels of communication and feedback. The institutions must also be seen by the different interested parties as being legitimate.

The need for collaboration between the authority and the interested parties is as important as collaboration between the institutions within the authority. Examines the pre-requisites for effective partnerships between the management authority and the interested parties and the different types of partnership which can be considered.

It is common and frequently desirable for the national government to devolve all or some fisheries management functions to local government or to smaller groups such as fishing communities. In such cases, it is essential to specify precisely the responsibilities and functions, including the geographical area, falling under this local authority or smaller group. The institutions within the local authority must follow the same principles as those for a national authority.

The Code of Conduct requires that fisheries management should be concerned with the whole stock over its entire area of distribution and therefore that States should cooperate in the management of transboundary, straddling, highly migratory and high seas fish stocks exploited by two or more states.

General rules for cooperation towards conservation of such fish stocks are foreseen in the United Nations Convention on the Law of the Sea of 10 December 1982, and in the 1995 UN Fish Stocks Agreement. The responsibilities, functions and structure of international or regional fisheries authorities will usually not differ substantively from those of national authorities.

GOALS AND OBJECTIVES

The over-riding goal of fisheries management is the long-term sustainable use of the fisheries resources. Achieving this requires a proactive approach and should involve actively seeking ways to optimise the benefits derived from the resources available.

This rarely happens, though, and fisheries management is still most commonly practised as a reactive activity, where decisions are made and actions taken largely in response to problems or crises. The resulting crisis decisions are then normally attempts merely to solve the immediate problems without properly considering the broader perspective and the longer-term objectives. Such an approach may succeed in maintaining dissatisfaction sufficiently low to avoid major conflict, but it is extremely unlikely to result in the best use of the marine resources being exploited by the fishery.

The first step in proactive fisheries management is to decide what is meant by optimising the benefits for each fishery - what can the State or the collection of legitimate interested parties agree on as being optimal benefits? This may be described in general terms in the national fisheries policy which must be the starting point for determining the specific objectives for each fishery. The broad goals stated in the fisheries policy may need to be tailored for a specific fishery, but the goals for each fishery should be consistent with the policy.

In general terms, the goals in fisheries management can be divided into four subsets: biological; ecological; economic and social, where social includes political and cultural goals. The biological and ecological goals may be more correctly thought of as constraints in achieving desired economic and social benefits but for simplicity and consistency with the terminology most commonly used in fisheries management, we will include them as goals in this Guidebook. Examples of goals under each of these categories include:

- To maintain the target species at or above the levels necessary to ensure their continued productivity (biological);
- To minimize the impacts of fishing on the physical environment and on non-target (bycatch), associated and dependent species (ecological);
- To maximize the net incomes of the participating fishers (economic); and
- To maximize employment opportunities for those dependent on the fishery for their livelihoods (social).

Identifying such goals is important in clarifying how the fish resources are to be used to benefit society, and they should be agreed upon and recorded, both at the policy level and for each fishery. Without such goals, there is no guidance on how the fishery should be operated, which results in a high probability of *ad hoc* decisions and sub-optimal use of the resources (resulting in lost benefits), and increases the probability of serious conflicts as different interest groups jostle for greater shares of the benefits. This is often seen in practice and one of the important causes of failures in fisheries management has been identified as the frequent absence of clear and precise objectives.

While setting goals is an essential first step, the goals stated above have two obvious limitations. Firstly, they have clear conflicts in intention as it is impossible, for example, to minimize impacts of the fishery on the ecosystem and simultaneously to maximize net incomes. Similarly, it is very probable that management strategies that aim to maximize net incomes will not also maximize employment opportunities. Some compromise between these goals has to be achieved before an effective management strategy can be devised. The second limitation of the goals is that they are too vague to be of much benefit to the manager. For example, the impacts of fishing can only be "minimized" by having no fishing at all, which is unlikely to have been the intention of those who stated the goal. Maximising employment opportunities could mean allowing as many fishers as possible to participate, regardless of whether or not they could make a living from the fishery, or it could mean maximising the number which could still earn some acceptable income, or many other such targets. Too much is left to the discretion of the manager with these examples of goals.

It is therefore necessary to refine the goals further and to develop operational objectives for each fishery. Operational objectives are very precise and are formulated in such a way that they should be simultaneously achievable in that fishery. In other words, the trade-offs between the biological, ecological, economic and social goals must have been agreed upon and the conflicts and contradictions resolved. The development of operational objectives is illustrate the difference between goals and operational objectives, two examples of objectives are:

- To maintain the stock at all times above 50 per cent of its mean unexploited level (biological);
- To maintain all non-target, associated and dependent species above 50 per cent of their mean biomass levels in the absence of fishing activities (ecological).

With operational objectives such as these, it is possible for any observer, including the manager, to establish whether or not they are being achieved and hence whether or not the management strategy is appropriate and being successfully implemented. These operational objectives can also easily be used as the foundation for reference points, which are essentially the operational objectives expressed in a way which can be estimated or simulated in a fisheries assessment. Once operational objectives have been agreed upon, a management strategy can be developed, made up of a suite of different management measures, to achieve those objectives.

All of this may sound complex, but in reality is no more than most people do in order to develop a budget for their personal finances. Most of us have realistic but imprecisely expressed hopes and needs for our lifestyle as well as a knowledge of the nature of the resource (in this case our net income). These hopes and needs are the goals of our budget but they will all compete for the same resource, our net income, so there will probably be conflicts which need to be resolved. Therefore we have to modify our goals and express them more precisely: we develop operational objectives in which we specify what we can realistically achieve in terms of food, housing, education etc. Thereafter, we need to decide on our budget strategy: how can we meet those objectives: what type and quantities of food and clothing should we be buying; what type of housing can we consider; can we consider an annual holiday, etc.

Clearly, our operational objectives must be consistent with the yield we can expect from the resource (our income). Normally the process of developing realistic objectives will require trade-offs and most of us find, for example, that we cannot allocate as much for entertainment or holidays as we would like and at the same time make our rental or mortgage payments. Therefore priorities are established and compromises made until eventually we arrive at realistic objectives that balance our desires with our income, and that provide a good guide on how to manage our finances from month to month and in the longer-term. At the end of this, we should have a feasible financial management strategy that, barring totally unexpected events, will have a predictable outcome. If we have done our calculations correctly and responsibly, the strategy should mean we enjoy a reasonable lifestyle without being sued for bankruptcy. This is little different from the basic task, and overall hope, of the fisheries manager!

MANAGEMENT PLANS, MEASURES AND STRATEGIES

There is a lot of terminology floating around in fisheries management that, unless clearly understood, can cause further confusion in an already confusing environment. In addition to the words 'goals' and 'operational objectives', the terms management plans, management measures and management strategies will crop up on many occasions in this Guidebook and we need to clarify what we mean by each of them and how they differ.

The Technical Guidelines on Fisheries Management (FAO, 1997) describe a management plan as "a formal or informal arrangement between a fisheries management authority and interested parties which identifies the partners in the fishery and their respective roles, details the agreed objectives for the fishery and specifies the management rules and regulations which apply to it and provides other details about the fishery which are relevant to the task of the management authority." A well formulated management plan should be prepared for every fishery and the Code of Conduct (Paragraph 7.3.3) states that: "Long-term management objectives should be translated into management actions, formulated as a fishery management plan or other management framework." Given the importance of management plans in fisheries.

The fisheries policy is translated into goals and the goals into objectives that indicate precisely what is expected to be achieved from the fishery. The objectives are achieved through the implementation of a management strategy which will also be a central element of a management plan. The management strategy is the sum of all the management measures selected to achieve the biological, ecological, economic and social objectives of the fishery. It is possible that in a single species fishery a management strategy could consist of a single management measure, such as a specified total allowable catch (TAC), but in practice the great majority of management strategies consist of a number of management measures, encompassing technical, input and output controls and a system of user rights.

An effective management strategy, however, should not contain so many management measures that compliance and enforcement become so difficult as to be practically impossible.

A management measure is the smallest unit of the fishery manager's tool kit and consists of any type of control implemented to contribute to achieving the objectives. Management measures are classified as technical measures, input (effort) and output (catch) controls, and any access rights designed around input and output controls. Technical measures can be sub-divided into regulations on gear-type or gear design and closed areas and closed seasons. A minimum legal mesh size, a seasonal closure of the fishery, a total allowable catch (TAC), a limit on the total number of vessels in a fishery, and a licensing scheme to achieve the limit are all examples of management measures. A substantial part of the Guidebook is intended to assist managers in considering and selecting different management measures for a given fishery.

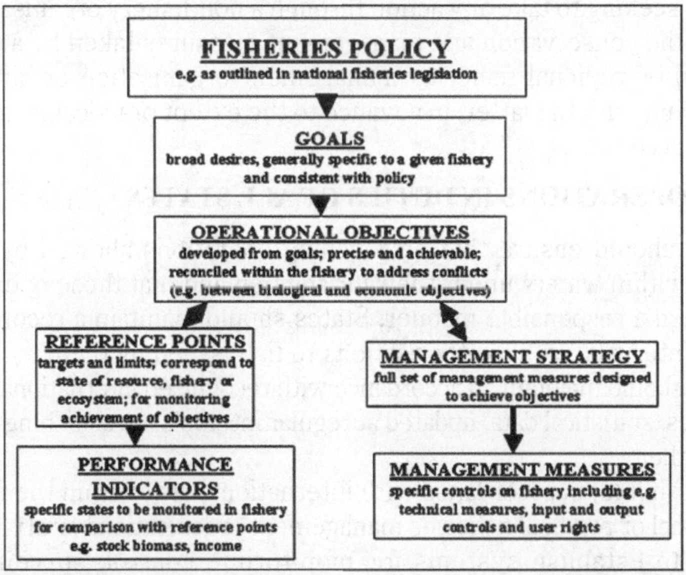

Fig. The hierarchical relationships between the different intentions (policy, goal, objectives), standards (reference points and indicators) and actions (management strategy and measures).

FISHERIES MANAGEMENT: FRAMEWORK AND PROCEDURES

To be effective, fisheries management should be concerned with the whole stock unit over its entire area of distribution and take into account previously agreed management measures established and applied in the same region, all removals and the biological unity and other biological characteristics of the stock. The best scientific evidence available should be used to determine, *inter alia*, the area of distribution of the resource and the area through which it migrates during its life cycle.

In order to conserve and manage transboundary fish stocks, straddling fish stocks, highly migratory fish stocks and high seas fish stocks throughout their range, conservation and management measures established for such stocks in accordance with the respective competences of relevant States or, where appropriate, through subregional and regional fisheries management organisations and arrangements, should be compatible. Compatibility should be achieved in a manner consistent with the rights, competences and interests of the States concerned. Long-term management objectives should be translated into management actions, formulated as a fishery management plan or other management framework. States and, where appropriate, subregional or regional fisheries management organisations and arrangements should foster and promote international cooperation and coordination in all matters related to fisheries, including information gathering and exchange, fisheries research, management and development.

States seeking to take any action through a non-fishery organisation which may affect the conservation and management measures taken by a competent subregional or regional fisheries management organisation or arrangement should consult with the latter, in advance to the extent practicable, and take its views into account.

FISHING OPERATIONS IN DUTIES OF ALL STATES

States should ensure that only fishing operations allowed by them are conducted within waters under their jurisdiction and that these operations are carried out in a responsible manner. States should maintain a record, updated at regular intervals, on all authorisations to fish issued by them.

States should maintain, in accordance with recognised international standards and practices, statistical data, updated at regular intervals, on all fishing operations allowed by them.

States should, in accordance with international law, within the framework of subregional or regional fisheries management organisations or arrangements, cooperate to establish systems for monitoring, control, surveillance and enforcement of applicable measures with respect to fishing operations and related activities in waters outside their national jurisdiction. States should ensure that health and safety standards are adopted for everyone employed in fishing operations. Such standards should be not less than the minimum requirements of relevant international agreements on conditions of work and service. States should make arrangements individually, together with other States or with the appropriate international organisation to integrate fishing operations into maritime search and rescue systems.

States should enhance through education and training programmes the education and skills of fishers and, where appropriate, their professional qualifications. Such programmes should take into account agreed international standards and guidelines.

States should, as appropriate, maintain records of fishers which should, whenever possible, contain information on their service and qualifications, including certificates of competency, in accordance with their national laws. States should ensure that measures applicable in respect of masters and other officers charged with an offence relating to the operation of fishing vessels should include provisions which may permit, *inter alia*, refusal, withdrawal or suspension of authorisations to serve as masters or officers of a fishing vessel.

States, with the assistance of relevant international organisations, should endeavour to ensure through education and training that all those engaged in fishing operations be given information on the most important provisions of this Code, as well as provisions of relevant international conventions and applicable environmental and other standards that are essential to ensure responsible fishing operations.

MAINTAIN RECORDS OF FISHING VESSELS

Flag States should maintain records of fishing vessels entitled to fly their flag and authorised to be used for fishing and should indicate in such records details of the vessels, their ownership and authorisation to fish. Flag States should ensure that no fishing vessels entitled to fly their flag fish on the high seas or in waters under the jurisdiction of other States unless such vessels have been issued with a Certificate of Registry and have been authorised to fish by the competent authorities. Such vessels should carry on board the Certificate of Registry and their authorisation to fish. Fishing vessels authorised to fish on the high seas or in waters under the jurisdiction of a State other than the flag State, should be marked in accordance with uniform and internationally recognisable vessel marking systems such as the FAO Standard Specifications and Guidelines for Marking and Identification of Fishing Vessels. Fishing gear should be marked in accordance with national legislation in order that the owner of the gear can be identified. Gear marking requirements should take into account uniform and internationally recognisable gear marking systems.

Flag States should ensure compliance with appropriate safety requirements for fishing vessels and fishers in accordance with international conventions, internationally agreed codes of practice and voluntary guidelines. States should adopt appropriate safety requirements for all small vessels not covered by such international conventions, codes of practice or voluntary guidelines. States not party to the Agreement to Promote Compliance with International Conservation and Management Measures by Vessels Fishing in the High Seas should be encouraged to accept the Agreement and to adopt laws and regulations consistent with the provisions of the Agreement.

Flag States should take enforcement measures in respect of fishing vessels entitled to fly their flag which have been found by them to have contravened applicable conservation and management measures, including, where appropriate, making the contravention of such measures an offence under national legislation.

Sanctions applicable in respect of violations should be adequate in severity to be effective in securing compliance and to discourage violations wherever they occur and should deprive offenders of the benefits accruing from their illegal activities. Such sanctions may, for serious violations, include provisions for the refusal, withdrawal or suspension of the authorisation to fish.

Flag States should promote access to insurance coverage by owners and charterers of fishing vessels. Owners or charterers of fishing vessels should carry sufficient insurance cover to protect the crew of such vessels and their interests, to indemnify third parties against loss or damage and to protect their own interests.

Flag States should ensure that crew members are entitled to repatriation, taking account of the principles laid down in the "Repatriation of Seafarers Convention, 1987". In the event of an accident to a fishing vessel or persons on board a fishing vessel, the flag State of the fishing vessel concerned should provide details of the accident to the State of any foreign national on board the vessel involved in the accident. Such information should also, where practicable, be communicated to the International Maritime Organisation.

Port State Duties

Port States should take, through procedures established in their national legislation, in accordance with international law, including applicable international agreements or arrangements, such measures as are necessary to achieve and to assist other States in achieving the objectives of this Code, and should make known to other States details of regulations and measures they have established for this purpose. When taking such measures a port State should not discriminate in form or in fact against the vessels of any other State. Port States should provide such assistance to flag States as is appropriate, in accordance with the national laws of the port State and international law, when a fishing vessel is voluntarily in a port or at an offshore terminal of the port State and the flag State of the vessel requests the port State for assistance in respect of non-compliance with subregional, regional or global conservation and management measures or with internationally agreed minimum standards for the prevention of pollution and for safety, health and conditions of work on board fishing vessels.

Fishing Activities

States should ensure that fishing is conducted with due regard to the safety of human life and the International Maritime Organisation International Regulations for Preventing Collisions at Sea, as well as International Maritime Organisation requirements relating to the organisation of marine traffic, protection of the marine environment and the prevention of damage to or loss of fishing gear. States should prohibit dynamiting, poisoning and other comparable destructive fishing practices. States should make every effort to ensure that documentation with regard to fishing operations, retained catch of fish and non-fish species and, as regards discards, the information required for stock assessment as decided by relevant management bodies, is collected and forwarded systematically to those bodies. States should, as far as possible, establish programmes, such as observer and inspection schemes, in order to promote compliance with applicable measures. States should promote the adoption of appropriate technology, taking into account economic conditions, for the best use and care of the retained catch. States, with relevant groups from industry, should encourage the development and implementation of technologies and operational methods that reduce discards. The use of fishing gear and practices that lead to the discarding of catch should be discouraged and the use of fishing gear and practices that increase survival rates of escaping fish should be promoted.

States should cooperate to develop and apply technologies, materials and operational methods that minimize the loss of fishing gear and the ghost fishing effects of lost or abandoned fishing gear. States should ensure that assessments of the implications of habitat disturbance are carried out prior to the introduction on a commercial scale of new fishing gear, methods and operations to an area. Research on the environmental and social impacts of fishing gear and, in particular, on the impact of such gear on biodiversity and coastal fishing communities should be promoted.

Fishing Gear Selectivity

States should require that fishing gear, methods and practices, to the extent practicable, are sufficiently selective so as to minimize waste, discards, catch of non-target species, both fish and non-fish species, and impacts on associated or dependent species and that the intent of related regulations is not circumvented by technical devices. In this regard, fishers should cooperate in the development of selective fishing gear and methods. States should ensure that information on new developments and requirements is made available to all fishers. In order to improve selectivity, States should, when drawing up their laws and regulations, take into account the range of selective fishing gear, methods and strategies available to the industry. States and relevant institutions should collaborate in developing standard methodologies for research into fishing gear selectivity, fishing methods and strategies. International cooperation should be encouraged with respect to research programmes for fishing gear selectivity, and fishing methods and strategies, dissemination of the results of such research programmes and the transfer of technology.

Protection of the Aquatic Environment

States should introduce and enforce laws and regulations based on the International Convention for the Prevention of Pollution from Ships, 1973, as modified by the Protocol of 1978 relating thereto (MARPOL 73/78). Owners, charterers and managers of fishing vessels should ensure that their vessels are fitted with appropriate equipment as required by MARPOL 73/78 and should consider fitting a shipboard compactor or incinerator to relevant classes of vessels in order to treat garbage and other shipboard wastes generated during the vessel's normal service. Owners, charterers and managers of fishing vessels should minimize the taking aboard of potential garbage through proper provisioning practices. The crew of fishing vessels should be conversant with proper shipboard procedures in order to ensure discharges do not exceed the levels set by MARPOL 73/78. Such procedures should, as a minimum, include the disposal of oily waste and the handling and storage of shipboard garbage.

Energy Optimisation

States should promote the development of appropriate standards and guidelines which would lead to the more efficient use of energy in harvesting and post-harvest activities within the fisheries sector. States should promote the development and transfer of technology in relation to energy optimisation within the fisheries sector and, in particular, encourage owners, charterers and managers of fishing vessels to fit energy optimisation devices to their vessels.

Protection of the Atmosphere

States should adopt relevant standards and guidelines which would include provisions for the reduction of dangerous substances in exhaust gas emissions. Owners, charterers and managers of fishing vessels should ensure that their vessels are fitted with equipment to reduce emissions of ozone depleting substances. The responsible crew members of fishing vessels should be conversant with the proper running and maintenance of machinery on board. Competent authorities should make provision for the phasing out of the use of chlorofluorocarbons (CFCs) and transitional substances such as hydrochlorofluorocarbons (HCFCs) in the refrigeration systems of fishing vessels and should ensure that the shipbuilding industry and those engaged in the fishing industry are informed of and comply with such provisions. Owners or managers of fishing vessels should take appropriate action to refit existing vessels with alternative refrigerants to CFCs and HCFCs and alternatives to Halons in fire fighting installations. Such alternatives should be used in specifications for all new fishing vessels. States and owners, charterers and managers of fishing vessels as well as fishers should follow international guidelines for the disposal of CFCs, HCFCs and Halons.

Harbours and Landing Places for Fishing Vessels

States should take into account, *inter alia*, the following in the design and construction of harbours and landing places:

- Safe havens for fishing vessels and adequate servicing facilities for vessels, vendors and buyers are provided;

- Adequate freshwater supplies and sanitation arrangements should be provided;
- Waste disposal systems should be introduced, including for the disposal of oil, oily water and fishing gear;
- Pollution from fisheries activities and external sources should be minimized; and
- Arrangements should be made to combat the effects of erosion and siltation.

States should establish an institutional framework for the selection or improvement of sites for harbours for fishing vessels which allows for consultation among the authorities responsible for coastal area management.

States should ensure that the standards and guidelines for the removal of redundant offshore structures issued by the International Maritime Organisation are followed. States should also ensure that the competent fisheries authorities are consulted prior to decisions being made on the abandonment of structures and other materials by the relevant authorities.

Fish Aggregation Devices

States, where appropriate, should develop policies for increasing stock populations and enhancing fishing opportunities through the use of artificial structures, placed with due regard to the safety of navigation, on or above the seabed or at the surface.

Research into the use of such structures, including the impacts on living marine resources and the environment, should be promoted. States should ensure that, when selecting the materials to be used in the creation of artificial reefs as well as when selecting the geographical location of such artificial reefs, the provisions of relevant international conventions concerning the environment and safety of navigation are observed.

States should, within the framework of coastal area management plans, establish management systems for artificial reefs and fish aggregation devices. Such management systems should require approval for the construction and deployment of such reefs and devices and should take into account the interests of fishers, including artisanal and subsistence fishers. States should ensure that the authorities responsible for maintaining cartographic records and charts for the purpose of navigation, as well as relevant environmental authorities, are informed prior to the placement or removal of artificial reefs or fish aggregation devices.

ENVIRONMENTALIST ADVOCACY AND FISHERIES MANAGEMENT

Environmentalists and fishermen rarely agree on anything. It's a pity, because conventional logic would say that, fundamentally, environmentalists and fishing people should stand shoulder-to-shoulder in a common cause for maintaining resources *sustainability*, while blending that with their sensible usage. This, especially, with respect to the damage to the environment due to pollution and coastal habitat destruction. Unfortunately, only too often over-eager environmentalist see fishing people as enemies of the environment, and a controversy between the two, at times on low fire, at times raging, is going on in many countries, and even globally.

For example, to some environmentalists *sustainability* means reducing commercial fishing to no more than a very small inshore one-man vessel industry with the interests of seaweed/fauna growing on the seabed being preferable to the development of an industry that over the generations has been producing top quality nutritional food. But, they say it's needed, for it is only by reducing the capacity of fishing fleets that a solution to the problem of over-exploitation of the marine environment can be found. "The fishing industry cannot exist if there are no fish left" – is the argument.

They believe that reduction of excess fishing capacity, creation of "no-take zones" covering about 20 or more per cent of marine habitats, and political enforcement of sustainable fishing levels would solve the problem of stocks impoverishment. But what they fail to see or often ignore are the dozens of toxic chemicals and excess nutrients that abound in upstream water and air pollution and their joint effect on coastal marine areas, and that the most deadly pollution that affects coastal habitats including fish nursery and feeding grounds, comes from industrial sources and, in particular, from the petro-chemical and electro-chemical sectors.

Other factors ignored by the environmentalists' advocacy are the crucial influence of climatic and oceanic processes and fluctuations on fish populations, well documented in the history. Species with narrow temperature preference limits, are affected by thermal anomalies that delay or hasten spawning and hatching, and displace spawning and feeding grounds. Survival of larvae and juveniles depends, apart from hydrographic conditions, also on availability of the right food, at the right place and time, as well as on the rate of predation. Changes in river flows raise or reduce salinity in estuaries, deplete and displace fish and aquatic plant species. Climate variability is the key controlling factor in fishing yields for about half of the world's large marine ecosystems, including the East and West Greenland shelves, the Benguela Current off Southwest Africa, the Canary Current off Northwest Africa and the Humboldt Current off the west coast of South America. Over the past decades, modes of oceanic variability such as the Pacific Decadal Oscillation and the North Atlantic Oscillation have been related to shifts in marine ecosystem structure, species composition, distribution and biogeochemical processes. Thus, since patterns of species abundances shift with the ocean climate, when climatic, biological and oceanographic conditions are just right, fish can respond with an extremely strong year class, or a series of them, and the other way around.

FISHERIES MANAGERS AND ECONOMICS

Environmental lobbying encourages fisheries managers to think that if they got hold of controlling the fishing, all their problems would be solved. Ignoring anthropogenic and natural environmental factors, which critically affect natural mortality is ridiculous. But to many of them all these ecological problems are only a noise, which creates confusion in their favored system. In that they're joined by some economists, who analyze fisheries in purely economic-financial terms, with hardly paying even lip service to non-fishing factors that affect the whole system, fishery resources included. A neo-liberal economic approach inserted the agenda of privatization of fishery resources as a medicine to overfishing. This agenda is often disguised as rights-based management. Politically it depends on who holds or is offered the rights, and economically-are those rights marketable, a solution promoted by neo-liberal economists.

Accordingly, the quota system has been introduced to fisheries management, particularly the individual transferable quotas (ITQ), which had great theoretical appeal to those economists. They embraced ITQ-system quickly and uncritically, and appeared to regard it as a cure-all for fisheries management problems. While the overall benefits of the ITQ-system are highly disputable, what is not is that it causes an ongoing concentration of quota in the hands of a smaller number of larger operators and a resulting displacement of fishermen owner-operators. Thus, the introduction of the ITQs has become also a political tool for redistribution of benefits from marine fishery resources away from the small to the hands of large firms and corporate interests. Notwithstanding, the whole idea of rationalization of fisheries through privatization is based on misperception and, hence, it fails to achieve the desired results of sustainability, all the more that for most fisheries any promise of true privatization is a hoax.

Evidence accumulated over many years shows that there's more than a single viable resource management option. Private, state, and communal property and fishing rights are all potential options and there's no panacea for fisheries management. Fishery laws and regulations should be separately tailored for every fishery and environment, and for the different socio-economic conditions. The tunnel vision of some economists, which disregards external costs and benefits, represents achievement of the highest profits and free marketing of fishing rights and quotas as also the highest social and national benefits. Often, consequences of such approach becoming actual policy have been social and economic devastation of fishing communities and dislocation of fishing people.

ECOSYSTEM-BASED MANAGEMENT

In the recent years, the fishery science started internalizing the notion that management by single species and only by controlling fishing is illogical and contrary to ecological realities. A new approach entered the domain of fisheries management under the name of "Ecosystem-based management". So what the new approach should be about? Let's consider the main elements of an ecosystem affected by commercial fishery (fishery ecosystem) and their changes in space, time and character. The first element is the *time factor*. Any aquatic ecosystem is a dynamic, pulsating, and ever-changing macro-organism. Thus, trends and fluctuations that have been occurring in the ecosystem throughout history must be taken into account. The second element embraces all the changes and physical, biological and chemical forces, including upstream and coastal pollution, imposed upon the ecosystem by *climatic variations* and the various *human activities*. Whatever happens with inshore and bottom habitats, and the water, affects the ecosystem's biota (*i.e.*, all living things). The third element is made up of the *relationships* between the various species occupying the ecosystem at all stages of their life. This runs from bacteria and phyto-plankton up to top predators, with special attention to the managed "target species", physical factors affecting them, their food, prey and predators. Last, but not least is *fishing*, which apart from massive removal of marine organisms from the system, also may influence the size, age and genetic composition of the fished populations. The fishing itself is influenced by the market and the socio-economic context of fishing people and their communities, and of fish consumers, as well as by the industries and technologies involved. No doubt, *controlling fish harvests is not enough to ensure sustainable fishery and healthy ecosystems*.

"The vastness of linkages between species and critical habitats in a coastal area requires comprehensive management of all its parts". An appropriate approach should incorporate institutional arrangements and cultural factors to provide for better analysis and prediction. The list of the factors other than fishing that affect the size, composition and well-being of populations of marine organisms would be extensive. Here're some examples:

Further expansion of dead anoxic zones, 150 of which were reported in 2003 in bays and semi-enclosed seas, some of which extended up to 27,000 square miles, may well be a greater peril than overfishing. A slowly killing mycobacteriosis epidemic was affecting the condition and size of the striped bass population in Maryland and Virginia and in the heavily polluted Chesapeake Bay. According to some estimates, the word's seabirds consume 70 million mt of food as compared to the 80-90 million mt of global marine landings, and the amount of fish eaten by marine mammals worldwide is several times the worldwide ocean fish harvest.

Climatic fluctuations and separate events cause boom-and-bust sequences among fish populations and other marine organisms. There may be umpteen sorts of association between the physical and biological elements. For example, studies show that the main factors critical for salmon abundance are distance to and size of oceanic areas with temperature and food critical to the survival of juveniles, such as the abundance of krill, which is their main food. Pollution of rivers and estuaries and longshore development that destroys inshore habitats, affect the reproduction of many fish species whose spawning and nursery areas are in inshore waters.

FISHERIES SUSTAINABILITY

In most coastal areas, rehabilitation of marine habitats and restoration or protection of essential upstream environments and coastal hydrology functions are essential to future fisheries sustainability. The fundamental message is that for such sustainability we must restructure general coastal management. Environmentalist NGOs and everyone involved in trying to secure sustainability of habitats must realize that there has to be a balance between the needs of the people and the conservation of living resources, and both sides need to be prepared to compromise. The environmentalists' and some scientists' advice that by only controlling fishing they'd achieve sustainability is counter-productive when it diverts attention from other, often more significant factors.

Only an intelligent *analysis and synthesis* of the interaction of all important elements involved can enable understanding of the *problematique* of ecosystem management and searching for solutions. We have to accept that the dynamics of the system is so complex that even the best existing models are of limited use for forecasting the outcomes of actual management actions. In this general context, "*ecosystem-based fishery management*" must address the particular elements. Those that require intervention must be defined and managed respectively, while the others, including those that are beyond the management's powers, must be taken into account. Flexibility and tailoring management for each specific fishery and area should become the rule. There's no rational way to impose a policy that doesn't take all the above into account, or a single "common" policy for different fisheries, ecosystems and fishing cultures. We have to analyze separately each fishery ecosystem to see, for example, if TACs are the right methodology to use or other options such as effort control should be considered.

Unfortunately, some authors and "green" zealots are trying to hijack the concept of "ecosystem management" by representing it as care-taking of the fishery that it doesn't affect the ecosystem. While paying lip service to other factors, they focus on commercial fishing in a way which stigmatizes it as the only factor affecting ecosystem that needs tackling and as the main villain to be constrained or eliminated in order to "protect" marine ecosystems. Their interest doesn't lie in cleaning up habitats and keep fisheries prosperous, but elsewhere. Where? – This depends on who's the "father" (or sponsor) of the particular "stewardship". The institutional and human inertia is strong and many NGOs as well as the fishery management system worldwide abound in scientists and environmentalists who preach sustainability, but keep talking of "saving the oceans" just by shutting down fisheries or by closing off major sea areas to fisheries, and hardly even mention the whole set of other vectors, whatever may be their relative roles in each separate ecosystem. They still ignore physical and biological-ecological environmental factors and upstream and marine pollution from industrial, municipal, and agricultural sources. They close the eye on inshore habitat destruction, and disregard or play down non-human predation, nowadays enhanced by the extensive protection bestowed upon marine mammals.

In fact, however, ecosystem management approach places fishing in its proper context, so it can't be blamed anymore for everything that happens in the sea. Ecosystem management doesn't allow managers and politicians to keep turning a blind eye to pollution, environmental variations, habitat destruction, etc. It carries fishery management from the current over-simplification into more complex concepts. This obviously worries some scientists and managers, who are concerned that with "ecosystem management" they'd be sailing in unknown waters and lose their control over fishing rights and quotas.

Doubtless, it won't be easy, but the point is that to manage fishery ecosystems using the existing methodologies, as they've practically been since the mid 20th century, is like looking under a streetlamp for a lost key, because that's where the light is, instead of looking for it where it may be-however dark is the place. The new approach may also require to get used to the fact that for a long time to come we won't be able to put numerical values to all acting factors, a current custom that sometimes borders on numerology, and relearn to talk also in qualitative terms and perhaps to employ fuzzy logic.

While ecosystem-based management is coming of age, institutional inertia and obstinacy, human conservatism, fear of the unknown and need to admit own misconstruction of the realities of the coastal, marine and living resources, impedes its application. The notion of positive development stems from the recognition that, climatic conditions permitting, sustainability of both, marine capture fisheries and marine aquaculture, can only be achieved by integrated and balanced approach to ecosystem management involving upstream and downstream influences, fisheries, and any other human activities that affect coastal and offshore habitats. There is a growing understanding of the complexity of the systems to be managed and of the futility of simplistic approaches, such as those of the still prevailing fishery management based on inadequate science and its mathematical models.

FISHERIES MANAGEMENT AND ITS PRIMARY CONSIDERATIONS

If marine living resources were infinite and indestructible, we could leave people to use and abuse them at will. However, this is not the case and we therefore need to manage fisheries to ensure that the resources are utilised in a sustainable and responsible way, and that the potential benefits are not inefficiently dissipated and possibly totally lost. Fisheries production and yield are constrained by a number of factors which can be classified as biological, ecological and environmental, technological, social and cultural, and economic considerations. There are frequently also considerations imposed by other users of the fishing grounds and neighbouring areas. These considerations are discussed in considerable detail in the Technical Guidelines on Fisheries Management.

BIOLOGICAL CONSIDERATIONS

As living populations or communities, aquatic living resources are capable of on-going renewal through the processes of growth in size and mass of individuals and additions to the population or community through reproduction (leading to what in fisheries is often called 'recruitment'). In a population at equilibrium, the additive processes of growth and reproduction on average equal the loss process of total mortality. In an unexploited population, total mortality consists only of natural mortality, made up of processes such as predation, disease, and death through drastic changes in the environment.

In a fished population, total mortality consists of natural mortality plus fishing mortality, and a primary task of fisheries management is to ensure that fishing mortality does not exceed the amount which the population can withstand, in addition to natural mortality, without undue harm or damage to the sustainability and productivity of the population. This requires not only that the total population is maintained above a certain abundance or biomass, but also that the age structure of the population is maintained in a state in which it is able to maintain the level of reproduction, and hence recruitment, necessary to replenish the losses through mortality. Further, fishing over a long period on selected portions of a stock, for example large individuals or individuals spawning at a specific time or locality within a wider spawning season or range, can reduce the frequency of the particular genetic characteristics giving rise to that feature or behaviour.

This has the effect of reducing the overall genetic diversity of the stock. With reduced genetic diversity, the production potential of the population can be adversely affected and it may also become less resilient to environmental variability and change. Fisheries management needs to be aware of this danger and avoid maintaining such selective pressures over a prolonged period.

Achieving an appropriate level and pattern of fishing mortality is hindered substantially by difficulties in estimating population abundance and population dynamics rates and the variability in these rates. The fisheries manager must, however, have sufficient knowledge to make good decisions. The Code of Conduct specifies: "...States... should, *inter alia*, adopt appropriate measures, based on the best scientific evidence available, which are designed to maintain or restore stocks at levels capable of producing maximum sustainable yield, as qualified by relevant environmental and economic factors..." and further "In implementing the precautionary approach States should take into account, *inter alia*, uncertainties relating to the size and productivity of the stocks, reference points, stock condition in relation to reference points...".

Fishery managers must also respect the stock structure of the resources. Fish populations are frequently made up of a number of different stocks, each of which is genetically largely isolated from the others through behavioural or distributional differences. The different stocks also reflect genetic diversity and if a particular stock is fished to extinction or to very low levels, this genetic diversity may be lost.

The stock will not readily be replenished from other stocks, because of the genetic isolation, and therefore the production it was generating will also be lost, leading to a permanent or at least long-term loss of benefits. Fisheries management should therefore attempt to address each stock separately and to ensure sustainable use of each stock and not just of the population as a whole. In this regard, the Code of Conduct states: "To be effective, fisheries management should be concerned with the whole stock unit over its entire area of distribution and take into account previously agreed management measures established and applied in the same region, all removals and the biological unity and other biological characteristics of the stock."

ECOLOGICAL AND ENVIRONMENTAL CONSIDERATIONS

The abundance and dynamics of a population place an important constraint on fisheries but aquatic populations do not live in isolation. They exist as components of a frequently complex ecosystem, consisting of biological components which may feed on, be fed on by, or compete with a given stock or population.

Even those populations which are not directly linked through the food web may indirectly affect each other through their direct interactions with predators, prey or competitors of the other. The physical component of the ecosystem, the water itself, the substrate, inflows of freshwater or nutrients and other non-biological processes may also be very important. Different substrates may be essential for the production of food organisms, for shelter, or as spawning or nursery grounds.

The environment of fish is very rarely static and conditions, particularly of the aquatic environment, can vary substantially over time, from hourly variability, such as the tides, to seasonal variability in, for example, water temperature and currents, to decadal variability as in the occurrence of El Niño events and regime shifts. These changes frequently affect the population dynamics of fish populations, resulting in variability in growth rates, recruitment, natural mortality rates or any combination of these. Such variability can also affect the availability of fish resources to fishing gear, not only affecting the success of the fishing industry, but also the way in which the fishery scientist must interpret catch and catch rate information from the fishery.

Changes in any of the biological, chemical, geological or physical components of the ecosystem can have impacts on the resource population and community. Some of these changes may be beyond human control, such as upwelling processes enriching some coastal ecosystems or large scale temperature anomalies, but they still need to be considered in the management of the resource. Others, such as the destruction of coastal habitats for development, or the direct impact of fishing on the substrate or on other species impacting the resources, are due to human action. In these cases, fisheries management should both take into account their impacts on the resource and, in consultation with other relevant agencies and parties, take steps to minimize their impacts on the fishery ecosystem.

The manager also needs to consider the impact of the fishery on the ecosystem as a whole. There are four types of impact of fisheries on the ecosystem: direct impact on the target species; direct impacts on the bycatch species; indirect impacts on other organisms transmitted through the food chain (*i.e.* by changing the abundance of predators, prey or competitors of a population); and direct impact of fishing on the physical or chemical environment. The manager needs to be aware of these potential impacts and to use management measures that minimise negative impacts.

The potential to address the ecosystem considerations will vary depending on whether they are caused by or independent of human action, but in both cases the constraints imposed on the resources and the fishery by biological and non-biological ecosystem factors need to be recognised. At the most fundamental level, these factors in combination with the biology of the species determine the maximum abundance, or carrying capacity, and productivity of the resources. Changes in the ecosystem can affect both and, where they are occurring, need to be considered by the fisheries manager. Again, these aspects are dealt with by the Code of Conduct. Amongst several references, Paragraph 7.2.3 specifies "States should assess the impacts of environmental factors on target stocks and species belonging to the same ecosystem or associated with or dependent upon the target stocks, and assess the relationship among the populations in the ecosystem." and Paragraph 7.6.9 affirms "States should take appropriate measures to minimize waste, discards, catch by lost or abandoned gear, catch of non-target species, both fish and non-fish species, and negative impacts on associated or dependent species, in particular endangered species.

Technological Considerations

The fishery manager has very little, if any, ability to influence directly the dynamics of the fish populations or communities which support a fishery. In some case, particularly inland waters, there may be opportunities and a desire to undertake stock and habitat enhancement and in some coastal fisheries, habitat destruction may have had an impact on fish production. In the latter case, restoration or stabilization may well be an issue the fisheries manager needs to consider.

However, in most fisheries, the only mechanism the fishery manager has to ensure sustainable utilization of the resources is by regulating the quantity of fish caught, when and where they are caught and the size at which they are caught. This can be done through directly regulating the catch taken, by regulating the amount of effort allowed in the fishery, by specifying closed seasons and closed areas and by regulating the type of gear and fishing methods used. However, there are constraints on how precise the manager can be in setting such regulations.

Catch controls are often difficult to monitor and therefore to implement. It is difficult to estimate fishing effort precisely, and normally improving technology and developing skills result in on-going increases in the efficiency of fishing operations, leading to continuing increases in effective effort, unless steps are actively taken to counter these improvements or their consequences. Fishing gear is rarely strongly selective and bycatch of non-target species or unwanted sizes of target species is frequently a problem. The uncertainties in fisheries management are not just at the level of predicting the status and dynamics of the resources, and uncertainties in the real consequences of implementing fishery measures is also a significant problem to the manager.

A fundamental problem in many fisheries is the existence of too much effort. The presence of excess effort will frequently result in on-going pressure on the fisheries manager to exceed the sustainable fishing mortality on a resource. The social and political pressure to provide employment and opportunities for all those with a stake in the fishery is often hard to resist and readily leads to over-exploitation. The Code of Conduct requires that States take measures to prevent or eliminate excess fishing capacity and such is the global level of concern that the FAO members have agreed on an International Plan of Action (IPOA) for the Management of Fishing Capacity.

Social and Cultural Considerations

Human populations and societies are as dynamic as other biological populations, and social changes take place continuously and on different scales, affected by changes in weather, employment, political circumstances, supply of and demand for fisheries products and other factors. Such changes can affect the appropriateness and effectiveness of management strategies, and therefore need to be considered and accommodated by them. However, again as with biological and technological factors, it can be difficult to identify and quantify the key social and cultural factors influencing fisheries management, generating additional uncertainties for the manager.

A major social constraint in fisheries management is that human societies and behaviour are not easily transformed and fishing families and communities may not be willing to move into other occupations, or away from their normal homes when there is surplus capacity in a fishery, even when their quality of life may be suffering as a result of depleted fish resources. The problem is much worse when there are no other opportunities outside of fisheries in which they could earn a basic living.

Under such circumstances, the political decision to reduce capacity in the fishery is an extremely unattractive option, as the short-term costs of excluding dependent people from the fishery will be much more visible and hence unpopular than a "hands-off" approach which allows the resource and fishery to dwindle in magnitude and quality under sustained excess fishing mortality. Nevertheless, the ecological, economic and social consequences of the latter choice are far more serious in the longer term.

This reluctance or inability to take decisions with serious, immediate social consequences for some has been one of the constraints most responsible for over-fishing around the world.

A key requirement for ensuring that social and cultural considerations are properly considered is to involve the interested parties in fisheries management, keeping them well-informed on the management aspects of the fishery and providing them with the opportunity to express their needs and concerns. The Code of Conduct suggests that "the interests of fishers, including those engaged in subsistence, small-scale and artisanal fisheries are taken into account;" and "Within areas under national jurisdiction, States should seek to identify relevant domestic parties having a legitimate interest in the use and management of fisheries resources and establish arrangements for consulting them to gain their collaboration in achieving responsible fisheries".

The relative balance between social and economic considerations in a fishery will depend on the priority given by the appropriate authority to social objectives and economic objectives.

Social and economic objectives can conflict: for example it is unlikely that maximising economic efficiency and maximising employment could be simultaneously pursued within a given fishery, and attempting to do so will result in conflict. A common example of such conflicts is that between a commercial fleet pursuing essentially economic objectives and an artisanal fleet fulfilling primarily social objectives, with both having an impact on the same stock, and possibly also interfering with each other's fishing operations. It is important for the management authority to have identified such potential conflicts and to have resolved them, identifying and specifying compromise objectives that achieve general support.

Economic Considerations

In a fishery for which sustainable economic efficiency had been specified as the sole benefit to be extracted and in which optimum circumstances prevailed, market forces could be anticipated to lead to the desired objective of economic efficiency. However, in reality such optimum conditions are rarely if ever found and uncertainties and externalities distort the natural selection of market forces.

Uncertainties include unpredictable variability in resources and other sources of imperfect information, and externalities can include the impacts of other fisheries on the target resources (*e.g.* taking them as bycatch), subsidies, trade regulations, fiscal regulations and variability in markets and demand. All of these introduce complexity and additional uncertainty into a fishery and, without proper management, will lead to sub-optimum economic performance. It is important for the management authority to consider the broad economic context of a fishery, including relevant macroeconomic factors. As with social considerations, this requires close consultation with the legitimate users who will be the ones most affected by and sensitive to these issues.

At one extreme, although still very common in fisheries especially in many developing countries, are the problems of open access fisheries, in which anyone is allowed entry into a fishery. Under these circumstances, people will continue to enter the fishery until the benefits from fishing are so low as to be unattractive to prospective new entrants.

How low this is will depend largely on the availability of other options and in many countries, especially developing countries, such alternatives may be extremely scarce. Even where there are reasonable alternatives, the inevitable result of open access fisheries is dissipation of rent leading to very poor economic efficiency and, unless strong and effective management measures are in place and enforced, to over-exploitation of resources. Such circumstances prevail in many fisheries around the world.

Recognizing this most elementary lesson in fisheries management, the Code of Conduct calls for the adoption of "measures to ensure that no vessel (by which should also be understood no shore-based fisher) be allowed to fish unless so authorised..", that "States should ensure that the level of fishing is commensurate with the state of fisheries resources.", and going further than that, that "Where excess fishing capacity exists, mechanisms should be established to reduce capacity to levels commensurate with the sustainable use of fisheries resources so as to ensure that fisheries operate under economic conditions that promote responsible fisheries."

Taken together, these three paragraphs specify that responsible fisheries require limited and authorised access by fishers, where actual and potential effort is appropriate to the productivity of the resource or resources being exploited.

CONSIDERATIONS IMPOSED BY OTHER PARTIES

Some offshore fisheries operate in effective isolation from any other users and the regional fisheries organisations charged with their management may be able to manage the fisheries without needing to consider conflicts with or interference from non-fishery users. However, the bulk of global fishery landings come from coastal waters and for many if not most of the fisheries producing these landings, other users are an important consideration and frequently a constraint.

Other users of the fishing grounds can include, for example, tourism, conservation, oil and gas extraction, offshore mining and shipping, while use of the intertidal and coastal area can include tourism again, aquaculture and mariculture, coastal zone development for housing, business or industry, and agriculture. All of these can impose significant constraints on fishing activities and may be impacted by fishing activities. The manager therefore needs to be aware of such activities and of real or potential impacts in both directions. When developing management strategies and formulating management measures, potential conflicts with other users need to be identified and addressed, and the potential impacts of other users on the efficacy of the management strategy and measures need to be considered. The strategy must be adapted so as to account for and be robust to these impacts.

An unavoidable implication of overlapping interests is that the fishery manager, through the management authority, must ensure that suitable structures and mechanisms are put into place for effective communication and decision-making with representatives of the other users. In addition to reference in Paragraphs 6.8 and 6.9, this is dealt with mainly in Article 10 of the Code of Conduct: Integration of Fisheries into Coastal Area Management, which includes the requirement that: "States should establish mechanisms for cooperation and coordination among national authorities involved in planning, development, conservation and management of coastal areas."

5

Fishery: Aquatic Species

A fishery is an organized effort by humans to catch fish or other aquatic species, an activity known as fishing. Generally, a fishery exists for the purpose of providing human food, although other aims are possible (such as sport or recreational fishing), or obtaining ornamental fish or fish products such as fish oil. Industrial fisheries are fisheries where the catch is not intended for direct human consumption.

Regardless of purpose, however, the term fishery generally refers to a fishing effort centered on either a particular ecoregion or a particular species or type of fish or aquatic animal, and usually fisheries are differentiated by both criteria.

Examples would be the salmon fishery of Alaska, the cod fishery off the Lofoten islands or the tuna fishery of the Eastern Pacific. Most fisheries are marine, rather than freshwater; most marine fisheries are based near the coast. This is not only because harvesting from relatively shallow waters is easier than in the open ocean, but also because fish are much more abundant near the coastal shelf, due to coastal upwelling and the abundance of nutrients available there.

FISHERIES HISTORICALLY

Fisheries have been important parts of human life and food production throughout history. Fish acts as one main food in people's everyday life as well as food security of the nation. Fisheries have become a part of human cultures and mythologies, providing a community identity and a subject for artists throughout the ages. Partially, this is because fisheries are irretrievably wrapped up in humanity's perpetual fascination with the sea, and partially, because they have been a major source of food and income for many communities throughout the ages.

One of the world's longest lasting trade histories is the trade of dry cod from the Lofoten area to the southern parts of Europe, Italy, Spain and Portugal. The trade in cod started during the viking period or before, has been going on for more than 1000 years and is still important.

In India, the Pandyas, a classical Dravidian Tamil kingdom, were known for the pearl fishery as early as the 1st century BC. Their seaport Tuticorin was known for deep sea pearl fishing. The paravas, a Tamil caste centred in Tuticorin, developed a rich community because of their pearl trade, navigation knowledge and fisheries.

FISHERIES IN THE PRESENT DAY

Today, fisheries are estimated to provide 16 per cent of the world population's protein, and that figure is considerably elevated in some developing nations and in regions that depend heavily on the sea. Fisheries are a huge global business and provide income for millions of people. Fisheries have been and continue to be culturally important for many communities as well.

According to the Food and Agriculture Organization of the United Nations, total world capture fisheries production in 2000 was 86 million tons. The top producing countries were, in order, the People's Republic of China (excluding Hong Kong and Taiwan), Peru, Japan, the United States, Chile, Indonesia, Russia, India, Thailand, Norway and Iceland. Those countries accounted for more than half of the world's production; China alone accounted for a third of the world's production. Of that production, over 90 per cent was marine and less than 10 per cent was inland. There are large and important fisheries worldwide for various species of fish, mollusks and crustaceans. However, a very small number of species support the majority of the world's fisheries. Some of these species are herring, cod, anchovy, tuna, flounder, mullet, squid, shrimp, salmon, crab, lobster, oyster and scallops. All except these last four provided a worldwide catch of well over a million tonnes in 1999, with herring and sardines together providing a catch of over 22 million metric tons in 1999. Many other species as well are fished in smaller numbers, both locally and globally.

Methods

Fishing methods vary according to the region, the species being fished for, and the amount of income and technology available to the fisher. A fishery can consist of one man with a small boat hand-casting nets, to a huge fleet of trawlers processing tons of fish per day. Some common commercial techniques today are trawling, seining, driftnetting, handlining, longlining, gillnetting, and diving.

Trawling

Trawling is a method of fishing that involves actively pulling a fishing net through the water behind one or more boats.

Structure of a Trawl Net

When two boats are used (pair trawling), the horizontal spread of the net is provided by the boats, with one warp attached to each boat. However, single-boat trawling is more common. Here, the horizontal spread of the net is provided by trawl doors (also known as "otter boards"). Trawl doors are available in various sizes and shapes and may be specialized to keep in contact with the sea bottom or to remain elevated in the water. In all cases, doors essentially act as wings, using a hydrodynamic shape to provide horizontal spread. As with all wings, the towing vessel must go at a certain speed for the doors to remain standing and functional. This speed varies, but is generally in the range of 2.5-4.0 knots. Nets for trawling in surface waters and for trawling in deep water and over the bottom. Note the "tangles" with all of the marine life caught up in them.

The vertical opening of a trawl net is created using flotation on the upper edge ("floatline") and weight on the lower edge ("footrope") of the net mouth. The configuration of the footrope varies based on the expected bottom shape. The more uneven the bottom, the more robust the footrope configuration must be to prevent net damage.

Environmental Impacts of Trawling

Although trawling today is heavily regulated in some nations, it remains the target of many protests by environmentalists. Environmental concerns related to trawling refer to two areas: a perceived lack of selectivity and the physical damage which the trawl does to the seabed.

Selectivity

Reports of the lack of selectivity of trawling have been present since it started (about the 1600's) and it became used more widely (about 1900). Trawl nets may be non-selective, sweeping up both marketable and undesirable fish and fish of both legal and illegal size. Any part of the catch which cannot be used is considered as by-catch. Size selectivity is controlled by the mesh size of the "cod-end" - the part of the trawl where fish are retained. Fishermen complain that a mesh size which allows undersized fish to escape also allows a proportion of legal-landing sized fish to escape as well. There are a number of "fixes", such as tying a rope around the "cod-end" to prevent the mesh from opening fully, which have been developed to work around technical regulation of size selectivity. One problem is when the mesh gets pulled into narrow diamond shapes (rhombuses) instead of squares.

The capture of undesirable species is a recognized problem with all fishing methods and unites environmentalists, who do not want to see fish killed needlessly and fishermen, who do not want to waste their time sorting unsellable fish from their catch. A number of methods to minimize this have been developed for use in trawling. Bycatch reduction grills or square mesh panels of net can be fitted to parts of the trawl, allowing certain species to escape while retaining others. Trawling for shrimps has specifically been cited as having high levels of bycatch in various parts of the world.

Ecological Damage

Because bottom trawling involves towing heavy fishing gear over the seabed at a speed of several knots, it is destructive to the ocean bottom. The primary sources of impact are the doors, which can weigh several tonnes and create furrows when dragged along the bottom, and the footrope configuration, which usually remains in contact with the bottom across the entire lower edge of the net. Depending on the configuration, the footrope may turn over large rocks or boulders, disturb or damage sessile organisms or rework bottom sediments. Published research has shown that benthic trawling destroys the cold-water coral *Lophelia pertusa*, an important habitat for many deep-sea organisms. The primary focus of dispute over the impact of trawl gear is on the magnitude and duration of these impacts. Opponents of trawl gear argue that the impact of trawl nets is widespread, intense and long-lasting. Defenders of trawl gear maintain that impact is mostly limited and of low intensity compared to natural events.

Pelagic trawling is a much "cleaner" method of fishing, in that the catch usually consists of just one species. However, some cases of it have been attacked for depleting resources which are important sources of food for certain sea birds. An instance of this was the RSPB linking a population crash of sea birds in the North Sea to pelagic fishing for sand eels, which are food for many seabird species. This led to political pressure for the closure of this fishery; the seabird populations subsequently improved. However, a second population crash of seabirds which occurred with no effect on the stocks of sand eel, cast doubt on this link.

Other uses of the Word "Trawl"

The noun "trawl" has many possibly confusing meanings in commercial fisheries. For example, two or more lobster pots that are fished together may be referred to as a trawl. In some older usages "trawling" meant "long-line fishing"; that usage occurs in Rudyard Kipling's book *Captains Courageous*. (This use is perhaps confused with trolling, where a baited line is trailed behind a boat) The word "trawling" has come to be used in a number of non-fishing contexts, usually meaning indiscriminate collection with the intent of picking out the useful bits. For instance, in law enforcement it may refer to collecting large records of telephone calls hoping to find calls made by suspects. The word "trawling" occurs frequently in general literature and is used to mean searching through literature for information more often than it means catching fish.

Hand-line Fishing

Handlining is one of the oldest forms of fishing and is still common. The method consists of a single fishing line with a weight and one or more lure-like hooks are attached. The line is jigged or moved up and down in a series of short movements, most often close to the sea floor. The motion attracts the fish, which are normally caught while trying to eat the lure but also as they move close to jigged the lure. The line is then hauled onboard and the fish removed. Handlining are most often used to catch groundfish and squid but also other species are sometimes caught, including pelagic species.

Long-line fishing

Long-line fishing is a commercial fishing technique that uses hundreds or even thousands of baited hooks hanging from a single line. Swordfish, tuna and Patagonian toothfish are commonly caught by this method. It is also practiced on a smaller scale in New Zealand, where a twenty five hook maximum is prescribed by law.

Longlines can be set to hang near the surface, for instance in tuna fisheries, or on the sea bottom, such as in the Patagonian toothfish fishery.

Long-line fishing is controversial because the lines can lead to significant bycatch, often of endangered species such as sea turtles, petrels and albatrosses. Methods to mitigate such incidental mortality have been developed and successfully implemented in some fisheries.

These include the use of weights to ensure the lines sink quickly, the deployment of streamer lines to scare birds away from the baited hooks as they are deployed, setting lines only at night with ship lighting kept low (to avoid attracting birds), limiting fishing seasons to the southern winter (when most seabirds are not feeding young), and not discharging offal while setting lines.

GILLNET

Gillnetting is a common fishing method used by commercial fishermen of all the oceans. Because gillnets can be so effective their use is closely monitored and regulated by fisheries and enforcement agencies, such as the National Marine Fisheries Service in USA. Mesh size, twine strength, as well as net length and depth are all closely regulated to reduce bycatch of non-target species. Most salmon fisheries in particular have an extremely low incidence of catching non-target species.

History

Gillnetting began with First Nations fishermen using canoes and cedar fibre nets. They would attach stones to the bottom of the nets as weights, and pieces of wood to the top, to use as floats. This allowed the net to suspend straight up and down in the water. Each net would be suspended either from shore or between two boats.

By around 1864, gillnetting had expanded to European, Japanese, and other international fisheries. The boats used by these fisherman were typically around 25 feet long and powered by oars. Many of these boats also had small sails and were called "row-sail" boats. At the beginning of the 1900s, steam powered ships would haul these smaller boats to their fishing grounds and retrieve them at the end of each day. However, at this time gas powered boats were beginning to make their appearance, and by the 1930s, the row-sail boat had virtually disappeared.

In 1931, the first powered drum was created by Laurie Jarelainen. The drum is a circular device that is set to the side of the boat and draws in the nets. The powered drum allowed the nets to be drawn in much faster and along with the faster gas powered boats, fisherman were able to fish in areas they had previously been unable to go into, thereby revolutionizing the fishing industry.

During World War II, navigation and communication devices, as well as many other forms of maritime equipment (ex. depth-sounding and radar) were improved and made more compact. These devices became much more accessible to the average fisherman, thus making their range and mobility increasingly larger. It also served to make the industry much more competitive, as the fisherman were forced to invest more into there boats and equipment in order to stay up to date with the current technology.

This type of net was heavily used by many Japanese, South Korean, and Taiwanese fishing fleets on the high seas in the 1980's. Because of their indiscriminate nature, catching near everything in their path, and lack of regulation as well as a growing concern for the plight of whales and dolphins, gillnets were banned by the United Nations in 1993 in international waters.

DESIRABLE FISH SPECIES FOR CULTURE

The choice of fish species is very important in maximizing production, both in terms of quantity and quality.Since considerable amount of energy is lost in successive trophic levels of the food chain, efficient fish culture always aims at making the chain as short as possible. Because of this, herbivorous fishes are always preferred to carnivorous fishes, the latter being mostly excluded because of their longer food chains. Mixed species farming or polyculture yields a higher production than single species farming.

It is obvious that any single species cannot utilize all the available food in a pond because of its specific feeding habit and hence a combination of compatible species with complementary feeding habits are usually stocked to make better use of the natural food available in the pond. Selection of the species should be based on the productivity of a pond, availability of artificial food resources, availability of seed and the marketing prospects. The principal considerations in species combination are that they have complementary feeding habits, they occupy different ecological niches, they attain marketable size at more or less the same time, they tolerate each other and they be non-predatory in nature. A combination of plankton and macrophyte feeders is most usual. Ungrazed phytoplankton is fed upon by zooplankton and to utilize them, the zooplankton feeders are included in the combination.

The combination of the phytoplankton-feeding silver carp (Hypophthalmichthys molitrix), the zooplankton-feeding bighead carp (Aristichthys nobilis) and the weed-eating grass carp (Ctenopharyngodon idella) is well known in China and Southeast Asia. In India, under composite fish culture, six species of fish *viz.* catla (Catla catla), rohu (Labeo rohita) and mrigal (Cirrhinus mrigala) along with three Chinese carps such as grass carp, silver carp and common carp (Cyprinus carpio) are stocked together so as to utilize most of the fish food organisms present in the pond Other similar combinations may work just as well, but the most important aspect is to try to establish a balance between the species based on the food spectrum of the pond

STOCKING DENSITY

Normally fish production increases with the increase in the number of fish stocked per unit area upto a level and then starts decreasing. Higher stocking density results in increased total production, as there is better utilization of the available food, but in such cases the individual weight and size is reduced. On the other hand, lower stocking density yields larger individual fish.

Proper stocking rate for a pond is that optimum level which results in a given time, usually a year, in a production which is highest in quantity and quality of fish and most profitable. In ponds where no artificial feed is used, the total crop becomes dependent on the primary production and in such cases simply by increasing the stocking density, the increase in the total production is not possible. Even with supplementary feeding the scope of increasing stocking density and fish yield is limited; it increases to an optimum level and then starts decreasing.

Under crowded conditions fish compete for food and space and are stressed due to aggressive interaction. Fish under stress exhibit decreased feed consumption and slow growth and are predisposed to many parasitic and microbial infections. Increase in stocking density simultaneously increases the total oxygen demand with obvious dangers. In undrainable ponds, accumulation of excretory products of the fish population also suppresses their growth rate. With efficient removal of such metabolites by aerating the pond water, the stocking rate can be increased further, thereby enhancing production.

LIVING SPACE

It has been observed that under identical conditions of management levels and stocking density fish grow bigger in larger ponds. In Malaysia, grass carp,

Puntius sp. and monosex Tilapia mossambica grew bigger in ponds of a larger area indicating the living space phenomenon In other words, the rate of production in a 0.2 ha pond will be more than double that of a 0.1 ha pond, despite the fact that the stocking rate per unit area is the same and all other management components including the genotype of the stocking materials and ecological conditions remain the same. The ponds having larger surface area are subjected more often to wind action resulting in greater rate of diffusion of atmospheric oxygen into the water.

Larger ponds have other advantages also, *viz.* better cooling action by wind. In smaller ponds, water tends to stagnate and in hot weather tends to heat up quickly. Though it is preferable to have ponds of a large size, there is a physical limitation. Large ponds are difficult to fill and even more difficult to harvest. There must be an optimum size and shape of the pond to balance size with practicability of management, *i.e.* large enough to allow proper growth of fish, but at the same time small enough to be manageable.

Supplementary Feeding

With the increase in carrying capacity of the pond either by aeration or circulation of water, fish growth can be increased further by supplementing the natural food with some artificial feed. This is the single most important management component for increasing production. In intensive and semi-intensive culture of fishes, supplementary feeding is indispensable. The quantity of feed and the form in which it is offered affect the rate of consumption. Temperature, dissolved oxygen level, crowding and health condition, etc., affect the rate of food consumption.

POND FERTILITY

Organic matter and mineral constituents of the pond soil supply the required nutrients for chemical and biochemical production processes. The pond bottom also provides a suitable environment for the decomposers like bacteria and fungi to mineralise organic components of the pond sediment and release soluble nutrients. Sometimes such nutrients are not available in sufficient quantity in the pond and hence they are added from outside in the form of fertilizers.

Since plankton production is often limited by inadequate quantity of phosphorus which is essential for the assimilation of nitrogen into cellular matter, phosphatic fertilizers are widely used in fish culture. Unlike phosphorus, availability of nitrogen does not depend on the inherent status of soil, since it is brought to the soil by different processes.

Nitrogen fixation by azotobacteria, blue-green algae, atmospheric electric discharges and photochemical fixation are some of the potential sources of pond nitrogen. In a tropical climate, the fixation of atmospheric nitrogen by blue-green algae is of considerable importance. However, when nitrogen is added from outside, its form, *viz.*, ammoniacal or nitrate is also very important. It is advisable to use the ammoniacal form of nitrogen in acid and neutral soils and the nitrate form in alkaline soil.

Though there is a considerable loss of nitrogen from the ammoniacal form in alkaline soil, the use of ammonium sulphate in low doses is usually recommended, keeping in view the role of sulphate in reducing the soil alkalinity. Potassium is the other essential nutrient for plant growth.

In ponds it is easily available both in soil and water and does not form insoluble salts and is rarely deficient except in acid peaty soil. Yet, a little potassium when added to the pond, stimulates the production of plankton.

Organic matter of the pond sediment is also an essential factor regulating the bacterial activity. In this context, the ratio of organic carbon to total nitrogen (C/N ratio) is important. Periodic application of organic manures ensures to a certain extent replenishment of nutrients and also provides an energy base for bacterial activities. Apart from this, the organic matter and the bacterial flora are also directly consumed by zooplankton and some fish species.

DISEASES AND THEIR CONTROL

Various intensification approaches such as increased stocking rates, increased feeding, fertilization programmes, etc., sometimes result in nutrient accumulation, frequent appearance of algal blooms, dissolved oxygen deficiency and other water quality problems in undrainable ponds. As a result of such water quality and environmental problems, the infectious diseases and their control assume importance.

A fish farming system is unique in that the farmed animal is poikilothermic and lives in water where respiratory oxygen level compared to air is limited and becomes critical at times. Further, metabolic waste products, left-out feed materials and organic load of the pond bottom can affect certain exposed vital organs and tissues of fish. All such factors affect fish health and contribute to the risk of disease outbreaks.

The above basic facts need careful consideration while planning for freshwater pond fish culture. The habitat of an undrainable pond is very varied and dynamic, but can be monitored and managed for increasing fish production.

FISH SPECIES

There are around 50 species of fish found for at least part of their lives in the freshwaters of the British Isles. This is quite a small number of species considering the diversity of the aquatic habitats available to them and the number of species in similar waters in continental Europe. Although many of the species are native to the British Isles, there are also many that have been successfully introduced over the centuries. Some of these have settled and become well established and are now generally considered ' native ', for example the carp. Some, however, still raise concerns among conservationists about the potential impact they may have, should they become more widespread; the zander and wels catfish for example, are described as ' non - native ' and are subject to regulation.

Fish species have developed and evolved to make the best use of certain habitats. Many of the species present in the British Isles are especially developed to live in rivers. These species are usually unsuited to living in still - waters as they are not adapted to this very different type of habitat. In this chapter we will concentrate on those species already adapted to the still - water, and those that are commonly stocked in still - waters with apparent success, such as the chub. The barbel has been included, as it is stocked commonly in still - waters, but it should be borne in mind that special conditions must be maintained for this species owing to its requirement for clear, oxygen - rich water.

This chapter sets out some detailed information about each species, which should allow fishery managers to understand better the species under their custody. The ecology of lakes, should allow the manager to establish the best conditions for the fish species and assess any other species for likely success in any given situation.

Cyprinidae

The barbel is a large river fish with a long, streamlined, slightly flattened body. The juveniles are an overall brown colour but as they get larger they develop a dark brown back with golden bronze flanks and a creamy white underbelly. Adults generally grow to around 70 cm, but can get up to 90 cm and weigh in excess of 6 kg (the British rod - caught record 2008 is 9.837 kg). The barbel is native to the southern UK and mainland Europe. It is widespread and relatively common.

The barbel will generally mature after 3 - 5 years. Spawning takes place once a year in the late spring, usually May - July. Barbel spawn in small groups among gravel and stones in fast - flowing rivers. The adhesive eggs stay within the gravel bed until they hatch 10 - 15 days later. The fry tend to congregate in slow flowing areas where they feed on zooplank-ton. As they mature and get larger they tend to move out into the main flow of the river, feeding on invertebrates and even small fish in among clean gravel and associated vegetation.

The barbel is a very popular coarse fish, being one of the most sought - after river fish. They are a hard fighting fish that can grow very large, attracting specialist anglers.

Barbel have increasingly been stocked in still - waters over several years. They appear to grow and survive reasonably well, but there is little evidence that they can successfully spawn in most still - waters. It is vital that any stocking is with barbel obtained from a reputable fish farm. Barbel can sometimes be introduced from fish poached from the wild. Not only is this very harmful to the wild populations but evidence suggests that these fish find it very difficult to make the transition from rivers to still - waters. Generally barbel should not be stocked in shallow still - waters with a predominance of bottom feeders such as carp.

Common Bream (Abramis brama)

The common bream is a large, bottom - feeding species with a deep thin body. When young it is a very silvery fish, but as it matures it becomes darker and more golden brown to green. It can grow to nearly a metre in length and weigh up to 8 kg (the British rod - caught record 2008 is 8.329 kg). The common bream is native to the UK and central Europe where it is widespread and common. It is a popular food fish in eastern Europe.

Bream generally mature after 4 years. Spawning takes place in May and June in dense vegetation in shallow water. The males develop white bumps (tubercles) over the body surface and become territorial. The females spawn at night in large groups and their sticky eggs attach to the vegetation. After 5 – 10 days the eggs hatch. The fry start by feeding on zooplankton such as rotifers and then larger zooplankton such as daphnia. They quickly move on to their normal adult diet of benthic invertebrates, preferentially worms, molluscs and insect larvae such as chironomid midge larvae. The adults feed by using their extendable tubular mouth to root around in the pond bottom, taking large mouthfuls and ' winnowing ' out the food items. They are strongly shoaling fish from larval fry to late adulthood. Some of the very large individuals appear to be solitary or in small shoals.

The common bream is one of the most popular of the coarse fish. It responds well to anglers ' baits and is readily caught. It grows quickly to a good size and survives well in many different conditions. As a bottom feeder it will disturb the bottom of the pond, causing suspended solids to cloud the water column. They are good in a mixed silver - fish population. The common bream should not be mixed with large numbers of carp as the species compete for the same food source.

The silver bream is a small mid - water species, with a deep, compressed body. When young it is a very silvery fish but as it matures its back becomes a darker olive/grey, although it still retains a very silvery look. Its maximum size is around 20 – 25 cm in length (the British rod - caught record 2008 is 0.425 kg). The silver bream is native to England, central and northern Europe, where it widespread and reasonably common. In England it is generally restricted to the southeast but is becoming more widespread. Silver bream mature at around 3 – 4 years old. Spawning takes place in May – July in dense vegetation in shallow water. They spawn in groups early in the morning, scattering their sticky eggs among the submerged weeds. The eggs hatch in 4 – 8 days and begin feeding on small planktonic invertebrates, moving to larger invertebrates and plant material as they grow. Silver bream form strong shoals with individuals of a similar size and age throughout their lives. The silver bream is not a popular species for anglers, largely because it is commonly mistaken for a small common bream. Indeed it is very similar to a common bream of the same size, except the silver bream is slightly thicker in the body and has larger scales. They do make useful additions to a lake as they feed in a very different manner.

The carp is a large, bottom - feeding species with a thickset rounded body. They are usually a dark olive brown on the back, lightening to a light yellowish brown on the belly. It can grow to very large sizes, sometimes exceeding 1 m in length (the British rod - caught record 2008 is 26.9 kg). The carp is native to eastern Europe and Asia, but has now achieved worldwide distribution. It is very widespread and common in the UK, where it was first introduced in the nineteenth century.

Carp mature after 2 – 3 years. Spawning takes place in June to July in dense vegetation on the margins of the water body. The males develop small white lumps (tubercles) on the flanks and head. The females spawn at dawn and the sticky eggs attach to the weed. The eggs will hatch after 5 – 7 days and the fry start feeding on zooplankton, particularly rotifers. They quickly move to feeding on the bottom - dwelling invertebrates that make up the bulk of their diet. Their mouth is well designed for this feeding technique, being protrusible. However, carp are a very adaptable species and they can often be seen feeding on invertebrates on marginal vegetation and even off the surface. They tend to move around in small shoals of similar - sized individuals. The carp is probably the most popular species for anglers on still - waters. It grows quickly to very large sizes and responds well to a variety of anglers ' baits. It is a very adaptable species so can survive and thrive in many different conditions. As a bottom feeder, it will disturb the sediment on the bottom of the water body, causing suspended solids to cloud the water.

Carp have been bred for food over many centuries and it is one of the main global species for aquaculture in ponds. This has led to several different varieties of carp being commonly found. The most obvious of these varieties is the common carp, which is the fully scaled type. Mirror carp were bred to make it easier to remove the scales before cooking. Ornamental varieties are also common, from full - colour varieties, known as koi, to slightly gold - tinged cross breeds known as ghost carp. These are all the same species of fish, however.

The chub is a large, mid - water and surface - feeding fish with a rounded, streamlined body. When young it is a very silvery fish with an olive green back;

as it gets larger its upper body darkens to a steel grey colour but retains the silvery flanks and belly. It is a large fish, attaining sizes of between 40 and 50 cm, rarely getting to up to 80 cm (the British rod - caught record 2008 is 3.9 kg). The chub is native to the UK and central Europe and is widespread and common. It is caught for food in some parts of Europe. Chub generally mature after 3 – 4 years. Spawning takes place during April – June among clean gravel and stones in flowing water. They spawn in the early morning in small groups of one female with several males in attendance. The eggs hatch within 6 – 8 days and start to feed on benthic invertebrates. As they grow older their diet changes to include larger invertebrates, fruit, vegetation and even small fish. When young, chub move around in shoals but as they mature they become much more solitary and even appear to be somewhat territorial. In rivers they migrate significant distances to feeding and spawning areas. Little is known about their activities in still - waters.

The chub is a popular fish among anglers because it is a large, hard - fighting fish that responds well to anglers ' baits. It grows quickly to a good size and appears to do very well in still - waters. Current evidence suggests that it does not successfully spawn in most still -waters, although it does spawn in large, clear - water lakes.

The crucian carp is a medium - sized, deep - bodied fish with marked lateral compression. Young fish are a golden bronze colour, which turns darker as they get older, with mature specimens being olive brown on the back through deep bronze on the flanks to a golden yellow on the belly. Adults can attain 20 – 30 cm in length and 1.5 kg in weight, although many crucian carp populations remain ' stunted ' with the mature adults rarely getting more than 15 – 20 cm and 0.5 kg (the British rod - caught record 2008 is 2.01 kg). The crucian carp is native to the UK, Europe and central Asia. There is some argument about whether it is a native to the UK and western Europe, but there seems little evidence to suggest it is introduced into these areas, where it is widespread.

Crucian carp generally mature after 2 – 3 years. Spawning takes place in May – June in shallow water, in thick vegetation. The fish shed sticky eggs onto the vegetation where they take between 5 and 7 days to hatch, depending on the vegetation. Once hatched, and after the yolk sac has been used, the fry tend to form loose shoals and feed on small zooplankton. As they grow they start to feed mainly on invertebrates, such as molluscs and worms on the bottom of the pond, as well as plant material. Both the juveniles and the adults tend to live in loose shoals. They tend to occupy the mid - water and bottom of still - waters. Crucian carp prefer still - waters and particularly thrive in rich, lowland still - waters with abundant vegetation. Crucian carp have a remarkable ability to survive very low dissolved oxygen situations for long periods, leading to situations where they are often the only fish species to survive. Here they form healthy populations dominated by small ' stunted ' individuals. In larger waters they can grow much larger and seem to adopt a slightly different body shape. This is a very popular angling species and is readily caught. It survives well in well -managed fisheries dominated by silver fish, but it is generally unsuitable for stocking in waters dominated by common carp. Crucians readily hybridise with goldfish and common carp. They are then displaced by the vigorous hybrid. They are also threatened by the non - native parasitic tapeworm *Bothriocephalus acheilognathi*. The goldfish is a medium – sized mid - water species with a relatively deep and laterally compressed body. Wild goldfish are a deep brown colour throughout their lives, although there are many colour variants from deep orange through to almost white. Adults can get to around 30 cm and 1 kg in size. The goldfish is native to Asia, but owing to its ornamental value it has achieved worldwide distribution, being found on most continents. It is an introduced species in the UK. Goldfish generally mature after 2 – 3 years. Spawning takes place during June and July in thick weed in the shallow margins. The eggs hatch in 4 – 7 days, depending on the water temperature, and the young feed on zooplankton. As they grow, the diet changes to small invertebrates and plant material. Goldfish tend to form loose shoals and prefer shallow, rich ponds with abundant vegetation. They are a hardy species, however, and appear to thrive in most still - water conditions.

The goldfish has become increasingly common in still - waters in the UK and Europe. It is apparently popular with some fishermen. Goldfish readily hybridise with common carp and crucian carp, producing vigorous offspring that can successfully outcompete the original parent stock. Stocking with goldfish or hybrid strains is advised against.

The grass carp is a large mid - water feeding species with a solid, rounded body. It has a dark blue - black back, shading to silver on the belly. It can grow quite large, with adults reaching up to 100 cm in length (the British rod - caught record 2008 is 20.185 kg). Grass carp are originally from Asia, but have been widely distributed around the world as a method of weed control. They were introduced into England in the 1960s to control weed growth in some still - waters. Since then they have become widely distributed, but because of their specialised breeding requirements there appear to be no breeding populations.

Grass carp mature after 3 – 4 years. Spawning takes place in fast - flowing water in the headwaters of large rivers. Temperatures must be around 23 – 25 ° C.

The eggs are unusual in that they are pelagic, being carried down river in mid - water until they hatch in the slower flows downstream. The fry start by feeding on small invertebrates, but as they get older they begin to feed on aquatic plants. Grass carp form loose shoals throughout their lives. Grass carp are not particularly popular among anglers as they are generally difficult to catch and do not fight as hard as their size might suggest. They are not very effective in controlling weed growth as they do not feed until the waters are quite warm.

The gudgeon is a small, rounded, bottom - dwelling fish. Its back is a dark olive green to brown with lighter flanks and a silvery belly. It has dark markings along the flank and upper body. It is a very small fish, rarely reaching over 15 cm although it can grow to about 20 cm. (the British rod - caught record 2008 is 0.141 kg). Gudgeon are widely distributed throughout Europe and Asia and they are native to the UK. Gudgeon mature at between 2 and 3 years old. They will spawn on stony or gravely bottoms, or among weed, and prefer flowing water, although they will spawn successfully in still - waters. They spawn during May or June and the eggs hatch in around 15 days. They feed on insects, molluscs, crustaceans and occasionally plant material. They are generally a solitary fish, but sometimes form into small shoals of perhaps a dozen individuals. The gudgeon is not a popular target species for anglers, but it does do well in some still -waters where it probably makes an important contribution to the health of the lake.

The minnow is a small mid - water species with a long rounded body. It has a brown - gold body with numerous brown and black spots down the flanks usually joining to form an obvious black line along the body. It is a small fish, rarely exceeding 10 cm in length (the British rod - caught record 2008 is 0.135 kg). The minnow is a native to the UK, Europe and Asia where it is very widespread and common.

Minnows mature after 1 – 2 years. Spawning takes place in June or July, usually over clean stones or gravels. The males particularly become more colourful during spawning, with a scarlet belly and black throat. The eggs take 5 – 10 days to hatch and immediately start feeding on small invertebrates. As they grow they continue to feed on a variety of invertebrates. Minnows generally aggregate into small, loose shoals. The minnow is not a target fish for anglers, although it can be important as a bait fish. It does well in lakes and ponds and can be a very useful addition to the lake ecology, particularly if predatory fish are present.

The orfe is a large, mid - water and surface - feeding fish with a rounded, streamlined body. When young it is a very silvery fish, but as it gets larger its upper body darkens to a brownish grey colour.

Coloured ornamental varieties are common, particularly golden and blue orfe. It is a medium - sized fish, attaining sizes of between 30 and 40 cm, although it can occasionally get up to 80 cm. (the British rod - caught record 2008 is 3.7 kg). The orfe is native to central and eastern Europe and parts of Asia, where it is widespread and common. It is caught for food in some parts of Russia. It was introduced into England and is now widespread and common.

Orfe generally mature after 3 – 4 years. Spawning takes place during April and May, among weeds and clean stones in shallow water. The eggs hatch within 15 – 20 days and start to feed on benthic invertebrates. As they grow older their diet changes to include larger invertebrates, although they will take fruit, vegetation and even small fish. Orfe move around in shoals of similar - sized and aged individuals. They are found equally in rivers and still - waters. The orfe is a popular fish among anglers because it is a good - sized, hard fighting fish that responds well to anglers ' baits. It grows quickly, to a good size and it appears to do very well in still - waters.

The roach is medium - sized, mid - water fish with a relatively deep body. The young fish are silvery, but they quickly develop a dark blue – green back and light underside. Adults generally get to 20 – 40 cm and between 1 and 2 kg (the British rod - caught record 2008 is 1.899 kg). The roach is native to the UK and Europe, where it is very widespread and common throughout the lowland catchments. Roach generally mature after 2 or 3 years. Spawning takes place once a year in the middle of spring, usually April – June. The roach spawn at dawn, shedding their sticky eggs on dense, submerged vegetation in the shallow areas of the lake. The eggs will hatch in 5 – 10 days. Once the yolk sac is used, the fry will feed on zooplankton and other small invertebrates. The juveniles prefer to live in large shoals in the shallow, marginal areas with plenty of vegetation, which provide cover and food. As they mature and get larger they move out into open water, shoaling in smaller groups of similar - sized individuals. These larger individuals feed on larger benthic invertebrates and pondweed, particularly attached algae (periphyton). They tend to occupy the mid - water to bottom of the pond.

The roach is one of the most popular coarse fish in the UK. It responds well to anglers ' bait and is readily caught. It grows steadily and survives well in many different conditions. It is an excellent species in any mixed fishery as it is very adaptable. In the right conditions, it can quickly overpopulate with a very large population of small fish.

The rudd is a medium - sized, top - feeding species, with a deep, laterally compressed body. It has a dark greenish - brown back, grading through to a silvery underside. The flanks are golden brown. The iris is a deep gold with a red fleck on the upper side. The fins are normally a bright red. It can grow to 20 – 25 cm and 0.5 – 1 kg (the British rod - caught record 2008 is 2.1 kg). The rudd is native to the UK and central Europe, where it is very widespread and common.

Rudd generally mature at 2 – 4 years and live to 10 – 14 years. They spawn in late spring, usually from April to July. Rudd spawn by shedding their eggs on submerged vegetation around the margins. The eggs hatch in around 5 – 10 days and the fry stay within the protection of the vegetation, feeding on small zooplankton. As they grow they form compact shoals, feeding on the surface and in midwater. They prefer zooplankton, weed - dwelling invertebrates and terrestrial insects on the surface. Rudd appear always to spend their time in fairly compact shoals, no matter how large they get.

The rudd is a popular fish to catch, being attractive and readily taking bait, which is particularly important if other species are more reluctant to feed on anglers ' bait. It grows steadily but rarely attains large sizes. It is a very good fish for a mixed fishery, as it does not compete directly with any other fish species. The tench is a large, bottom - feeding species, with a thickset, slightly laterally compressed body. The tench is a beautiful olive to dark green throughout its life, with small orange to red eyes. Adults generally grow slowly to a maximum length of 60 – 70 cm and can weigh up to 7 kg. (the British rod - caught record 2008 is 6.9 kg). The tench is native to the UK and Europe, although absent from the northern parts of both. The species has been widely introduced into Asia and North America.

Tench generally mature at 3 – 4 years old. Owing to their slow growth, they may only be 15 cm at this age. Spawning takes place once a year in spring, usually between May and July. They spawn among aquatic plants in shallow waters, to which their sticky eggs attach. The eggs will hatch in 4 – 5 days, and once the yolk sac is used the fry will feed on zooplank-ton, before switching to grazing among the bottom of water plants on a variety of aquatic invertebrates and attached algae. Tench prefer still - waters, or very slow flowing rivers with an abundance of macrophytes. The juveniles may form loose shoals, but as they mature they become more solitary, almost appearing to have preferred territories.

The tench is one of the most popular and easily recognisable of the coarse fish in the UK and Europe. Its popularity relates to its size and its beauty. It is generally a difficult fish to catch on rod and line. It is quite adaptable to a mixed fishery, but does not thrive in waters without good communities of aquatic macrophytes. The pike is a large predatory fish, with a slim streamlined body and a large head with an enormous mouth full of teeth. It has a dark green, mottled back, grading through light green flanks to a creamy yellow underbelly. It is a very large fish, routinely growing to 50 – 100 cm and occasionally 140 cm and 30 kg (the British rod - caught record 2008 is 21.2 kg). The pike is widespread and abundant throughout the Northern Hemisphere in Europe, Asia and North America. It is a popular food fish wherever it is found.

Pike generally mature after 3 – 4 years, the males earlier and smaller than the females. They spawn among weed during February – May. The eggs attach to the weed and hatch after 10 – 15 days. When they hatch they start by feeding on invertebrates but quickly turn to small fish and then onto larger prey, including other vertebrates such as ducks and water rats. They are very partial to other pike and are, unsurprisingly, very solitary and territorial. It appears that females grow much larger than males, and it is said that any pike over 5 kg will be a female. They are an ambush predator, laying in wait for their prey and only striking at the very last minute when the prey is within one to two body lengths. The pike is one of the most popular freshwater fish in the UK. It grows exceptionally quickly to a large size and is a ferocious fighter, particular in the first moments as it attacks the bait.

Percidae

The ruffe is a small fish with an obvious spiny dorsal fin, large eyes and mouth. Its back is a dark green - brown colour with irregular dark blotches, whereas its underside is pale yellow to cream in colour. It usually grows to around 15 cm but can exceptionally grow to 25 cm (the British rod - caught record 2008 is 0.142 kg). The ruffe is native to much of Europe but was confined to eastern England, although its range has spread considerably in recent decades.

The ruffe matures after 1 to 2 years. They spawn in shallow water among stones and vegetation, mainly in April to May, although they probably spawn several times in a year. Initially the fry grow quickly on a diet of small invertebrates before moving on to larger invertebrates and other food such as fish eggs and young fry. The ruffe is a shoaling fish, moving around in groups throughout its life.

The ruffe is not a popular fish for anglers, being such a small size and attacking baits destined for other larger target species. It has numerous alternative common names such as pope, tommy and daddie.

Perch (Perca fluviatilis)

The perch is a beautiful, deep - bodied fish with four to six dark bands over olive - green flanks. The abdomen is creamy silver with prominent red pelvic and anal fins. It can grow to 20 – 40 cm and weigh 1 – 2.5 kg (the British rod - caught record 2008 is 2.523 kg). The perch is native to the UK and Europe and is now widespread and common in the UK, northern Europe and Asia. It is a popular food fish in many countries; in England it used to be canned and sold as ' perchines '. Perch generally mature after 3 – 4 years and live to around 10 years.

They spawn in early spring, usually March to May. Perch tend to spawn in the margins, producing long strings of eggs which lie wrapped around submerged vegetation. The eggs hatch after 10 days and the juveniles feed on small invertebrates as well as fish fry, including other perch fry. As they get older they start to feed on larger invertebrates and begin to feed actively on other fish. Small perch shoal in groups but as they get bigger they do become more solitary, with large individuals tending to move around in small shoals of just a few individuals.

The perch is a popular fish for coarse fisherman, being one of the most attractive of the freshwater fish species. It responds well to anglers ' baits and is readily caught. As a predator it is a useful fish to control the populations of other fish species. However, they can mature at a very small size (10 – 15cm) and in certain circumstances they can create an abundance of small perch. It appears that perch only grow to a large size where there is a plentiful supply of small prey fish.

Zander (Sander lucioperca)

The zander is a large predatory species with a long, thick body. The back is a dark brown – green with obvious dark brown vertical stripes running to the middle of the body. It grows quite large, reaching average sizes of 50 – 70cm, occasionally much bigger to a maximum of 120 cm (the British rod - caught record 2008 is 8.7 kg). The zander is common throughout Europe. It was deliberately introduced into England (the River Great Ouse) in 1963 and has spread widely since.

Zander generally mature after 3 – 5 years. Spawning takes place from April to June in among marginal vegetation. Pairs of fish spawn together at dawn and lay sticky eggs on vegetation and stones on the bottom. Unusually, both parents will guard the eggs until they hatch 5 – 10 days after spawning. The fry start on a diet of invertebrates but move quickly on to eat mainly of other fish. The zander is a hunter, patrolling open waters and chasing down small prey fish. Occasionally it appears to hunt as a group, although it mainly hunts as an individual.

The zander is a very popular fish with anglers, being a fast - growing, large and aggressive fish. It survives well in larger, clear still - waters and may be a useful addition to a specimen water as it prefers small fish as prey. Licences are required to stock this species.

Gasterosteidae

Three - s pined s tickleback *(Gasterosteus aculeatus)*

The stickleback is one of the most common and recognisable species in freshwaters. It is a small, thin - bodied fish with an olive - brown back and silvery sides and underside. The body is covered in large bony plates and there are three obvious strong spines on the back. The stickleback is a very small fish that rarely exceeds 10 cm in length (the British rod -caught record 2008 is 7 g (0.007 kg)). Sticklebacks are widely distributed and common throughout Europe.

Sticklebacks mature after 1 – 2 years. Spawning takes place in March – June. They are unusual in that the male builds a nest of fibrous plant material and attracts females to spawn within it. The male also develops a vivid red throat to help attract a mate.

The eggs take 10 – 20 days to hatch and are guarded constantly by the male. This guarding behaviour continues until the fry are a few weeks old. The fry feed on small invertebrates. As they get older they continue to feed on invertebrates but may extend their diet to include fish fry. Sticklebacks tend to aggregate into small shoals, only becoming solitary and territorial during spawning times. The stickleback is not a target species for anglers. It is common in most still - waters and will almost certainly appear without help.

Nine - s pined s tickleback *(Pungitius p ungitius)*

This is a rare species. It is similar in most respects to the three - spined stickleback, except that it has 7 – 12 spines running along its back. It also goes dark with a black throat when in breeding condition.

DIVERSIFIED FISH SPECIES BREEDING

Like major carps, both endemic and exotic in nature, breeding techniques of few important minor carps, catfishes/perches as well as shell fishes have been developed and seeds are available commercially in many parts of this country and in the world. The easy availability of stocking material is always considered important for successful culture of any fish species. Though the collection of natural seed for the purpose may be an alternative, it is not sustainable for intensive culture. So the seed production in hatchery will be the only alternative for obtaining optimum quantities of seed for the purpose through induced breeding operations. The injection of different inducing agents in fish breeding is adopted for successful ovulation and collection of eggs in different cultivable fish species.

USE OF MINOR ENDEMIC CARP IN AQUACULTURE

Some other minor endemic carps like L. bata, C. reba and L. gonius are also most suitable species which can easily be cultured in all sorts of ponds to support additional income to the farmers. In the recent past, the natural stock of these species has become threatened by habitat destruction etc, which is likely to cause a gradual loss of genetic diversity. The availability of hatchery-produced seed of these species for farming is a major trust area of aquaculture activity.

Table. Endemic Diversified Species in Culture in India

Family	Species	Common name	Local name
Cyprinidae	Labeo rohita	Rohu	Ruhu
	Catla catla	Catla	Katla
	Cirrhinus mrigala	Mrigal	Mrigal
	Cirrhinus reba	Reba	Laachu, Bhangan
	Labeo calbasu	Calbashu	Kalibaush
	Labeo bata	Bata	Bata
	Labeo boga	Boga labeo	Bhangan
	Labeo gonius	Gonius	Gonnia
	Labeo nandina	Nandina labeo	Nandil
	Bengala elonga	Bengala barb	Along
	Puntius sarana	Barb	Sarpunti
	Tor tor	Tot mahseer	
	Tor putitora	Putitor mahseer	Mahashoal

Table. Exotic Fishes in culture in India

Species	Common name	Status	Seed production
Ctenopharyngodon idellus	Grass carp	In poly culture	Seed produced in hatchery produced seed
Hypophthalmichthys molitrix	Silver carp	Do	Do
Aristichthys nobilis	Bighead carp	Do	Do
Cyprinus carpio var. communis	Scale carp	Do	Do
Cyprinus carpio var. specularis	Mirror carp	Do	Do
Cyprinus carpio var. nudus	Common carp	Do	Do
Barbodes gonionotus	Silver barb	Do	Do
Pangasius sutchi	Pangus	In poly and monoculture	Do
Clarias gariepinus	African magur	In monoculture	Do
Piaractus brachypomus	Pacu	Do	Do

Table. Development of Artificial Propagation Techniques for Minor Carps etc.

Species	Preliminary dose (PG mg/kg)	Interval between two doses (hours)	Decisive dose (PG mg/kg)	Ovulation (hours)	Hatching (hours)
Labeo calbasu	Female 2.0	6	Female 6.0 Male 2.0	6–7	18–20
Labeo gonius	Female 2.0	6	Female 5.0 Male 2.0	7–8	16–18
Labeo bata	Female 1.0	6	Female 5.0 Male 1.0	7–8	16–18
Cirrhinus ariza/reba	Female 1.0	6	Female 5.0 Male 1.0	7–8	14–16
Puntius sarana	-	6	Female 5.0 Male 2.0	6–7	14–16
Tor putitora	No requirement of hormone injection. Water flushing during spawning season induce female to be ripe which are stripped to collect ripe eggs.				72 -80

BREEDING MINOR CARPS

C. REBA (REBA)

C. reba is a bottom feeding omnivore although the young feed voraciously on zooplankton and grow very quickly, even faster than the young of catla and mrigal. C. reba does not spawn in ponds even though they attain full maturity there. Currently, C. reba is considered as 'vulnerable in natural waters' due to a decline in its abundance, extent of occurrence, area of occupancy and habitat.

Recently, C. reba has drawn attention as one of the potential new candidate species for aquaculture and captive breeding. C. reba is an annual breeder with a single spawning period restricted to south-west monsoons extending from May to July in Assam and Bangladesh, and June to August with a peak in June in West Bengal.

The shallow waters affording the optimum range of temperature (approx. 28-30 C) may be a factor that induces the fish to spawn. The average fecundity was 420,000. The average diameter of eggs was 2.24 mm and average weight was 0.0042 mg.

LABEO BATA

Labeo bata, locally called as ilish bata, bhangon bata or bata, is one of them belonging to the Family Cyprinidae. It is a non-migratory fish and remains in one habitat throughout its life. The fish matures during monsoon season (April to July) in NE region and attends first maturity at 18.62 cm in total length.It breeds in floodplains during rainy season as Indian major carps. It spawns from May to July in at the range of water temperature 26.2–30.3^{o}C.

LABEO GONIUS

Inhabits rivers. Spawns during the southwest monsoon. Does not normally breed in ponds. Artificial breeding done through hypophysation. Cultured in ponds along with other carp species.

BREEDING OF SARPUTI (PUNTIUS SARANA)

Puntius sarana locally known as Sar Punti is widely distributed fish found in India. P. sarana is a freshwater fish common in ponds and rivers, prefers shallow waters of floodplains for breeding, column-bottom dwelling nature and omnivorous in feeding habit, have good consumer demand as food fish for its high biological value.

It is a profilic breeder and breeds during monsoon. In July and August it spawns in shallow water. However, poor survival of egg and larvae were noticed. Like many commercially important indigenous fish species P. sarana also needs urgent attention from conservation angles, as the population of this commercially important species is reported to be in drastic decline. Artificial propagation of seed of this commercially important fish species was done using Ovaprim @ 1 ml/kg weight of both male and female fish as an inducing agent with success.

It was also found that a dose fish PG of 5 mg/kg to 6 mg/kg body weight of female was suitable for breeding.

INDUCED SPAWNING OF THAI PUTI (PUNTIUS GONIONOTUS)

Thai puti is an exotic species which breeds normally in streams and rivers like most tropical cyprinids. They can also breed in captivity like pond and tank water. Their breeding season starts from April and lasts till August. The natural source provides a negligible amount of fish seed because of higher mortality rate, mixture of cultivable and non- cultivable species and shrinkage of spawning ground which impede the extension and expansion of fish culture.

After the first attempt of induced spawning in early thirties this technique had been successfully tried in many countries of the world. The best ovulation, fertilization, hatching and survivability rates were achieved under higher dose of PG as used @2.00–5.00 mg/kg body weight 2 mg/kg weight of fish in first injection and 4 mg/kg in second injection) were found to be most effective for induced spawning of P. gonionotus. Slightly higher dose of hormone was required at the beginning and latter part of the spawning season and comparatively lower dose was required at the middle of the breeding season.

CAT/AIR BREATHING FISH BREEDING

Important cultured species are:

- Clarias batrachus
- Heteropneustes fossilis
- Anabas testudineus
- Pangasius sutchi
- Ompok spp.

ASIAN CATFISH (CLARIAS BATRACHUS)

Asian catfish, Clarias batrachus, is considered as a potential aquaculture species in Indian subcontinent. The Asian cat fish, locally known as Magur fish, is an important air-breathing cat fish with good markets especially in North-Eastern parts of India where it fetches a higher price than the major carps. The scarcity of marketable fish as well as seed from the natural ground has been felt in this catfish.

The potential to obtain magur seed from natural sources has become low due to the increasing use of pesticides in the paddy fields-which are the main breeding grounds of this fish. The breeding performance is an important parameter to evaluate the breeding success in captive condition, which depends on the type of hormone used and its potency, dose of hormone and maturity status of the fish Human chorionic gonadotropin (HCG) at 14–23 h latency in combination with 3000–4000 IU HCG dose is one among them and is reported successful in catfish during induced ovulation. Appropriate combinations of the proper dose of inducing agent and stripping time always yield maximum egg output during induced breeding. A single injection of 0.6ml/kg body weight of ovaprim was the most effective. The males were given a single dose of 0.1–0.2 ml/kg body weight.

Again administration of fish PG of dosage varied from 12 to 30 mg/kg weight of fish given in two doses, a provocative dose of 5–10 mg/kg and a final dose of 8–20 mg/kg and 5–6 hours interval was found successful in spawning. In hapa nursing of magur, we achieved an average survival of 51 per cent while feeding with rice bran and mustard oil cake mixture at 1:1 ratio and termite twice daily. Before the female are stripped male fish with gravid testis are to be sacrificed, and testes are taken out and macerated in normal saline (0.9 per cent NaCl). The spermatozoa become inactive in this medium and this extract can be maintained for few hours in refrigerator. After 16 hours of latency period female fish is stripped and ova are collected in to dry enamel tray. Before fertilization milt (spermatozoa) extract medium is activated by addition of fresh water. Sperms become active and motility of sperms can be confirmed in microscope. Sperm preparation thus obtained will be sufficient to fertilize the ova stripped from 2 females. Sperm extract is sprinkled over the ova and gametes are mixed gently with bird feathers and allowed to 2 to 3 minutes for fertilization. After repeated washing with fresh water fertilized eggs are transferred to hatching trays for incubation.

FLOW THROUGH SYSTEM OF MAGUR BREEDING

This is a simple device comprising a stand on which are placed a row of plastic tubs (12 cm dia, 6 cm high). Water supplied from the overhead tank through a common pipe to all the tubs with individual control tabs. Each tub is provided with an outlet at a height of 4 cm and connected to a common conduit to drain off water. In this model of flow through system the temperature monitoring system has not been used which seems to be necessary to increase the rate of survivality of magur larvae.

INNOVATIVE MODEL OF FLOW THROUGH SYSTEM

This is a modification in the CIFA flow through system by adding temperature monitoring system which is necessary to increase the rate of survivality of magur larvae. This innovative model device comprises a stand on which are placed a row of plastic tubs (12 cm diameter and 6 cm high). Water supplied from the overhead tank through a common pipe to all the tubs with individual control tabs. Each tub is provided with an outlet at a height of 4 cm and connected to a common conduit to drain off water. Lights are fixed over each tub for maintaining the temperature in the tubs during incubation. The wattage of bulbs is selected depending on the need of raise in temperature. Normally 100 Watt bulb is sufficient to maneuver the temperatures in Vidarbha

Region where, during the monsoon the average minimum temperature is found to be 16 °C which may decline up to 6° C in extreme conditions. But the ideal water temperature required for the rearing of magur larvae is 22 ° C to 30 °C.

SINGHI (HETEROPNEUSTES FOSSILIS)

This is a common catfish found in freshwater swamps, ponds and tanks throughout the country. It is also suitable for pond culture. It reportedly attains a length of 200 mm at the end of the first year and a maximum length of about 450 mm. This fish breeds in ponds and confined waters almost throughout the year, peak season being monsoon. During rainy days, fishes move from wells to shallow inundated areas of paddy fields for breeding. The eggs are greenish in colour and are usually found attached to weeds. This fish has been successfully induced to breed in India by administering in one injection 75–100 IU of human chorionic gonadotrophin.

It is also possible to induce this fish to breed 8 to 10 weeks ahead of peak spawning season by administering pituitary gland injections. By hypophysation these fishes can be induced to breed several times in the same season. Even the spawning season could be prolonged by 2–3 months when the fishes are kept exposed to light during this period for about 12 hours every day. The incubation period extends from 18–20 hours and the newly hatched larvae measure about 2–7 mm in length. At this stage, the larvae feed voraciously on zooplankton. Therefore, it is suggested that before stocking the larvae, the nursery ponds have to be prepared to have abundant zooplankton to get better survival of hatchlings.

BREEDING OF KAI (ANABAS TESTUDINEUS)

The adults are solitary and aggressive. It can gain weight up to 52gm in one year. Maturity occurs at the age of one when the fishes reach a size of 10–12cm in total length. The sexual dimorphism in A. testudineus is more apparent during breeding season. The mature male acquires a reddish hue on the body, particularly on the pectoral and ventral fins. The female shows only a faint reddish colour. Further in the male a distinct diamond shaped black spot appears in the caudal peduncle. In the female this black spot is oblong and somewhat diffused. Moreover, the female in contrast to the male, has a prominently bulging abdomen. The ventral distance between the bases of the two pectoral fins in the female is significantly greater than the male. In the breeding season, the female exhibits a prominent bulge at the vent, resembling the genital papillae while in the male this structure is absent. Mature males ooze out white milt and mature females ooze out ova even at a gentle pressure at the abdomen during breeding season.

In nature the eggs are scattered in open water at the onset of the rains without any nest. The male wraps itself in the female body, fertilizing the eggs as they are laid. Each time 200 colourless eggs are released until about 5000 nos are laid. The fecundity varies from 5000-35000 nos. The eggs rise to the surface and float. The eggs hatch in 24 hrs and the fry are about 2-3mm long. They are free swimming within two days of hatching.

While in artificial breeding with pituitary or synthetic hormone, a single dose of injection for both the male and female spawning actively and courtship behaviour starts after 6 hrs of injection. The water temperature to be maintained at 28° C + 1°C. Good spawning was reported with 8.0-12.0 mg/kg PG to female and 4.0 mg/kg of body weight to male admistration in hapa 7-8 hours after second injection in the temperature of 27-30°C. Fertilized eggs float on the surface of the water. It takes 18-19 hrs for hatching after spawning and newly hatched larvae measure 1.9-2.0 mm in length without any movement. Yolk sac completely absorbs on third day after hatching and settles at the bottom. Egg custard, plankton and Artemia are supplied as artificial feed for those frie up to 20-25 days. The survivability varies from 70-75 per cent.

BREEDING OF PANGAS (PANGASIUS SUTCHI)

Pangasiidae (order: Siluriformes) is a family of fresh water catfish common to southern and south-eastern Asia. Catfish of the genus Pangasius have been cultured in earthen ponds and other waters on the Indo-Chinese Peninsula since ancient times. The most important of these is Pangasius sutchi, which is commonly known as shark catfish or Thai pangas and reaches weights of 3 kg and lengths of 150 cm within 2 years of birth.

The fertilized eggs are adhesive and spherical with a yellowish or greenish-brown egg capsule. The yolk sac is yellowish-brown in colour and 1.20-1.80 mm in diameter. Nine hours post-fertilization, the first cleavage stage, embryonic shield, head, tail region, neural grooves and somites were evident. The incubation period ranges from 24-36 h at a temperature of 20-30°C.

The newly hatched larvae are quite transparent and light yellowish in colour with a body length of 2.98-3.10 mm. Eye pigments appear and the heart starts to work within 12-14 h of hatching. In 1-day-old pro-larvae, the mouth becomes well developed; barbules are elongated, prominent and look like tiny threads. The yolk sac is fairly well absorbed and the palatine teeth are fully developed during the 3 day pro-larval stage. At the end of 12 days of larval development, the stomach becomes functional and aerial respiration starts. After 2 weeks, the young fry is well-developed, and is of an adult appearance, that is, measuring up to 13.56 mm in length.

OMPOK (PABDA) SPP

Ompok pabda/bimaculatus (Ham.) popularly known as 'butter cat fish' or pabda is a freshwater species native to India specially in North East States of India. Open beels/mauns connected with rivers are common habitats. Pabda has fine flesh with a soft meat texture, good taste and high nutritional value. Presently Ompok spp has been listed as an endangered fish species in India due to its decrease in abundance and restricted distribution. Causes of the decline are likely to be indiscriminate fishing during the breeding season, wide use of pesticide and insecticides from agricultural fields causing pollution and siltation in habitat. The fish attained maturity at the end of the first year. Males matured earlier than females, which became mature at 30 -40 g in weight.

Fertilization is external and spawning occurs once a year during the monsoon season (June - August) with a peak in July. Fully ripe females and males were segregated and used in induced breeding. Females can be distinguished by a rounder, fuller abdomen, reddish vent colour and rounded genital papilla.

Males have an elongated and pointed genital papilla. Used Ovaprim to promote induction of spawning. Ovaprim was applied at 1 - 1.5 ml/kg body weight for females and 0.5-1.0ml/kg body weight for males, applied in a single injection. Females were stripped for spawning 8 - 10 hours after hormone injection and the eggs were collected in a tray. Milt was obtained from males by surgically removing the testes, which were macerated to produce a suspension to be mixed with the eggs for fertilisation. Eggs were subsequently washed thoroughly with clean water and transferred to a fibreglass/cement tank for hatching, with constant aeration.

SPECIES FOR AQUACULTURE AND RESEEDING

Although we remain hopeful that more effective methods of fisheries management can be found in time to restore natural resources, I accept that aquaculture is very important for the future supply and affordability of fish and other aquatic products.

Therefore, we will have to seriously develop aquaculture. Becoming serious means domesticating more species for aquaculture and, since there is a large cost to domestication, carefully choosing the species.

Domestication is at the heart of making aquaculture more productive and fish more affordable, for three reasons: domestication allows us to develop improved breeds, and this usually contributes about one-third of the long-term productivity improvement in aquaculture — farm management and better feeds are the other contributors; species choice and domestication co-evolve with farming practices and therefore tend to drive farm and feed improvements to get the best out of the breeds; and domestication, coupled with the conservation of the diversity of genetic resources, provides the long-term safety net for weathering production crises such as devastation from fish diseases and the impacts of climate change.

Despite the great desirability of domestication, many farmed species are far from being domesticated, illustrating the rudimentary state of much aquaculture.

CHOOSING SPECIES TO CULTURE AND DOMESTICATE

Too little attention is given to this step in aquaculture development, and species choices are typically made on the basis of a few, albeit important, criteria — usually market value and/or growth rate. In the long term, farmers and consumers need to be able to breed varieties of the farmed species with characteristics suitable for a range of farm conditions and markets. The breeding must be backed up by *in situ* and *ex situ* genebanks to provide the raw material for further breeding. A wide range of economic, biological and environmental criteria should be considered in the choice of species.

Choice of species by the fish farmer is a dynamic process influenced by factors at different scales. At the farmers' level, determinants include the farmer's own know-how, local practices, markets, likely profitability and access to the support infrastructure for aquaculture such as availability of seed, feed and technical support. Indeed, most of the small-scale fish farmers in the developing world will start with growing the species that their government research agencies are studying and those for which the development assistance organisations offer project technical help. In some cases, such as the Malaysia cockle farming industry, the fishers themselves pioneered the farming system which is based on spat collection and grow-out. Research agencies and development assistance agencies have a responsibility to do their own careful planning in choosing aquaculture species for research and dissemination — because not only are their research programmes dependent on making sensible choices, but their choices have a large bearing on the farmer's choices of species.

One major challenge for species choice is to balance the investment in domesticating and improving breeds of known desirable species with that of bringing new species into culture. Research information and more formal decision support and priority-setting tools can help decision-makers and stakeholders set objectives and multiple criteria, and weigh quantitative and qualitative factors, for several potential aquaculture species. The species choice process, if rigorous, also provides good information on gaps in knowledge that need to be filled if culture of the chosen species is to succeed.

Food security objectives can readily be used to guide species choice in aquaculture. The poor can benefit from choice of appropriate species as consumers and/or producers: if more low-value fish are farmed, then fish will be more affordable; and if more species of fish are able to be farmed with little capital input, then more of the poor can become fish farmers. In designing its aquaculture research programmes, WorldFish Centre placed emphasis on species choice, and developed a programme that covered species from pearl oysters to tilapia, depending on the conditions in which aquaculture was practiced.

Environmental and feed requirements — *e.g.* habitat needs, carnivorous vs herbivorous species — can also be defined to guide decisions on those species for which aquaculture is more likely to be sustainable in the long term. The list of candidate aquatic organisms appears large, *e.g.* FishBase lists nearly 30 000 finfish species alone. However, only 130 finfish are farmed in such quantities that they receive a mention by name in the official FAO global statistics, and of these, only 30 species of carps, tilapias and salmonids produce most of the world's cultured finfish. Few new species, however, will become major global producers because the exploratory development of aquaculture to date has picked the 'easy' species and already brought them into culture. Indeed, many of the recent attempts to domesticate fish have chosen high-value and over-fished marine species such as the northern cod (*Gadus morhaus)* and Asia-Pacific groupers in desperate attempts to fill gaps in market demand. None of these species are 'easy'; this could have been predicted advance by taking a well-considered approach to their choice. But ease of culture may still not deter attempts at domestication if the species is special enough. Even so, the more considered approach to species selection will be valuable, as it will enable the proponents to identify the bottle-necks and pay special attention to these.

With a more considered approach to species choice, more species can become important national and local culture species, even if few go on to become globally prominent. For example, the culture of the Australian silver perch (*Bidyanus bidyanus)* is an excellent example of careful and well-planned species selection using a native species. In Bangladesh, small native freshwater species are being chosen for culture along with the large carps, catfish and tilapia that have dominated the early days of aquaculture. The price of the small, locally-preferred species is now high, and some are found to have very high vitamin A content.

Domestication through Selective Breeding

Following choice of species for culture, domestication of a species starts with closing its life cycle, *i.e.* breeding the species and growing it to breed again in captivity. At the present early stage of aquaculture development, many farmed species still have open life cycles, including many of the species of fish and other aquatic organism that produce the bulk of the world aquaculture harvest. Freshwater fish, such as carps and tilapias, and some fish that migrate between salt and freshwater, such as salmons and trouts, have proven the easiest to breed in captivity and are now also the most advanced in domestication. All fish species for which the life cycle is closed are domesticated to some extent, since they are amenable to growth in captivity and therefore could be classified as forms 'more useful to man'. An advance of the last 30 y in aquaculture is artificial selection that is directed to create strains more suitable for widespread and intense human use.

The leading examples are Atlantic salmon in Norway (begun in the 1970s), Nile tilapia, and Chinese carps. Other species are now in the early stages of rigorous selective breeding but it is still relatively rare to have a properly conducted selection programme for major aquaculture species. At the same time, investments are also in train to produce genetically modified fish in an effort to leapfrog the more standard approaches to genetic improvement through selective breeding.

Species choice and domestication cannot occur without strong research backing and strong international sharing of experience.

Many of the species, exotic and endemic, are shared across national borders, and most of the biological, engineering, economic and social research developments benefit from science as a global public good. In the case of fish domestication, aquaculture science has another deep additional pool of knowledge and experience on which to draw, namely that from terrestrial animal and plant domestication which are much more advanced compared to fish.

6

Genetically Modified of Fisheries

INTRODUCTION

Genetically modified fish pose economic benefits to aquaculture, but also pose many ecological risks. Since most of the risks are unknown, further research, review, and monitoring is important. Conducting thorough studies under near natural environmental conditions provides our only hope of assessing the risks associated with the introduction of genetically modified fish. Demand to produce transgenic fish is only increasing, so to improve the chances that decisions to use transgenic fish outside the laboratory are made in an ecologically sound manner, ecological assessments and studies need to be initiated at this time. Minimization of the risks associated with genetically modified organisms can be addressed through the processes of risk assessment and risk management, and by the acceptance of precautionary principles. If we do not approach this subject with caution, the introduction of genetically modified fish could have detrimental affects that are uncontrollable, permanent and irreversible.

In the field of transgenics, there have been numerous methods employed in the transfer of foreign DNA to target organisms, and each has had varying success depending upon the recipient animal. To date, microinjection is still the preferred method for aquatic species, and many of the techniques are modified versions of those used in mammalian microinjection. However, significant differences in fish egg physiology (*i.e.*, a large yolk, an impenetrable outer membrane, and overall opaqueness) make it impossible to inject DNA directly into the nucleus, which renders this method time consuming, labour intensive, and technically challenging.

Electroporation is an alternative that alleviates some of these difficulties and could greatly facilitate research and commercial development of transgenic animals. However, techniques for electroporation have not been standardized, and considerable variation exists among methods. Initial studies involving electroporation in aquatic species used a direct current (DC) with either a pulse of exponential decay or multiple rectangular pulses; however, levels of transfer were low, and expression questionable. As a modification to cell culture electrotransfection techniques, Chang combined the properties of a DC field and an oscillating field to produce a new waveform, called DC-shifted radio frequency (RF) pulses. The idea is that this new waveform would be gentler to the membrane and therefore increase the probability of the membrane resealing. We recently tested the efficacy of DC-shifted RF pulses to improve gene transfer in fish embryos and to determine if transgene expression could be achieved. The Japanese medaka (Oryzias latipes) was chosen as the study organism. Medaka offer several advantages as model organisms. For example, the medaka is a small, egg-laying freshwater teleost with a rapid generation time, large number of offspring, and external fertilization. Many aspects of this species have been well characterized, including physiology, genetics, and development. Medaka are easy to maintain in a laboratory setting, fertilization time can be predicted, and the fertilized embryos develop externally.

We used the commercially available Gene Pulser II and RF module (Bio-Rad Laboratories, Hercules, CA) with the reporter gene constructs pCMV-SPORT-ß-gal (Invitrogen, Carlsbad, CA) and the pEGFP-1 promoterless plasmid linked to a gene of agricultural importance. The pCMV-SPORT-ß-gal plasmid contains the ß-galactosidase gene from E. coli driven by the CMV promoter and followed by the SV40 polyadenylation signal. The EGFP construct consisted of the CMV promoter driving expression of both the egfp gene and the phyA phytase gene from Aspergillus niger. Plasmid DNA was purified using a commercial kit. Following fertilization, embryos were collected as quickly as possible. Embryos were rinsed with deionized water, separated into groups, and placed into a 0.4cm gap-width cuvette with supercoiled plasmid DNA resuspended in buffer.

Over 15,000 embryos were electroporated with pCMV-SPORT-ß-gal in order to determine how each parameter (buffer choice, buffer volume, quantity of DNA, total voltage, per cent modulation of the wave, the radio frequency of the wave, number of bursts, length of bursts, time between bursts, and number of embryos) affected gene transfer. Following electroporation, embryos were rinsed with deionized water, placed within a homemade hatchery, and allowed to develop.

At two weeks of age, fry were sacrificed, fixed, and stained overnight to detect ß-galactosidase activity. Transgenic fry were compared to wild type controls, and blue tissue staining was used as an indicator of transgene expression. Total voltage significantly affected survival of electroporated embryos, and this effect was influenced by buffer choice and volume. The radio frequency significantly affected the number of transgenics obtained, and this effect was most significant with 100 per cent modulation of the wave. The length of the bursts as well as the amount of time between bursts also significantly affected the number of transgenic fry obtained.

Based upon these results, we concentrated on the effects of voltage, radio frequency, burst duration, and burst interval on gene transfer in embryos electroporated in groups of 50 with 4mg of plasmid DNA resuspended in 400ml of HEPES buffered saline solution. From these results, it is evident that voltage will not only affect survival, but in turn will also affect the probability of surviving fry being transgenic.

For the most part, survival decreased as voltage increased, yet the percentage of fish with transgene expression increased as voltage increased up to 20-25V and then decreased. Similarly, as burst duration increased, survival decreased. However, the effect of burst duration on the production of transgenic fish was dependent upon the radio frequency. When the radio frequency was between 35 and 45KHz, the highest percentage of transgenics was obtained with a burst duration of 10msec; for a radio frequency of 30 or 50KHz, the highest percentage of transgenics occurred with a burst duration of 50msec. In contrast, the effect of the burst interval on the production of transgenic fish was linear and did not appear to be influenced by any other factor. As the burst interval increased, the efficiency of gene transfer decreased.

Since the expression patterns in the ß-galactosidase stained fish displayed a high level of mosaicism, we decided to test for germ-line integration, transmission, and expression of the transgene in subsequent generations. The EGFP construct was utilized because its expression can be observed in living organisms with minimal discomfort to the fish. Following analysis of the above parameters and their effects, we decided to use the same DNA concentration resuspended as above, 25V, 100 per cent wave modulation with a radio frequency of 35KHz, and 3 bursts for 10msec each with a 1.0sec pause between bursts. These fish were grown to sexual maturity and a double back-cross performed. Approximately 85 per cent of the founders that survived to sexual maturity demonstrated germ-line transmission to their offspring3. The observance of green fluorescent protein indicated transgene expression, and Southern blots demonstrated heritability of both the copy number and junction fragments of the transgene in a Mendelian fashion.

It is evident that electroporation has the potential to increase greatly the efficacy of transgenic fish production. We were able to use an electroporation device based upon the principle of a direct current with an oscillating field, called DC-shifted RF pulses, to produce effectively and efficiently germ-line transgenic medaka. Unlike microinjection, this technique is very rapid and easy to use, allowing for as many embryos as can be collected to be electro-porated in a day. Although some time is required to optimize the electroporation condition, once a set of conditions has been determined, it can be used repeatedly to produce transgenic fish with varying transgenes. The high percentage of transgenic fish obtained should allow for an abundant number of founders to be screened for proper or ideal expression, as well as to decrease the number of embryos needing to be sacrificed in order to obtain one transgenic one. Unfortunately, the RF module from Bio-Rad Laboratories is no longer commercially available.

GENETIC IMPROVEMENT TECHNOLOGIES

Genetic improvement technologies cover a range of techniques requiring different levels of expertise and resources. Chromosome-set manipulation (*i.e.* polyploidy induction) is an established technique to increase the number of chromosome-sets (ploidy number) in an organism. Temperature, chemical and pressure shocks applied to fish eggs can be used to produce triploid (3 chromosome-sets) individuals that have desirable culture traits. Sex-reversal and the production of single sex groups of fish is also a simple technology that combines hormone treatment and chromosome-set manipulation. Hybridisation, *i.e.* the mating of genetically different groups from the same species (intra-specific hybridisation) or from different species (inter-specific hybridisation), is a simple technique that is now easy to accomplish due to our increased knowledge of reproductive biology.

It can be used to combine good traits from two different species into one group of fish or to transfer a characteristic of one group to another. A problem is that breeding hybrids with hybrids results in a non-uniform and unpredictable group of fish that is generally not well suited for culture. Therefore, for hybrid production, the parent-lines must be maintained pure. The above genetic improvement techniques are considered short-term strategies, where the gains are seen in one or two generations. Selective breeding is a longer-term strategy where gains are accumulated at each generation of selection.

Molecular markers may now increase the efficiency of selective breeding by facilitating the identification of quantitative trait loci (QTLs), *i.e.* genes that control complex characters such as growth rate and environmental tolerance and, secondly, by making it possible to use molecular markers linked to QTLs to identify desirable individuals or families. Genetic engineering and the production of transgenic organisms is an active area of research and development in aquaculture. This is a medium-long term strategy in that development and testing of stable transgenic lines requires time. The large size and hardy nature of many fish eggs allows them to be manipulated rather easily and facilitates gene transfer by direct injection of a foreign gene or by electroporation, where an electric field assists gene transfer. We will briefly discuss currently available biotechnologies in the context of fishery management, aquaculture and conservation respectively.

GENETICALLY DISCRETE GROUPS

This substructuring into different, relatively genetically discrete groups may take various forms. For example, the migratory salmonids return to the rivers in which their parents spawned and this effectively creates genetic groups that are associated with particular rivers or even particular regions of a river. In another example, some lake fish have autumn and spring spawners, and as long as this character is inherited, two genetically distinct groups can evolve.

In many marine fish, there are particular sites where spawning aggregations occur and these can lead to genetic differentiation. In the case of sedentary shellfish, dispersal is usually mainly via a larval phase, and hydrographic factors will constrain the direction and distance of dispersal. Shellfish such as flat oysters with a relatively short larval phase or other species with direct development will be more likely to be genetically differentiated than shellfish such as cupped oysters or mussels with an extended larval phase. What should we call these genetically differentiated groups and what qualifies as 'genetically differentiated'?

It is possible to quantify levels of genetic differences using various indices, but for the moment, let us consider the terminology that is available. Partly or strongly genetically differentiated groups within a species have been called (1) 'varieties', 'races', 'breeds' or 'strains' if they are cultivated and (2) 'stocks', 'demes', 'populations', 'subpopulations', 'types' or 'ecotypes' if they are wild. All of these terms have been used in the past to describe genetic differentiation within species, but they have often not been clearly defined.

In the case of fisheries, the word 'stock' has often been defined by fishery managers as a group of fish exploited by a specific method or existing in a particular area. Although this may be convenient for the analysis of landings or catch and effort data, and for the enforcement of management measures such as quotas or net size, it may bear little relation to the true genetic substructuring of the fish species. The important point to realise is that there is a continuum of genetic differentiation.

In some species there may be clearly genetically distinct groups, while in others (or in other parts of their range) there will be groups which are virtually indistinguishable genetically. Thus, the use of a single word such as 'stock' to define the units of such substructuring is not often appropriate. Here, we will use the less prescriptive term of 'population' to define an intraspecific (within a species) group of randomly mating individuals which exist (and can therefore be sampled) in a defined geographic position or at a defined time.

A key point to note here is that we are assuming that all individuals comprising a population are able to mate randomly with one another, and therefore, there can be no further genetic subdivision within a population. The main types of genetic markers were outlined, and we now need to show how these markers can be used to identify any population substructure within species of fish or shellfish. We will start with markers such as allozymes, microsatellites and single nucleotide polymorphisms (SNPs) that are co-dominant, that is they allow direct identification of homozygotes and heterozygotes.

How do we handle this information on genotypes in a population? Firstly, we should note that the process of meiosis breaks up existing genotypes and that new genotypes are reassembled when egg and sperm combine at syngamy. Therefore, although there will be the same range of genotypes in an offspring generation as in a parent generation, the two are not directly linked by inheritance. What is linked by inheritance, however, is the presence of an allele and the frequency of that allele in the population. And it is the allele frequency (or gene frequency) that is used to investigate the structure of populations within species.

Frequencies Estimated

When genotypes at a co-dominant locus are scored from a sample of individuals, the frequencies of the alleles at the locus can easily be calculated from these data.

Remember that every diploid individual has pairs of chromosomes, so they must also have pairs of alleles at each locus, that is a homozygote at a locus has two of the same allele and a heterozygote has two different alleles. Although a diploid individual can only exhibit two alleles at a locus, there may be many different alleles at that locus present in the population as a whole. Allele frequencies are the critical starting point for all further analyses of genetics in populations. By convention, the frequencies of alleles at a locus are symbolised using the lower-case letters *p*, *q*, *r*, *s* and the frequency of an allele is given by:

$2H_o + H_e p = 2N$

where H_o is the number of homozygotes for that allele, H_e is the number of heterozygotes for the allele and N is the number of individuals scored at the locus.

Alleles and Genotypes

Considering a single locus, it is convenient to envisage a population as a 'pool' of alleles. Haploid gametes are produced by each generation, and each of these gametes contains a single allele from this pool. Let us assume that all adults in the population provide equal numbers of gametes and that each gamete has an equal chance of combining with all other gametes. Once we know the frequencies of the alleles in the population, it is possible to calculate the frequencies with which the genotypes will be present in the offspring from that generation. This principle was first quantified in 1908 by both Godfrey Hardy, a British mathematician, and Wilhelm Weinberg, a German doctor, and is called, unsurprisingly, the Hardy–Weinberg model.

The random mixing of eggs and sperm the proportions of the genotypes will be:

AA AB BB

p^2 $2pq$ q^2

which, in mathematical terms, is equal to $(p + q)^2$. As long as nothing upsets the Hardy–Weinberg model, allele frequencies should remain constant from generation to generation. The frequencies of the genotypes predicted by the model are dependent on the assumptions of equal and random parental contributions and equal and random mixing of gametes. However, if this is not the case, the model will not hold true. Also, we do not usually sample animals at the beginning of their lives; normally fish or shellfish are sampled as adults. In order for the Hardy–Weinberg model to be appropriate in populations of adults, further assumptions need to be made. We must assume that there is no selection that causes one or other genotype to suffer differential mortality.

We must also assume that our sample taken does not include individuals that have migrated into the population from some other population with different genotype frequencies. So both migration and selection are factors that can cause deviation from the genotype frequencies predicted by the Hardy–Weinberg model. If the number of parents that reproduce in a population is significantly smaller than the whole adult population, allele frequencies in these parents might differ from the whole population and the allele frequencies in the following generation will therefore change.

A further consideration is that very few fish or shellfish species exist as discrete generations, most populations being mixtures of animals from different overlapping generations.

Allele Frequencies Change

If a population is in agreement with the Hardy–Weinberg model, then allele frequencies at a locus are not being driven (by selection or migration) to change significantly from generation to generation. However, there is always bound to be some variation in allele frequency from one generation to the next because of the element of chance. Contrary to the idealised situation required to make mathematical predictions, in real life all individuals of all genotypes will not produce exactly the same number of gametes. Neither are all gametes likely to undergo truly random mixing. Therefore, there will be variation from the model in every generation. This is a fact of biological variability, called random genetic drift. In order to quantify this natural variation, allele frequencies can be given a variance as indicated in the formula:

$$p(1\text{-}p) \text{ Variance of frequency of allele} = 2N_e$$

where p is the frequency of the allele and N_e is the effective population size. The concept of the effective population size is an important one. It is the number of individuals in the population that contribute genetically to the next generation. It will exclude juveniles, individuals too old to reproduce and those that provide non-contributory gametes. These may be individuals that have infertile gametes, or those whose gametes never come into contact with the gametes of other members of the population due to geographic position or timing of spawning.

Thus it can be seen how the effective population size could, in certain circumstances, be very much smaller than the total number of individuals in the population.

If the effective population size (N_e) in the expression above is a very large number, then the allele frequency variance between successive generations will be very small. Conversely, allele frequency variance will be large when N_e is small. This means that natural fluctuations in allele frequency between generations will be much greater in small populations. We shall encounter this concept again when dealing with various aspects of genetics in small populations.

Allele frequencies in a population can therefore change over time owing to random genetic drift. However, they may also change owing to pressure of selection (one genotype or one allele survives better than others at a locus) or to patterns of migration or dispersal that may fluctuate in direction or in strength over time.

Population Structure Arise

The differentiation of a species into genetically different populations is a fundamental part of the process of evolution. For a number of physical or biological reasons, the distribution of a species may become fragmented. For example, during the last ice ages, aquatic species in the temperate regions of the northern hemisphere were driven south and many became restricted to local areas in southern habitats. Where species were fragmented into different areas, many of these populations remained isolated for long periods of time in such refugia. Following the retreat of the last glaciation some 10 000–13 000 years ago, aquatic and terrestrial species went through the process of gradual recolonisation of habitat and this has provided plenty of opportunity for further fragmentation.

Once fragmentation has occurred, allele frequencies at most loci will be subject to random genetic drift in the fragmented populations. As we have seen, random genetic drift produces more rapid allele frequency change in small, compared with large, populations. If only a few individuals are involved initially in founding a population, then allele frequencies in the new population may be very different from the source population, and if numbers remain small, further allele frequency changes may be rapid.

In addition to random genetic drift, localised adaptation will occur involving selection at some loci for particular characteristics and these will cause further differences between populations. These loci under selection, and to a lesser extent those linked to them, can show higher patterns of differentiation between populations than neutral markers and are sometimes called 'outliers'. These processes of random genetic drift and adaptation will tend to increase differences between populations, while migration or larval dispersal between populations will tend to reduce it. So the population differentiation we can identify today in a species is essentially the result of the historical interplay between the environment and the forces of dispersal, adaptation and random genetic drift.

COMPARATIVE OF FISH DEVELOPMENT

Comparative of fish development constitute one of the glories of nineteenth century embryology. The comparative method as a formal concept in morphology has its roots in German Naturphilosophie and was extended to embryology by Dollinger and von Baer. Subsequently, Johannes Muller and others incorporated it into physiology.

Already well established, comparative embryology was thrust into a position of prominence with the publication of Darwin's On the Origin of Species. Darwin stated that much could be learned about evolution through embryological studies. Fritz Mller and Haeckel considered that embryology, especially comparative embryology, was paramount in understanding evolution, *i.e.*, "ontogeny recapitulates phylogeny".

The new evolutionary impetus combined with the pre-existing research agenda drove comparative studies of fish development ahead at a rapid clip. Fishes provided a intellectual feast for evolutionary comparative embryologists. The four major groups of fishes occupy key positions in vertebrate evolution. Agnaths (hagfish, lampreys) are the most primitive representatives of the craniate-vertebrate lineage.

Chondrichthyans (sharks, rays, chimaeras) are among the oldest extant jawed vertebrates and incorporate the definitive vertebrate Bauplan and developmental programme. Sarcopterygians comprise lungfishes, coelacanths, and tetrapods. The Actinopterygian or ray-finned fishes (Polypterus, sturgeons, gars, Amia, and teleosts) represent a group of bony fishes that evolved in a lineage that culminated in the teleosts, one of the most successful groups of vertebrates. Not only was there evolution at the phyletic level, but the process of development itself underwent evolutionary change.

COMPARATIVE VENTURE

Once embarked upon the comparative venture, the availability of study material became a problem. Many fishes of interest were found only in the fresh waters of the tropics, and some, such as the Australian lungfish Neoceratodus, were only discovered in the last quarter of the nineteenth century. Coincident with the rise of interest in comparative embryology, geographical regions that harboured fish species of interest became more accessible, the fishes themselves became better known, and the technology of travel improved.

Even so, studying the embryology of fishes under primitive field conditions was a major task. Individuals such as Budgett, Kerr, and Semon are part of the golden age of exploration. The hagfishes and lampreys are the most primitive representatives of the craniatevertebrate lineage.

Both are jawless. Hagfishes are common, marine, bottom-dwelling fish in cold, inshore waters and in deeper waters off continental shelves. Recently, hagfishes have been considered to be the sister group to all remaining vertebrates.

Virtually everything that is known about their embryonic development is derived from collections of Eptatretus (=Bdellostoma) stout eggs obtained by Bashford Dean and Franz Doflein in Monterey Bay, California, on the Pacific coast of North America in the 1890's. For all intents and purposes, there have been no modern embryological studies of hagfish except for Gorbman, Gorbman and Tamarin, and Wicht and Northcutt, who used Dean's material. For this discussion, research on the Atlantic hagfish Myxine will not be considered because there is so little of it. Doflein and Dean (1898, 1899) described embryonic development. Dean's 1899 extraordinary monograph gives a definitive account, sumptuously illustrated with colour lithographs, of hagfish development from early cleavage through hatching. Unfortunately, because the monograph is not readily accessible, this research has been overlooked.

Most of Dean's account is based on the observation of whole mounts. Sections of blastula and gastrula stages are illustrated. The eggs are large ellipsoids about 22 mm in length by 8 mm in width. They are heavily yolked, and there is a germinal disc at the animal pole. Cleavage is meroblastic. The process of embryo formation coincides with the epibolic movement of the blastoderm over the yolk mass. The equivalent of a germ ring is present and the embryo is formed along an anterior-posterior axis as the blastoderm moves over the yolk mass. The only section of a gastrula reveals the absence of bottle cells, although this could be a function of the plane of section.

Both a cellular "periblast" and an underlying yolk syncytium are depicted. The neural tube is formed by the closure of the medullary folds. Much information is given on organogenesis and the later phases of embryonic development. Additional descriptions of early cleavage stages are given by Gudger and Smith. A description of development of the head, brain and associated organs based on the analysis of sectioned material was published by von Kupffer. Lampreys are widely distributed throughout the waters of the northern and southern temperate zones.

Chondrichthyan Development

They were known to zoologists such as Home, Rathke, and Miller who worked on aspects of their reproductive anatomy. It is surprising, then, that embryological research was only undertaken in the mid-nineteenth century and that comprehensive studies only appeared in the latter part of the nineteenth and in the early twentieth centuries. The first substantive description of lamprey development was that of Schultze, who amongst other observations demonstrated the somewhat unequal holoblastic cleavage of the egg. Aspects of gastrulation were described by Balfour, Goette, and Hatta. Both Goette and Hatta demonstrated the presence of bottle cells and involution of surface cells through the blastopore. Other contributions of note are those of Scott, von Kupffer, and Selys-Longchamps. Older literature on lamprey development is listed in Ziegler. Piavis provides a modern account of development and a list of the more recent literature. Two main lines of evolution are recognized within the class Chondrichthyes: the holocephalans and elasmobranchs.

When chondrichthyan development was discussed previously, only the elasmobranchs (sharks, rays, and skates) were considered. Now the holocephalans (chimaeras or ratfishes) will be considered. Chimaeras are oviparous, bottom-dwelling marine fishes usually found in the deep waters off the continental shelf, except in those regions where the inshore waters are cold, *e.g.*, the northwest coast of North America and New Zealand. Because of their deep water habitat, it has been difficult to procure their eggs for study.

The major sources of information on chimaeroid development are Schauinsland's and Dean's monographs. Schauinsland studied Callorhinchus mil, whereas Dean's study was mostly based on the eggs and embryos of Hydrolagus (=Chimaera) colliei collected in Monterey Bay, California. Dean's monograph is remarkably complete. Dean begins with an account of the breeding habitats of Hydrolagus and egg case formation and then describes in detail development from fertilization through hatching. Chimaeras are oviparous.

Cleavage and Subsequent Development

Their eggs, moderately large, oblate spheroids (25 x 20 mm), are enclosed in an elaborate egg case composed of structural proteins that differ considerably from those of elasmobranchs. Cleavage and subsequent development is meroblastic and closely resembles that of sharks. A closely spaced series of stages from early cleavage through the mid-phases of development is illustrated with surface views of the blastoderm and drawings of the embryos. This series is supplemented with many illustrations of sectioned material, especially from the blastula and gastrula stages. One developmental characteristic that sets chimaeras apart from elasmobranchs is the pronounced elongation of the post-anal region of the body, which begins at the tailbud stage and soon gives the young embryo an almost eel-like appearance. The studies of Schauinsland and Dean remained unchallenged for many years.

Only in the late twentieth century has interest in chimaeroid development revived. The osteichthyans or bony fishes include the sarcopterygians and actinopterygians. The sarcopterygians (fleshy-finned fishes) are now considered to include the tetrapods, two extinct groups of fishes, and two extant groups of fishes: coelacanths and dipnoans (lungfishes). These fishes are of considerable interest because the "lungfishes, coelacanths, or both together are the closest living relatives of tetrapods". The living coelacanth Latimeria chalumnae is the sole surviving representative of a once common group. The only known population occurs in the Comoros Islands off the east coast of Africa. No embryological research was carried out on Latimeria during the nineteenth century because it was not discovered until 1938. However, in 1975 Smith *et al.* discovered that Latimeria is viviparous when they found five nearterm pups in the oviduct. Up to this time only two gravid females have been collected. Wourms *et al.* described aspects of viviparity and the maternal-embryonic relationship using the embryos and maternal tissues from the Smith *et al.* specimen.

This material was also used by Bemis and Northcutt in their study of the innervation of cranial muscles and Northcutt and Bemis in their study of cranial nerves. Fricke and Frahm described full-term pups obtained from the second gravid female. Coelacanth eggs are enormous, up to 9 cm in diameter and with a dry weight of 184 g. They are heavily yolked and contain yolk platelets. Although no information is available on early embryonic development, it is reasonable to assume that development is meroblastic. Because the coelacanth is on the verge of extinction, it is highly unlikely that any substantial body of embryological knowledge will be forthcoming. The dipnoans or lungfishes comprise the other extant group of sarcopterygian fishes.

TELEOSTEAN EMBRYOLOGY

The history of teleostean embryology. The main emphasis of early studies was placed on defining the meroblastic pattern of teleostean development and piscine features of embryogenesis and organ and tissue formation. Some attention was given to the diverse embryonic adaptations for viviparity in different taxa. By the end of the nineteenth century, it was apparent that the early development of most teleosts was very similar but that mid-and late-phases diverged, yielding diverse embryonic morphology and larval forms adapted to specific life styles and habitats.

Thus, the later phases of embryonic development, larval development, and life histories became the subjects of comparative studies of teleostean development during the late nineteenth century and the twentieth century. Several factors favoured the growth of a comparative approach, especially the advent and rise of marine biology, biological oceanography, and fisheries biology. Fishes are the dominant group of marine vertebrates and are commercially important. Thus, the study of life histories and the embryonic and larval stages of inshore, pelagic, and deep-sea fishes became a research agenda for the marine sciences.

The results were often quite spectacular, *e.g.*, the leptocephalus larvae of eels and the bizarre larvae of the stomiatoid fish Idiacanthus with its stalked eyes and trailing gut. Studies of this type were pioneered by Alexander Agassiz and Ryder in the United States, McIntosh and Prince in Great Britain, and

Ehrenbaum in Germany, amongst others. Similar activities were undertaken at limnological stations and in freshwater fisheries biology. Popularization of the aquarium hobby and the successful reproduction in captivity of freshwater fishes imported from Africa, South America, and Asia such as the zebrafish, Danio rerio, established another source of material for comparative studies. Given their numbers and diversity, a wealth of information, mostly of a descriptive nature, was produced on the development of a great many species of teleosts. Increased activity in the study of teleostean development was accompanied by the elaboration of several concepts and theoretical approaches which both aided and impeded further progress.

In 1877, Haeckel set forth his Gastrea theory. Based on his observations of teleostean development, he applied the concept to both teleosts and chondrichthyans. Much of the literature on fish development from his time to the present has been concerned with the morphogenetic movements and embryo-forming mechanisms that are associated with gastrulation, a literature too voluminous to review. One major problem that arose from overzealous and inept efforts to use embryological studies to support evolutionary theory was the attempt to homologize the events and processes of gastrulation in teleosts and chondrichthyans with amphibians and amniotes.

In this respect, it was Goette who first proposed that involution, *i.e.*, flowing of a sheet of cells over an inpocketing such as a blastopore, has a prominent role in teleost gastrulation. At the risk of oversimplification, many of these studies were comparative in name only. There was little or no conceptual basis for interpreting the mass of information. Attempts, such as that of Schultz, to establish a well-defined conceptual basis for comparative embryological research were overlooked. (In passing, Schultz's 1910 monograph appears to be a direct precursor of de Beer's 1930 study of embryology and evolution.) Although the body of evolutionary theory was available, the influence of Haeckel's biogenetic law interfered with the productive application of it to many developmental issues.

A growing anti-evolutionary bias tended to discourage this type of enquiry. Studies of individual species were often exceedingly well done, and the development of a single organ system was often compared in several different taxa and interpreted in the context of the evolutionary paradigm.

Examples of the latter include Ryder's study of heterocercy and the evolution of the fins and fin rays of fishes and Eigenmann's study of the abortive development of the eye in blind cave fishes. Eigenmann compared the development and degeneration of the eye in the blind cave fish Amblyopsis with that of the surfperch Cymatograster, a fish with a well-developed eye. In Amblyopsis, development of the eye begins normally, but then the lens degenerates and the entire eye regresses. Recently, Jeffery, using the embryos of another blind cave fish Astyanax, has shown that programmed cell death of the lens eliminates lens induction from the cascade of inductive interactions required for normal eye development.

In general, however, the comparative method was not used to explore the evolution of development and the factors that brought about evolutionary change. It was not until the maturation of evolutionary thought in the twentieth century that a new set of concepts and approaches were produced and used to exploit the potential of comparative studies. Paramount among these are: (1) revived interest in the evolution of development and the role of development in evolution; (2) application of evolutionary theory to life histories; and (3) attempts to order the bewildering diversity of fish reproduction in terms of systematics or reproductive guilds.

CYTOGENETIC AND FISH ANALYSIS

The differential diagnosis between 'true' SAA and hypoplastic MDS is often difficult because of a reduced bone marrow cellularity.1,2 Fundamental discriminant clues can be provided by trephine biopsy and by the identification of a chromosome aberration,3 that, however, has been reported in SAA patients too.

We report on five patients, aged 20 59 years, observed at our Institution between March 1989 and August 1995. Their main clinico-hematological characteristics. Cytogenetics and FISH results are report. At diagnosis an initial cytogenetic analysis showed a normal chromosome pattern in all the patients. All of them evolved into AML showing clonal karyotype defects described according to ISCN4 (trisomies and monosomies were considered clonal when present in at least two and three metaphases, respectively). We decided to employ FISH retrospectively in order to establish if any minor subclone, carrying the chromosome abnormality detected by cytogenetics at the time of AML transformation, was already present at diagnosis. In order to reinforce the interphase FISH analysis of small subpopulations of cells we decided to apply the probe discovering the clonal chromosome defect along with an additional probe used as an internal control (dual-colour FISH). All probes were commercially obtained.

The digoxygenated 5q31 DNA probe was applied to metaphase cells only along with the 5 probe. Its cut-off value was obtained by screening 1000 mitoses from 10 normal controls. We determined the one-sided 95 per cent confidence limit using a binomial distribution for the proportion of metaphase cells that were normal or that carried the del(5)(q13q31). We detected the probability of discovering 0, 1, 2, 3 cells with del(5)(q13q31) by using the upper boundary of the 95 per cent confidence interval.5 As in normal subjects, 3 was the highest number of cells lacking the 5q31DNA probe signal, probably because of a hybridization failure, the normal range for the cells with this karyotypic defect was fixed at 0.8 per cent.

Monosomy 7 or trisomy 8 or other numerical defects were considered clonal by metaphase and interphase FISH when the percentages of the cells with such abnormalities were above the cut-off value determined for each numerical change. The cut-off value was obtained by screening 25 mitoses and 200 interphase cells from 10 normal controls. Monosomy 7 cut-off was determined by applying the 7 probe together with a 12 probe. We calculated the mean percentage of mitoses or cells showing two spots due to the internal control and only one spot due to the 7 probe plus three times the standard deviation. Monosomy 7 cut-off value for metaphase FISH was 8 per cent; that for interphase FISH was 5%. Trisomy 4 and 8 cut-offs were obtained in the same way and were fixed at 0 per cent for both the numerical defects when considering mitoses, at 2.3 per cent and at 2.5 per cent, respectively, when examining interphase cells.

Despite the high interphase FISH cut-offs for monosomies and trisomies making the identification of minor subclones marked by such abnormalities difficult, this technique succeeded in demonstrating that the clonal defect was already present at disease onset in a few interphase cells obtained from four of our patients.

This result was confirmed by metaphase FISH, that detected similar percentages of clonogenic cells in the same patients, suggesting that, initially, the chromosome defect was really present in a small subpopulation of cells. Moreover, a careful review of the karyotypes, obtained at disease onset and considered normal on an initial conventional cytogenetics investigation, demonstrated that few mitoses of the same four patients carried the clonal abnormalities observed on leukemic transformation and retrospectively identified by FISH.

These cytogenetics and FISH results might be explained by the very small size of the abnormal clone and not by the low mitotic rate with poor quality metaphases often observed in patients with hypoplastic marrows. In both situations, however, FISH plays an important role in identifying clonogenic cells that may easily escape cytogenetic detection.

An intriguing point in patients with hypocellular marrow is the differential diagnosis between 'true' SAA and hypoplastic MDS.1,2,3 In our patients FISH alone was unable to discriminate between true SAA and hypoplastic MDS, as the presence of a chromosome abnormality per se does not help to make a discriminatory diagnosis. However, karyotypic defects such as monosomy 7, trisomy 8 and sporadically trisomy 6 have been observed in SAA evolving into MDS or into AML.3 Therefore, an overlap between SAA and MDS may actually exist.2 This possibility is further illustrated by our patient No. 5, who showed an abnormality identifying a particular subgroup of MDS with a very low probability of evolving into AML, ie a del(5)(q13q31), accompanied by an increased marrow reticulin on trephine biopsy, a sign predictive of AML evolution.1 This case initially classified as hypo-MDS ultimately developed into AML-M4 88 months after initial diagnosis.

In conclusion, the present FISH study was made possible by conventional cytogenetics, the only reason that the abnormalities present in each case were known. Cytogenetics and FISH were complementary; the latter succeeded in discovering minor subclones at diagnosis and, demonstrating their expansion, it was able to predict AML transformation.

A POPULATION GENETICS MODEL

Now that you have seen what happens in a situation of no evolution (Hardy-Weinberg Equilibrium), let's develop a model of natural selection. Remember that natural selection occurs if genotypes don't have equal fitness. We will model a situation in which natural selection is the ONLY form of evolution occurring (there will be no mutation, genetic drift, non-random mating, or gene flow--remember, these are the other forms of evolution, as introduced in the last lecture.)

So for this model, we will assume (as we did for Hardy-Weinberg Equilibrium) infinite population size, no movement of individuals among populations, no mutation, and random mating. However, we will see what happens when the different genotypes for the trait differ in fitness. First, consider the fitnesses of genotypes. Remember that fitness is a measure of how well individuals with a certain genetic trait are expected to survive and reproduce. We will still consider a single gene with two alleles (A and a) and three genotypes (AA, Aa, and aa.) Natural selection will occur if individuals with different genotypes differ in fitness. So to understand and model natural selection, a first important point is to determine how to measure fitness.

Remember that natural selection occurs because individuals with some traits (those with higher fitness) survive and therefore reproduce more than do other individuals. The important feature here is reproduction--it is those traits that are reproduced most that necessarily become more common from generation to generation.

So we will measure fitness based on the degree to which traits (in this case, different genotypes) reproduce. A first measure of the fitness of a genotype is absolute fitness: the number of offspring an individual with a particular genotype has on average. Absolute fitness could be studied in natural populations; one could determine that, for example, individuals with a certain genotype have on average six offspring.

A problem with this measure is that there is no way to determine, just looking at this number, whether having an average of six offspring means that this form has high or low fitness. If AA individuals have six offspring, Aa have three offspring, and aa have one offspring, then six is the best, and we would say it represents high fitness. On the other hand, if AA individuals have six offspring, Aa have twelve, and aa have thirty, then we would say six represents very low fitness. The important point to note here is that whether a particular absolute fitness is high or low depends on the fitnesses of other genotypes in the population. So we will develop a second measure of fitness that accounts for this.

A second measure of the fitness of a genotype is relative fitness: the degree to which individuals with a particular genotype reproduce in proportion to individuals with other genotypes. Typically, relative fitness is measured with respect to the genotype that has the highest fitness. The genotype with highest fitness has a relative fitness value of one; the other fitnesses have relative fitness values that are fractions of one, telling us how well these individuals reproduce with respect to the individuals of the genotype that reproduces best.

At this point, you should have all the information you need to work all the problems in Chapter VI of your lab manual, and you should try to start working on them. Here are some tips on how to work the problems: Your first step should be to determine whether you're working a problem for a population in Hardy-Weinberg Equilibrium or a problem in which natural selection is occurring. Remember that the difference between the two models is in whether or not different genotypes have different fitness. If the genotypes all have the same fitness (all survive and reproduce equally well) that should tell you you're looking at a Hardy-Weinberg Equilibrium problem. If the genotypes differ in fitness (if they don't survive and reproduce equally well) that should tell you you're looking at a natural selection problem.

If you have a Hardy-Weinberg Equilibrium problem there are two places the problem could start. You could be given allele frequencies to start out or you could be given genotype frequencies to start out. So your next step in solving the problem is simply to figure out, and write down, which you've got: a llele frequencies or genotype frequencies.

In a Hardy-Weinberg Equilibrium problem remember that if you have an allele frequency, you can figure out the other allele frequency (since $p+q=1$) and you can figure out any genotype frequency (Freq(AA)=p2, Freq(Aa)=2pq, Freq(aa)=q2.) So if you're given an allele frequency, use it, and get whatever information the question asks for. If you're given a genotype frequency rather than an allele frequency, your first step should be to calculate an allele frequency, because once you have the allele frequencies you can figure out anything else the question might require. To calculate an allele frequency from a genotype frequency, you need the genotype frequency of a homozygote (that is, either AA or aa.) Once you have that, take the square root to get the allele frequency of the allele that makes up that genotype.

If you have a natural selection problem then there are three places the problem could start, and you need to figure out which one you have. As with Hardy-Weinberg problems, things go more smoothly if you have allele frequencies, so your first step is to get an allele frequency (if you're not already given one.) Here are the three places a natural selection problem could start, and what your first step should be for each possible starting place (once you've completed the first step, you should be able to use the natural selection formulas to work the rest of the problem--it is often the first step that is hardest.)

1. You could be given an allele frequency in gametes at the start of a generation. If you are, use the allele frequency to determine the other allele frequency (remember p+q=1) and use the fitness information you are given (be sure you take this and calculate relative fitnesses if you're not already given them) and use the formulas you have to get the information required by the question.
2. You could be given a genotype frequency in zygotes. If you are, remember that genotype frequencies in zygotes are p2, 2pq, and q2, just like in Hardy-Weinberg Equilibrium. If you have the genotype frequency of a homozygote in zygotes, take the square root to get the allele frequency that was present at the start of the generation, and proceed as you did in the first case where you were given the allele frequency directly.

You could be given a genotype frequency in adults. If you are, then you are in a situation where the population is NOT in the proportions of Hardy-Weinberg Equilibrium. To calculate the allele frequencies in these adults, which are also the allele frequencies in the gametes that will start the next generation, use the formula for the allele frequencies: Freq(A)=Freq(AA) + (1/2)Freq(Aa.) Once you have the allele frequencies that start the next generation, proceed as you would in the first case where you were given the allele frequencies directly.

When e-mailing me problems, show your work as clearly as you can. You can use the following ways of representing things to make typing the formulas (which is tedious, as I know, just having typed out a bunch of them for this lecture) easier: To represent p squared (p2) type p^2. To represent w bar, the average population fitness, type wbar.

To represent things with subscripts, like the absolute and relative fitnesses, you don't have to put the subscripts as subscripts--it's OK to type:

wAA for wAA

It will probably help to work stuff with pen and paper first, then type it out. Get into the habit of writing down all formulas and steps clearly and legibly--you'll make many fewer mistakes, you'll be able to go back and study from what you've done, and I'll expect you to write down all formulas and steps clearly and legibly on exams so you'll do better if you get into the habit of doing so now. Finally, from time to time look at the questions and the answers and think about what you'd really expect to happen in the situation you're given, through natural selection. Do the numbers you're getting makes sense? Can you see how they might relate to a real situation? The goal, really, is to be able to translate evolution into math and then the math back into evolution--don't get so bogged down in algebra that you forget what you're really trying to study.

Now that you've learned the basic model, let's consider some more aspects of natural selection as it affects situations such as those you have modeled: natural selection occurring because of different fitnesses of genotypes for a single gene with two alternate alleles in a diploid, sexually reproducing population. Depending on the traits being studied, and the environment, fitness relationships among genotypes vary. They also depend on just how the traits are coded--whether one allele is completely dominant to the other (recessive) allele or whether there is some form of codominance or incomplete dominance such that the heterozygote has a different phenotype from either homozygote. (If these terms--dominance, recessiveness, incomplete dominance, codominance--are not completely familiar to you, be sure to review some genetics before proceeding!)

An important point to remember is that fitness depends on the phenotype--the appearance, structure, function of an organism. If two different genotypes result in the same phenotype (as when one allele is dominant) then both of those genotypes will have the same fitness--they look, act, function just like each other, so they survive and reproduce just like each other. Here are the possible ways the fitnesses of different genotypes could be related to each other: If one allele is completely dominant to the other, recessive, allele, so that the heterozygote has same phenotype as the dominant homozygote, there are two ways fitnesses could be related:

1. The recessive phenotype could have highest fitness (it would have a relative fitness value of 1; the dominant homozygote and heterozygote would have fitness values that are equal to each other and that are less than 1.)
2. The dominant phenotype could have highest fitness (in this case, the dominant homozygote and the heterozygote would both have relative fitness values equal to one, and the recessive homozygote would have a relative fitness value equal to something less than 1.)

If neither allele is completely dominant (in a case of codominance or incomplete dominance), so that the heterozygote has different phenotype from either homozygote, there are three ways that fitnesses could be related to each other:

1. Fitness codominance occurs when the heterozygote has fitness that is intermediate between the fitnesses of the two homozygotes (one homozygote has highest fitness, the heterozygote has lower fitness than it, and the other homozygote has still lower fitness.)
2. Heterosis occurs when the heterozygote has higher fitness than either homozygote (the heterozygote would have a relative fitness value of one, the two homozygotes would have fitness values of less than one.)

3. Underdominance (negative heterosis) occurs when the heterozygote has lower fitness than does either homozygote (one homozygote would have a relative fitness value of one, the other homozygote might also have a fitness value of one or, more likely, would have a somewhat lower fitness value, and the fitness value of the heterozygote would be even lower.)

You can use the formulas you've learned to calculate the effect of natural selection over one or two generations for any of these situations. If you repeated calculation of these formulas for 50 or 100 generations (I don't recommend doing this by hand!) you could learn what happens in each of the situations, in the long run. It turns out that the different situations listed above do differ in the expected result of natural selection. To learn about these, you will complete a computer exercise to study the different situations. In this assignment, you will look at specific instances of the forms of natural selection and of one other form of evolution, genetic drift. These specific instances illustrate general patterns--for example, what you learn for the specific case of heterosis you study will show you patterns that are generally true for heterosis. Your goal will be to learn these general patterns.

LABORATORY TECHNIQUES

Novel laboratory techniques are often the driving force behind new ideas in science. Certainly the use of cytogenetic studies for clinical testing literally exploded in the 1960s and 1970s because of three new techniques:

(1) Peter Nowell discovered that the plant lectin phytohaemagglutinin could stimulate lymphocytes to grow in culture;

(2) TC Hsu used hypotonic shock to prepare chromosomes so that they could be counted accurately;

(3) T. Caspersson and Marina Seabright developed chromosome banding techniques that allow accurate pairing and identification of structural abnormalities.

In the 1980s the techniques of molecular biology were applied to cytogenetic preparations.

We call this "hybrid" technology molecular cytogenetics, and it is transforming the way we study chromosomal changes in humans. It has improved the detection of, indeed in some cases defined, microdeletion syndromes. De novo derivative chromosomes in patients with chromosome imbalances can now be accurately characterized: the clinician now knows the identity of the partial monosomy and trisomy in these patients, and the molecular geneticist has accurate information from which to find genes relevant to the phenotype. The chromosomal origin of supernumerary markers can be identified and we now have a real potential of predicting phenotype for marker carriers, benign or adverse.

With molecular cytogenetic techniques, we can now detect some chromosomal abnormalities in non-dividing cells with interphase nuclei. Standard cytogenetics requires actively dividing cells with metaphase nuclei. Some constitutional chromosomal abnormalities, and phenomena such as mosaicism and chimerism can be addressed without growing cells in culture or in cell types that do not adapt well to tissue culture.

Potentially, chromosomal aneuploidy studies (*i.e.* studies looking for abnormalities in chromosome number) can be done more quickly. Preserved, rather than fresh, tissue can be investigated for retrospective studies. We can ask questions of chromosome organization, its relationship to gene expression and tissue specificity in ways that were not possible a few years ago.

Does it replace standard cytogenetics? No, molecular cytogenetic techniques focus on specific chromosomes, chromosome regions, and unique DNA sequences or genes. Standard cytogenetic studies, including high resolution analysis, allow us to survey the whole genome for abnormalities of chromosome number or structure. But as complementary studies or for certain targeted abnormalities, molecular cytogenetic techniques expand our capabilities for making more accurate and refined cytogenetic diagnoses, both for constitutional abnormalities and acquired chromosomal changes in cancer cells.

BASIC TECHNIQUES

The most commonly used molecular cytogenetic technique is fluorescence in situ hybridization, or FISH. FISH is usually applied to standard cytogenetic preparations on microscope slides, but it can be used on slides of formalin-fixed tissue, blood or bone marrow smears, and directly fixed cells or other nuclear isolates. The basic principle of the method is that single-stranded DNA will bind or anneal to its complementary DNA sequence. Thus, a DNA probe for a specific chromosomal region will recognize and hybridize to its complementary sequence on a metaphase chromosome or within an interphase nucleus. Both have to be in single-strand conformation, therefore the DNA probe and the target DNA must be denatured, usually by heating them in a formamide-containing solution.

The probe is hybridized to the target DNA under conditions that allow the DNA to reanneal in double-strand form. Added to the hybridization mixture is an excess of repetitive sequence DNA to block non-specific binding of the probe to the target. After hybridization is complete (often after 2-18 hr at 37 C), the slides are washed in formamide-saline citrate solutions to remove excess or non-specifically bound probe. To detect the location of the probe on the target DNA, the probe DNA can be directly labeled with a fluorescent tag. It can also be chemically modified by the addition of hapten molecules (biotin or digoxigenin) that can then be indirectly fluorescently labeled with immunocytochemical techniques. The target DNA is counterstained with another fluorochrome of a complementary colour.

The probe DNA can be observed on its target by using a fluorescent microscope with filters specific for the fluorochrome label and the counterstain. Special filters have been developed to allow simultaneous visualization of several fluorochromes.

Digital cameras designed to detect low light level emissions and computer imaging are used to increase the sensitivity of probe detection. Because fluorescent dyes are subject to photobleaching (fading), the preparations are not permanent and must be stored away from light. Use of an antifade solution (phenylenediamine) has improved the capacity to observe and document fluorescently labeled samples.

Three different types of probes are typically used in clinical FISH studies:

1. Probes that bind to specific chromosome structures typically recognize repetitive DNA sequences, such as within centromeres (alpha satellite DNA) or telomeric sequences. Within the repeat sequence are nucleotide patterns that are unique for specific chromosomes. There are now available centromeric probes that can identify most of the individual chromosome homologues. Similarly, there are probes that specifically recognize the telomeres (chromosome ends) of the long and short arms of many of the homologues, and more are rapidly being developed. Most alpha satellite centromeric probes give a large, bright signal and are useful for both chromosome identification in metaphase preparations and chromosome enumeration in interphase nuclei. Chromosome-specific telomere probes can be used for the above, for detection of cryptic translocations, and to define interstitial and terminal deletions.
2. Unique sequence probes hybridize to single copy DNA sequences in a specific chromosomal region or gene. In clinical cytogenetics these probes are usually referred to as cosmids, named for their cloning vector. These are the probes used to identify the chromosomal critical region or gene associated with microdeletion syndromes. On metaphase chromosomes, they hybridize to each chromatid, usually giving two small, discrete signals per chromosome.
3. Whole chromosome paints are cocktails of unique sequence probes that recognize the unique sequences spanning the length of a particular chromosome. At metaphase, both chromosome homologues are "painted" or fluoresce brightly. Among other applications, paint probes are used to define the chromosomal origin of derivative segments on translocation chromosomes or supernumerary markers.

A new nomenclature to describe FISH findings has been introduced by the standing committee for the International System on Cytogenetic

Nomenclature. It is designed to be compatible with standard cytogenetic nomenclature and to provide precise information about FISH results. Many laboratories will be incorporating the new nomenclature into their reports, together with text to explain their findings.

The Genetic Drift Newsletter is not copyrighted. Readers are free to duplicate all or parts of its contents. The Genetic Drift Newsletter is published semiannually by the Mountain States Genetics Network for associates and those interested in Human Genetics. In accordance with accepted publication standards, we request acknowledgement in print of any article reproduced in another publication. The views expressed in the newsletter do not necessarily reflect local, state, or federal policy.

FISH APPLICATIONS IN CANCER CYTOGENETICS

FISH analysis can identify selected acquired genetic changes in non-dividing (interphase) cells and can detect masked translocations on metaphase chromosomes. However, FISH is informative only for the specific probes used, while cytogenetic analysis can detect a wide range of abnormalities and provides both diagnostic and prognostic information for patients with a variety of malignancies. The two techniques are complementary, and FISH has proven a valuable adjunct to cytogenetic analysis in the following ways:

FISH ANALYSIS OF INTERPHASE CELLS

This application requires that a probe be available for the abnormality in question and that the laboratory has established normal background ranges for that specific probe. Interphase cells may show lack of signal or may demonstrate multiple signals because of various technical artifacts. It is important to establish the range of signals observed in normal cells for each probe used, in order to determine what this background rate is. Given that these conditions have been met, FISH analysis is very useful for:

Identification of Abnormalities in Specimens with a Low Mitotic Index

Diseases such as the chronic lymphoproliferative disorders are characterized by a very low proportion of mitotically active abnormal cells. In these cases traditional cytogenetic analysis is more likely to identify the karyotype of the normal dividing cells, and may miss the rare abnormal cell in mitosis.

FISH on interphase cells from these patients is often helpful in detecting abnormalities when there is a high suspicion of a specific abnormality associated with the disease in question-for example, trisomy 12 or a deletion of 13q14 in patients with CLL. In cases of cytogenetic culture failures, FISH may also be helpful if an abnormality, such as the t in CML, is suspected.

Single Cytogenetically Abnormal Cell is Detected

Because cytogenetically abnormal cells may arise as artifacts of the tissue culture or slide making processes, the determination of clonality (*i.e.* that all of the abnormal cells originated from a single aberrant cell) requires that multiple cells share the same aberration. When only a single abnormal cell is observed in the course of a cytogenetic analysis, FISH on interphase cells may be used to confirm the presence of an abnormal clone, if the appropriate probe is available and if the laboratory has established normal ranges for that probe.

Treatment and Detection of Minimal Residual Disease (MRD)

If a cytogenetic abnormality has been identified at diagnosis and a FISH probe is available to detect that abnormality, FISH may be used to screen interphase cells in subsequent studies. However FISH alone is not sufficient for monitoring, because cytogenetic analysis may also detect additional acquired changes, which may have important prognostic significance, or may uncover the development of secondary disease with a different set of abnormalities.

The sensitivity of cytogenetic analysis of mitotic cells and FISH analysis of interphase cells is roughly equivalent-*i.e.* a population of about 5 per cent abnormal cells can be detected by either approach-although FISH allows a greater sampling of cell types since mitotic cells are not required.

The ability of FISH to be used to screen hundreds of interphase cells may increase sensitivity for the detection of MRD, especially when samples can be enriched for the presumptive abnormal population. However, the clinical significance of abnormal cells which are not actively dividing is not established and may vary with both the disease and the therapy used to treat it.

FISH ANALYSIS OF METAPHASE CHROMOSOMES

This technique employs the use of whole chromosome paints, which are now commercially available for every chromosome, or cosmid probes on metaphase spreads prepared in the course of cytogenetic analysis. This applications allows:

Variant Translocations or in Cytogenetically Normal Cells

The application of molecular techniques to cancer diagnosis has taught us that some patients may have apparently normal chromosomes in their neoplastic cells but nevertheless have acquired genetic changes which are detectable only by molecular methods. FISH analysis with cosmid probes is useful for detecting masked bcr/abl rearrangements in CML, or pml/rara rearrangements in suspected APL. These cosmid probes may also be used for interphase cell analysis, with sensitivity similar to southern blotting, but with results more rapidly obtained.

Clarifying Complex Rearrangements and Breakpoints

Whole chromosome paints or appropriately located cosmids may be hybridized to metaphase chromosomes to identify the origins of complex marker chromosomes, or to identify cryptic translocations which may appear as simple deletions.

For example, some cases of myeloid leukemias with apparent deletions of 11q23 may actually have cryptic translocations, often involving chromosome 6. Delineation of disease groups and prognosis may hinge on this information.

The selective application of FISH techniques to cancer cytogenetic analysis has the ability to increase the resolution, sensitivity and informativeness of each analysis. In order to be more widely applied, there must be a greater selection of commercially available probes, and issues of quality control and quality assurance still need to be addressed.

FISH FOR GENE AMPLIFICATION

Role of Gene Amplification in Cancer

Gene amplification is a characteristic of cancer cells that allows increased production of specific proteins used for acquisition and maintenance of the malignant phenotype. Amplification of certain oncogenes has an important role in the progression of many tumors. Detection of such amplifications may be of diagnostic and prognostic importance.

The HER-2/neu or erbB-2 oncogene codes for a 185 Kd transmembrane oncoprotein (p185). Approximately 25-30 per cent of breast and ovarian carcinomas have amplification of this gene. Studies have demonstrated that HER-2/neu is amplified and/or overexpressed in 10-30 per cent of invasive breast cancers and in 40-60 per cent of intraductal breast carcinomas.

Amplification and overexpression of this gene were found to be associated with rapid proliferation, low estrogen receptor content, and high grade of ductal carcinomas, which suggests that this oncogene plays an important role in the progression of breast cancer.

Amplification or overexpression of the HER-2/neu gene was shown to be an indicator of poor prognosis in node-positive breast cancer. In node negative breast cancer patients, the subgroup for which accurate prognostic factors could make a significant contribution to treatment decisions, the prognostic value of HER-2/neu amplification or overexpression has been controversial.

The technical difficulties in using standard immunohstochemical staining (IHC) and Southern blot analysis may explain not only the differences in the observed clinical-genetic correlation, but also the varied frequency of HER-2/neu overexpression reported in tumors.

Fluorescence in situ hybridization (FISH) has been used to demonstrate gene amplification in human breast carcinoma cell lines in both interphase and metaphase cells. FISH appears to be a useful technique as it can overcome many of the inherent limitations of other techniques and can provide the most reliable and accurate data. HER-2/neu amplification appears to be a strong indicator of breast cancer recurrence in women under 40. This gradient of risk demonstrated by FISH with a DNA probe and the more consistent recent findings of the prognostic importance of amplified HER-2/neu is evidence of probable superiority of this technique compared to standard Southern blot or IHC.

7

Developments in Fisheries Biotechnology

There exists a gradient of biotechnologies, depending on the degree of sophistication, complexity, stage of development and application. The lower side of the gradient comprises simpler but widely used techniques such as in vitro culture, rhizobium technology, fermentation. The upper side of the gradient includes advanced techniques involving genetic engineering. The gradient of biotechnologies may be matched with the gradient of national capabilities, economic investment and efforts to provide the possibility of choosing the appropriate techniques and approaches with the most positive impacts. The pattern of use and development of biotechnologies in developed and developing countries thus varies considerably.

THE PATTERN IN DEVELOPED COUNTRIES

In the industrialized countries, a new pattern of biotechnological research funding has emerged. With the availability of property right protection of biotechnologies and prospects of vast markets for biotechnology products and the techniques, the bulk of the research is funded, carried out, and controlled by the private sector. For instance, since 1976 when GENENTECH, the first biotechnology company, was established, the new techniques have spawned a variety of industries that now comprise more than 400 start-up firms, more than 200 established firms that have diversified into biotechnology, and more than 200 supply firms in the United States alone.

The new biotechnology industry in the United States produced pharmaceutical, diagnostic tests and agricultural products worth close to US$2 billion in 1990. A similar trend is seen in Europe and Japan. It is estimated that about 60 per cent of the biotechnology research and development funding in industrialized countries is from the private sector. Thus, the private sector has been a major force in enhancing the capability of these countries in this field.

Research institutions in the public sector are now generally required to raise a substantial part of their budget from non-government sources, via contractual research, licensing agreements and royalties. This is tending to increase secrecy over research findings and to hinder free scientific communication. University professors, researchers and government institution scientists are increasingly becoming entrepreneurial and are entering private industry.

Another important trend is that large multinational corporations are purchasing smaller seed and biotechnology companies and diversifying their holdings. This allows them to develop a package sale of chemicals, seeds and equipment.

Heavy involvement of the private sector and market considerations greatly influence the topics and commodities chosen for research. Major crops, commodities and farming systems of great socio-economic importance to the developing world, but of little international market importance, do not figure in the biotechnology research agenda of industrialized countries. Furthermore, these countries are keen to reduce their production costs, increase the productivity, quality and value of their products and, thus, improve their overall competitiveness in the world market.

Biotechnology facilities are being established in most developing countries. However, the level of research, development and use of biotechnology for agriculture, forestry and fisheries in the developing countries is generally far below the level in the industrialized countries. Among developing countries, the status varies considerably. A few, such as Brazil, Mexico, India, China and The Republic of Korea, have sought to gain full scientific and technological capacity, especially in agricultural biotechnology. Others, such as Indonesia, Malaysia, the Philippines and Thailand and a few countries of Latin America, have built the capacity to apply biotechniques and develop biotechnologies useful for their agriculture and food industries. The participation of the private sector in gaining biotechnological capacity is not significant in most of these countries.

Many developing countries have inadequate funding, poor human resources and limited access to information, resulting in a relatively low-level capacity for research and technology development and exploitation, especially in the field of modern biotechnology research, which is costly and requires highly trained personnel. Most developing countries are vague as to their immediate aims in agricultural biotechnology. Few have appropriate proprietary-right protection systems or mechanisms to increase their access to protected techniques and products. Furthermore, there is negligible involvement of the private sector, which accentuates the problem of insufficient attention to biotechnology.

One of the major constraints on biotechnological development in developing countries is the poor quality and extent of higher education in frontier sciences, especially molecular biology.

Besides, there are no or very weak links between universities and research institutions to reinforce each other and to utilize synergistically the scarce trained personnel resources. The university experts play a negligible role in national policy formulation, including that on biotechnology. Furthermore the universities are generally not oriented for efficiency in commercialization and are therefore not able to market biotechnology products of their own or others' inventions.

Some international and donor-country public sector institutions strive to ensure that attention is given to solving, through biotechnology, the food and agriculture problems of developing countries. Among this group are the International Agricultural Research Centres (IARCs) located or operating in developing countries. Capacity exists in several of these centres for utilization of advances in biotechnologies to solve certain problems of plant production and protection and of livestock production and health, and capacity is being built in others.

For example, the International Rice Research Institute (IRRI) is incorporating modern molecular biology in its rice research activities. Its programme is linked closely to the Rockefeller Foundation Biotechnology Network. The World Bank, the International Service for National Agricultural Research (ISNAR) and the Australian Government undertook a major study on the likely impact of modern biotechnology on agriculture. This study is being followed up by the participants by an expansion in the World Bank lending for biotechnology and by ISNAR's establishing an Intermediary Biotechnology Service to provide advisory services to national agricultural research systems.

APPLICATIONS, IMPACT AND POTENTIAL

Biotechnological research and development are moving at a very fast rate. For instance, three years ago, transgenics in rice, especially in japonica rices, were considered rather difficult because of the problem of regeneration through protoplast culture. But today, a large number of transgenics both in indica and japonica types are available and are being tested at various stages. It is therefore difficult to predict the potential and impact of a given technology beyond five years or so. This section gives a brief account of the current level of technology and refers to the developments likely to occur in the next three to five years.

The potential of genetic engineering in medicine has received much attention. The potential for advances in agriculture, forestry and fishery are similarly bright. Biotechniques are already being used to create new strains of crop plants, new plant and animal diagnostic products, animal vaccines, biological pesticides and herbicides, other biological control agents, and modifications in domestic animals used for food production.

In some cases, applications are being held in check by the need for still more research to ensure that there are no harmful effects (or, if there are, they are greatly outweighed by the benefits) and by the slow pace of evolution of regulations governing the release of genetically modified organisms or products for general use or acquisition. Biotechnological research, especially genetic engineering, on problems of field and tree crops, forest species and fisheries has a relatively short history. The knowledge of biological aspects of species and ecosystems needs to be expanded in may cases before new biotechnologies can be applied effectively. Even where transfer of one or more genes can be achieved reliably, expression of the transferred gene(s) may not occur in the expected way. The search for and identification and cloning of useful genes, effective vector systems, methods of gene transfer and promoter mechanisms should be intensified.

A perspective on both the difficulties and intensity of the research effort suggests that diagnostic tools will speed solutions in the next five to ten years to certain disease problems in several crop, forest, animal and fish species, such as black sigatoka of banana and plantain, and virus/viroid diseases of coconut and rice.

Improved tolerance to certain physical stresses, such as heat tolerance in potatoes, may also be achieved, but prospects for improved resistance of varieties and clones to most abiotic stresses are longer term.

Livestock

Among agricultural and allied fields, animal production and health have benefited the most from biotechnology, although practical use of transgenic livestock is only a future possibility. Wide use of monoclonal antibodies for efficient diagnostics, leading to safe and specific treatments of animal diseases, is a major breakthrough.

Through genetic engineering, vaccines for the prevention of viral, bacterial, and parasitic animal diseases are rendered more effective and safe. Tailored vaccines exist for pig scours, chicken bursar disease and cattle tickborne diseases. Pathogen-specific vaccines are attractive goals. Other interesting possibilities are endocrine-directed vaccines to stimulate twinning in beef cattle, immunocastration, livestock growth rate increase and vaccines that compensate for various stress-induced production losses.

Advances in genetic engineering will also facilitate the production of male-only populations of screwworms, tsetse flies, ticks and various other ectoparasites for use in the sterile release technique of control or eradication. Furthermore mammalian tissue culture may replace whole animals in the 1990s for toxicity testing of certain chemicals. The culture technique can also be exploited for studying and analyzing pesticide metabolism and for herbicide pre-screening. In vitro fertilization and embryo sexing techniques have considerably increased the use of embryo transfer techniques for cattle breeding and trade. The value of the approach will be further enhanced if embryo cloning techniques can be reliably employed. Microbial and enzymatic treatment of roughages and genetic engineering of rumen bacteria both have great potential to improve animal nutrition. Growth hormones can be produced by genetically engineered microorganisms in quantities and at the low cost necessary for widespread use to speed and increase milk and lean meat production. Biotechnological tools (embryo culture, gene cloning, etc.) may also be used for conservation of genetic resources.

Forestry

Successful regeneration through micropropagation or somatic embryogenesis has been achieved for about 100 forest species although, for most, considerable development work would be required before commercial propagation could be contemplated. In breeding programmes incorporating clonal testing, inclusion of a micromultiplication phase may facilitate more rapid deployment of superior genotypes than that afforded by sequential multiplication by cuttings.

This will particularly be the case when gene mappling techniques are sufficiently advanced to permit accurate identification of superior genotypes without replicated clonal testing in the field, especially within a breeding line where substantial genetic disequilibrium exists. Furthermore, gene mapping may allow eventual identification of valuable genes, including those that contribute to quantitative traits.

As regards the application of genetic engineering, many major traits of commercial importance to forestry are under polygenic control, and much remains to be learned about the operation of the genes involved before this technique can have a major impact for these characters. An earlier application of genetic engineering in some forestry operations may be the introduction of genes, some already available, known to confer insect of disease resistance. Other applications of biotechnology with obvious value for forestry, but as yet not widely supported by experimental successes, include: in vitro manipulation of the maturation state, *e.g.* the promotion of early flowering to reduce generation intervals, in vitro selection for traits such as disease resistance and tolerance to salinity; and the use of haploid cultures.

Fisheries

Two broad areas of biotechnology exist within the fisheries sector, namely natural products biotechnology (including mostly marine species); and aquaculture biotechnology. Commercially valuable products such as pharmaceutical compounds, pigments, oils, sterols, alginates and agarose are being extracted from micro-and macro-algae in many parts of the world. Aquatic invertebrates are currently being screened for biologically active compounds that may have, inter alia anti-carcinogenic or antiviral properties, whereas marine bacteria are currently utilized in treatments of oil spills and holding tanks in tanker ships.

Within aquaculture, induced increases in the chromosome complement (polyploidy) of commercially important species such as salmon and oysters have increased the growth and marketability of these species. Genetically engineered microbes can be used to produce fish growth hormones, which might then be used to improve feed conversion and growth rate. Synthetic reproductive hormones are produced commercially and used to regulate fecundity, breeding cycles, growth rates and sex determination in certain cultured species. In attempts to increase desirable culture qualities such as growth rate, disease resistance, temperature tolerance and marketability, transgenic fishes containing introduced genes from other species have been produced on an experimental scale. The application of advanced biotechnology to the fisheries sector is a relatively recent practice. Therefore, continued research can be expected to reveal additional commercially viable applications and products within this sector.

PROCESSING AND PRODUCT QUALITY AND USES

Biotechnology could have great potential for improving the quality and diversifying the uses of agricultural, forestry and fisheries products. This technology could be used for processing products by both traditional and new methods in order to:

- Improve the value, safety and quality of processed and unprocessed foods, such as genetically engineered tomatoes which soften more slowly and which could be processed at lower temperatures, resulting in a higher proportion of solids to liquid in canned tomatoes;
- Enhance non-food uses of farm products and thereby increase their market value;
- Develop new uses for farm products, especially those often producing surpluses, including energy production from biomass and recycling of wastes and by products. An example of such an application is found in ethanol production from cassava and sugar cane;
- Produce algal cells from, for instance, Spirulina or Chlorella in mass culture for proteins;
- Produce enzymes on a commercial scale, especially using the microbial system, as substitutes for enzymes isolated from animal or plant sources. For example, chymosin, the enzyme used in the manufacture of cheese, traditionally taken from the cow, can now be made from specially engineered microorganisms. Mass production of amino acids from molasses and other agricultural resources is another example. These amino acids can improve the nutritional value of food and animal feed;
- Produce and use new probes for rapid detection and accurate identification of specific microbial pathogens in food, especially diagnostics for staphylococcal enterotoxins, and others; and

- Enhance productivity through the application of newly developed processes such as the immobilized enzyme and plant tissue culture systems which are being used to produce useful secondary metabolites. Examples are diosgenin, a female contraceptive commonly used in China and India and shikonin, a natural pigment used for lipstick in Japan.

Biotechnology is being used in a number of countries to characterize the indigenous germplasm variability for therapeutic and biologically important substances. The use of biotechnology for the removal of toxic and antinutritional factors and for improving the quality of food products is gaining momentum.

These techniques include the elimination or reduction of cyanogenic compounds in cassava and the incorporation of high protein in potato and sweet potato.

BACTERIOLOGICAL CHANGES

THE BACTERIAL FLORA ON LIVE FISH

Microorganisms are found on all the outer surfaces (skin and gills) and in the intestines of live and newly caught fish. The total number of organisms vary enormously and Liston (1980) states a normal range of 10^2–10^7 cfu (colony forming units)/cm^2 on the skin surface. The gills and the intestines both contain between 10^3 and 10^9 cfu/g.

The bacterial flora on newly-caught fish depends on the environment in which it is caught rather than on the fish species. Fish caught in very cold, clean waters carry the lower numbers whereas fish caught in warm waters have slightly higher counts. Very high numbers, *i.e.*, 10^7 cfu/cm^2 are found on fish from polluted warm waters. Many different bacterial species can be found on the fish surfaces. The bacteria on temperate water fish are all classified according to their growth temperature range as either psychrotrophs or psychrophiles. Psychrotrophs (cold-tolerant) are bacteria capable of growth at 0°C but with optimum around 25°C.

Psychrophiles (cold-loving) are bacteria with maximum growth temperature around 20°C and optimum temperature at 15°C. In warmer waters, higher numbers of mesophiles can be isolated.

The microflora on temperate water fish is dominated by psychrotrophic Gram-negative rodshaped bacteria belonging to the genera *Pseudomonas, Moraxella, Acinetobacter, Shewanella* and *Flavobacterium.*

Members of the *Vibrionaceae (Vibrio* and *Photobacterium)* and the *Aeromonadaceae (Aeromonas* spp.) are also common aquatic bacteria and typical of the fish flora. Gram-positive organisms as *Bacillus, Micrococcus, Clostridium, Lactobacillus* and coryneforms can also be found in varying proportions, but in general, Gram-negative bacteria dominate the microflora. Shewan (1977) concluded that Gram-positive *Bacillus* and Micrococcus dominate on fish from tropical waters. However, this conclusion has later been challenged by several studies which have found that the microflora on tropical fish species is very similar to the flora on temperate species. A microflora consisting of *Pseudomonas, Acinetobacter, Moraxella* and *Vibrio* has been found on newly-caught fish in several Indian studies. Several authors conclude, as Liston (1980), that the microflora on tropical fish often carry a slightly higher load of Gram-positives and enteric bacteria but otherwise is similar to the flora on temperate-water fish.

Aeromonas spp. are typical of freshwater fish, whereas a number of bacteria require sodium for growth and are thus typical of marine waters. These include *Vibrio, Photobacterium* and *Shewanella*. However, although *Shewanella putrefaciens* is characterized as sodium-requiring, strains of *S. putrefaciens* can also be isolated from freshwater environments. Although *S. putrefaciens* has been isolated from tropical freshwaters, it is not important in the spoilage of freshwater fish.

Table: Bacterial flora on fish caught in clean, unpolluted waters

Gram-negative	Gram-positive	Comments
Pseudomonas	*Bacillus*	
Moraxella	*Clostridium*	
Acinetobacter	*Micrococcus*	
Shewanella putrefaciens	*Lactobacillus*	
Flavobacterium	Coryneforms	
Cytophaga		
Vibrio Photobacterium		*Vibrio* and *Photobacterium*
Aeromonas		are typical of marine waters; *Aeromonas* is typical of freshwater

In polluted waters, high numbers of *Enterobacteriaceae* may be found. In clean temperate waters, these organisms disappear rapidly, but it has been shown that *Escherichia coli* and *Salmonella* can survive for very long periods in tropical waters and once introduced may almost become indigenous to the environment. The taxonomy of S. *putrefaciens* has been rather confused. The organism was originally associated with the *Achromobacter* group but was later placed in the Shewan *Pseudomonas* group IV.

Based on percentage of guanine+ cytosine (GC %) it was transferred to the genus *Alteromonas,* but on the basis of 5SRNA homology it was reclassified to a new genus, *Shewanella*.

It has recently been suggested that the genus *Aeromonas* spp. which was a member of the *Vibrionaceae* family be transferred to its own family, the *Aeromonadaceae*. Japanese studies have shown very high numbers of microorganisms in the gastrointestinal tract of fish, and as such numbers are much higher than in the surrounding water, this indicates the presence of a favourable ecological niche for the microorganisms.

Similarly, Larsen *et al.* (1978) reported up to 10^7 cfu/g of vibrio-like organisms in the intestinal tract of cod and Westerdahl *et al.* (1991) also isolated high numbers of vibrio-like organisms from the intestines of turbot. *Photobacterium phosphoreum* which can be isolated from the surface can also be isolated in high numbers from the intestinal tract of some fish species. On the contrary, some authors believe that the microflora of the gastrointestinal tract is merely a reflection of the environment and the food intake.

Microbial Invasion

The flesh of healthy live or newly-caught fish is sterile as the immune system of the fish prevents the bacteria from growing in the flesh. When the fish dies, the immune system collapses and bacteria are allowed to proliferate freely. On the skin surface, the bacteria to a large extent colonize the scale pockets. During storage, they invade the flesh by moving between the muscle fibres. Murray and Shewan (1979) found that only a very limited number of bacteria invaded the flesh during iced storage.

Ruskol and Bendsen (1992) showed that bacteria can be detected by microscope in the flesh when the number of organisms on the skin surface increases above 10^6 cfu/cm^2. This was seen at both iced and ambient temperatures. No difference was found in the invasive patterns of specific spoilage bacteria (*e.g.*, S. *putrefaciens)* and non-spoilage bacteria.

Since only a limited number of organisms actually invade the flesh and microbial growth mainly takes place at the surface, spoilage is probably to a large extent a consequence of bacterial enzymes diffusing into the flesh and nutrients diffusing to the outside.

Fish spoil at very different rates, and differences in surface properties of fish have been proposed to explain this. Skins of fish have very different textures. Thus whiting *(Merlangius merlangus)* and cod *(Gadus morhua)* which have a very fragile integument spoil rapidly compared to several flatfish such as plaice that has a very robust dermis and epidermis. Furthermore, the latter group has a very thick slime layer, which includes several antibacterial components, such as antibodies, complement and bacteriolytic enzymes.

METHOD OF FISHING TECHNIQUES

Fishing techniques are methods for catching fish. The term may also be applied to methods for catching other aquatic animals such as molluscs (shellfish, squid, octopus) and edible marine invertebrates. Fishing techniques include hand gathering, spearfishing, netting, angling and trapping. Recreational, commercial and artisanal fishers use different techniques, and also, sometimes, the same techniques. Recreational fishers fish for pleasure or sport, while commercial fishers fish for profit. Artisanal fishers use traditional, low-tech methods, for survival in third-world countries, and as a cultural heritage in other countries. Mostly, recreational fishers use angling methods and commercial fishers use netting methods. There is an intricate link between various fishing techniques and knowledge about the fish and their behaviour including migration, foraging and habitat. The effective use of fishing techniques often depends on this additional knowledge. Which techniques are appropriate is dictated mainly by the target species and by its habitat.

POSSIBLE OF HAND FISHING

It is possible to fish and gather many sea foods with minimal equipment by using the hands. Gathering seafood by hand can be as easily as picking shellfish or kelp up off the beach, or doing some digging for clams or crabs. The earliest evidence for shellfish gathering dates back to a 300,000 year old site in France called Terra Amata. This is a hominid site as modern Homo sapiens did not appear until around 50,000 years ago.

- Flounder tramping-Every August, the small Scottish village of Palnackie hosts the world flounder tramping championships where flounder are captured by stepping on them.
- Noodling: is practiced in the United States. The noodler places his hand inside a catfish hole. If all goes as planned, the catfish swims forward and latches onto the noodler's hand, and can then be dragged out of the hole.
- Pearl divers-traditionally harvested oysters by free-diving to depths of thirty metres. Today, free-diving recreational fishers catch lobster and abalone by hand.
- Trout binning-is another method of taking trout. Rocks in a rocky stream are struck with a sledgehammer. The force of the blow stuns the fish.
- Trout tickling-In the British Isles, the practice of catching trout by hand is known as trout tickling; it is an art mentioned several times in the plays of Shakespeare.

Fishing of Netting

Fishing nets are meshes usually formed by knotting a relatively thin thread. About 180 AD the Greek author Oppian wrote the *Halieutica*, a didactic poem about fishing. He described various means of fishing including the use of nets cast from boats, scoop nets held open by a hoop, and various traps "which work while their masters sleep". Netting is the principal method of commercial fishing, though longlining, trolling, dredging and traps are also used.

- Artisanal techniques
- Chinese fishing nets-are shore operated lift nets. Huge mechanical contrivances hold out horizontal nets with diameters of twenty metres or more. The nets are dipped into the water and raised again, but otherwise cannot be moved.

- Lampuki nets-are an example of a traditional artisanal use of nets. Since Roman times, Maltese fishers have cut the larger, lower fronds from palm trees which they then weave into large flat rafts. The rafts are pulled out to sea by a luzzu, a small traditional fishing boat. In the middle of the day, lampuki fish (the Maltese name for mahi-mahi) school underneath the rafts, seeking the shade, and are caught by the fishers using large mesh nets.
- Cast nets-are round nets with small weights distributed around the edge. They also called *throw nets.* The net is caste or thrown by hand in such a manner that it spreads out on the water and sinks. Fish are caught as the net is hauled back in. This simple device has been in use, with various modifications, for thousands of years.
- Drift net-are nets which are not anchored. They are usually gillnets, and are commonly used in the coastal waters of many countries. Their use on the high seas is prohibited, but still occurs.
- Ghost nets-are nets that have been lost at sea. They can be a menace to marine life for many years.
- Gillnets-catch fish which try to pass through by snagging on the gill covers. Trapped, the fish can neither advance through the net nor retreat.
- Hand nets-are small nets held open by a hoop. They have been used since antiquity. They are also called scoop nets, and are used for scooping up fish near the surface of the water. They may or may not have a handle–if they have a long handle they are called *dip nets*. When used by anglers to help land fish they are called *landing nets*. Because hand netting is not destructive to fish, hand nets are used for tag and release, or capturing aquarium fish.
- Seine nets-are large fishing nets that can be arranged in different ways. In purse seining fishing the net hangs vertically in the water by attaching weights along the bottom edge and floats along the top. Danish seining is a method which has some similarities with trawling. A simple and commonly used fishing technique is beach seining, where the seine net is operated from the shore.
- Surrounding net-
- Trawl nets-are large nets, conical in shape, designed to be towed in the sea or along the sea bottom. The trawl is pulled through the water by one or more boats, called trawlers. The activity of pulling the trawl through the water is called trawling.

Methods of Spearfishing Fishing

Spearfishing is an ancient method of fishing conducted with an ordinary spear or a specialised variant such as a harpoon, trident, arrow or eel spear. Some fishing spears use slings (or rubber loops) to propel the spear.

- Bowfishing-uses a bow and arrow to kill fish in shallow water from above.
- Gigging-uses small trident type spears with long handles for gigging bullfrogs with a bright light at night, or for gigging suckers and other rough fish in shallow water. Gigging is popular in the American South and Midwest.
- Hawaiian slings-have a sling separate from the spear, in the manner of an underwater bow and arrow.
- Harpoons-Spearfishing with barbed poles was widespread in palaeolithic times. Cosquer cave in Southern France contains cave art over 16,000 years old, including drawings of seals which appear to have been harpooned.
- Polespears-have a sling attached to the spear.
- Modern spearguns-traditional spearfishing is restricted to shallow waters, but the development of the speargun has made the method much more efficient. With practice, divers are able to hold their breath for up to four minutes and sometimes longer. Of course, a diver with underwater breathing equipment can dive for much longer periods.
- Tridents-are three-pronged spears. They are also called leisters or gigs. They are used for spear fishing and were formerly also a military weapon. They feature widely in early mythology and history.

Methods of Angling and Line Fishing

Angling is a method of fishing by means of an "angle" (hook). The hook is usually attached to a line, and is sometimes weighed down by a sinker so it sinks in the water. This is the classic "hook, line and sinker" arrangement, used in angling since prehistoric times. The hook is usually baited with lures or bait fish. Additional arrangements include the use of a fishing rod, which can be fitted with a reel, and functions as a delivery mechanism for casting the line. Other delivery methods for projecting the line include fishing kites and cannons, kontiki rafts and remote controlled devices. Floats can can also be used to help set the line or function as bite indicators. The hook can be dressed with lures or bait. Angling is the principal method of sport fishing, but commercial fisheries also use angling methods involving multiple hooks, such as longlining or commercial trolling.

Line fishing is fishing with a fishing line. A fishing line is any cord made for fishing. Important parameters of a fishing line are its length, material, and weight (thicker, sturdier lines are more visible to fish). Factors that may determine what line an angler chooses for a given fishing environment include breaking strength, knot strength, UV resistance, castability, limpness, stretch, abrasion resistance, and visibility. Modern fishing lines are usually made from artificial substances. The most common type is *monofilament*, made of a single strand. There are also *braided fishing lines* and thermally fused *superlines*.

- Droplining-a dropline consists of a long fishing line set vertically down into the water, with a series of baited hooks Droplines have a weight at the bottom and a float at the top. They are not usually as long as longlines and have fewer hooks.
- Handlining-is fishing with a single fishing line, baited with lures or bait fish, which is held in the hands. Handlining can be done from boats or from the shore. It is used mainly to catch groundfish and squid, but smaller pelagic fish can also be caught.
- Longlining-is a commercial technique that uses a long heavy fishing line with a series of hundreds or even thousands of baited hooks hanging from the main line by means of branch lines called "snoods". Longlines are usually operated from specialised boats called longliners. They use a special winch to haul in the line, and can operate in deeper waters targeting pelagic species such as swordfish, tuna, halibut and sablefish.
- Slabbing-involves repetitively lifting and dropping a flat lure, usually made of 1 to 2.5 oz of lead painted to look like a baitfish, through a school of actively feeding fish that the angler has located on a fish finder. Used on white and striped bass in the reservoirs of the southern USA.
- Trolling-is fishing with one or more baited lines which are drawn through the water. This may be done by pulling the line behind a slow moving boat, or by slowly winding the line in when fishing from the land. Trolling is used to catch pelagic fish such as mackerel and kingfish.
- Trotlining-a trotline is like a dropline, except that a dropline has a series of hooks suspended vertically in the water, while a trotline has a series of hooks suspended horizontally in the water. Trotlines can be physically set in many ways, such as tying each end to something fixed, and adjusting the set of the rest of the line with weights and floats. They are used for catching crabs or fish, such as catfish, particularly across rivers.

Angling with a Rod

Fishing rods give more control of the fishing line. The rod is usually fitted with a fishing reel which functions as a mechanism for storing, retrieving and paying out the line. Floats may also be used, and can function as bite indicators. The hook can be dressed with lures or bait.

- Bank fishing-fishing from river banks and similar shorelines. Bank fishing is usually performed with a rod and reel, alhough nets, traps, and spears can also be used. People who fish from a boat can sometimes access more areas in prime locations with greater ease than bank fishermen. However many people don't own boats and find fishing from the bank has its own advantages. Bank fishing has its own requirements, and many things come into play for success, such as local knowledge, water depth, bank structure, location, time of day, and the type of bait and lures.

- Casting-the act of throwing the fishing line out over the water using a flexible fishing rod. The usual technique is for the angler to quickly flick the rod from behind towards the water. Casting is also a sport adjunct to fishing, much as shooting is to hunting. The sport is supervised by the International Casting Sport Federation, which sponsors tournaments and recognizes world records for accuracy and distance.
- Float tubes-small doughnut-shaped boats with an underwater seat in the "hole". Float tubes are used for fly fishing and enable the angler to reach deeper water without splashing and disturbing stillwater fish.
- Fly fishing-the use of artificial flies as lures. These are cast with specially constructed fly rods and fly lines. The fly line (today, almost always coated with plastic) is heavy enough cast in order to send the fly to the target. Artificial flies vary dramatically in size, weight and colour. Fly fishing is a distinct and ancient angling method, most renowned as a method for catching trout and salmon, but employed today for a wide variety of species including pike, bass, panfish, and carp, as well as marine species, such as redfish, snook, tarpon, bonefish and striped bass. There is a growing population of anglers whose aim is to catch as many different species as possible with the fly.
- Rock fishing-fishing from rocky outcrops into the sea. It is a popular pastime in Australia and New Zealand. It can be a dangerous pastime and claims many lives each year.
- Surfcasting-fishing from a shoreline using a rod to cast into the surf. With few exceptions, surf fishing is done in saltwater, often from a beach. The basic idea of most surfcasting is to cast a bait or lure as far out into the water as is necessary to reach the target fish from the shore. This may or may not require long casting distances and muscular techniques. Basic surf fishing can be done with a surfcasting rod between seven and twelve feet long, with an extended butt section, equipped with an appropriate spinning or conventional casting reel. Dedicated surfcasters usually possess an array of terminal and other tackle, with rods and reels of different lengths and actions, and

lures and baits of different weights and capabilities. Depending on fishing conditions and the fish they are targeting, such surfcasters tailor bait and terminal tackle to rod and reel and the size and species of the fish. Reels and other equipment need to be constructed so they resist the corrosive and abrasive effects of salt and sand.

Trapping

Traps are culturally almost universal and seem to have been independently invented many times. There are essentially two types of trap, a permanent or semipermanent structure placed in a river or tidal area and pot-traps that are baited to attract prey and periodically lifted.

- Dam fishing-An artisanal technique called dam fishing is used by the Baka pygmies. This involves the construction of a temporary dam resulting in a drop in the water levels downstream.
- Basket weir fish traps-were widely used in ancient times. They are shown in medieval illustrations and surviving examples have been found. Basket weirs are about 2 m long and comprise two wicker cones, one inside the other — easy to get into and hard to get out.
- Fishing weir-In medieval Europe, large fishing weir structures were constructed from wood posts and wattle fences. 'V' shaped structures in rivers could be as long as 60 metres and worked by directing fish towards fish traps or nets. Such fish traps were evidently controversial in medieval England. The Magna Carta includes a clause requiring that they be removed: *"All fish-weirs shall be removed from the Thames, the Medway, and throughout the whole of England, except on the sea coast"*.
- Fish wheels-operate alongside streams, much as a water-powered mill wheel. A wheel complete with baskets and paddles is attached to a floating dock. The wheel rotates due to the current of the stream. The baskets on the wheel capture fish travelling upstream and transfer them into a holding tank. When the holding tank is full, the fish are removed.
- Lobster traps-also called lobster pots, are traps used to catch lobsters. They resemble fish traps, yet are usually smaller and consist of several sections. Lobster traps are also used to catch other crustaceans, such as crabs and crayfish. They can be constructed in various shapes, but the design strategy is to make the entry into the trap much easier than exit. The pots are baited and lowered into the water and checked frequently. Historically lobster pots were constructed with wood or metal. Today most traps are made from checkered wire and mesh. It is common for the trap to be weighted down with bricks. A bait bag is hung in the middle of the trap. In

theory the lobster walks up the mesh and then falls into the wire trap. Bait varies from captain to captain but it is common to use herring. In commercial lobstering five to ten of these traps will be connected with line. A buoy marks each end of the string of pots. Two buoys are important to make retrieval easier and so captains don't set their traps over each other. Each buoy is painted differently so the various captains can identify their traps.

Other Angling

- Bottom fishing-is fishing the bottom of a body of water. In the United Kingdom it is called "legering". A common rig for fishing on the bottom is a weight tied to the end of the line, with a hook about an inch up line from the weight. The method can be used both with hand lines and rods. There are fishing rods specialized for bottom fishing, called "donkas". The weight is used to cast or throw the line an appropriate distance. Bottom fishing can be done both from boats and from the land. It targets groundfish such as sucker fish, bream, catfish, and crappie.
- Fishing cannon-
- Ice fishing-is the practice of catching fish with lines and hooks through an opening in the ice on a frozen body of water. It is practised by hunter-gatherers such as the Inuit and by anglers in other cold or continental climates.
- Kayak fishing-has a long history, and has gained popularity in recent times. Many of the techniques used are the same as those used on other fishing boats, apart from difference is in the setup, how each piece of equipment is fitted to the kayak, and how each activity is carried out on such a small craft.
- Kite fishing is said to have been invented in China. It was, and still is, used by the people of New Guinea and other Pacific Islands-either by cultural diffusion from China or independent invention. Kites can provide the boatless fishermen access to waters that would otherwise be available only to boats. Similarly, for boat owners, kites provide a way to fish in areas where it is not safe to navigate such as shallows or coral reefs where fish may be plentiful. Kites can also be used for trolling a lure through the water. Suitable kites may be of very simple construction. Those of Tobi Island are a large leaf stiffened by the ribs of the fronds of the coconut palm. The fishing line may be made from coconut fibre and the lure made from spiders webs. Modern kitefishing is popular in New Zealand, where large delta kites of synthetic materials are used to fish from beaches, taking a line and hooks far out past the breakers. Kite fishing is also emerging in

Melbourne where sled kites are becoming popular, both off beaches and off boats and in freshwater areas. The disabled community are increasingly using the kites for fishing as they allow mobility impaired people to cast the bait further out than they would otherwise be able to.

- Boat anglers-Fishing is usually done either from a boat or from a shoreline or river bank. When fishing from a boat, pretty much any fishing technique can be used, from nets to fish traps, but some form of angling is by far the most common. Compared to fishing from the land, fishing from a boat allows more access to different fishing grounds and different species of fish. Some tackle is specialised for boat anglers, such as sea rods.
- Remote control fishing-Fishing can also be done using a remote controlled boat. The boat is usually one to three feet long and runs on a small DC battery. A radio transmitter controls the boat. The fisherman connects the fishing line/bait to the boat; drives it; navigating the water by manipulating the remote controller. The technique is growing in popularity. The methods of remote control vary, from tying a piece of fishing line and bait to the boat, and driving, (retrieving) the hooked fish, with the boat. Another method is using an apparatus designed so that once the fish is hooked the line disconnects from the boat, and the fish is retrieved with the fishing rod.

Animals

- Cooperative human-dolphin fisheries date back to the ancient Roman author and natural philosopher Pliny the Elder. A modern human-dolphin fishery still takes place in Laguna, Santa Catarina, Brazil. Here, dolphins drive fish towards fishermen waiting along the shore and give them a signal when they can cast their nets. The dolphins then feed off the fish that manage to escape the nets.
- Cormorant fishing-In China and Japan, the practice of cormorant fishing is thought to date back some 1300 years. Fishermen use the natural fish-hunting instincts of the cormorants to catch fish, but a metal ring placed round the bird's neck prevents large, valuable fish from being swallowed. The fish are instead collected by the fisherman.
- Frigatebirds fishing-The people of Nauru used trained frigatebirds to fish on reefs.
- Portuguese Water Dogs-Dating from the 1500s in Portugal, Portuguese Water Dogs were used by fishermen to send messages between boats, to retrieve fish and articles from the water, and to guard the fishing boats. Labrador Retrievers have been used by

fishermen to assist in bringing nets to shore; the dog would grab the floating corks on the ends of the nets and pull them to shore.

- Remora fishing-The practice of tethering a remora, a sucking fish, to a fishing line and using the remora to capture sea turtles probably originated in the Indian Ocean. The earliest surviving records of the practice are Peter Martyr d'Anghera's 1511 accounts of the second voyage of Columbus to the New World. However, these accounts are probably apocryphal, and based on earlier, no longer extant accounts from the Indian Ocean region.

Other Techniques

- Artisanal techniques
- Basnig-
- Electrofishing-is another recently developed technique, primarily used in freshwater by fisheries scientists. Electrofishing uses electricity to stun fish so they can be caught. It is commonly used in scientific surveys, sampling fish populations for abundance, density, and species composition. When performed correctly, electrofishing results in no permanent harm to fish, which return to their natural state a few minutes after being stunned.
- Fish aggregating devices-are man-made objects used to attract pelagic fish such as marlin, tuna and mahi-mahi (dolphin fish). They usually consist of buoys or floats tethered to the ocean floor with concrete blocks.
- Dredging-There are types of dredges used for collecting scallops, oysters or sea cucumbers from the seabed. They have the form of a scoop made of chain mesh and they are towed by a fishing boat. Dredging can be destructive to the seabed, because the marine life is unable to survive the weight of the dredge. It is extremely detrimental to coral beds since they take centuries to rebuild themselves. Unmonitored dredging can be compared to unmonitored forest clearing, where it can wipe out ecosystems. Nowadays, this method of fishing is often replaced by mariculture or by scuba diving.
- Fish finders-are electronic sonar devices which indicate the presence of fish and fish schools. They are widely used by recreational fishermen. Commercially, they are used with other electronic locating and positioning devices.
- Fishing light attractors-use lights attached to some structure to attract fish and bait fish. Fishing light attractor are operated every night. After a while, fish discover the increased concentration of bait surrounding the light. Once located, the fish return regularly, and can be harvested.

- Flossing-
- Harvesting machines-have recently been developed for commercial fishing. Harvesting machines use pumps to pump fish out of the sea. Dredges have also been mechanized so that they directly transfer mollusks to the surface as are dredged.
- Payaos-a type of fish aggregating device used in Southeast Asia, particularly in the Philippines. Payaos were traditionally bamboo rafts for handline fishing before World War II, but modern steel payaos use fish lights and fish location sonar to increase yields. While payaos fishing is sustainable on a small scale, the large scale, modern applications have been linked to adverse impacts on fish stocks.
- Shrimp baiting-is a method used by recreational fisherman for of catching shrimp. It uses a cast net, bait and long poles. The poles are used to mark a specific location and then bait is thrown in the water near the pole. After several minutes the cast net is thrown as close to the bait as possible and shrimp are caught in the net. In the 1980s the sport became popular in the south eastern coastal states of the USA.

Destructive Techniques

Destructive fishing practices are practices that easily result in irreversible damage to aquatic habitats and ecosystems. Many fishing techniques can be destructive if used inappropriately, but some practices are particularly likely to result in irreversible damage. These practices are mostly, though not always, illegal. Where they are illegal, they are often inadequately enforced. Some examples are:

- Explosives-Dynamite or blast fishing, is done easily and cheaply with dynamite or homemade bombs made from locally available materials. Fish are killed by the shock from the blast and are then skimmed from the surface or collected from the bottom. The explosions indiscriminately kill large numbers of fish and other marine organisms in the vicinity and can damage or destroy the physical environment. Explosions are particularly harmful to coral reefs. Blast fishing is also illegal in many waterways around the world.
- Bottom trawling-
- Cyanide fishing-Cyanides are used to capture live fish near coral reefs for the aquarium and seafood market. This illegal fishing occurs mainly in or near the Philippines, Indonesia, and the Caribbean to supply the 2 million marine aquarium owners in the world. Many fish caught in this fashion die either immediately or in shipping. Those that survive often die from shock or from massive digestive damage. The high concentrations of cyanide on reefs harvested in this fashion

damages the coral polyps and has also resulted in cases of cyanide poisoning among local fishermen and their families.

- Fish toxins-
- Muroami-is a destructive artisan fishing method employed on coral reefs in Southeast Asia. An encircling net is used with pounding devices, such as large stones fitted on ropes that are pounded onto the coral reefs. They can also consist of large heavy blocks of cement suspended above the sea by a crane fitted to the vessel. The pounding devices are repeatedly lowered into the area encircled by the net, smashing the coral into small fragments in order to scare the fish out of their coral refuges. The "crushing" effect on the coral heads has been described as having longlasting and practically totally destructive effects.

Ancient remains of spears, hooks and fishnet have been found in ruins of the Stone Age. The people of the early civilization drew pictures of nets and fishing lines in their arts. Early hooks were made from the upper bills of eagles and from bones, shells, horns and plant thorns. Spears were tipped with the same materials, or sometimes with flints. Lines and nets were made from leaves, plant stalk and cocoon silk. Ancient fishing nets were rough in design and material but they were amazingly, as if some now use. Literature on the indigenous fishing practices is very scanty. Baines documented traditional fisheries in the Solomon Island. Use of the herbal fish poisons in catching fishes from fresh water and sea documented from New Caledonia. John documented fishing techniques and overall life style of the Mukkuvar fishing Community of Kanyakumari district of Tamilnadu, India. Tribal people using various plants for medicinal and various purposes extends the use notion for herbal fish stupefying plants. Use of the fish poisons is very old practice in the history of human kind. In 1212 AD King Frederick II prohibited the use of certain plant piscicides, and by the fifteenth century similar laws had been decreed in other European countries as well. All over the globe, indigenous people use various fish poisons to kill the fishes, documented in America and among Tarahumara Indian.

8

Genetic Biotechnologies in Aquaculture

Genetic biotechnologies in aquaculture focus primarily on increasing growth rate, but also include disease resistance and increased environmental tolerance. There are several biotechnologies that can be applied to farmed aquatic species.

Selective breeding, *i.e.* traditional animal breeding, started with the common carp several thousand years ago. However, it has only recently been applied to a handful of other species of food fish such as catfish, trout and tilapia. Therefore, many farmed aquatic species are very similar to their wild relatives. Selective breeding programmes have yielded significant and consistent gains of 5-20 per cent per generation in species of, inter alia, Atlantic salmon, catfish and tilapia. Hybridisation is a simple genetic technology that has become easier with the development of artificial breeding techniques, such as the use of pituitary gland extract and other hormones to initiate gamete development and induce spawning (*i.e.* the depositing of eggs), and an increased understanding of environmental cues that influence reproduction, such as day length, temperature or water current. Many of the natural reproductive isolating mechanisms that species develop in the wild can now be overcome by fish farmers.

These improvements in reproductive technologies have also assisted aquaculturists greatly in their efforts to domesticate aquatic species. In addition, by making it possible to remove the natural constraints and timing of breeding, farmers are able to mate many more species at the times that are most beneficial, and thus help to ensure a steady and consistent supply of fish to the market. Chromosome-set manipulation can be used to produce triploid organisms that generally do not channel energy into reproduction because of problems associated with development of reproductive organs. Initially it was thought that this energy saving would result in increased growth rate, but this seems not to be the case. The real advantage of triploids seems to be in their functional sterility.

For example, triploid oysters do not produce gonads (*i.e.* reproductive glands) and are therefore marketable at times of the year when mature oysters have an off-taste because of production of gametes (*i.e.* sex cells - the ovum, or egg (female), and sperm (male)). In aquaculture, one sex is often more desirable than the other. For example, female sturgeon produce caviar, male tilapia grow faster than females whereas it is the female trout and salmon that generally grow faster than the males. The production of single sex groups of fish takes advantage of these differences between the sexes and can be accomplished by manipulation of the developing gametes and embryo.

The manipulation can be in the form of denaturing (*i.e.* destroying) the DNA in gametes followed by chromosome-set manipulation or by hormonal sex-reversal and subsequent breeding. The phenotypic sex of many aquatic species can be changed by administering appropriate hormones.

For example, genetically male tilapia can be turned into females through estrogen treatments. These genetic males when mated with normal males produce a group of all-male tilapia that grow faster and have less unwanted matings (that lead to overcrowding and stunting) than a group of mixed-sex tilapia. Some of the all-male offspring would have two male chromosomes and these could be used as broodstock for subsequent generations, thus avoiding the use of hormones in the broodstock. Hybridisation can also be used to produce single sex groups of fish, when the sex-determining mechanisms in the parental lines are different (for example, hybridisation of Nile tilapia and the blue tilapia). Genetic engineering is a vague term that has come to be nearly synonymous with gene transfer *i.e.* the production of transgenic fish or genetically modified organisms (GMOs). This technology is progressing rapidly and it is now possible to move genes between distantly related species. Gene transfer in fish has usually involved genes that produce growth hormone and has been shown to dramatically increase growth rate in carp, catfish, salmon, tilapia, mudloach and trout.

A gene from the winter flounder that produces an anti-freeze protein was put into salmon in the hope of extending the farming range of the fish. The gene did not produce enough of the protein to extend the salmon's range into colder waters, but it did allow the salmon to continue growing during cold months when non-transgenic salmon would not grow. Transgenic technology is currently in the research and development stage. To our knowledge there are no transgenic aquatic plants or animals available to the consumer.

CRYOPRESERVATION

The development of cryopreservation or low-temperature technology allows the short- and long-term storage of gametes. Currently, these low-temperature techniques can only be used on male gametes; eggs and embryos can generally not be stored in this way. Freezing gametes can increase the flexibility of a fish breeder, especially when breeding species where the sexes mature or migrate at different times, when the breeding season is very short, when the breeders are far apart or when one sex is exceptionally rare.

Fish Health

Genetic biotechnologies are being used to improve fish health through conventional selection for disease resistance and through the use of molecular investigation of pathogens for characterisation and diagnosis.

DNA-based technologies are being used now to characterise different species and strains of pathogens. Genetic characterisation of the pathogen may also reveal information about its origin, *e.g.* DNA analysis revealed two strains of crayfish plague fungus in Sweden: one from the local species and one originating in Turkey. Once the pathogen is characterised, DNA probes can be developed to screen for specific pathogens in tissue, whole animals and even in water and soil samples. These techniques are being used to detect viral diseases of marine shrimp throughout the world and for bacterial and fungal pathogens in fishes in many areas.

Genetically engineered vaccines are also being developed to protect fish against pathogens. Genetic immunisation of rainbow trout with a glycoprotein gene from the virus causing viral haemorrhagic septicaemia has recently been shown to induce high levels of protection against the virus. Work is also underway on immunising carp, salmon and other fishes with genetically engineered vaccines for other diseases. The new molecular techniques are extremely sensitive and can identify pathogens in fish long before there are any clinical signs of the disease. This has implications for quarantine and the trade of aquatic species, which is currently governed by the World Trade Organisation and the Office International des Epizooties. Trade can be restricted based on the disease status of a product or a region; identification of minute quantities of a pathogen or of a new strain of an existing pathogen could change or influence existing trade patterns.

Farming Systems

Farming systems for aquatic species are diverse and include industrial scale farms, family ponds and culture based fisheries (stocking), in both developed and developing countries. Often, there is a division of the production process where fingerlings (*i.e.* small fish, especially up to one year of age) or eggs are produced by the seed-supplier, but the grow-out to market size is done elsewhere. In the case of sea going salmon, there is often a seed supplier operating a hatchery near a river, a fingerling producer in a freshwater lake, and another group that grows the fish to market size in the sea. Marine shrimp hatcheries in Asia are usually small family owned ventures, whereas in Latin America they are more industrial in scale. Appropriateness of genetic biotechnologies must take these different systems into consideration.

Biotechnologies in Conservation

Genetic biotechnologies can be used to reduce the impacts of farmed fish on wild populations, to identify and manage endangered species and to manage captive populations in aquaria or in species recovery programmes. In several areas, farmed fish must be made triploid, *i.e.* sterile, in order to reduce their impact on wild populations should they escape from the fish farm.

Generally, the planned use of transgenic fish also includes the provision that they are sterile, to reduce the chance of mixing with other fishes. Genetic manipulation and polyploidisation can be combined to regenerate endangered species. This can be done from frozen sperm by denaturing the DNA in an egg of a related species, fertilising with frozen sperm from the endangered species and then duplicating the chromosome-set of the fertilised egg.

CELL CULTURE IN AQUACULTURE

Development and characterization of cell lines from selected finfish and shell fish was undertaken at CIFE, Mumbai and a cell culture system was developed from the fish Lates calcarifer (Sea bass). At CUSAT, the cell lines developed from eyestalk sub-cultured and made available to develop such cell lines as and when required.

The cells shown differentiation in to a proliferating bunch of cells and subsequently got detached as a lump of cell aggregates. The development of cell lines from seabass, Lates calcarifer was attempted at CAH Abdul Hakeem College, Melvisharam and CUSAT. The kidney cells shown fibroblastic and formed a monolayer. The cells were were deposited at NCCS.

Growth Promoting Factor(s)/Signal Transduction

A collaborative project was undertaken on identification, isolation and characterization of growth promoting and differentiation factor(s) from perivitelline fluid of developing embryos of the Indian horseshoe crab at Agharkar Research Institute, Pune, National Centre for Cell Science (NCCS), Pune and National Institute of Oceanography (NIO), Goa. Active fraction identified shown significant enlargement and enhanced compartmentalization of the heart in cardiac development and promoting activity. In another project on large-scale cultivation of amoebocytes in vitro from Indian horseshoe crab implemented by NCCS and NIO, regeneration of gill lamellae of the Indian horseshoe crab was successful in amoebocyte production. A molecular signal intervention mechanism was developed as an alternative to eyestalk ablation at the Departments of Zoology and Biochemistry, University of Madras. A specific inhibitor that intervenes in this pathway has been shown to reduce the molt cycle of the prawn and reduces the turnover time and rearing cost and maximizes the economic returns. By decreasing the molt cycle duration, it can accelerate the growth rate of the prawn resulting in early maturation.

Studies on feed supplementation of highly unsaturated fatty acids (HUFAs) and immunostimulants for disease resistance in freshwater prawn was carried out at the Department of Aquaculture, College of Fisheries, Mangalore. HUFAs namely Eicosapentaenoic acid (C20: 5n-3) and Docosahexaenoic acid (C22: 6n-3) are important for larval growth. The supplementation of PUFA incorporated feed could enhance growth, survival and disease resistance in freshwater prawn. A project on prototyping of raceway based third generation shrimp production technology was implemented at the Fisheries Biotechnology Centre, Fisheries College and Research Institute, Tuticorin. The protocol has been developed to increase survival of post-larvae. This in-door shrimp farming facility will be eco-friendly, economically viable and technically useful for large-scale adoption in aquafarming systems in India.

The work on development of Artemia franciscana culture in the solar salt ponds and processing of Artemia cyst and biomass was undertaken at Centre for Marine Science and Technology, Manonmaniam Sundaranar University, Rajakamangalam, Tamil Nadu. Artemia production was initiated in condenser ponds and inoculated in culture ponds and the efforts are being made to utilize the abandoned area of the saltworks for Artemia cultivation. Studies were undertaken at NIO, Goa to isolate, purify and characterize new natural fluorescent dyes and fluorescent molecules from tissues of sea cucumber Holothuria scabra and to test them as bioactivities compounds for therapeutic and industrial applications.

At Kerala Agriculture University, Kochi, attempts were made to isolate bioactive substances such as antibacterial, antiviral and anticancer agents from the accessory nidamental gland and ink of cuttlefish (Sepia pharaonis ehrenberg). An antitumour peptidoglycan was isolated from cuttlefish ink and the crude preparation showed antitumour activity against mice following intraperitonial administration. The peptidoglycan was made up of protein and uronic acid rich with polysaccharide fraction and was found to be made up of five amino acids. The screening of marine Acinetobacter genospecies for production of biosurfactant/s, purification and antimicrobial activity was undertaken at Pune University. Untapped natural sources were screened for novel biosurfactant/s and bioemulsifier-producing microorganisms using Acinetobacter strains, which showed emulsification of toluene, diesel, hexadecane and crude oil, haemolysis of human RBC's and anionic biosurfactant/s production.

At the department of biotechnology - CUSAT, the work on molecular cloning was undertaken to develop a technology for production of alkaline protease enzyme using marine fungus, Engyodontium alba. The optimal conditions were studied for enzyme production using solid-state fermentation of wheat bran as the solid substrate. The enzyme was found relatively stable for one year. At NIO, Goa, fungi from deep-sea sediments were explored as new sources for protease. Fungal growth and protease production at low temperature and elevated hydrostatic pressure was studied to understand their adaptations to extremophilic conditions.

SEAWEED CULTIVATION

At CSMCRI, Bhavnagar, the project was undertaken on scale-up cultivation and processing of phycocolloid seaweeds (Gelidiella acerosa and Eucheuma). Multilocational trials undertaken to validate different culture methods for large-scale cultivation of Eucheuma proved that the raft cultivation method consistently yields better harvest. This method has been successfully demonstrated in the Gulf of Mannar, Tamil Nadu coast as well as at Okha, Gujarat coast. High quality agar was extracted from Gelidiella acerosa and Gracilaria sp. The Gracilaria agar had very high gel strength (1200 g cm-2) with low gelling temperature. This agar will be useful in bacteriological and molecular biology applications.

The nitrifying bioreactor technology developed at CUSAT paves the way for transforming the open prawn/shrimp larval rearing systems to closed re-circulation systems. The reactor, on properly activating and deploying in the hatchery system, can take care of the entire water quality problems. Apart from nitrification this duel capability lowers down the biological oxygen demand, total bacterial population along with stabilization of Vibrio population. The training programme for fisheries scientists was undertaken at three institutes namely Central Institute of Freshwater Aquaculture (CIFA), Bhubaneshwar, Central Institute Fisheries Technology (CIFT), Cochin and Central Institute of Fisheries Education (CIFE), Mumbai to train in service fisheries scientists on aspects of modern biology, health management and conservation of resources etc. Trainees are being given both theoretical hands-on training and independent project work on molecular biology aspects relevant to fisheries topics. After successful completion of the training programme, the trainees have started working in the area of molecular biology in marine sciences at their institutes.

New Programme Support

The programme on aquaculture and marine biotechnology has been identified for support after a detailed discussion under the Task Force on Aquaculture and Marine Biotechnology. Two proposals from the UAS, College of Fisheries, Mangalore and the Cochin University of Science and Technology (CUSAT), Cochin have been supported for attention on brood stock and larval health management of black tiger shrimp and freshwater prawn and screening for potential anticancer agents from marine Cnidarians, bacteria and fungi. Genotypic characterization and sequencing of genes of interest of marine bacteria, fish and shellfish immunology and screening for useful natural products from microorganisms, capacity building through hands-on training programmes for scholars and technicians on molecular techniques for detection of pathogens and health management in shrimp hatchery system, microbial taxonomy, crustacean immunology and screening and characterization of marine microbes for useful products etc. are also the part of the programme.

Shrimp Genomics

Shrimp (Penaeus monodon) is a very important species for the country from the commercial viewpoint. Unfortunately, the species is not domesticated and the harvests are mainly from the wild. The reproductive biology is complex and the disease burden very high, especially viral diseases. There are populations, which are naturally resistant to viral attack and could be tapped to our advantage. The network programme on shrimp genomics has been developed covering the aspects *viz.* functional genomics in disease resistance of Penaeus monodon, gene regulation of maturation and breeding in P. monodon, microsatellites and physical mapping of P. monodon and genomics of Penaeus indicus for comparative genomics.

TECHNOLOGIES/PRODUCTS

(a) Development of a heat killed whole cell vibrio vaccine using a virulent strain of Vibrio harveyi was developed at College of Fisheries, Mangalore. This has shown immune response in shrimp (Penaeus monodon). The technology has been transferred to Mangalore Biotech Lab.

(b) A polyclonal antibody based immunodiagnostic kits for detection of different bacterial pathogens in finfish and shellfish has been developed by CIFE, Mumbai. The technology has been transferred to GlaxoSmithKline Pharmaceuticals, Mumbai without any modifications for commercialization. The kits are useful as on-farm, rapid diagnostic kits to detect bacterial and viral diseases of finfish and shellfish.

(c) To overcome the problem of viral diseases in shrimp aquaculture and for simultaneous detection of WSSV and MBV, highly sensitive method "Combi kit – WSSV, MBV", a test kit, for specific detection of pathogens is developed by the Department of Microbiology, UAS, College of Fisheries, Mangalore. The test kit can detect all genotypes of WSSV and can be used to detect the presence of virus in shrimp, pond water, sediment, carrier animals etc. The technology has been transferred to Mangalore Biotech Laboratory for packaging and commercialization.

(d) A polyclonal antibody-based immunodiagnostic assay for the detection of white spot syndrome virus - a simple diagnostic test kit developed in joint collaboration with the Centre for Biotechnology, Anna University and C. Abdul Hakeem College, Melvishram was transferred to an aquaculture-based company (Poseidon Biotech, Chennai)

Patent Obtained

In vitro production of amoebocytes from Tachypleus gigas in leibovitz culture medium (U patent # 6,790, 659 dated 14 September 2004) by Ramesh R. Bhonde and Anil Chatterji (2002).

AQUACULTURE TECHNOLOGY

The technology employed in aquaculture has developed over many centuries but has done so more rapidly during the last half century. Aquaculture systems, and the technology used, vary from very simple systems, used for family ponds in tropical countries, where production is for domestic consumption, to high technology systems, such as intensive closed systems, like those used for rearing stripped bass. Herbivorous and filter feeding fish, reared mostly in simple systems of small freshwater ponds, however, account for about half of global aquaculture production.

Much of the technology used in aquaculture is relatively simple, amounting to small modifications that improve the growth and survival rates of the target species, such as providing additional food, adding seed animals collected elsewhere, managing water exchange to maintain adequate oxygen levels, and protecting the stock from predators. Greater understanding of complex interactions between nutrients, bacteria and cultured organisms, together with advances in hydrodynamics applied to pond and tank design, have enabled the development of closed systems. These have the advantage of isolating the aquaculture systems from natural aquatic systems, thus minimizing the risk of disease or genetic impacts on the external systems.

Developments in engineering, some learnt from offshore oilrig construction, increase the possibilities for offshore aquaculture using robust cages. Sea ranching, the release of young fish into the wild to improve the harvest in capture fisheries, has also made a start but its long term viability is still to be assessed. Major advances are also being made in the technology of the production of aquafeeds, which generally require the combining of a large number of ingredients into very small feed pellets.

AQUACULTURE ENGINEERING

Aquaculture draws on well-established engineering fields for most of the design and construction needs of its production facilities. Building earth ponds is similar to building roads - a knowledge of the characteristics of soils and the limits of safe design are the basis of good construction. Similarly, the buildings used for hatcheries and other support activities are no different from those common in the housing, agricultural and commercial sectors. Sometimes ponds are lined with plastics or other impermeable materials, and here the techniques are similar to those for civil structures such as potable water reservoirs or sludge tanks.

The design and installation of water control gates, including in unstable soils, benefits from the long experience in this field in the agriculture and irrigation sectors. An understanding of hydrodynamics allows ponds and tanks to be built with good water circulation, oxygen mixing and without 'dead spots' where sediments might accumulate and cause health problems to fish.

For installations in the sea, the situation is somewhat different and many of the important engineering solutions, such as for fish cages or suspended shellfish growout systems, have had to be developed by aquaculturists themselves. They have benefited however from the accumulated knowledge of seafarers in general and fishermen in particular, in the design and operation of mooring and buoyage systems.

More recently, when fish farmers have turned their attention to how to operate fish cages in locations further offshore where seas are rougher, the experience of the oil exploration industry has proven very valuable. Techniques have been developed in recent years for the production of fish and other aquatic products in closed recirculation systems. To make these work, aquaculturists have needed to develop a knowledge of the biological processes operating - such as how bacteria can be used to neutralise and re-cycle the nitrogenous waste products produced by growing fish - and how to engineer the systems to meet the biological requirements. Knowledge of bio-engineering from the waste treatment and water treatment industries has made contributions to the development of closed aquaculture systems and there is probably more that could be usefully transferred from the sewage treatment sector to help solve problems in fish rearing.

Modern materials have brought many benefits to aquaculture. For instance, custom made plastic joints have simplified the construction of sea cages, and made them more reliable in high stress conditions. Experiments with huge free-floating or sunken net cages operated in the open ocean were begun several decades ago, for instance in the Caspian Sea. These showed some promise, but more reliable construction materials will make the farming of fish in such structures increasingly feasible.

Modern materials and production methods have been important also, in the construction of plastic filter substrates for indoor recirculating systems. The fine detail of these has been found to make substantial differences to the efficiency of biological filters.

In shrimp farms, specially designed matting materials that stand upright on pond bottoms, with a structure that promotes the growth of the small animals and plants that the shrimp can thrive on, have recently been developed and shown to boost production.

Engineering skills are important in the design of most aquaculture facilities and good engineering can affect the efficiency and economics of production. If capital costs can be minimised while still maximising productivity and reducing risk, the farming operation will be more profitable. Aquaculturists have proven very innovative over the past fifty years, constantly developing new technologies to support their farming operations. As new production methods and species for farming are developed, the engineering solutions needed to support them will continue to evolve.

Aquaculture Facilities

Aquaculture began with man making small modifications to natural habitats so as to improve the survival and growth of target species. Some of the oldest examples are in the rearing of freshwater fish in ponds, which has been practiced for thousands of years in Asia and at least for many centuries in Europe. The simple act of placing a mesh barrier across the outlet of a small pond or lake to prevent fish from escaping can make a big improvement in the supply of food. Similarly, along coasts, some tidal lagoons can be easily turned into ponds. Closing off such naturally occurring water bodies was the start, centuries ago, of much fish and shrimp aquaculture in Asia and, in modern times, in South America.

Removing predators and improving the conditions within the pond, (for instance by providing more area of preferred water depth), supplying additional food and, later, by adding seed animals collected outside, were further steps that moved aquaculture production close to where it is today. The farming of seaweeds and molluscs (oysters, clams, mussels etc) developed similarly, as people made improvements such as providing more settlement areas for the young, or the removal of predators from the growing area.

Farmers had a natural desire to improve the productivity of their systems and, as knowledge grew, they learned to stock more animals, increase feeding and manage the exchange of water to maintain the conditions, such as adequate oxygen levels, that the animals needed to survive. The range of facilities used for aquaculture subsequently broadened for a number of reasons. Farmers encountered difficulties with more intensive rearing because of the uncontrolled influence of pond soils, local water quality, weather. Some of these problems could be resolved by rearing in ponds built of concrete, or lined with plastic, by bringing the ponds indoors under cover, or treating the water before flowing it to the culture ponds.

Secondly, as the naturally occurring ponds and lagoons all became used, prospective farmers had to take a broader approach and develop the technology and engineering to be able to use less naturally-favored sites. Net cages floating in protected coastal or inland waters were developed for fish culture, or fish were stocked in fenced areas of the sea or of large lakes. At the same time, the need for supplies of young animals (fry, seed) to stock these systems led to the development of hatchery techniques and dedicated hatchery facilities. For most species this aspect of production has proved more successful when conditions can be more closely controlled, for instance in indoor concrete and fibreglass tank systems, rather than in outdoor ponds. Often, the younger stages of aquatic animals are more sensitive than adults to physical and chemical conditions and these have to be managed within a smaller range, if production is to be successful. Thus hatchery facilities developed as a separate branch of the industry.

More recently, our knowledge has improved greatly regarding the complex interactions that occur in a rearing system, between nutrients, bacteria and the cultured organism. This and technological developments have allowed many aquatic organisms to be reared in completely closed recirculating facilities, including the farming of marine organisms at locations far from the sea. Closed systems have the added advantage of offering greater protection from the danger of disease entering from the natural environment and also of minimizing adverse effects of the production system on that external environment. Technology has also begun to open up the possibilities of growing fish in enclosures in the open ocean, something that could one day transform the nature of human food production on the planet. With 70 per cent of the earth's surface covered by water, the potential is clear. Earlier technology has restricted the cage farming of fish to sheltered coastal waters. Here the number of available sites is limited, environmental damage is more likely and conflicts exist with other users. As cages are developed that can withstand the demanding conditions of the open ocean, or which can be operated below the ocean surface, farming could move further offshore.

A small start has been made, notably in Japan, through so-called 'ranching' programmes', the farming of the sea without enclosures where fry are released in large numbers into the ocean with the aim of improving returns from the capture fishery. Sometimes artificial reef structures are created underwater as well, to increase the available habitat and natural food for the fish.

Aquaculture Systems

Aquaculture - the growing of aquatic animals and plants - covers a wide range of species and methods. Some of the simplest production systems are the small family ponds in tropical countries where carp are reared for domestic consumption. At the other end of the scale are high technology systems, such as the intensive indoor closed units used in the USA for the rearing of striped bass or the sea cages used in Chile and Europe for growing salmon and bream. Nearly half of the world's aquaculture however is of herbivorous and filter-feeding fish such as carp.

Practised in freshwater, in ponds made of earth, and often managed by a single household, production systems are simple and in many cases have changed little over many centuries. A farmer will excavate a small pond near his house; sometimes, as for instance in the flood river deltas of countries like Vietnam, using the spoil to build a raised foundation for the house itself. The pond will typically be fed by natural rainfall or groundwater, or sometimes by diverting a nearby stream or irrigation canal. Some stocking occurs naturally, but more commonly a farmer will buy young fish from a breeder and stock them in his pond, often after holding them for a time in a small floating net known as a 'hapa' to check that they are in good condition before release in the pond. Production will improve if the farmer can stock a good balance of different species to make the best use of the varied kinds of food available in the pond. Typically the fish will be fed with household or agricultural by-products, and harvested when the family needs a meal.

Stocking and harvesting is often continuous, where knowledge of the best stocking level is learned from experience and where the pond is not drained for many years. For most such farmers, fish production is a secondary activity, a useful additional source of protein to add to the supply or income from his main agricultural or commercial activities.

Outdoor freshwater fish farming is practised commercially in many countries, including in the developed nations. The density of stocking may be much higher, the control of feeding, water quality and fish health more closely monitored, but even in intensively operated systems, the key parameters that need to be monitored and balanced for success are similar to those in the traditional household pond system.

Over the last half-century, systems for the indoor rearing of many species of fish have also been developed. Holding of fish in controlled conditions indoors has been important in the development of seed production (hatcheries). Also, as knowledge has increased of nutrient cycles, bacterial action and water chemistry, it has become possible to rear fish, both for food and for ornament, in 'closed' indoor systems, where the water is recirculated. Passing the water through filters that use bacteria to naturally break down and recycle the waste products produced by the fish allows a production system to be run in almost total isolation from the outside. Such systems have been important in the control of disease and also in maintaining the stable conditions that some species need to flourish and reproduce.

A fifth of current world aquaculture production is of plants - mainly seaweeds, that for the most part are grown on the seabed or on raft or racks in shallow coastal waters and used directly for food or for the production of alginate or carageenan (agar-agar). This sector of aquaculture is another largely run by small-scale growers, mainly in Asia but in some parts of the South America, who attach seedlings of marine plants to simple structures built close to shore and constructed from natural materials and then harvest the plants once they have grown. A further fifth of world production is of molluscs such as oysters, clams and mussels.

Again the majority of production is small-scale and by coastal people who often combine fishing activities with farming. Oysters and mussels are mainly grown on structures built above the seabed - poles or racks on the shore, or ropes suspended from rafts or floating lines. The farmer's role is to supply suitable places for seed to settle or to add to natural production by bringing seed from a hatchery - and then to maintain the conditions of waterflow and freedom from predators that the shellfish need to grow. Most commercially grown molluscs feed on microscopic algae floating in the water, so the farmer does not need to provide any feed.

Fish are also grown in coastal areas, in ponds or in floating cages. As technology advances, there is the potential to develop systems for rearing fish in the open ocean, either in sturdy cages or by so called 'ranching', where young fish are released to the wild and then collected by normal fishing or by training them to respond to specially generated sounds.

The tropical coastal zones of Asia and Latin America are where most shrimp farms are found. Shrimp farming is mainly carried out in earth-bottomed ponds built on flat land close to the sea. Shrimp are raised in ponds at a range of different densities. At low densities the systems need only limited inputs of feed and fertilizers. As the density increases, more feed has to be supplied and at the higher end of the range, so-called 'intensive' farming, machines have to be put in the ponds to mix and aerate the water.

Aquaculture is practised from the cold waters of the far north and south, where fish like salmon, arctic char and sturgeon are grown in ponds, flowing raceways and cages in the sea, down through the latitudes to the tropics, where carp and tilapia flourish in freshwater and shrimp and seabass are farmed along the coasts. It ranges from production of fish in naturally occurring ponds in rural areas to the intensive culture of ornamental fish in plastic tanks in the middle of a city. It is practised by the poorest farmers in developing countries as a livelihood and to supply much needed protein for their families - and by urban sports shop owners in Europe and the U.S.A. producing baitfish for weekend anglers. Systems can range from an intensive indoor system monitored with high-tech equipment through to the simple release of baby fish to the sea - but all with the same aim, of helping boost Nature's natural productivity

Biotechnology Development

Biotechnology - any technological application that uses biological systems, living organisms, or derivatives thereof, to make or modify products or processes for specific use 1994 UNEP Convention on Biological Diversity - has a wide range of useful applications in fisheries and aquaculture. It creates opportunities, for instance, to increase growth rate in farmed species, boost the nutritional value of aquafeeds, improve fish health, help restore and protect environments, extend the range of aquatic species and improve the management and conservation of wild stocks.

Some biotechnologies are simple with a long history of application such as the fertilization of ponds to increase feed availability. Others are more advanced and take advantage of increasing knowledge of molecular biology and genetics, *e.g.* genetic engineering and DNA disease diagnosis.The field of genetic biotechnology similarly ranges from simple techniques such as hybridization, to more complex processes such as the transfer of specific genes between species to create GMOs (genetically modified organisms). Over the years, our knowledge of fish breeding requirements has improved and the ability to induce artificial breeding developed through the use of natural or synthetic hormones and/or environmental manipulations. (For example changing photoperiod or water temperature can induce some fish to spawn). These have been key factors facilitating the application of more advanced biotechnologies.

Selective breeding, the maintenance of stocks genetically improved by chromosome manipulation, line crossing, and sex reversal all depend on the controlled breeding of farmed species. These improvements in reproductive technologies have also assisted aquaculturists greatly in their efforts to domesticate aquatic animals. In addition, by making it possible to remove the natural constraints and timing of breeding, farmers are able to mate many more species at times that are most beneficial, and thus helping to ensure a steady and consistent supply of fish for consumption.

GENETIC AQUACULTURE RESOURCES

Genetic resources are the foundation on which species, stocks and genetically-improved strains are based. At the species level, more aquatic animals are being farmed now than ever before. Although the common carp, Cyprinus carpio and goldfish, Carasius auratus, were domesticated several thousand years ago into a variety of shapes and colours, most of the farmed fish today are very similar to their wild relatives. Improvements in our knowledge of artificial reproduction, reproductive biology, early larval rearing (training series) and basic genetics have recently allowed fish breeders to improve genetically species such as rainbow trout, coho and Atlantic salmon, channel catfish, Nile tilapia, as well as common carp.

The culture of several important species still relies on the collection of brood stock or seed from natural populations. Perhaps the most important group of species whose culture is dependent on natural populations is the marine shrimp Penaeus spp. Shrimp farming in South and Central America stock production ponds with wild-caught larvae. Hatcheries that produce shrimp larvae exist in Asia and the Americas, but the broodstock are generally collected from the wild. Culturists recognise the problems associated with this harvest of wild resources and are taking steps to domesticate marine shrimp. Other culture systems dependent on wild resources include milkfish in the Philippines, yellow tail in Japan, and eel in Asia and Europe.

However, simply having a domesticated species or genetically improved species is not sufficient to guarantee optimum production from an aquaculture facility. In addition to proper husbandry, *i.e.*, water quality, nutrition, health etc., broodstock must be managed to ensure conservation of genetic resources, to maintain the desirable characters of the farmed species and to avoid problems of inbreeding.

CURRENT STATUS OF AQUACULTURE GENETICS

Domestication and Strain Evaluation

When wild fish are moved to aquaculture settings, a new set of selective pressures comes into play that often changes gene frequencies. Thus an organism better suited for the aquaculture environment begins to evolve. This process, termed domestication, occurs even without directed selection by the fish culturist. Domestication effects can be observed in some fish within as few as one to two generations after removal from the natural environment. In channel catfish (Ictalurus punctatus) an increased growth rate of three to six per cent per generation was observed.

The oldest domesticated strain of channel catfish (89 years), the Kansas strain, has the fastest growth rate of all strains of channel catfish. Although most domesticated strains usually perform better in the aquaculture environment than wild strains, there are exceptions, *e.g.*, wild Nile tilapia, Oreochromis niloticus, and rohu, Labeo rohita, grow better in the aquaculture environment.

The explanation for this appears related to a lack of maintenance of genetic quality and genetic degradation in domesticated strains. Poor performance of some domestic tilapia is related to poor founding (parental) lines, random genetic drift, inbreeding and introgression with slower growing species, such as O. mossambicus and slower growing strains such as Nile tilapia from Ghana. Channel catfish strains differ in growth, disease resistance, body conformation, dressing percentage, vulnerability to angling and seining, age of maturity, time of spawning, fecundity and egg size. Strains of rainbow trout, Oncorhynchus mykiss, show similar variability. Domestication of farmed shrimp (penaeids) has been relatively slow compared to that of finfish.

This can be attributed to use of wild broodstock and postlarvae, a lack of understanding of shrimp reproductive biology for domestication of the species and perceptions of low potential for genetic improvement. Current reliance on wild broodstock is risky and negates the opportunity to enhance disease resistance (as well as other production traits) through selective breeding. Efforts to domesticate broodstock are now hampered by endemic disease challenges; however, recent collaborative research between the Commonwealth Scientific and Industrial Research Organisation (CSIRO) in Australia and the shrimp culture industry has resulted in successful captive breeding of Penaeus japonicus. Economic analysis has demonstrated that domesticated broodstock are more cost-effective than wild broodstock and that reproductive performance of domesticated P. monodon can match that of wild broodstock of a similar sise.

Use of established, high-performance domestic strains is the first step in applying genetic principles to improved aquaculture mana-gement. Strain variation is also important, since there is a strain effect on other genetic enhancement approaches, such as intraspecific crossbreeding, interspecific hybridisation, sex control and genetic engineering.

Inbreeding and Maintenance of Genetic Quality

It is as important to prevent production losses due to inbreeding as it is to increase production from genetic enhancement. This applies especially to species with high fecundity, *e.g.* Indian and Chinese carps, where few broodstock are necessary to meet demands for fry and broodstock replacement. The detrimental effects of inbreeding are well documented and can result in decreases of 30 per cent or greater in growth production, survival and reproduction.

Intraspecific Crossbreeding

Intraspecific crossbreeding (crossing of different strains) may increase growth rate but heterosis (differences between offspring and parents) may not be obtained in every case. Increases of 55 per cent and 22 per cent in growth rate of channel catfish and rainbow trout crossbreeds, respectively, were achieved using this technique. Chum salmon crossbreeds, however, have shown no increase in growth rates compared with parent strains.

Common carp crossbreeds generally express low levels of heterosis, however, those that exhibited positive heterosis are now the basis for carp aquaculture in Israel, Vietnam, China and Hungary.

The crossing of common carp lines in Szarvas, Hungary is a good example of the relative success of crossbreeding. During the last 35 years, more than 140 crosses have been tested.

Three were chosen, based on ~20 per cent improvement in growth rate (and other qualitative features), compared to parent and control carp lines, for culture purposes. Now approximately 80 per cent of common carp production comes from these "Szarvas" crossbreeds. Production of gynogenetic female lines and gynogenetic sex-reversed inbred male lines from common carp with the best combining ability was an important part of the Hungarian crossbreeding programme. A higher heterosis was expected from crossing inbred lines, but the growth rate of F1 crossbreeds was only 10 per cent higher than controls.

Kirpichnikov successfully produced a new strain of cold resistant carp - the "Ropsha" carp - for cold zones in northern Russia using local carps and Siberian wild carps from the River Amur. The Czech Republic also had a national common carp breeding programme and improved growth rates with crossing, "South Bohemian" x "Northern mirror" carp and the "Hungarian 15" x "Northern mirror". Likewise in Israel, over 20 years of crossing common carp strains revealed that the cross using the strain "DOR-70" and the Croatian line "Nawice" produced fast growth, and this is now one of the most popular crosses for Israeli carp production.

In Indonesia, strain development using artificial gynogenesis and sex-reversal resulted in 10 common carp inbred lines, which were later used for crossbreeding. In Vietnam, eight local varieties of common carp, along with "Hungary", "Ukraine", "Indonesia" and "Czech" strains are maintained, with significant heterosis observed in F1 generations of crossbreeds. Double crosses among Vietnamese, Hungarian and Indonesian strains have subsequently been used for carp selection and crossbreeding programmes throughout Vietnam.

The Vietnamese x Hungarian common carp crossbreed is particularly popular, due to fast growth and high survival rates under different production conditions. Under various rice-field conditions, growth rates of different strains of Nile tilapia and their crosses showed that the crosses were superior to pure Senegal strains. Breeding programmes are also under development in several countries for the Java or silver barb, Barbodes (formerly Puntius) gonionotus, another economically important fish species in Southeast Asia. The Bangladesh programme used three strains: "Bangladesh", "Thailand" and "Indonesian". The growth rate of females from six crosses was 23 per cent higher than the average growth rate of the parent strains. Even higher growth rates (35 per cent improvement) were found in the three crosses using the Thailand strain as either the sire or dam. In the Vietnamese breeding programme, six different strains were used to produce a population ideally suited for culture.

Cross-breeds of different strains of European catfish, Silurus glanis, are characterised by outstanding adaptability under warmwater holding conditions and mixed diet feeding regimes. In addition, crosses with the walking catfish, Clarias macrocephalus, have shown improved resistance to Aeromonas hydrophila infections. Studies on "domestic a" × "domestic b" channel catfish also showed greater heterotic growth rates than "domestic" × "wild" crosses (Dunham and Smitherman, 1983. The same was found in rainbow trout crosses. Strain mating incompatibilities, however, can occur and can impede fry output.

Interspecific Hybridisation

Interspecific hybridisation has been used to increase growth rate, manipulate sex ratios, produce sterile animals, improve flesh quality, increase disease resistance, improve tolerance of environmental extremes, and improve a variety of other traits that make aquatic animal production more profitable. Although interspecific hybridisation rarely results in an F1 suitable for aquaculture application, there are a few significant exceptions.

Channel catfish females x blue catfish, I. furcatus, males ("channel-blue") is the only cross (between 28 catfish hybrids examined) that exhibits superiority for growth rate, growth uniformity, disease resistance, tolerance of low oxygen levels, dressing percentage and harvestability. However, mating problems between the two species have prevented commercial utilisation. The "sunshine" bass is a cross between white bass, Morone chrysops, and striped bass, M.

saxatilis, and grows faster, with better overall culture characteristics than either parent species. In addition, crosses of the silver carp (Hypophthalmichthys molitrix) and bighead carp, black crappie and P. annularis and African catfish hybrids all show faster growth than parent species. Numerous crosses of common carp with rohu, mrigal and catla; tambaqui and Piaractus brachypoma and P. mesopotamicus green sunfish crossed with bluegill, and gilthead seabream with red seabream, have also resulted in improved overall performance for aquaculture systems. In the family Sparidae, hybrids of P. major and common dentex,Dentex dentex, also grow faster than parent stocks.

Hybridisation in commercial Thai oysters was carried out to explore the possibility of producing hybrid oysters with superior traits. Hybridisation of C. belcheri × C. lugubris was only successful to the spat stage, and growth rates of the hybrids and reciprocal crosses were significantly lower than their parents. Intergeneric hybridisation was only successful with female C. lugubris and male S. cucullata. Growth rates of this hybrid were significantly higher than those of S. cucullata, but did not differ significantly from those of C. lugubris. Shell morphology of the hybrid was intermediate between the two parental types. Effects of intergeneric hybridisation on the genetic diversity of natural oyster populations.

Hybridisation between some species, such as Nile tilapia and blue tilapia, Oreochromis aureus, result in predominantly male offspring. Other tilapia crosses, which produce mainly male offspring, include Nile tilapia × O. urolepis honorum or O. macrochir, and O. mossambicus × O. urolepis honorum. Conversely, the cross between striped bass and yellow bass produced 100 per cent females. This can be desirable for culture purposes where i) there are: growth differences between the sexes; ii) sex-specific products such as caviar are wanted; or iii) reproduction needs to be controlled (*e.g.*, overpopulation and stunting in tilapia production ponds).

Hybridisation between species can also result in offspring that are sterile or have diminished reproductive capacity. As with monosex production, the production of sterile hybrids can reduce unwanted reproduction or improve growth rate by energy diversion from gametogenesis. Karyotype analysis can be used as a general predictor of potential hybrid fertility. For example, hybrid Indian major carps are generally fertile because they share similar chromosome numbers (2N = 50). When crossed with common carp (2N = 102), the hybrids are triploid and sterile. A natural triploid results from the cross between grass carp, Ctenopharyngodon idellus, and bighead carp. Grass carp are commonly produced for aquatic weed control, but there is concern about spread to natural water bodies and the potential impact on desirable vegetation. The triploid hybrids have reduced fertility, but some progeny maintain diploidy and could be fertile. Other exceptions to the chromosome number-fertility rule are crosses of some sturgeon species with different chromosome numbers that produce fertile F1 offspring. Investigated hybridisation of coho salmon, which is considered resistant to several salmonid viruses. Disease resistance in the hybrids was improved, but overall viability was poor.

Viability increased when hybridisation was followed with triploidisation. The same authors also reported that triploid hybrids from rainbow trout and char were resistant to several salmonid viruses, but grew more slowly than their diploid counterparts. Similar results were found with rainbow trout and coho crosses. Hybrid triploids of Atlantic salmon x brown trout showed survival and growth rates comparable to those of Atlantic salmon monospecific diploids. Triploid Pacific salmon hybrids have also shown earlier seawater acclimation.

Increased environmental tolerance may also be imparted to hybrids where one parent species has a wide or specific physiological tolerance or due to increased heterozygosity. Hybrid red tilapia, O. mossambicus, (high salinity tolerance) and Nile tilapia, O. niloticus, (low salinity tolerance) show enhanced salinity tolerance. Florida red-strain hybrids can reproduce in salinities of 19 ppt and O. niloticus × O. aureus hybrids also show enhanced salinity tolerance. Reciprocal hybrids of O. niloticus (N) × O. mossambicus (M) have different salinity tolerances.

The hybrid with an O. niloticus mother (N×M) had a higher survival rate after salinity challenges at 20 ppt than pure O. niloticus, but lower survival rates than those of the reciprocal hybrid (M×N). At 30 ppt salinity, a direct transfer killed all tilapia with O. niloticus maternal genes. Growth rates of N×M hybrids were comparable to those of Nile tilapia, while those of the N×M hybrids and O. mossambicus were comparable, but lower, than the first two groups. There were no statistical differences in carcass percentages of the four groups. Back-crosses were also evaluated. MN×N showed the highest salinity tolerance (comparable to that of O. mossambicus), but no significant differences in salinity tolerances were found in the remaining backcross (N×NM, NM×N, N×MN) or pure O. niloticus. Carcass percentage of the back-cross hybrids, however, tended to be higher than those of the parent species.

Hybrids between marine species, and between marine and freshwater spawning species, have produced surprising results. Hybrids between Sparus aurata and Pagrus major (both belonging to the Sparidae) developed vestigial gonads at two to three years and were sterile. Similar vestigial gonads were observed in offspring of the reciprocal crosses. No consistent growth or survival superiority, compared with the parent species, was detected until sexual maturity in the reciprocal crosses. Hybridisation between European sea bass, females and striped bass resulted in viable larvae; however 28 per cent were triploids, and only the triploids appeared to survive to six months of age. At eight months, the survivors showed poor growth compared to diploid D. labrax.

Such hybrids may be of commercial value where reproduction needs to be restricted for ecological reasons.

Sometimes an interspecific hybrid does not exhibit heterosis for specific traits, but may still be important for aquaculture if it expresses other useful traits from the parent species. The main catfish cultured in Thailand is the hybrid between African (Clarias gariepinus) and Thai catfish. This combines the fast growth of the African catfish and the desirable flesh characteristics of the Thai catfish. Although it does not grow as fast as pure African catfish, overall production rates are improved and the flesh is still acceptable to Thai consumers. Likewise the rohu x catla hybrid grows almost as fast as pure catla, but has the small head of the rohu considered desirable in Indian aquaculture. Catla catla × Labeo fimbriatus (fringe-lipped peninsula carp) hybrids have the small heads of L. fimbriatus, plus the deep body and growth rate of catla. The "sunshine" bass has a suite of advantageous traits from the parent species (white and striped bass) including good osmoregulation, high thermal tolerance, resistance to stress and certain diseases, high survival under intense culture, and ability to use soy bean protein in feed. Interspecific backcrossing has also been used to successfully introgress (merge) genes from one closely related species into another. Cold tolerance and colour genes have been transferred among tilapia in this manner.

Genetic Selection

Very little was done in this area prior to 1970, however, the field has grown significantly in the past three decades and is now extremely active. In general, the response to selection for growth rate in aquatic species is very good compared to that with terrestrial farm animals. Fish and shellfish often have higher genetic variance compared to farmed land animals, notes the genetic variation for growth rate is seven to ten per cent in farmed land animals and 20-35 per cent in fish and shellfish. Fecundity is also higher in aquatic organisms than land organisms. This allows for higher selection intensity for aquaculture production improvement, and over 200 heritability estimates have been obtained for several traits of cultured fish and shellfish.

There are few national breeding programmes in fish and shellfish which aim at improved aquaculture production. In 1975, a National Breeding programme for Atlantic salmon and rainbow trout was started in Norway, and today this supplies about 75 per cent of the Norwegian industry with improved eyed eggs. In Canada, a similar breeding programme is operated by the Atlantic Salmon Federation. In 1993, The Philippines National Tilapia Breeding programme (PNTBP) was started with broodstock from the GIFT programme (Genetically Improved Farmed Tilapia) and is now operated by the GIFT Foundation. In Israel and Hungary, crossbreeding programmes with common carp (Cyprinus carpio) exist. In addition, some private companies in several countries, including the United States and Chile, now have their own breeding programmes.

Selection for body weight and disease resistance in salmonids has been particularly successful. By 1925, three generations of selection of brook trout (Salvelinus fontinalis) survivors of endemic furunculosis (caused by Aeromonas salmonicida) improved survival from 2 per cent to 69 per cent. Ehlinger further increased resistance to furunculosis in brown trout and brook trout with selective breeding programmes. An infectious pancreatic necrosis virus (IPNV)-resistant strain of rainbow trout showed 4.3 per cent mortality compared with 96.1 per cent in a highly sensitive strain.

With respect to body weight, a 30 per cent increase in rainbow trout was achieved within six generations of selection. In Atlantic salmon, an increase of seven per cent was achieved within a single generation and an increased growth rate of 50 per cent was achieved within ten generations in coho salmon. Body weight has also been improved in channel catfish, by 12-20 per cent over one to two generations of genetic selection. The best line grew twice as fast as non-selected lines.

After three generations, the growth rate of channel catfish in ponds was improved by 20-30 per cent. Four generations of selection in a Kansas strain of channel catfish resulted in 55 per cent improvement in growth rate. Four generations of selection also increased body weight by 50.5 gm and total length by 0.88 cm in walking catfish, C. macrocephalus. Genetic selection in gilthead seabream (Sparus aurata) has also been successful despite early difficulties with producing single-pair offspring groups. This led to the conclusion that family mating designs were inappropriate for group spawning of S. aurata. Mass selection proved more effective and resulted in significant heritability estimates for growth.

Different strains of common carp appear to possess varying amounts of additive genetic variation. Heritabilities for body weight of 0.15-0.49 in a Czechoslovakian strain of common carp. Vietnamese common carp also show significant heritability (0.3) for growth rate.Successful selection programme, which started in 1965, against dropsy (spring viremia of carp) in common carp.

Responses can differ depending on the direction of selection. Body weight of common carp in Israel was not improved over five generations, but could be decreased in the same strain selected for small body sise. Virtually identical results for Nile tilapia has also been reported.

Several authors reported that, in tilapia, mass selection improved body weight in Oreochromis mossambicus, red tilapia and O. aureus. However, selection for increased body weight in other red tilapia has been less successful. This is similar to the situation in Nile tilapia. This may reflect a narrow genetic base in the founder stock or sole use of mass selection. Selection for increased growth in GIFT Nile tilapia gave much different results, with 77 per cent to 123 per cent growth improvement. The genetic gain was superior to results from crossbreeding experiments.

The 11 per cent genetic gain per generation in GIFT tilapia is better than that obtained in most other species of fish; the channel catfish increased body weight by 14 per cent per generation over four generations. However, a more typical genetic gain is five to seven per cent per generation, as demonstrated by salmonids following approximately ten generations of selection. The only other exceptions that come close to the results with GIFT tilapia and the channel catfish study of Padi are the 13-14 per cent increase per generation observed by Gjerde, and five per cent per generation for common carp after six generations of selection.

Production trials and socio-economic surveys in five Asian countries show that cost of production per unit fish is 20-30 per cent lower for GIFT strain tilapia than other Nile tilapia strains in current use.

Body weight of common carp appears unresponsive to selection; however, body conformation can be dramatically changed. Selection for carcass quality and quantity has also been initiated for salmonids and catfish. In Thailand, selection results are not yet available for many species and traits, but numerous heritability estimates have been obtained, *e.g.*, for growth and disease resistance in pangasiid freshwater catfish, rohu (Labeo rohita), Thai walking catfish (Clarias macrocephalus), Java barb (Barbodes gonionotus), bighead carp (Aristichthys nobilis) and Asian rock oyster (Saccostrea cucullata).

Selective breeding has also improved growth of the shrimp Penaeus japonicus in laboratory and pilot-scale farm trials using offspring from CSIRO broodstock. In 1998/1999, comparative trials demonstrated significant improvements in the growth, survival and total yields in two selected lines (10-15 per cent increase in mean yields). In a related species, P. vannamei, estimated a response within one generation of selection of 4.4 per cent for growth rate and 12.4 per cent for survival of the viral disease Taura syndrome. A genetic improvement programme was recently started for Pacific oysters, Crassostrea gigas, in Australia. This followed demonstrations that little genetic diversity had been lost since the Pacific oyster industry was founded in Australia with imports from Japan some 50 years ago. The improvement programme aims to combine family and mass selection with molecular genetics. Two generations of mass selection and two generations of family selection have been completed, with a growth rate improvement of about eight per cent in the first generation from a mass selection. Based on work with a congeneric oyster species, C. virginica, Mass selection of adult oysters gave an apparent strong response to selection for growth rate.

CULTURE-BASED FISHERIES AQUACULTURE

In contrast to aquaculture which involves the cultivation of aquatic life within controlled environments or the commercial production of certain aquatic species by managing the major part of their life history under strict control, culture-based fisheries increase production in natural environments by controlling a part of the life history of certain species and transplanting or releasing their seed or fry into the open waters. The juvenile fish, which are produced in hatcheries and are released into fresh-, brackish-, or marine waters, are allowed to propagate or grow on natural foods until they reach harvestable size.

Unlike aquaculture, culture-based fisheries are not limited by land or population pressures and do not have to modify or manage the culture system to approximate the natural environment since it uses the natural environment itself. Also, unlike aquaculture, harvests are uncertain and returns are more difficult to predict as the "release of fish to sea involves the number harvestable ultimately being reduced to 1-15 per cent of the number released, depending on species and locality".

Nonetheless, culture-based fisheries have been increasingly resorted to as means of enhancing the fishery resources, replenishing natural stocks whose populations have declined through over-exploitation or environmental degradation, or simply maximizing the productivity of a water body, be it an open bay, a coastal lagoon, or a freshwater reservoir. Their adoption or application on an expanded scale has in fact been identified as a high-priority item in the agenda for development in a number of regions in the world in the coming years. The major types of culture-based fisheries include: (i) sea/ocean ranching as practised in Japan with various marine finfishes and the Kuruma prawn, and in the Pacific Ocean and Baltic Sea with salmon; (ii) coastal lagoon farming, as exemplified by valliculture in the Mediterranean; (iii) stocking and restocking in freshwater lakes and reservoirs; and (iv) floodplain fisheries management.

Sea/Ocean Ranching

Sea ranching, in which juvenile fish are released to grow unprotected on natural foods in marine waters where they are harvested at marketable size, takes advantage of the sea as a large aquatic pasture. While it is practised in slightly differing forms around the world, in its distinctive form, young fish are released to the sea through ponds, enclosures or channels, and allowed to grow until they are ready for the market.

Salmon

Sea ranching of salmon is widely practised in countries such as the United States (mainly Alaska, Washington and Oregon), Canada, Japan, USSR, New Zealand, Iceland, and the Baltic countries.

The most widely used species for ocean ranching is the Pacific salmon (Oncorhynchus sp.) because of the success of its artificial spawning coupled with the rapid growth and the high degree of its homing precision that makes it amenable to harvesting at maturity. The practice of salmon ranching was initially carried out more than 100 years ago in the Nordic countries where salmon smolts were released into the Baltic Sea area.

Hatchery production of salmon in the United States dates back to 1872 when the US Fish Commission established its first hatchery on the McCloud River in California. This was followed by the first private salmon hatchery on the Rogue River, Oregon in 1877. The technology for artificial propagation of salmon was introduced to Japan in 1877 and to western Canada in 1884.

In Japan, while salmon hatching and release have been carried out for nearly 100 years, the results were not considered very successful. It was only with the new method of intermediate feeding and timely release of salmon fry, starting in 1961, that significant advances in salmon production have been achieved. Most Japanese hatcheries use gravel-lined raceways to incubate larval salmon (alevins) and practise short-term feeding of newly-emerged chum fry on artificial diets.

Pink and chum salmon are raised in equal numbers in Soviet hatcheries using technology similar to that of Japan. In the Pacific Northwest, chinook and coho salmon are the predominant species used in hatcheries where raceways and ponds for feeding juvenile fish are prominently featured.

In Alaska, floating raceways in protected saltwater bays had to be innovated to suit Alaskan conditions. Canada's salmon farming industry has grown tremendously in the last five years as a result of its successful hatchery operations. Canadian hatchery workers have pioneered development and application of spawning and egg incubation channels which provide favourable environmental conditions for eggs and alevins. These techniques have been applied most successfully to sockeye, pink, and chum salmon.

The spawning channels produce fry with a capacity for rapid growth and high survival because they simulate high-quality natural spawning beds. Incubation channels, shallow raceways with a silt-free gravel bed, enable the alevins from artificially fertilized and hatched eggs to complete their development in a natural substrate.

Salmon fry that need to be raised in low-salinity or fresh water before release into marine waters (*e.g.*, sockeye, coho, and chinook) have to be transferred from the incubation system to feed-lot systems consisting of tanks, raceways, ponds, floating pens, or a combination or modification of these. The newly emerged fry are given frequent feedings of high-protein diets containing vitamin supplements and certain fats.

Other Species

Aside from the widely popular Pacific salmon, other marine species have been used for ocean ranching in Japan. The Japanese National Culture-Based Fishery Project, which was started in 1953, has succeeded in developing techniques for mass seed production and subsequent release of juveniles of commercially valuable fish/shellfish, such as the Kuruma prawn, red sea bream, blue crabs, sole, flounder, and yellowtail, into the Seto Inland Sea. The Project has now reached the stage where the fishermen themselves carry out the release of fry and manage the propagation work. The Project, based on its earlier successes, has been expanded on a national scale with the construction of a large number of Prefectural Centers for Culture-Based Fisheries all over Japan. The Ezo abalone, Haliotis discus Hanai, is one of the most important species for ocean ranching in Japan, with about 1.15 million hatchery-produced juveniles released in 1980 in rocky areas of the Sea of Japan around Hokkaido. Likewise, the giant Ezo scallop, Patinopecten yessoensis, is propagated in the Okhotsk Sea, the Nemuro Channel, and in other areas of the Hokkaido coast.

COASTAL LAGOON FARMING

Extensive lagoon farming is a traditional activity in various European and Mediterranean countries with a production of about 10 000 t/y. Among the Mediterranean countries, Italy has the largest areas of brackish water that are exploited for lagoon farming of commercially valuable species like Anguilla anguilla, Mugil cephalus, Liza aurata, Liza saliens, Liza ramada, Chelon labrosus, Dicentrarchus labrax, and Sparus aurata. Restocking of the valli/coastal lagoons is carried out by anadromous, natural, and annual migration and by artificial restocking. Catches from the valli primarily depend on the quantity of fingerlings which entered the lagoons some years before and on the quantity of fingerlings stocked.

Valliculture

Valliculture, as the practice is called in view of its being fish culture-based, is one of the most ancient forms of aquaculture in the Mediterranean region. Its origins date back to the first rudimental fish pond and fattening systems used along the Adriatic and Tyrrhenian coasts. This technique was developed by the upper Adriatic populations to exploit the seasonal migrations of some fish species from the sea into the lagoon and delta areas which were more suitable for their growth. The fish returned to the sea because of altered environmental conditions (temperature) of the sea or for reproduction. To exploit these periodic movements, large brackish areas were enclosed to prevent the fish returning to the sea and complex permanent capture systems, fish barriers, were developed consisting of barriers in the channels communicating with the sea to catch the adults. Later, from the simple ponding of fry freely entering the lagoon from the sea, came a man-made seeding of fry fished elsewhere and introduced into the basins to be reared for a few years.

The successful management of coastal lagoons using hatchery-bred fry of important species is thought to hold considerable promise world-wide for expansion in the future.

Brush-park Fisheries

Brush-park fisheries are a traditional form of low-technology aquaculture which is practised in coastal lagoons and brackish waters in many areas of the world. The brush parks are constructed in a variety of forms and sizes, but basically a brush park consists of an inner core, or concentric circles, of densely packed tree branches or other material surrounded by an outer, more substantial wooden framework which is fished periodically, usually by encirclement.

In coastal lagoons the most sophisticated forms of brush-park fisheries occur in Benin. There are several basic types of brush-park fisheries in Benin where they are known collectively as "acadjas". They vary from each other in configuration, construction and fishing characteristics. The acadjas are constructed of tree branches with harder woods forming the peripheral structure and with soft wood branches with many ramifications forming the interior of the acadja. Acadjas are preferentially placed in shallow, quiet waters of no more than 1.5 m depth.

Fishing is accomplished by surrounding the smaller types of acadjas with a net after which all of the branches are removed and the net is then pursed. For the larger brush parks the surrounding net is fished in a step-wise process by gradually moving the net inwards as branches are removed until the fish are concentrated in small areas and can thus be removed with traps, baskets, and hand-nets. After fishing, the used branches are replaced and new ones added as necessary.

Elsewhere in Africa, brush-park fisheries are found in coastal lagoons in Nigeria, Côte d'Ivoire, Ghana, Togo, and Madagascar. Elsewhere in the world, brush-park fisheries are found in Negombo lagoon in Sri Lanka and have been introduced in some Mexican lagoons.

Stocking of Inland Waters

Among the most advocated and widely used practices for the management of the fisheries resources of lakes and reservoirs throughout the world is the stocking and recapture technique.

Species stocked are either indigenous or exotic and either herbivorous, carnivorous, or omnivorous. In the developing countries of the tropics, where the production of more fish for food is the goal of any fisheries activity, high-yielding herbivores, detritivores and plankton feeders (like tilapia and carp), are commonly stocked in lakes and reservoirs. This is in direct contrast with the developed countries in temperate zones where carnivores like trout and bass are stocked in lakes and reservoirs to support the recreational or sport fishery.

The major lakes and reservoirs in ASEAN countries, for example, have been stocked with hatchery-produced fingerlings of a wide variety of species including tilapia, various Chinese and Indian carps, milkfish, mullet and catfish.

In China, around 65 per cent, or 1.4 million ha, of reservoir area out of a total of two million ha are farmed and managed like fish ponds. They are stocked with fingerlings and following a period of growth, mature fish are harvested. The species used are the common carp, grass carp, silver carp, bighead carp, mud carp, and Wuchang bream (Megalobrama amblycephala) in varying densities and species ratios. Reservoir fisheries in China are almost entirely dependent on the regular release of large quantities of fingerlings because the Chinese carp do not spawn outside their area of origin. In many instances, therefore, stocked fish make up over 90 per cent of fish catches from reservoirs.

In Israel, many water storage reservoirs (10-40 ha area, 5-7 m depth) originally constructed for irrigation, are now stocked with a range of species including tilapia, mullet and carp, usually grown in intensively managed polyculture systems. Sri Lanka's large perennial reservoirs and small seasonal tanks constitute the country's main freshwater resource. These are regularly stocked with fingerlings of the different carp species (Indian, Chinese, and common) which are produced at Government-run hatcheries spread all over the country. Since the Indian and Chinese carps do not spawn in the reservoirs/ tanks, they have to be stocked regularly to sustain the fisheries. There is thus large pressure on the State to accelerate its seed production programme to keep up with the large demand for fingerlings. It is interesting to note that unlike the Philippines and Thailand, for example, where fish seed production is largely a private sector undertaking, the Sri Lankan Ministry of Fisheries is primarily responsible for the production of carp fingerlings for distribution among the various reservoirs and seasonal tanks.

In Cuba, most of the freshwater fish is produced from seeding of the country's small to medium size reservoirs; in Colombia, some dams are stocked and restocked with mullets.

African small reservoirs are stocked mainly with tilapias and Clarias. In Zambia the most important species for stocking reservoirs are Tilapia melanopleura, T. macrochir, T. andersonii, and Haplochromis spp. In Zimbabwe the fish most commonly used for dam stocking are Oreochromis mossambicus, O. macrochir, T. rendalli, and several exotics like black bass and rainbow trout.

AQUACULTURE AND MARINE BIOTECHNOLOGY

Diagnostics and vaccine development in aquaculture are a major priority apart from development of suitable cell culture systems, immunostimulants, anti-bacterial and anti-cancerous agents. Studies have been supported on isolation of novel enzymes from deep-sea fungi, molecular cloning and gene expression for alkaline protease and molecular epidemiology of white spot shrimp disease in brackish water system.

DNA vaccines developed against Aeromonas are being studied for the efficacy and challenge experiments. Immunodot-based diagnostic kit is being used for detection of white spot syndrome virus (WSSV) in shrimp and prawn. An ELISA-based kit has been developed for detection of IgM of Indian major carps against Aeromonas hydrophila infection. An anti-WSSV formulation was made as a prophylactic measure in shrimp health management. Biosurfactants production was standardized from marine wastes employing the acinetobacter strains.

New source of molecular fluorescent dyes has been attempted from sea cucumber tissues for bioactive compounds and use in biomedical applications. Bioactive properties of ink gland of cuttlefish have been studied for antibacterial, antiviral and anticancer agents. Cell culture attempted on brackish water species, seabass, could lead to establish stable species-specific cell lines useful in virus isolation.

The growth-promoting factor studied on development of embryos of Indian horseshoe crab showed significant enlargement of organ development. Development of culture technology in non-conventional species like seaweeds and product and process development of commercial importance was also the part of the programme. A protocol on better aquaculture management practices was developed through recirculatory and raceway system. In service training programme in molecular biology for fisheries scientists was received greater attention in the programme funded at CIFT, CIFA, CIFE. Two programme supports on Aquaculture/Marine Biotechnology have been supported.

DIAGNOSTICS AND VACCINES DEVELOPMENT

At College of Fisheries, Mangalore, work was carried out on the cloning and expression of virulence genes of Aeromonas hydrophila, as an important fish pathogen and the attempts were made to isolate the proteins and study the immunogenicity. At Centre for Biotechnology, Jawaharlal Nehru University, New Delhi, recombinant porin has been expressed and purified in large quantity for maintaining the consistency of the porin vaccine. The efficacy study and challenge experiments are being undertaken on immunization of mice and fish with porin DNA vaccine. Studies were undertaken on pathogenecity of the Epizootic Ulcerative Syndrome (EUS) in fish at Viswa Bharti University, Santiniketan; North Bengal University, Darjeeling and Center for Cellular and Molecular Biology (CCMB), Hyderabad.

A project was undertaken at College of Fisheries, Mangalore on expansion of panel of monoclonal antibodies and standardization of immunodot test kit for detection of white spot virus of shrimp. A simple monoclonal antibody (MAb)-based Immunodot kit for detection of WSV of shrimp at the farmers level has been developed, which is a cheap and effective alternative for expensive and complex DNA based tests. Development of DNA– and protein-based diagnostic methods of white spot disease of shrimp, their field evaluation and monitoring were undertaken at Anna University. The purified viral protein was used as diagnostic assay kit and transferred to Posideon Aquatech Limited, Chennai for commercialization. An ELISA test has been developed using rabbit antisera against carp IgM for the detection of IgM in IMC. Studies were undertaken on development of anti-WSSV formulation against anti-white spot syndrome virus compound as a prophylactic measure in shrimp health management at CAH Abdul Hakeem College, Melvisharam. A process to purify the compound responsible for inactivating the WSSV was optimized.

THE FISHERIES SECTOR

Bangladesh is endowed with vast marine, coastal and inland waters having great fisheries potential: a 480 km long coastal line and approximately one million hectares of territorial waters extending 19 km up to the sea. The nation's economic zone extends 320 km out into the sea from the coast line. Total fish production in 1989–90 amounted to 847,000 tons, of which 72 per cent was derived from inland fisheries and 28 per cent from marine fisheries. Of inland fisheries, 69 per cent was from open water capture fisheries and 31 per cent from closed water culture fisheries (ponds, beels, baors and brackish water aquaculture). Clearly inland open water capture fisheries are the most important part of the fisheries sector, accounting for 49 per cent of total fish production. So even small improvements in the average yield of inland open water capture fisheries could significantly affect national fish production and consumption.

LEVELS OF GENETIC DIFFERENTIATION IN AQUATIC ORGANISMS

Many studies have been carried out to estimate the amount of genetic subdivision within aquatic species. Levels of population substructure in various groups. On average, these levels of G_{ST} (which is equivalent to F_{ST}) are not too far from 0.2, suggesting that, in general, subdivision of populations within species is close to that which allows genetic drift to change allele frequencies in local populations in the face of gene flow by migration. However, these average values hide a wide range of variation in population structure between species. For example, let us take two contrasting cases – the salmon, *Salmo salar*, and the mussel, *Mytilus edulis*. The salmon has a life history involving extensive juvenile and adult migration, with mature adults returning to their natal rivers to spawn.

Thus, although salmon can be found over a very wide area, they are genetically very much restricted to local populations in their own rivers as this is where the transmission of genes between generations occurs. There are strong barriers to gene flow because very few fish return by mistake to non-natal rivers. In addition, each local population consists of relatively few individuals and the population can be sometimes even further subdivided into year classes that return to spawn in the same year as one another. Values of

F_{ST} for salmon, calculated from extensive allozyme data, are in the region of 0.4 and indicate that, as expected, there is very little gene flow ($N_e m = 0.38$) and strong genetic differentiation into local populations in this species. On the other hand, the mussel is a sedentary organism and adults never actively move more than a very short distance.

As with salmon, mussels release eggs and spermatozoa into the water, but, in contrast to salmon, mussel larvae are small and planktonic and are at the mercy of currents that can disperse them over great distances. Larval life, from egg to metamorphosis, in mussels lasts around 4 weeks and can be further extended in two ways. Firstly, if a suitable habitat for settlement is not discovered, metamorphosis can be delayed for more than a week, allowing further dispersal. Secondly, once metamorphosed, these very young mussels (spat) can detach, secrete a very thin byssal thread and be transported in currents by a process known as byssal drifting, which is analogous to the aerial dispersal of spiders by gossamer threads. Typically, F_{ST} values from allozyme studies in mussels are very low (<0.001) and clearly reflect extensive gene flow ($N_e m > 250$) and a lack of any population substructure.

It is also interesting to compare genetic differentiation in marine pelagic fish such as Atlantic herring (*Clupeus harengus*) with that in anadromous fish such as salmon. The herring has a very large effective population size because all fish return to the same region to spawn and there are therefore few, if any, barriers to gene flow. Average F_{ST} for herring is 0.01 and $N_e m$ is 24.8.

Therefore, the conclusion is that where the effective population size and/ or migration is large, gene flow will tend to dominate over random genetic drift, there will be little differentiation and F_{ST} will be close to 0. Where $N_e m$ is small, random genetic drift will tend to dominate over gene flow, allele frequencies will differ strongly between populations and F_{ST} will be large.

Although information about population differentiation is very valuable to fishery managers, it is important to recognise that a *lack of evidence* for local genetic populations does not always mean a *lack of substructure*. If populations are genuinely genetically isolated from one another, then we would expect random genetic drift to be acting to change allele frequencies at all polymorphic loci. However, for reasons of chance, not all loci will show different allele frequencies in different populations. If the loci screened in limited surveys happen to be these invariant loci, then the true variation remains hidden. It is therefore important to examine sufficient loci to be sure that an apparent lack of genetic differentiation can be relied upon.

POTENTIAL PROBLEMS WITH ALLOZYMES AND CODING MARKERS

There is a risk that allozyme markers could fail to detect genetic isolation because, as enzymes, they can be vulnerable to selection operating at the biochemical level, either directly on them or on the biochemical pathways within which they operate. This can be also the case for SNP markers located in exons or any marker closely linked to another one that is subject to selection.

If the selection is such that it is in the same direction in two genetically isolated populations, that is an allele is at high frequency because the individuals carrying it are favoured in both populations, then the allozyme data will be interpreted as indicating that the populations are not genetically different. On the other hand, two populations with habitat differences but which regularly exchange genes via larval flow may have different allele frequencies at a locus which is under selection where one allele is favoured in one population but is deleterious in the other. Differential mortalities in the two populations will cause allele frequency differences between samples taken from the two populations and this will give a false impression about the degree of reproductive separation of the two. This is why the use of several markers and, even better, different types of markers is recommended.

Here is a good example of how different makers can deliver a different message. The American oyster, *Crassostrea virginica*, occurs in estuarine habitats throughout the east coast of the USA, from Maine in the north to the Gulf of Mexico in the south. It has a larval phase lasting several weeks and might be expected to be relatively genetically homogeneous as a result of this. Allozyme studies detected no significant genetic differentiation into local populations anywhere in the species' range. However, mtDNA markers and some neutral, non-coding nuclear DNA markers demonstrated a very distinct division into a southern group and a northern group of populations separated at a zone of demarcation near to Cape Canaveral on the Florida Atlantic coast.

This evidence makes it clear that there is practically no gene flow between the southern and northern regions, probably owing to the characteristics of a major oceanic current – the Gulf Stream – which emerges from the Gulf of Mexico around the tip of Florida. On the basis that evolution is faster in the mtDNA molecule than at protein coding loci, it could be suggested that, although differences in the mtDNA molecule have evolved, insufficient time has elapsed since the divergence of the two groups of oysters for allozymes to reflect the division.

However, the non-allozymic single copy nuclear DNA markers also show this divergence, and the most convincing conclusion is that selection at the studied allozyme loci is maintaining the same alleles at similar frequencies on both sides of the break point. It is notable that several other species such as the horseshoe crab (*Limulus polyphenus*), the black sea bass (*Centropristis striata*) and the seaside sparrow (*Ammodramus maritimus*) also exhibit a fundamental mtDNA divergence in the same region, and this is congruent with the biogeography of the region. What then are we saying here? Is it really the case that allozyme data, and more generally coding markers, should not be trusted at all? This is a vexed question, but the answer is that ideally, a large number of loci of different types should be used to provide a reliable picture of gene flow and population differentiation. Fortunately, selectively neutral markers such as mtDNA, microsatellites and SNPs, generally more rapidly evolving than allozymes, are now the tools of choice for studies of population differentiation.

mtDNA Variation

An example of the use of mtDNA variation to detect population structure. The anadromous fish *Coregonus artedii*, the cisco, is important in the local fisheries of the river systems of the James and Hudson Bays in Canada. Allozymes were just not variable enough to be able to reveal differences between local river populations; therefore, a mtDNA approach was used by Bernatchez and Dodson to investigate population structure. The frequencies of three mtDNA clonal groups (A, B and C) of cisco from rivers feeding into the Hudson and James Bays.

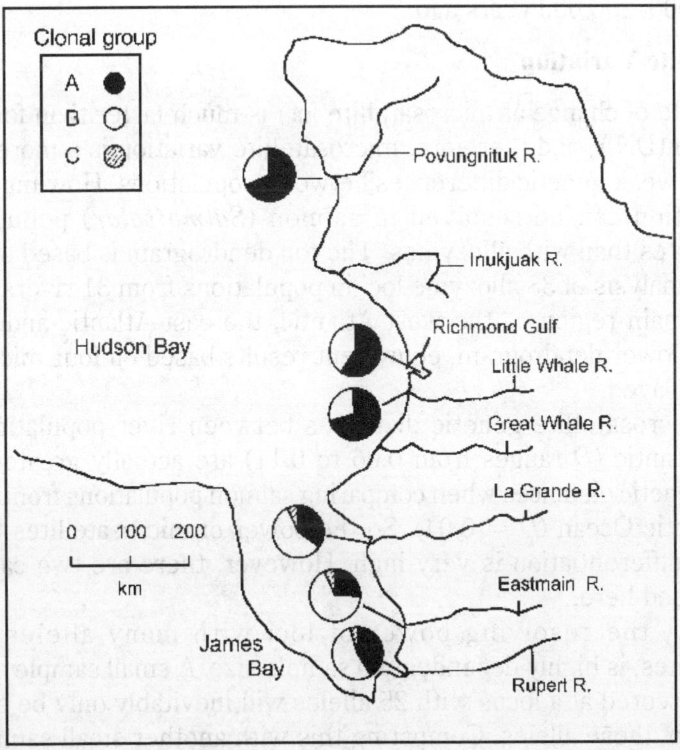

Fig.: Mitochondrial DNA markers used to identify genetic differentiation in cisco.

The clonal groups are not individual mtDNA haplotypes, but come from three clear clusters on a dendrogram of the 19 haplotypes detected from the 141 fish sampled in the study. Different mtDNA haplotypes can be compared to estimate their relatedness to one another and this is what provides clusters of more closely related haplotypes. The genetic pattern revealed by a detailed mtDNA analysis of the different haplotypes within the clonal groups suggests that the cisco of this region, which was covered by ice in the last glaciation, were actually derived from two quite separate glacial refugia (clonal groups A and B) and have recolonised the area by different routes.

Since recolonisation, there has been some merging between the two types but this has not obscured the historical geographic pattern. The source of clonal group C which is strongly diverged from both the A and B clonal groups is not clear – it might even represent introgressed mtDNA from a closely related hybridising species. In this example, we see how mtDNA analysis can not only tell us about the current population structure of a species, but also can point to historical processes which have influenced the pattern observed in the present day. In human genetics, this valuable characteristic of mtDNA has been used to provide evidence for the 'out of Africa' theory, since it appears that we are all descended from a single 'mitochondrial Eve' lineage that inhabited Africa some 140 000–290 000 years ago.

Microsatellite Variation

The rate of change at microsatellite loci is much faster than for allozyme loci or for mtDNA, and therefore, microsatellite variation is a more sensitive measure of weak genetic differences between populations. How much genetic differentiation can be resolved in salmon (*Salmo salar*) populations by microsatellites than with allozymes. The top dendrogram is based on an allele frequency analysis of 38 allozyme loci in populations from 31 rivers that drain into three main regions – the west Atlantic, the east Atlantic and the Baltic Sea. In the lower dendrogram, equivalent results based on four microsatellite loci are displayed.

The microsatellite genetic distances between river populations in the western Atlantic (D ranges from 0.06 to 0.11) are actually greater than the allozyme genetic distances when comparing salmon populations from both sides of the Atlantic Ocean ($D = 0.04$). So the power of microsatellites to identify population differentiation is very high. However, there are two caveats that must be added here.

Firstly, the resolving power of loci with many alleles, such as microsatellites, is highly dependent on sample size. A small sample of, say, ten individuals scored at a locus with 25 alleles will inevitably only be sampling a proportion of those alleles. Comparing this with another small sample from a different population that also has the same alleles at similar frequencies could show quite large genetic differences based on chance alone. Some alleles sampled from one population will be absent in the sample from the other population, leading to the mistaken conclusion that the two populations are very different. Secondly, Nei's genetic distance measure *(D)* was devised on the basis of estimated point mutation rates at allozyme loci (around 10^{-7} mutations per gene per individual). As mutation in microsatellites is due to slippage during replication (around 10^{-3} mutations per gene per individual) rather than point mutation, it would not be safe to use Nei's formula (time of divergence = $5 \times 10^6 D$) to extrapolate any times of divergence between taxa based on microsatellite data.

FISHERIES AND AQUACULTURE PRODUCTS

Fisheries and aquaculture products are globally important sources of much needed, high quality, aquatic animal proteins, and invaluable providers of employment, cash income, and foreign exchange. Fisheries products are the world's most widely traded foods, with commerce dominated by the developing countries.

Fisheries products are the primary protein sources for some 950 million people worldwide, and are an important part of the diet of many more. In comparison to other sectors of the world food economy, however, the fisheries and aquaculture sectors are poorly planned, inadequately funded, and neglected by all levels of government. This neglect occurs in a paradoxical situation: fishing is the largest extractive use of wildlife in the world; and aquaculture is the most rapidly growing sector of the global agricultural economy.

Our vision is one in which the USAID is a world leader in channeling high quality, "needs directed" kinds of technical assistance in fisheries and aquaculture to developing countries, mainly in the form of capacity-building though education and training opportunities, but also in applied research. Considering the status, priority issues and future trends we have identified in this study, we recommend seven strategic approaches and investments to USAID:

1. USAID needs to substantially increase its programmatic emphasis and enlarge its financial and human resource commitments to global fisheries and aquaculture.
2. USAID needs to play a central role in mobilizing America's considerable human and institutional resources in fisheries and aquaculture to assist developing countries.
3. USAID needs to bridge the "digital divide" to develop solutions to fisheries and aquaculture *issues in developing countries.*
4. USAID should prioritize the improved management of coastal marine and inland fisheries by providing technical assistance to evolve innovative fisheries management schemes in developing countries, including but not limited to, property rights, co-management, and the use of marine protected areas; plus assist in the development of more accurate and reliable fisheries data reporting systems.

5. USAID needs to substantially increase its support to develop more comprehensive, sustainable, ecologically and socially compatible, and economically viable aquaculture systems in developing countries that have the long-term goals of poverty alleviation and food security.
6. USAID should prioritize its assistance to fisheries and aquaculture activities that are more integrated, comprehensive, community-based, and use "systems approaches"-such as ecological and integrated farming/fishing systems research and extension approaches-in both rural and urban settings. The current agriculture emphasis of USAID is on plant commodity research, not on comprehensive, agro/aqua-ecosystems research/extension approaches. We urge the USAID to support long-term, applied research and development that makes expanded use of participatory ecological and social science tools to empower community control of fisheries and aquaculture systems; and to better integrate aquaculture and fisheries activities into the comprehensive management of natural and social resources of its missions, target nations and regions.
7. USAID needs to develop comprehensive strategic and implementation plans and regular impact assessments of an expanded fisheries and aquaculture portfolio. USAID missions and regions should include fisheries and aquaculture into their strategic plans for the comprehensive management of natural resources-or they will be incomplete-especially in regards to USAID plans for involvement in the issues of water allocation and quality, and plans for the management of marine and inland coastal areas.

We believe our case for increased strategic engagement and substantially increased investments in priority issues of importance to the future sustainability of global capture fisheries and aquaculture by all levels of the USAID bureaucracy (headquarters, regions, missions, etc.) cannot be overlooked. America has an accelerating trade deficit in fisheries products that now exceeds $9 billion per year-a deficit surpassed only by those in oil and automobiles-and the US remains the 4th largest exporter of fisheries products in the world (~$2.8 billion). The lack of US engagement in international fisheries and aquaculture not only compromises America's financial position: and an important part of our Nation's food security is at risk; and our domestic fisheries and aquaculture industries are rapidly losing their competitive position.

STATUS, TRENDS AND ISSUES IN FISHERIES AND AQUACULTURE

We suspect that living in true harmony with the natural world, in a manner sustainable over the long run, is something no modern human society has yet learned how to do. The survival of the natural world, however, and likely our survival as a species, depends on our learning to do this. It will be a unique experience in human history.

MARINE FISHERIES RESOURCES AND POTENTIAL

Reported global production of marine capture fisheries increased from 17 million tons in 1950 to about 80 million tons in the mid-1980s, oscillating since then between 78 and 88 million tons (excluding discards), representing 60 per cent of the overall fisheries production including aquaculture in 2001. The annual rate of increase of marine catches decreased to almost zero in the 1990s, indicating that the world oceans have reached their maximal production under the present fishing regime.

An estimated 25 per cent of the major marine fish stocks for which information is available are underexploited or moderately exploited. Stocks or species groups in this category represent the main source for the potential expansion of total marine catches. About 47 per cent of the main stocks or species groups are fully exploited and are therefore producing catches that have reached, or are very close to, their maximum sustainable limits. Thus, nearly half of world marine stocks offer no reasonable expectations for further expansion.

Another 18 per cent of stocks or species groups are reported as overexploited. Prospects for expansion or increased production from these stocks are negligible; and there is an increasing likelihood that stocks will decline further and catches will decrease, unless remedial management action is taken to reduce overfishing. The remaining 10 per cent of stocks have become significantly depleted, or are recovering from depletion and are far less productive than they used to be (or than they could be) if management can return them to the higher abundance levels commensurate with their pre-depletion catch levels. Recovery usually implies drastic and long-lasting reductions in fishing pressure and/or the adoption of other management measures to remove conditions that contributed to the stock's overexploitation and depletion. In most areas, overfishing is certainly a significant factor responsible for the declines. The information available tends to confirm the estimates made by FAO in the early seventies that the global potential for marine fisheries is about 100 million tons of which only 80 million tons were probably achievable for practical reasons. It also confirms that despite local differences, overall, this limit has been reached.

Developed countries are faced with fully or overexploited stocks so their management objectives concentrate on stock rebuilding and capacity reduction, although most countries also have significant aims regarding markets and social conflict. The most urgent objective is to scale fleet sizes so that they become commensurate with sustainable exploitation of the resources. Management plans also increasingly recognize the need for a policy that integrates fisheries with management of the coastal zone or inland waters. Developing countries tend to concentrate on fisheries development in terms of new resources and technology. Although it is recognized that some stocks are overfished, objectives are concentrated more on enhancing and diversifying fisheries rather than on limiting fishing efforts. This is perhaps because the underlying concern for many countries is the relatively important role fisheries play in employment and food security for some of their poorest people. More specific aims include building infrastructure (particularly for processing to reduce post-harvest losses and increase the value added); fishery enhancement, through restocking; and reducing social conflicts, not only among different fishing groups but also between fisheries and other sectors.

The principal policy challenge is to bring the capacity of the global fishing fleet back to a level at which fish stocks can be sustainably harvested. Fisheries based on clearly defined rights of access will need to become more common: experience shows that when these rights are not merely in place but are understood and observed by users, conflicts tend to be minimized. The need is to blend innovation, research, conservation and educational awareness into a goal of aquatic sustainability, and to demonstrate this via successful commercial enterprises.

The "great trends" of the past 20 years in marine fisheries worldwide are the: (1) globalization of both production and labour in marine fisheries, (2) the overcapacity of fleets both nearshore and offshore, resulting in dramatic and widespread declines in catches per unit efforts, (3) the movement of the bulk of the world's fishing capacity from the developed to developing countries, resulting in (4) declining catches and economic hardships worldwide in small scale artesanal and inshore fisheries resulting in less fish for poor consumers, and (5) infant success with various property rights schemes and use of protected areas to sustain stocks.

Inland Fisheries Resources and Potential

Four current strategies in the use of inland waters for fisheries can be distinguished: (1) food fisheries based on wild stocks; (2) enhancement of food fisheries in smaller water bodies and reservoirs; (3) recreational fisheries, which are becoming more common in many areas of the world, and, where they develop, tend to supplant commercial food fisheries; and (4) locally very intense exploitation of juvenile or small adults for stocking into other water bodies and/ or aquaculture ponds, or for the ornamental fish trade.

In 2001, inland capture from 129 countries reached 8.7 million tons. Regionally, Asia dominates inland capture, accounting for nearly 66 per cent (about 5.8 million tons) of the total in 2001, with Africa second at 24 per cent (nearly 2 million tons). In comparison, the remaining regions are relatively insignificant. The capture from inland waters is very diverse. Apart from fish, other groups included in inland capture that are tabulated by weight are freshwater shrimps and prawns, frogs, terrapins, turtles, crayfishes, mussels, mussel shells, pearl oyster shells, swamp crabs, marine worms, manatees and green seaweeds.

There is an enigma concerning the status of inland fishery resources. On the one hand, it is widely accepted and well documented that freshwater resources and environments are deteriorating rapidly and widely. On the other hand, harvests from freshwater environments are stable or on the upswing among countries that account for 93 per cent of the total inland capture.

The increases are due to two factors: (1) enrichment of aquatic systems from land based human activities that until now have been a counterweight to habitat losses and pollution; (2) enhancements of inland fisheries (*e.g.*, stocking, introductions) that increase the output per unit of area; and (3) the increased number of reservoirs with capture fisheries enhancement activities. Inland fisheries enhancement methods, often combined with conventional fisheries management practices, are widely applied, and are becoming a central theme in the management of inland waters in developing countries The exact contribution of enhancements to the total inland capture fisheries production is, however, difficult to estimate.

INLAND CAPTURE IN DEVELOPING COUNTRIES

About two-thirds of inland capture is from developing countries and about one-fourth is from China. The countries in Africa and Asia that are among the top 20 in inland capture production also rank low in the Human Development Indices.

This comparison underlines the need to sustain inland fisheries in the countries where inland capture is relatively important in its own right, where inland capture contributes significantly to food security, and where levels of human development are lowest. In contrast, inland recreational fisheries are pre-eminent in most developed countries; however, almost every country with inland waters has some recreational fisheries that often play an important role in subsistence. Indications are that freshwater recreational effort is perhaps one-half of the food fishing effort from a worldwide perspective.

Output from inland food fisheries will continue to increase slowly overall. In the short term most of the gains will be realized where enhancements are already common, namely in Asia. In Africa, where enhancements have been slow to be implemented, output may actually decrease due to overfishing and a deteriorating environment in the most populous countries, but increase as enhancements become more widely implemented. Likewise, in Latin America, inland fisheries enhancements are practiced and are growing, but the demand for inland fish is weak in many countries, while in others degradation of the environment is causing a decline in production.

Degradation of the environment is the main underlying issue, and the consequent loss of fishery habitat is the pre-eminent concern. A closely related concern is that loss of habitat that, along with the intense and widespread exploitation of fishery resources, negatively impacts aquatic biodiversity. In practical terms, the resiliency of resources to fishing, and often the quality of the resources, is lessened. Additionally, in most countries the main challenges to maintaining and enhancing inland fish production and small-scale aquaculture and their associated social and economic benefits are increasing competition for resources and insufficient institutional and political recognition.

Reporting and Statistical Issues in Fisheries

Without reliable statistics, effective fisheries management and policy-making are impossible. During the last decade, financial support for the development and maintenance of national fishery statistical systems have decreased sharply in real terms, while statistical requirements have been increasing dramatically for by-catch and discards, fishing capacity, illegal fishing, vessels authorized to fish in the high seas, economic data (costs, revenues, prices, subsidies), employment, management systems, inventories of stocks and fisheries, aquaculture, etc.

Despite FAO's efforts, the available fisheries data are not fully reliable. The outcome is far from perfect in terms of coverage, timeliness, and quality. Statistics from artisanal and subsistence fisheries are still a concern, and many key statistics are missing, *e.g.* economic and social data, discards, fishing capacity, etc. The result is that the general trends are probably reliably reflected, but the annual figures and the assessments involve a degree of uncertainty, and small changes from year to year are probably not statistically significant. Illegal, unreported and unregulated fishing is found in all capture fisheries, irrespective of the location, species targeted, fishing gears employed or level and intensity of exploitation. Working with the countries is the only way to improve fishery statistics, primarily to meet national needs with regard to food security and fisheries management. Unlike capture fisheries, the separate monitoring of aquaculture is relatively new in most countries, and often there are less well-established systems of data collection as compared to capture fisheries.

Actual inland capture fisheries production is considerably greater than the amounts reported to FAO. The factor is at least two overall, but may be as high as three in some instances. There is an urgent need for better data on inland fisheries that can be interpreted in both economic and ecological terms. Although the cost of improving inland fishery data collection may be high, failure to fully account for inland capture also is costly in terms of lost opportunities to increase food security and other economic and social benefits from enhanced management of inland fisheries resources.

A recent chapter in *Nature* indicated that China's marine capture fishery production for 1995-1999 has been overstated in Chinese statistics submitted to and published by FAO. The paper states that as a consequence of this, global marine capture fishery production—excluding Peruvian anchoveta—has likely been declining since 1988 rather than remaining fairly constant as indicated by the statistics. According to the authors, this would have led to understating the degradation of world fisheries, and produced unfortunate policy and investment decisions. However, the FAO maintains that despite likely errors in the data sets, the main global trends have not been masked, and that the most important conclusions have emerged, nevertheless. These findings, together with similar ones emerging at regional and national level, have been the foundation for the governance and institutional changes observed since 1990.

Aquaculture Status and Potential

Aquaculture is more akin to farming and animal husbandry than to fishing, as it involves the rearing and management of living aquatic resources in a restricted environment. Tenure of production facilities, and property rights to the produce, are as important to the success of aquaculture as land tenure is to agriculture. Aquaculture has been developed to serve a variety of purposes: (1) producing high nutritional value food for human consumption; (2) contributing to rural income and employment through farming and related activities; (3) enhancing capture and sport fisheries; (4) cultivating ornamental species for aesthetic purposes; (5) controlling aquatic weeds or pests hazardous to humans or crops; and (6) desalination and other forms of soil recuperation.

Meeting basic human needs for protein foods in the future will be a difficult challenge. Approximately 1.3 billion people live on less than a dollar a day—the cost of a half a pint of beer—and half of the world's population lives on less than 2 dollars a day.

Since 1950, there's been a 100 per cent increase in the per capita demand for fish, a 40 per cent increase for grain, and 33 per cent for wood. If world fish consumption will increase from 16 kg (1997) to 19-20 kg by 2030, total human use of aquatic foods will increase to 150-160 million tons. Capture fisheries can provide no more than 100 million tons, so the bulk of the increase will need to come from aquaculture.

In 2001, 48.4 million tons of aquatic products (including plants) valued at US$ 61.5 billion were produced, with half of the production being finfish. Aquaculture is growing more rapidly than all other animal food producing sectors. Worldwide, the sector has increased at an average compounded rate of 9.2 per cent per year since 1970, compared with only 1.4 per cent for capture fisheries and 2.8 per cent for terrestrial farmed meat production systems. Over half of global aquaculture production originated from marine and brackish coastal waters, while the remainder (45 per cent) was from freshwater.

Aquaculture will soon overtake cattle ranching as a global food resource, possibly signaling a basic shift in diets. Over the last century, the world relied heavily on two natural systems—oceanic fisheries and rangelands—to satisfy a growing demand for animal protein, but that era is ending as both systems are reaching their productive limits. Between 1950 and 1990, beef production, four-fifths of it from rangelands, nearly tripled, climbing from 19 million to 53 million tons before leveling off. Since 1990, there has been little growth in either beef production or the oceanic fish catch. Additional production of beef or seafood now depends on placing more cattle in feedlots or more fish in ponds.

PRODUCTION EFFICIENCIES OF AQUACULTURE

Comparisons of energy and production efficiencies of aquaculture versus an array of fisheries and terrestrial agriculture systems confirm that aquaculture is an efficient mass producer of animal proteins for a crowded, coastal planet. Production efficiencies of edible mass for aquaculture range from 2.5 to 4.5 kg dry feed/kg edible mass compared with 3.0 to 17.4 for conventional terrestrial animal production systems. Beef cattle require over 10 kg of feed to add 1 kg of edible weight, whereas catfish can add a kg of edible weight with less than 3 kg of feed. To produce 1 kcal of catfish protein about 34 kcal of fossil fuel energy is required—lobster and shrimp capture fisheries use more than 5 times this amount of energy. Energy costs for even the most intensive salmon cages are less than lobster and shrimp fishing, but are comparable to beef production in feedlots. Aquaculture also has a comparable advantage in water efficiency, since a comparatively smaller amount of water for aquaculture is required. For example, catfish ponds managed using multiple harvest strategies use 1.50 m^3 of water per 1 kg of product while conventional soybean production takes 1.63 m^3 of water to produce 1 kg.

In a world of land and water scarcity, the advantages of aquaculture over capture fisheries and other land-based protein production systems to produce low-cost animal protein are clear. However, care must be taken to ensure that aquaculture is not viewed as a panacea—since most analysts agree that aquaculture will never completely replace capture fisheries—and that increased aquaculture production will not be associated with higher rates of environmental damage and harvest rates of forage fish species used to produce fish meals and oils, which would lead to a net loss of fish production (*e.g.* the capture for fish meals and oils would exceed the amount of fish produced for consumption).

There are many cases where aquaculture expansion has fueled the hope of fragile coastal and inland rural communities that have undergone unprecedented changes in their traditional ways of life. Aquaculture has provided significant multiplier effects on the local economies increasing both direct and indirect personal spending in these coastal communities. And yet, communities in many parts of the world actively oppose aquacultural development because such development is perceived as a threat to local social and/or ecological systems. If intensive aquaculture operations—no matter how advanced technically—have no community roots; and feeds, seeds, supplies, equipment and human expertise are procured from great distances from the sites of production; community opposition will continue to occur. In these cases it is easy to see why some community members view aquaculture development as "all we get is your pollution". Planning for aquaculture development as community development and environmental enhancement must thereby encompass regional planning processes to accommodate aquaculture's vital support industries (inputs), and for the use of aquaculture resources and wastes in agriculture or in environmental enhancement projects (outputs). Regional planning for "ecological aquaculture" developments will have much higher positive impacts on jobs and the environment, and will eventually dissolve the opposition from communities who will see the newcomers as one of their own.

Aquaculture production systems, aquatic environments, and the feeds to produce fish must be environmentally benign and ecologically sound in order for the advantages of aquaculture as a food production system to be embraced and supported. Indeed, the expansion of aquaculture can never be justified on the destruction of the world's capture fisheries. The future protein needs of millions of people—and the sustainability of aquaculture itself—depend on the conservation, good management and recovery of the world's capture fisheries and the environments on which they depend.

GLOBAL ENVIRONMENTAL THREATS TO FISHERIES AND AQUACULTURE

We live on a human-dominated planet, and the momentum of human population growth, together with the imperative for further economic development in most of the world, ensures that our dominance will increase.

SUSTAINABLE DEVELOPMENT AND MANAGEMENT OF AQUACULTURE AND FISHERIES SYSTEMS

The sustainable development and management of aquaculture and fisheries systems can only occur if these activities are well planned and integrated into the natural and social resource, ecosystems, and farming systems contexts of the larger global context of which they are a part. Population and natural resource constraints in a crowded future demand that aquaculture "fits" as a part of a larger strategy for the non-consumptive, multiple uses of water; and that fisheries be managed sustainably as part of the larger trends affecting the marine environment.

In the past 50 years there has been a massive migration—called the "greatest human migration of all time"—from rural, inland areas to the world's coasts, resulting in about 60 per cent of the Earth's people living within 100 km of the coast. Massive growth of coastal cities has raised issues of the future survival of coastal and estuarine ecosystems and habitats, and has put at risk the livelihoods of millions of people in traditional coastal communities that depend upon the sustainable capture and culture of aquatic living resources. Upwards of 35 per cent of the primary production of the temperate continental shelves is being harvested in fisheries, or discarded back to the sea as waste ("bycatch"). Coastal margins and oceans are among the most heavily used and modified areas of the planet, suffering disproportionate amounts of habitat destruction and pollution.

Humans have removed about 50 per cent of the world's mangroves. Human activities in the coastal zone deliver sewage, solid wastes, refuse (marine debris), sediments, dust, pesticides, and oil hydrocarbons to rivers, estuaries, and coastal areas. Assessing the range, magnitude and delivery of land-based sources of pollution to coastal oceans is a major global effort. It is estimated that about 80 per cent of marine pollution originates from land-based sources and activities. Inputs of nutrients to the coastal zone from development and agriculture have caused an increase in toxic algae blooms, some of which have caused human disease and neurological impairment. In Shanghai, China, an estimated 13,000 factories discharged 10.55 million tons of waste in 1989, nearly twice the amount in 1980; about one-fifth was toxic waste. The Songhua River in China contains 10 tons of mercury and has waterborne mercury concentrations higher than those reported after the disaster in Minamata Bay, Japan. About one-third of China's coastal waters are polluted with oil; mercury and cadmium have been detected in 60 per cent and 33 per cent of seawater samples, respectively. In Poland, 92 per cent of the nation's rivers are "beyond classification", meaning that the level of pollution is greater than that described by any existing pollution category.

Humanity is the now one of the major driving forces in the Earth's hydrological cycle, using more than half of the world's freshwater run-off. Agricultural water use accounts for about 75 per cent of total global consumption, mainly through crop irrigation, while industrial use accounts for about 20 per cent, and the remaining 5 per cent is used for domestic purposes. Most of the world's rivers are dammed—there are 36,000 dams—and the number of dams is increasing.

Many major rivers (Colorado, Nile and Ganges) are so heavily used that little or no water reaches their deltas and the sea. Only 2 per cent of rivers in the USA run free. Major inland water areas (Aral Sea, Lake Chad, etc.) have nearly dried up or been greatly reduced to small lakes. It is estimated that two out of every three people will live in water-stressed areas by the year 2025. In Africa, it is estimated that 25 countries will be experiencing water stress (below 1,700 m^3 per capita per year) by 2025. About 450 million people in 29 countries suffer from water shortages. Clean water supplies and sanitation are major problems in many parts of the world, with 20 per cent of the global population lacking access to safe drinking water. Water-borne diseases from fecal pollution of surface waters are a major cause of illness in developing countries. Polluted water is estimated to affect the health of 1.2 billion people, and contributes to the death of 15 million children annually.

Losses of biodiversity are occurring at alarming rates. Rates of loss are estimated at 100—1000 times greater than natural rates of extinctions. Extinction rates are even higher on remote islands, such as Hawai'i, USA. Due to the ease and rapidity of global transportation, the world's ecosystems are becoming "homogenized" due to "biological invasions": the exotic introductions of plants and animals, bacteria and other pests to natal ecosystems. After land transformations, exotic species impacts are the second major cause of species extinctions and population losses. About 11 per cent of birds, 18 per cent of mammals, 5 per cent of fish and 8 per cent of the Earth's plants are threatened with extinction, and exotic species have contributed greatly to their demise.

Given these immense global challenges, Vitousek *et al.* recommend:

- A slowing the rate of population growth since humanity's growth drives all resource use and waste generation,
- A reduction in the rate of human impacts since ecosystems can react to lower rates of impacts and stabilize with moderate levels of human-induced changes,
- Accelerating ecosystem level research and management understanding. Human impacts must be included in all analyses of global and ecosystem change. Ecological science must include development of new methodologies to assist humanity in this global crisis, requiring development of true interdisciplinary environmental scholarship, and education of the "informed generalist."

THE GLOBAL IMPORTANCE OF FISHERIES AND AQUACULTURE

Fisheries play an important role in the world food economy. Fisheries are a source of employment for about 200 million people who depend directly upon ocean fishing for their livelihoods. Fish is the primary source of protein for some 950 million people worldwide and represents an important part of the diet of many more.

In less than 50 years, the world's average per capita consumption of fish has almost doubled. Globally, fish provide about 16 per cent of the animal protein consumed by humans, and are a valuable source of minerals and essential fatty acids.

Fish is the primary source of omega-3 fatty acids in the human diet. Omega-3 fatty acids are critical nutrients for normal brain and eye development of infants, and have preventative roles in a number of human illnesses, such as cardiovascular disease, lupus, depression and other mental illnesses.

The reported production of fish for direct human consumption doubled between 1950 and 1970, and has stabilized since then at an average of 9.0 to 10 kg of fish per capita, notwithstanding world population growth. Fish consumption per person is expected to continue to rise. Supply will probably be limited by environmental factors, and a likely range for demand is 150 to 160 million tons, or between 19 and 20 kg per person in 2030. Global increases in consumption of food fish will take place predominantly in the developing countries, where population is growing and higher incomes are allowing purchase of high value fisheries items for the first time by many people. However, fish production in least developed countries where fish protein is needed to prevent malnutrition is a key element of food security in these regions and a critical area where innovative programmes are needed to increase production.

Today, fishing is the largest extractive use of wildlife in the world. The value of world total fishery production in 1999 was US$ 125 billion. World production of fish, crustaceans, mollusks and plants reached 142 million tons in 2001. Capture fisheries production, which accounted for 66 per cent of the total, was 93.7 million tons, of which inland capture was 8.7 million tons, while aquaculture production was 48.4 million tons including plants. Marine and freshwater fish are also an increasingly important recreational resource, both for active users such as anglers and for passive users such as tourists, sports divers and nature-lovers.

PREDOMINATES IN CAPTURE FISHERIES AND AQUACULTURE PRODUCTION

Asia predominates in capture fisheries and aquaculture production, with China the leading nation worldwide. In 1999, over three-quarters (or 97 million tons) of the global production of fish, crustaceans and mollusks were utilized for direct human consumption. Fish utilized as raw material for the production of animal feed, *e.g.*, fish meal and fish oil, represented about one-quarter of the total fishery production in 1999; and this amount has remained relatively static for the past 15 years. Most growth in the fisheries sectors is projected to occur in developing countries, which will account for 79 per cent of food fish production in 2020.

Increased production of fish from aquaculture has occurred primarily as a result of increasing feed inputs into ponds and other production systems, thereby increasing yields per hectare by an order of magnitude compared to extensive production systems in which rearing water is fertilized only. Higher inputs mean two things to the aquaculture feed industry; more feed and higher quality feed. Currently, global feed production for farmed fish and crustaceans is approximately 13 million tons, and predictions are for feed production to increase to over 37 million tons by the end of the decade, an increase of 24 million tons. Feeds for salmonids and marine fish have always been complete feeds, *i.e.*, ones that supply all of the nutritional needs of the fish. Pond-reared fish, in contrast, obtain a significant proportion of their nutritional needs from pond biota. The degree to which feeds must supply essential nutrients to pond-reared fish increases as rearing densities increase beyond the capacity of natural foods in ponds to supply them. Fish farmers around the world have found that as they increase feed inputs, the biomass and economic yields from ponds increase as well. Thus, great areas of low-input, pond-based aquaculture mainly in Southeast Asia and China are being converted from low-input systems to high-input systems that depend upon high quality feeds to supply an increasing proportion of nutrients used by the fish.

The effects of the aquaculture industry's growth and of changes in feed input in pond-based aquaculture have been dramatic with respect to the use of marine proteins by the aquaculture feed industry. In the mid-1980s, less than 10 per cent of annual fish meal production was used by the aquaculture feed sector. Today, that proportion is over 40 per cent. Similarly, aquaculture now uses nearly 75 per cent of annual global fish oil production, up from less than 10 per cent seventeen years ago, but this change is mainly due to the adoption of high lipid feeds by the salmon farming industry, rather than increasing the inputs into pond-based aquaculture systems.

Fish meal and oil are produced from species of fish that are not generally utilized directly for human food, *e.g.*, herring and capelin in Norway and Iceland, sand eel in Denmark, capelin in South Africa, anchovies in Peru and northern Chile, jack mackerel in central Chile, sardines in Japan, and menhaden in the USA. The rapid increase in fish meal and oil use in aquaculture feeds over the past 15 years has not resulted in over-exploitation of the stocks of fish harvested primarily to produce fish meal and oil. Production of fish meal has averaged between 6-7 million tons per year since the mid-1980s, except in El Nino years, when production has been lower. Fish oil production has averaged between 1.2-1.3 million tons. No significant changes in annual harvest or fish meal/oil production associated with increased aquaculture production or increasing intensification of aquaculture and concomitant higher feed inputs is evident. Increased fish meal/oil use in the aquaculture sector has come at the expense of other uses.

Estimates of future protein requirements for aquaculture feeds depend upon future production from various segments of the aquaculture industry and on annual production levels of fish meal. As aquaculture production expands, it will be essential to replace portions of fish meal and oil in fish feed formulations with alternative ingredients derived from alternative sources, primarily grains and oilseed products.

Because 70 per cent of the fish meal used in diets for fish and crustaceans is used to produce diets for salmonids, marine fish and shrimp, these production sectors are the focus of most research with respect to the use of alternative protein sources. Numerous studies have been conducted to evaluate the effects of replacing various percentages of fish meal in diets for these fish, and, without exception, none has successfully replaced 100 per cent of fish meal without reducing fish performance. At best, 50 per cent of fish meal in diets for salmon and trout can be replaced by soy protein concentrate, and 25-30 per cent with soybean meal. Similar findings have been reported in studies of wheat gluten meal, corn gluten meal, and rapeseed protein concentrate. For the most part, formulated fish diets are used to produce high-value fish for export. In underdeveloped countries, increased production of lower-value fish that are consumed by local populations will depend upon the use locally-available, low-cost feed ingredients that can be combined to produce prepared feeds to increase productivity of community ponds and waterways.

This is an area that requires substantial investigation and development, and is a logical target for USAID support. Another logical target for USAID efforts is the development and testing of feeds that are based upon sustainable plant-derived protein sources for use in developing countries where fish are grown both for domestic consumption and export, such as China. Partnerships with US commodity groups could be a mechanism to extend USAID efforts. It is critical that USAID become a leader in this area, given the perception that increased aquaculture production leads to higher fish meal use and greater pressure on stocks of fish that are captured to produce fish meals and oils.

Fisheries products have become the most internationally traded food, as some 37 per cent (by quantity) of all fish for human consumption is traded across borders. In 1999, international trade (in live weight equivalent) represented 34 per cent of the total production. In 1999, foreign trade earnings amounted to US$ 52.9 billion. Most fishery exports were destined to developed countries, with Japan the world's leading importer, and the USA second. The US balance of trade deficit in seafood products is approximately $9 billion.

Exports of fisheries products to the developed countries have become so lucrative that nations like Argentina, a traditional, globally important exporter of meat products and livestock have turned to seafood exports as the major source of foreign exchange earnings. In 2002, exports of raw and processed fish and shellfish from Argentina surpassed meat products and livestock, with beef earning US$ 574 million in export revenue, while seafood—mostly prepared products—earned US$ 714 million. Argentina's main consumers of domestic seafood products were Spain, Brazil and the US.

9

Conservation and Utilization of Genetic Resources in Fisheries

New biotechnologies offer not only techniques to improve the conservation of genetic resources, but also new methods to identify, clone, transfer and express genes in different organisms. This has profound implications for the utilization of genetic resources, could broaden the germplasm base from which new genetic combinations can be created, and will allow scientists to pursue their breeding efforts with greater focus and speed.

In vitro conservation and the use of techniques for germplasm exchange of certain plant species are already proving considerably more efficient than conventional methods. Furthermore, the generation of gene libraries provides a valuable adjunct to the conventional germplasm conservation methods. Molecular methods such as Restriction Fragment Length Polymorph (RFLP), isozyme and protein analyses are already being used for the characterization of genetic resources and the identification of useful genes. However, massive use of crop varieties reproduced through in vitro culture, which contain genetically identical copies of the parent, could provoke increasing genetic erosion.

RESISTANCE/TOLERANCE TO STRESSES

Biotechnologies have been particularly effective in and could have great potential for developing genotypes resistant/tolerant to biotic and abiotic stresses commonly affecting crop, livestock, forest and fish species, and can therefore contribute to reducing inputs of pesticides and to stabilizing agriculture in marginal lands and inhospitable habitats. Genetically engineered de novo synthesis of biopesticides by host species for their own defence, development of biocapsules containing genetically engineered biopesticides and virus coat protein-mediated resistance represent tremendous opportunities for pest management.

It is anticipated that genetically engineered vegetable and cereal crops, resistant to certain insects and viruses or tolerant to herbicides, will be commercially available by 1993. Genetically engineered biopesticides are near approval for sale in some countries. The efficiency of insect-based control of pest arthropods, pathogens and weeds and the production of sterile males for insect control can be enhanced considerably through genetic engineering. Furthermore, biotechnologies are aiding conventional breeding in developing genotypes resistant/tolerant to high and low temperature regimes, drought and excess water conditions and saline and other problem soil conditions. A major concern about these solutions, however, is their sustainability if the improved attributes are based on one or only a few genes, as has often been the case.

SUSTAINABLE PRODUCTION

Biotechnology may be used as a tool in the sustained production of crops, livestock, forest and fisheries by providing opportunities to:

- develop genetically broad-based varieties/breeds resistant/tolerant to biotic and abiotic stresses;
- increase efficiency in the conservation and enhanced use of natural resources, including genetic resources and systems;
- reduce use of off-farm inputs such as pesticides;
- develop populations adapted to marginal land and problem soil conditions; and
- produce genetically engineered organisms for degradation of toxic wastes and detoxification of chemical residues on produce or land.

In order to be not only environmentally friendly but also socio-economically viable and attractive, a more vigorous and focused research and development approach, especially by the public sector, is necessary. The private sector should also be encouraged to achieve the desired goal of sustainable development through the use of sound biotechniques.

STATUS AND MANAGEMENT OF FISHERY RESOURCES

The Yangtze valley is the most developed freshwater fisheries area in China, with abundant fish resources and long history of fisheries. The area has been called "the cradle of freshwater fisheries production", with production accounting for about 60 per cent of the national total freshwater fish catch. The Yangtze fish catches have decreased or fluctuated after a historical record of 0.45 million tonnes in 1954. In the last decade, the catch has fallen below 0.10 million tons, with a notable depletion of migratory and semi-migratory fish stocks, the primary reasons being the destruction of the aquatic ecosystem and overfishing. This book focuses on measures taken for strengthening fishery administration at various levels, for comprehensive harnessing of water resources and for research as a way of rehabilitating the Yangtze fisheries.

MATERIALS AND METHODS

Fishery resources of the Yangtze River were investigated between 1971 and 2000. Statistical data were obtained from the Fishery Bureau of Agricultural Ministry of China. Local and national monitoring stations provided environmental and hydrological data. All data were analysed by SAS software.

RESULTS AND DISCUSSION

Fish Fauna and its Distribution

The fish fauna of the Yangtze River system comprises over 370 species (178 genera, 52 families, 17 orders), of which cyprinids (Cyprinidae) account for 51 per cent, loaches (Cobitidae) 6.9 per cent, bagrids (Bagridae) 6.9 per cent, Homalopteridae 5.5 per cent, gobies (Cobiidae) 4.4 per cent and other families 24.9 per cent (Wu 1984).

The major species of economic importance are black carp (*Mylopharyngodon piceus* (Rich.), grass carp (*Ctenopharyngodon idella* (C. et V.), silver carp (*Hypophthalmichthys molitrix* (C. et V.), bighead carp (*Aristichthys nobilis* (Rich.), common carp (*Cyprinus carpio* (L.), crucian carp (*Carassius auratus* (L.), blunt snout bream (*Megalobrama amblycephala* Yih), whitefish (*Hemisalanx brachyrostralis* (Fang), silurid catfish (*Silurus asotus* (L.), copper fish (*Coreius heterodon* (Bleeker), Chinese shad (*Macrura reevesii* (Rich.), anchovy (*Coilia mystus* (L.), Chinese sturgeon (*Acipenser sinensis* Gray), paddle fish (*Psephurusgladius* (Martens), Chinese sucker (*Myxocyprinus asiaticus* (Rich.) and eel (*Anguilla japonica* Temm. et Schl.). The distribution of the fish species varies from section to section of the river.

There are 126 fish species, most of them migratory, in the lower Yangtze. In the fisheries of Jiangsu Province, anchovy accounts for about 50 per cent of the catch, shad and eels for 20 per cent, common carp, silurid catfish, black carp, grass carp, silver carp, big-head, whitefish, etc. for 30 per cent. The catch from the lower Yangtze accounts for 63 per cent of the total.

There are over 140 fish species in the middle Yangtze most of which are semi-migratory (black carp, grass carp, silver carp, bighead carp and some other) and resident species (common carp, crucian carp, etc.). The catch from the middle Yangtze accounts for 34 per cent of the total. There are over 180 fish species in the upper Yangtze. Copper fish is the main species, accounting for about 40 per cent of the catch, common carp and Chinese sturgeon (before the damming of the Yangtze River at Gezhouba) acount for up to 15 per cent each, *Leiocassis longirostris* accounts for 10 per cent. Other major species are *Procypris rabaudi, Spinibarbus*, *Varicorhinus simus*, grass carp and *Elopichthys bambusa*. The catch from the upper Yangtze accounts for 3 per cent of the total.

MAJOR FISH SPECIES

Anchovy

Anchovy is found mainly in Shanghai City and Jiangsu Province. In both places the production accounts for about 70-80 per cent of the total catch. The annual catch fluctuates between 250 and 400 tonnes. A historical maximum of 4 000 tonnes was reached in 1973. Although the catch has been fluctuating in the last decade to some extent, it has generally been stable.

Chinese Shad

Chinese shad is an anadromous fish species. Before 1962 its annual catch from the Yangtze River was about 500 tonnes. After 1968 the catches decreased, with only 70 tonnes captured in 1971. In 1974, a record of 1 570 tonnes were harvested, this to be followed by a dramatic decline to 12 tonnes in 1986. Chinese shad is now endangered to the point of extinction.

Chinese Sturgeon

This is also an anadromous species. Before the Yangtze River was dammed at Gezhouba, the annual catch fluctuated between 391 and 636 individuals, averaging 517 annually. After the damming, the annual mean catch from 1981 to 1987 was 378 individuals, representing 73 per cent of that before damming (due to the ban on sturgeon fishing). There is great concern that when the Three Gorges Dam is completed, the spawning grounds of Chinese sturgeon below the dam may disappear or become dysfunctional.

Black Carp, Grass Carp, Silver Carp and Bighead Carp

The percentage of black carp, grass carp, silver carp and bighead carp in the total catch from the Yangtze River has been declining. While in 1982 these carps accounted for 84 per cent of the catch in Anhui Province on the lower Yangtze, they decreased to 36.8 per cent in the 1990s. In the middle reach of the river in the Yichang section of Hubei Province the carps accounted for 80-90 per cent of the catch in the 1960s, but only 22 per cent in 1974 and 0.52 per cent to 5 per cent in the recent decade.

Copper Fish

The copper fish dominates the catch from the upper Yangtze. In 1974, it represented 60.8 per cent of the catch in the Wanxian and Yibin sections. Before the damming the catches were stable, but afterwards there was a steep decrease. In 1982, the fish accounted for about 10 per cent and in 1986 for only 4.7 per cent of the total catch. During the period 1981 to 1987 catches in the Yichang section below the dam increased to 50-60 per cent of the total catch.

Common Carp, Crucian Carp and Silurid Catfish

These are the most widely distributed resident species. They account for 40-50 per cent of the total catch from the middle and lower Yangtze and for 60.6 per cent of the total from the Jialing River (the upper Yangtze). The proportion of these species in the catch remains relatively stable in spite of the decreasing total catch.

Paddlefish

Stocks of paddlefish are gradually declining and the individual size is becoming smaller. According to statistics, only about ten individuals are caught annually in the Yichang section. The average weight of most individuals is now below 30 kg. Only rarely is an individual over 50 kg captured. And the species is now rated as one of the rare fish species.

Leiocassis longirostis: This is another rare fish species. It is distributed in all sections of the river. Its flesh is tender and the taste delicious. The swim bladder, when dried, can be processed into fish maw, a well-known Chinese dish. The pen-holder-line fish maw produced in Shishou City, Hubei Province has enjoyed fame at home and abroad. Previously, several thousand kg of fish maw was processed for export, but now it cannot be found in the markets and catches of the adult fish have declined.

Chinese Sucker

The Chinese sucker is also rated as rare. Formerly, in the Yangtze it represented about 13 per cent of the total catch from the Mingshan section. In the last decade its stocks have been gradually depleted. Only ten old fish have been caught annually from the section from Yichang to Shishou, Hubei Province. Few individuals weigh over 10 kg and the majority are about 5 kg.

OWNERSHIP OF GENETIC RESOURCES

National systems for ownership of genetic resources are often very much at odds with traditional community practices. Most traditional communities in developing countries have continued to apply their own tenure system for biological resources, while the state enforces private and public property rights on goods and resources, and intellectual property laws on industry and commerce. Some traditional tenure systems regarding genetic resources are grounded on collective ownership or heritage, and sometimes, particularly in the case of medicinal plants, on religious and mystical considerations.

In many cases where governments have asserted sovereign rights over genetic resources, the land remains under traditional community tenure. The end result is that the state reaps the benefits from agreements for the use of resources, while the burden of conservation might be said to rest with the communities. The danger is that, once communities have lost control over local resources as well as the ability to practise traditional livelihoods, they may lose as well both the knowledge and the motivation to take care of local ecosystems. The choice between doing whatever it takes to feed one's children and conserving an endangered fish population is no choice at all.

Although the CBD's provisions apply to agreements at the national level, they also take into account the role of traditional communities in conserving and using biodiversity. Article 8(j) requires Parties to the CBD to 'respect, preserve and maintain knowledge, innovations and practices of indigenous and local communities embodying traditional lifestyles relevant to the conservation and sustainable use of biological diversity' and to encourage the equitable sharing of benefits arising from the use of such knowledge, innovations and practices. Article 8(j) confers no rights to communities but is based on the premise that sharing in benefits from the use of genetic resources will help contribute to their conservation and sustainable use.

How to implement Article 8(j) has been one of the greatest challenges for CBD Parties. The Conferences of the Parties have generally assumed (a) that the use of genetic resources generally depends on traditional knowledge and (b) that those using genetic resources are usually based in countries other than the provider country. As we'll explain in the following chapter, the first, critical point is far less true for aquatic than for plant genetic resources. Indigenous peoples, local communities and their advocates have high hopes that Article 8(j) will mean greater recognition of community rights over traditional resources, but this may not be the result for fishing communities if these rights are tied to an intimate knowledge of genetic resources.

RECOGNITION OF INDIGENOUS PEOPLES' RIGHTS

In the traditional cultures of indigenous peoples in widely separated parts of the world, the concept of 'ownership' has little meaning. First Nations participants at a workshop we hosted during the preparation of this book emphasized that they consider it inappropriate to refer to fish as 'resources' – genetic or otherwise. Indigenous peoples' attitudes about equality or 'oneness' of all living creatures, while they may be an essential part of spiritual beliefs, are likely to be rooted in a common sense recognition that surviving in a natural ecosystem requires maintaining the cycles of species, and that ownership is superfluous where there is abundance to be shared.

But times change. Today, claims of ownership make a frequent appearance in the rhetoric of the indigenous rights movement – but mainly as matter of political necessity in campaigns to win legal recognition of the right to use lands and biodiversity in traditional areas of occupation. 'Ownership' and 'title' are words well understood by courts that may have more difficulty relating spiritual beliefs to Western property law.

Ownership of land and control over aquatic life has become a contentious issue in coastal and riparian indigenous communities because of the broad extent of and fragility of fish habitat, the traditional importance of fish for sustenance, and frequent uncertainty about rights of access to fisheries. Recent attention to fish as genetic resources has added a new twist that isn't an issue for plant genetic resources: in the case of migratory fish, several indigenous communities may claim traditional ownership and the right to be consulted by a collector regardless of where broodstock is collected if a fish passes through their territory at some stage in its life cycle.

Most countries have made little progress towards resolving indigenous rights issues. This will undoubtedly impede efforts to facilitate access to genetic resources in indigenous communities. One notable exception is the Philippines, which under the 1997 Indigenous Peoples Rights Act extends a prior informed consent requirement to virtually all potential uses of natural resources in recognized indigenous territories. Another is Canada, where court decisions recognizing indigenous rights have led government negotiations of treaties with some indigenous peoples. Case Study 3 at the end of this chapter, although it describes an unsuccessful negotiation with indigenous communities for access to broodstock, illustrates one useful model for access negotiations with communities with co-management or ownership rights.

Although there is no unanimity among indigenous groups about the approach proposed by the CBD – some have turned their backs on the Convention, while others are actively working with national governments to develop workable access laws – there is naturally widespread scepticism about how Article 8(j) will be interpreted to ensure fair treatment and meaningful benefits for communities.

In 1993, the Draft United Nations Declaration on the Rights of Indigenous Peoples confirmed their right to 'own, develop, control and use the land and territories, including the total environment of the lands, air, waters, coastal seas, sea ice, flora and fauna and other resources which they have traditionally owned or

The CBD's recognition of national sovereignty over genetic resources represented an about-face from another international agreement more than a decade earlier. In 1981, member countries of the UN FAO adopted the International Undertaking on Plant Genetic Resources as an instrument to promote international harmony in matters regarding access to plant genetic resources for food and agriculture. The purpose of the Undertaking, to be monitored by the Commission on Genetic Resources for Food and Agriculture (CGFRA), was to 'ensure that plant genetic resources of economic and/or social interest, particularly for agriculture, will be explored, preserved, evaluated and made available for plant breeding and scientific purposes'.

The International Undertaking's recognition of genetic resources as the 'common heritage of mankind' was in large part a response to a demand from developing nations to keep plant genetic resources in the public domain and to put a brake on further privatization of agricultural genetic resources. Their concerns included gene banking in northern countries of seeds produced by southern farmers; the accumulation of seed companies under the control of transnational corporations; and the implementation of monopoly Plant Breeders' Rights (essentially a patent) over crop varieties, limiting farmers' access to breeders' lines and finished varieties.

ACCESS TO PLANT BREEDERS

Conflict over access to plant breeders' lines in the years following the approval of the International Undertaking led to a 1989 annex recognizing farmers' rights as a counterbalance to plant breeders' rights. Among other things, farmers' rights established the rights of farmers and their communities to participate fully in the benefits derived from plant genetic resources. By the early 1990s, as the privatization of agricultural research and patenting of plant genetic resources in industrial countries increased, developing countries were expressing disillusionment about the effectiveness of the International Undertaking and promises to implement farmers' rights. Consequently they proposed replacing the concepts of common heritage and open access with national sovereignty and benefit sharing to allow nation states to better control and benefit from their biological resources. The enshrinement of these principles in the CBD necessitated a renegotiation of the International Undertaking to ensure harmony between the two agreements.

The result was the International Treaty on Plant Genetic Resources for Food and Agriculture, approved by FAO member countries in 2001 after seven years of difficult negotiation. The treaty is intended to meet the needs of both plant breeders and farmers, guarantee the future availability of plant genetic resources for food and agriculture, and ensure fair and equitable sharing of benefits.

The agreement, which covers 64 food crops accounting for 85 per cent of global human nutrition, places some constraints on intellectual property over the seeds in the multilateral system and imposes obligations for benefit sharing when accessed seeds are commercialized. Civil society organizations such as Genetic Resources Action International (GRAIN) and the Erosion, Technology and Concentration Group (ETC), while acknowledging the treaty as a step forward, also criticize it for not guaranteeing farmers' rights and doing too little to ensure equity and benefit sharing. The history of the International Undertaking illustrates the increasing tension between developed and developing countries over the expansion of intellectual property rights and the demands of developing countries and farming communities for greater control over their genetic resources and the use of traditional knowledge developed by farmers. It also underscores the almost exclusive emphasis on plant genetic resources in international negotiations on access and benefit sharing. The International Undertaking and the treaty that succeeded it were made necessary by the interdependence among countries for access to crop germplasm needed to ensure global food security.

While there is currently no parallel interdependence in access to fish germplasm, the expanding importance of aquaculture in meeting global food needs may ultimately create the need to address similar issues to those that have dominated the negotiations towards the revised International Undertaking–most notably the compatibility between intellectual property rights protection and the protection of communities providing aquatic genetic resources for international aquaculture development.

otherwise occupied or used'. In 2001, the International Indigenous Forum on Biodiversity told the CBD Working Group on Access and Benefit Sharing that the 1993 UN Declaration represented the minimum acceptable standards and that the trust needed to meet the CBD objective of access, and that benefit sharing wouldn't come without recognition of the rights of indigenous peoples. How far to go in that direction remains a challenge for countries intent on facilitating access to genetic resources. Some indigenous groups see the CBD encouragement of benefit sharing with communities as a way to avoid tackling the hard issues that come with recognition of indigenous rights, especially if benefit sharing is limited only to those communities that can prove genetic resources users need their knowledge – and if benefits are solely tied to conservation objectives. The growing litany of 'biopiracy' complaints suggests that countries may find it increasingly hard to separate access issues from indigenous rights issues.

ADOPTION OF CONSERVATION AND MANAGEMENT MEASURES

When considering the adoption of conservation and management measures, the best scientific evidence available should be taken into account in order to evaluate the current state of the fishery resources and the possible impact of the proposed measures on the resources. Research in support of fishery conservation and management should be promoted, including research on the resources and on the effects of climatic, environmental and socio-economic factors. The results of such research should be disseminated to interested parties.

Studies should be promoted which provide an understanding of the costs, benefits and effects of alternative management options designed to rationalise fishing, in particular, options relating to excess fishing capacity and excessive levels of fishing effort. States should ensure that timely, complete and reliable statistics on catch and fishing effort are collected and maintained in accordance with applicable international standards and practices and in sufficient detail to allow sound statistical analysis. Such data should be updated regularly and verified through an appropriate system. States should compile and disseminate such data in a manner consistent with any applicable confidentiality requirements.

In order to ensure sustainable management of fisheries and to enable social and economic objectives to be achieved, sufficient knowledge of social, economic and institutional factors should be developed through data gathering, analysis and research. States should compile fishery-related and other supporting scientific data relating to fish stocks covered by subregional or regional fisheries management organisations or arrangements in an internationally agreed format and provide them in a timely manner to the organisation or arrangement.

In cases of stocks which occur in the jurisdiction of more than one State and for which there is no such organisation or arrangement, the States concerned should agree on a mechanism for cooperation to compile and exchange such data. Subregional or regional fisheries management organisations or arrangements should compile data and make them available, in a manner consistent with any applicable confidentiality requirements, in a timely manner and in an agreed format to all members of these organisations and other interested parties in accordance with agreed procedures.

PRECAUTIONARY APPROACH

States should apply the precautionary approach widely to conservation, management and exploitation of living aquatic resources in order to protect them and preserve the aquatic environment. The absence of adequate scientific information should not be used as a reason for postponing or failing to take conservation and management measures. In implementing the precautionary approach, States should take into account, *inter alia*, uncertainties relating to the size and productivity of the stocks, reference points, stock condition in relation to such reference points, levels and distribution of fishing mortality and the impact of fishing activities, including discards, on non-target and associated or dependent species, as well as environmental and socio-economic conditions. States and subregional or regional fisheries management organisations and arrangements should, on the basis of the best scientific evidence available, *inter alia*, determine:

- Stock specific target reference points, and, at the same time, the action to be taken if they are exceeded; and
- Stock-specific limit reference points, and, at the same time, the action to be taken if they are exceeded; when a limit reference point is approached, measures should be taken to ensure that it will not be exceeded.

In the case of new or exploratory fisheries, States should adopt as soon as possible cautious conservation and management measures, including, *inter alia*, catch limits and effort limits. Such measures should remain in force until there are sufficient data to allow assessment of the impact of the fisheries on the long-term sustainability of the stocks, whereupon conservation and management measures based on that assessment should be implemented. The latter measures should, if appropriate, allow for the gradual development of the fisheries. If a natural phenomenon has a significant adverse impact on the status of living aquatic resources, States should adopt conservation and management measures on an emergency basis to ensure that fishing activity does not exacerbate such adverse impact.

States should also adopt such measures on an emergency basis where fishing activity presents a serious threat to the sustainability of such resources. Measures taken on an emergency basis should be temporary and should be based on the best scientific evidence available.

LEVEL OF FISHING PERMITTED IN MANAGEMENT MEASURES

States should ensure that the level of fishing permitted is commensurate with the state of fisheries resources. States should adopt measures to ensure that no vessel be allowed to fish unless so authorised, in a manner consistent with international law for the high seas or in conformity with national legislation within areas of national jurisdiction.

Where excess fishing capacity exists, mechanisms should be established to reduce capacity to levels commensurate with the sustainable use of fisheries resources so as to ensure that fishers operate under economic conditions that promote responsible fisheries. Such mechanisms should include monitoring the capacity of fishing fleets.

The performance of all existing fishing gear, methods and practices should be examined and measures taken to ensure that fishing gear, methods and practices which are not consistent with responsible fishing are phased out and replaced with more acceptable alternatives. In this process, particular attention should be given to the impact of such measures on fishing communities, including their ability to exploit the resource.

States and fisheries management organisations and arrangements should regulate fishing in such a way as to avoid the risk of conflict among fishers using different vessels, gear and fishing methods.

When deciding on the use, conservation and management of fisheries resources, due recognition should be given, as appropriate, in accordance with national laws and regulations, to the traditional practices, needs and interests of indigenous people and local fishing communities which are highly dependent on fishery resources for their livelihood. In the evaluation of alternative conservation and management measures, their cost-effectiveness and social impact should be considered.

The efficacy of conservation and management measures and their possible interactions should be kept under continuous review. Such measures should, as appropriate, be revised or abolished in the light of new information. States should take appropriate measures to minimize waste, discards, catch by lost or abandoned gear, catch of non-target species, both fish and non-fish species, and negative impacts on associated or dependent species, in particular endangered species.

Where appropriate, such measures may include technical measures related to fish size, mesh size or gear, discards, closed seasons and areas and zones reserved for selected fisheries, particularly artisanal fisheries. Such measures should be applied, where appropriate, to protect juveniles and spawners. States and subregional or regional fisheries management organisations and arrangements should promote, to the extent practicable, the development and use of selective, environmentally safe and cost effective gear and techniques.

States and subregional and regional fisheries management organisations and arrangements, in the framework of their respective competences, should introduce measures for depleted resources and those resources threatened with depletion that facilitate the sustained recovery of such stocks. They should make every effort to ensure that resources and habitats critical to the well-being of such resources which have been adversely affected by fishing or other human activities are restored.

EFFECTIVE LEGAL AND ADMINISTRATIVE FRAMEWORK

States should ensure that an effective legal and administrative framework at the local and national level, as appropriate, is established for fisheries resource conservation and fisheries management. States should ensure that laws and regulations provide for sanctions applicable in respect of violations which are adequate in severity to be effective, including sanctions which allow for the refusal, withdrawal or suspension of authorisations to fish in the event of non-compliance with conservation and management measures in force.

States, in conformity with their national laws, should implement effective fisheries monitoring, control, surveillance and law enforcement measures including, where appropriate, observer programmes, inspection schemes and vessel monitoring systems. Such measures should be promoted and, where appropriate, implemented by subregional or regional fisheries management organisations and arrangements in accordance with procedures agreed by such organisations or arrangements.

States and subregional or regional fisheries management organisations and arrangements, as appropriate, should agree on the means by which the activities of such organisations and arrangements will be financed, bearing in mind, *inter alia*, the relative benefits derived from the fishery and the differing capacities of countries to provide financial and other contributions. Where appropriate, and when possible, such organisations and arrangements should aim to recover the costs of fisheries conservation, management and research.

States which are members of or participants in subregional or regional fisheries management organisations or arrangements should implement internationally agreed measures adopted in the framework of such organisations or arrangements and consistent with international law to deter the activities of vessels flying the flag of non-members or non-participants which engage in activities which undermine the effectiveness of conservation and management measures established by such organisations or arrangements.

Financial Institutions

Without prejudice to relevant international agreements, States should encourage banks and financial institutions not to require, as a condition of a loan or mortgage, fishing vessels or fishing support vessels to be flagged in a jurisdiction other than that of the State of beneficial ownership where such a requirement would have the effect of increasing the likelihood of non-compliance with international conservation and management measures.

MINNESOTA DEPARTMENT OF NATURAL RESOURCES FISHERIES POLICY AND REGULATION

The primary goal of fishery management in Minnesota is to protect, maintain and/or enhance the fishery resources and aquatic communities for long-term recreational, ecological and economic benefits to the state. To reach this goal, each water body and its watershed must be protected and managed for its ecological integrity and recreational value. Two statutes set the framework for the mission of the Minnesota Department of Natural Resources (MDNR), Division of Fisheries (DF). Minnesota Statutes, section 84.941 states, "It is the policy of the state that fish and wildlife are renewable natural resources to be conserved and enhanced through planned scientific management, protection and utilization."

Minnesota Statutes, section 97A.045 states, "The commissioner shall make special provisions for the management of fish and wildlife to ensure recreational opportunities for anglers and hunters." Specifically, it is the mission of the DFW "to protect and manage Minnesota's fish, wildlife, native plants, and their communities for their intrinsic values and long-term benefits to the people of Minnesota." Through the Division of Fisheries, the Commissioner of the MDNR is responsible for the management of fisheries within the state. This responsibility is exclusive to the MDNR and extends to no other group, private individual or agency. Participation in fishery management in waters of the state by other agencies, individuals or groups must be with the agreement of the MDNR. On certain federal and Indian lands, the MDNR's authority to manage fisheries is modified by federal authority, treaty or agreement.

The Division of Fisheries believes formalized planning is an essential step in most fisheries management activities and these activities are guided by strategic, long-range and operational plans. Strategic and long-range plans are updated every six years and operational plans are updated annually. Coordination with other public agencies and input from the general public is required. Minnesota Statutes, section 84.942 states that "planned scientific management" prescribes specific planning activities required for fish and wildlife management. As such, research is an integral component of successful fishery management. Research leading to new ideas, better understanding of aquatic ecology and fisheries biology and better methods must be part of the fishery management programme.

The Division of Fisheries in the MDNR uses the concepts of watershed, ecosystem, and biological community based management. These concepts recognize that a myriad of physical, biological, chemical and human induced factors affect fisheries. The ecosystem and/or community approach to fisheries management improves the chances of success and the information gathered in the process will continually lead to improved techniques. As such, the MDNR views individual species management as an integral component of ecosystem or community based management. In addition to scientific literature, fishery management principles are derived from a number of documents that describe goals, plans and procedures. Included are the Plan for Minnesota Fish and Wildlife resources, the long range planning document, the Lake Management Planning Guide, the Stream Management Planning Guide, the Department Guidance Document, and various lake and stream survey guidelines.

Recreational Fishing

It is the policy of the MDNR to continue to see that the rights of the public to the recreational use of state waters will be preserved and extended to all waters capable of supporting game fish populations. The MDNR opposes recreational fishing methods that are incompatible with successful fishery protection and maintenance and will support additional restrictions of methods if biologically justified.

In general, the State endorses and promotes catch and immediate release of fish as a management tool and as a general philosophy. Although fishing regulations are recognized as an essential fishery management tool, the potential benefits, whether biological, social or economic, must be identified before setting a regulation. Subsequent determination of a positive effect of the regulation is needed for its continuance.

For in-house review and evaluation, fishing regulations are categorized into four types: 1) experimental, 2) special, 3) border waters and 4) general statewide. All proposals to change fishing regulations must be reviewed at several department levels regarding rationale, value, and evaluation. Regulations affecting fisheries may be passed by statute or rule. Statutory proposals may originate with the legislature, the public or a State agency such as the MDNR, but they are established by the state legislature. Statutes encompass a variety of laws, but are generally used for broad policy regulations to set fees for licenses, to appropriate money and to give State agencies authority to promulgate rules pertaining to a specific topic.

Rules are generally used for laws that require more detail or technical review than the statutory process normally provides. Fisheries use four different categories of rules: 1) permanent, 2) emergency, 3) expedited emergency and 4) exempt. Promulgation of permanent, emergency, and emergency game and fish rules must be done according to provisions of the Administrative Procedures Act (APA) in Minnesota Statutes. Exempt rules are so named because they are promulgated outside of the APA and are usually based on an alternative process established in statute.

The MDNR neither advocates nor promotes fishing contests (tournaments), but recognizes that tournament fishing is a legitimate recreational use of the resource. Tournaments that cause adverse impacts on aquatic resources or interfere with other resource users will not be permitted. Tournament participants are subject to the same fishing regulations as the general public. Minnesota Statutes, section 97C.081 and Minnesota Rules, part 6212.2400 govern the permitting of tournaments and contests. It is the responsibility of the DNR, as Minnesota's natural resource management agency to ensure the protection of endangered species. Area fishery supervisors must make sure fishery management activities do not conflict with the protection or enhancement of threatened and endangered species. Minnesota Statutes, sections 84.0894 and 84.0895 specify requirements for the protection of threatened and endangered species and enforcement of the regulations. Minnesota Rules, part 6134.0200, lists species in Minnesota that fall into the categories of endangered, threatened and/or special concern. Minnesota Rules, parts 6212.1400-.1800, provide details on regulations for the issuance of special permits dealing with endangered or threatened species.

Fish Stocking

Fish stocking by the MNDR is done according to individual lake and stream management plans. Fish stocking can be justified by meeting one or more of the following criteria:

- In newly created or rehabilitated waters.
- In potential high use lakes which experience winterkill where winterkill does not occur annually.
- Where investigation has shown that an introduced desirable species is suitable for the water body and compatible with indigenous fishes.
- To maintain a species of game fish where all elements of required habitat exist but spawning success is poor.
- Where reproductive success of predatory species is too variable to establish a proper balance with prey.

- Where the carrying capacity of an intensively managed water is inadequate to supply angler demand.

Every effort is made to use strains of fish most suited for the intended body of water and to maintain the genetic integrity of the existing population. MDNR Fisheries, along with neighbouring states, are cooperatively funding a major genetic study that will be used to help set stocking guidelines for maintaining genetic integrity of existing fish stocks within the State of Minnesota.

The MDNR cooperates with private fish hatchery and aquatic farm operators to facilitate development of aquaculture in Minnesota in an environmentally sound manner. The MDNR has the authority to license operations to ensure the protection of natural aquatic resources from potential harmful impacts of aquaculture. Private fish hatchery and aquatic farm operators must obtain an annual license through the MDNR, but waters may not be licensed if they contain game fish populations of significant public value. The MDNR may allow the taking of fish from state waters for commercial purposes as a legitimate use of the fishery resource.

Exotic Fish Management

The Division of Fisheries regulates the introduction of fish species into State waters. The introduction of exotic species into state waters is generally not permitted by the MDNR without thorough evaluations of the impacts to aquatic communities. In addition, the MDNR Fisheries Programme adheres by the American Fisheries Society (AFS) policy on introduction of aquatic species and follows the AFS protocol for evaluation. MDNR Fisheries will also not permit the release of genetically engineered aquatic species into natural waters. Introductions of transgenic fishes into production-scale fish culture facilities, public or private, are not permitted without the completion of risk assessment studies and a demonstration of minimal environmental risk on a case-by-case basis.

Habitat Restoration and Improvement

Management of biological communities consists of activities that directly involve fish populations and associated aquatic organisms. The MDNR strongly emphasizes habitat management as a means of maintaining and enhancing fisheries. Habitat management involves protection, rehabilitation and improvement of lake and stream habitats. Minnesota DNR routinely conducts fisheries surveys that provide information on physical, chemical and biological components of a lake or stream and population assessments that focus primarily on the status of fish species in the aquatic community. These surveys provide the fundamental information on which lake and stream management plans are developed. Lakes and streams that receive high use are given a higher priority in assessment frequency than those with low use. Creel surveys are used to provide data on fishing pressure, catch and catch rates, fishing quality, angler demographics and angler opinions on management programmes. The MDNR may use lake rehabilitation techniques to improve a fishery when justified by a favorable benefit/cost ratio or as part of a general watershed management plan. Chemical treatments are approved only in situations where control of undesirable species and restoration of a fishery by other means is not feasible. Prior to the implementation of any lake rehabilitation project, the MDNR identifies and seeks to correct watershed problems that have contributed to changes in the fishery resource.

Aquatic plant management is also integrated into lake management planning. Watershed and community based approaches are considered by MDNR as means for controlling undesirable plant species. Minnesota Statutes, section 84.092 and Minnesota Rules, part 6280 provide the MDNR with the permitting authority to control the introduction and spread of exotic plant species.

Bibliography

A.C. Long: *A-Z of Industrial Marine Fisheries in Asia*, Cyber Tech Publications, New Delhi, 2011.

A.D. Dholakia: *Fisheries and Aquatic Resources of India*, Daya Publication, Delhi, 2004.

A.K. Roy and A.D. Upadhyay: *Fisheries Resource and Production Statistics of NE States of India: An Analytical Value Added Presentation*, Narendra Publishing House, Delhi, 2014.

Ajit Kumar Roy and Niranjan Sarangi: *Applied Bioinformatics Statistics and Economics in Fisheries Research*, New India Publication Agency, Delhi, 2008.

Ajit Kumar Roy: *Evaluation and Impact Assessment of Technologies and Developmental Activities in Agriculture, Fisheries, and Allied Fields*, New India Publishing Agency, Delhi, 2011.

Amita Saxena: *Fisheries Resources and Food Security*, Narendra Publishing House, 2014.

Arnold C. Long: *Deep Sea Demersal Fish and Fisheries*, Cyber Tech Publication, Newe Delhi, 2009.

Arvind N Shukla: *Encyclopaedia of Fish and Fisheries, Vols. 1 to 5*, Discovery Publishing House, Delhi, 2008.

B K Singh: *Applied Fisheries and Aquaculture*, Swastik Publication, Delhi, 2008.

B. N. Pandey and G.K. Kulkarni: *Fisheries and Fish Toxicology*, APH Publication, Delhi, 2011.

B.N. Pandey, Sunil P. Trivedi, Kamal Jaiswal and Navneet Kaur Sethi: *Fish and Fisheries*, Sarup Book Publishers, Delhi, 2009.

B.R. Selvamani and R.K. Mahadevan: *Fisheries Management*, Campus Books, Delhi, 2008.

C.B.L. Srivastava: *A Text Book of Fishery Science and Indian Fisheries*, Kitab Mahal, Delhi, 2013.

D.K. Pandey and H.K. De.: *Fisheries Governance and Legislation in India*, Narendra Publishing House, Delhi, 2014.

K.D. Bhardwaj: *A-Z of Fisheries and Aquaculture Technology*, Cyber Tech Publication, New Delhi, 2011.

K.D. Bhardwaj: *Business Management in Fisheries and Aquaculture*, Cyber Tech Publication, New Delhi, 2012.

K.P. Biswas: *Advancement of Fish Fisheries and Technology*, Narendra Publishing House, Delhi, 2012.

K.P. Biswas: *Ecological and Fisheries Development in Wetlands : A Study of Chilka Lagoon*, Daya Publication, Delhi, 1995.

K.P. Biswas: *Economics in Commercial Fisheries*, Daya Publication, Delhi, 2006.

M Lakshmi Narasaiah and G. Bala. Rangaiah: *Fresh Water Fisheries* , Discovery Publishing House, Delhi, 2011.

O.P. Sharma: *Fisheries Extension and Administration*, Agrotech Publication, Delhi, 2011.

Rekha R. Gaonkar, R.B. Patil and Maria D.C. Rodrigues: *Fishes and Fisheries : Conservation and Sustainable Development*, A P H Publication, Delhi, 2011.

S.K. Pandey: *Fisheries in the Marine Ecosystem*, Bio Green Books, Delhi, 2012.

Tomi Petr: *Fisheries in Irrigation Systems of Arid Asia*, Daya Publication, Delhi, 2007.

V R P Sinha: *Fisheries Research Planning and Management in Developing Countries*, Narendra Publishing House, Delhi, 2005.

Vishal Anand: *Encyclopaedia of Fish and Fisheries*, Anmol Publication, Delhi, 2006.

Vishwas B Sakhare: *Applied Fisheries*, Daya Publication, Delhi, 2007.

Yougesh Kumar and Rajeev Tyagi: *Aquaculture Fisheries Biotechnology and Genetics*, Manglam Publishers, Delhi, 2013.

Index

G

H

I

J

L

M

N

O

P

Q

R

S

T

U